Advance Praise for

From Education to Incarceration

"How did we become a society that handcuffs its young and warehouses them in penal institutions instead of educating them? *From Education to Incarceration* answers that question and offers an intelligently crafted overview of how ill-advised and inhumane practices and policies in the United States have betrayed generations of young persons, with suggestions for how we can up-end these transgressions. Educators, attorneys, youth organizers, and many others write with authority and conviction in this timely, relevant, and eminently readable book."

—Heidi Boghosian, Executive Director, National Lawyers Guild

"The authors, activists, and educators who gather their voices in *From Education to Incarceration* paint a clear, devastating picture of the way systems and the people who profit from their corruption create and then target disenfranchised youth. But what makes this book unique is that they do more: they equip us with the tools to fight back. That is invaluable and why everybody who cares about youth should read this book."

—Paul C. Gorski, author of *Reaching and Teaching Students in Poverty: Strategies for Erasing the Opportunity Gap*

"*From Education to Incarceration* addresses a complex, entrenched, and socially debilitating issue, one that needs to be placed within the context of inequitable power relations, social (in)justice, neoliberalism, and the position of the United States as a global hegemonic force. The editors have skillfully brought together a range of scholars and activists to examine and critique the meaning of incarcerating such unparalleled numbers of young people and have focused on the disproportionate and insidious reality of who is being victimized. This is an important book for those concerned that education help to diminish the use of imprisonment as a viable strategy for constructing a society and a cause of marginalization and disenfranchisement."

—Paul R. Carr, Lakehead University, Orillia

"Nocella, Parmar, and Stovall have assembled an impressive group of authors for this amazing collection. Although the fearful defenders of corporate rule will condemn the critical linkage of scholarship and activism represented here, anyone who still believes in a hopeful humanist vision will find these essays invaluable when contemplating the scale of the challenges ahead."

—David Gabbard, co-editor of *Education as Enforcement: The Militarization and Corporatization of Schools*

"Public schooling is divided along razor-sharp lines. Schools do skills training and, depending on where a child is, some limited intellectual training. In public schools, the key issues of life: work, production and reproduction, rational knowledge, and freedom are virtually illegal. The sorting machine of schools serves to train the next generation of workers—from pre-med or pre-law in affluent neighborhoods, to middle-class pre-teacher training, and for many others pre-military and pre-prison education. Contributors to *From Education to Incarceration* describe and deconstruct how, for many students, the promise of public education is merely bigger cages and longer chains."

—E. Wayne Ross, Professor, Department of Curriculum and Pedagogy, University of British Columbia

"As a social worker who mentors and consults youth on probation, I have been in desperate need of a book that articulates all the problems of schools and the juvenile justice system to city policy makers. *From Education to Incarceration* is a must-read for educators and policy makers and a 101 manual for community organizers working with youth to dismantle once and for all the school-to-prison pipeline."

—Joanna Lowry, Social Worker, Neighborhood House

"This book provides a serious and necessary investigation and critique of an inhumane and morally bankrupt system. The combination of a broken education system and a for-profit prison system leaves innocent kids to fend for themselves. *From Education to Incarceration* cuts through the propaganda and exposes the complexity of issues that contribute to one of America's biggest problems. This book will arouse the passions and incite a righteous indignation."

—Jason Del Gandio, author of *Rhetoric for Radicals: A Handbook for 21st Century Activists*

From Education to Incarceration

COUNTERPOINTS

Studies in Criticality

Shirley R. Steinberg
General Editor

Vol. 453

The Counterpoints series is part of the Peter Lang Education list.
Every volume is peer reviewed and meets
the highest quality standards for content and production.

PETER LANG
New York • Bern • Berlin
Brussels • Vienna • Oxford • Warsaw

From Education to Incarceration

Dismantling the School-to-Prison Pipeline

Second Edition

EDITED BY
Anthony J. Nocella II,
Priya Parmar, & David Stovall

FOREWORD BY WILLIAM AYERS

PETER LANG
New York • Bern • Berlin
Brussels • Vienna • Oxford • Warsaw

Library of Congress Cataloging-in-Publication Data

Names: Nocella, Anthony J., editor. | Parmar, Priya, editor. | Stovall, David, editor.
Title: From education to incarceration: dismantling the school-to-prison pipeline /
edited by Anthony J. Nocella II, Priya Parmar, and David Stovall.
Description: Second edition. | New York: PETER LANG, 2018
Series: Counterpoints; Volume 453 | ISSN 1058-1634
Includes bibliographical references.
Identifiers: LCCN 2017019782 | ISBN 978-1-4331-3517-0 (paperback)
ISBN 978-1-4331-4510-0 (ebook pdf) | ISBN 978-1-4331-4511-7 (epub)
ISBN 978-1-4331-4512-4 (mobi)
Subjects: LCSH: School discipline—United States.
Public schools—Security measures—United States.
School management and organization—United States.
School violence—Law and legislation—United States.
School violence—Law and legislation—United States.
Juvenile justice, Administration of—United States.
Discrimination in juvenile justice administration—United States.
Imprisonment—United States.
Crime and race—United States.
Minorities—United States—Public opinion.
Minorities—United States—Social conditions.
Educational equalization—United States.
Classification: LCC LB3012.2 .F76 2018 | DDC 371.5—dc23
LC record available at https://lccn.loc.gov/2017019782
DOI 10.3726/b11313

Bibliographic information published by **Die Deutsche Nationalbibliothek**.
Die Deutsche Nationalbibliothek lists this publication in the "Deutsche
Nationalbibliografie"; detailed bibliographic data is available
on the Internet at http://dnb.d-nb.de/.

The paper in this book meets the guidelines for permanence and durability
of the Committee on Production Guidelines for Book Longevity
of the Council of Library Resources.

29 Broadway, 18th floor, New York, NY 10006
www.peterlang.com

Printed in the United States of America

This book is dedicated to those who are currently incarcerated and to those who have died while incarcerated because they were pushed out of school and society.

Table of Contents

Foreword

WILLIAM AYERS

We seem somehow destined to be confined for a time in a lockup-state-of-mind. Perhaps because we've lived so long in a culture of discipline and punish, or perhaps because the traditional American Puritanism became ravenous once again and demanded to be fed, or perhaps because our go-to-jail complex developed obsessive-compulsive hyper-activity—whatever the reasons, many Americans hardly noticed as we slipped down the proverbial slope that Angela Davis and Ruthie Gilmore, Erica Meiners and Bernardine Dohrn had predicted, and we woke up living in a full-blown prison nation. There's no sense denying it: we are now marked indelibly as a carceral state (look it up), with mass incarceration the defining fact of life in the United States today (whether acknowledged or not) just as slavery was the fundamental reality in the 1800s (whether acknowledged or not).

And that fact points to the true and deep-seated reason underneath the phenomenon of mass incarceration: white supremacy dressed up in modern garb, structural racism pure and simple. The system has been dubbed "the new Jim Crow" by the brilliant lawyer and activist Michelle Alexander, who notes that there are now more Black men in prison or on probation or parole than there were living in bondage as chattel slaves in 1850; that there are significantly more people caught up in the system of incarceration and supervision in America today—more than six million folks—than inhabited Stalin's Gulag at its height; that the American Gulag is the second largest city in this country, and that while the United

States constitutes less than 5% of the world's people, it holds more than 25% of the world's combined prison population; that in the past twenty years the amount states have spent on prisons has risen six times the rate spent on higher education; and that on any given day tens of thousands of men, overwhelmingly Black and Latino men, are held in the torturous condition known as solitary confinement. You get the picture.

All of this indicates that we seem destined to be confined in that lockup-state-of-mind for the foreseeable future, or until we change the frame or flip the script, and—fed up—rise up.

That's precisely the assignment courageously taken on by Anthony J. Nocella II, Priya Parmar, and David Stovall—they want to revolutionize the conversation. And with *From Education to Incarceration: Dismantling the School to Prison Pipeline* they've done just that, leaping into the whirlwind full force and constructing a powerful weapon for the forces of prison abolition, and an essential handbook for educators.

This book maps in devastating detail the treacherous path constructed by the powerful for the children of formerly enslaved human beings, recent immigrants, first-nation people, and the poor—a path that's earned the colorful metaphoric phrase "the school to prison pipeline." A pipeline runs in a single direction, and once entered into the mouth, destiny sweeps everything before it to the bottom; a pipeline offers no exits, no deviations or departures, no way out—unless it fractures. *From Education to Incarceration* is not focused on prison reform or tinkering with the mechanisms of the pipeline to make it "fairer" or more efficient; it's aimed, rather, at ripping open the pipeline, upending the assumptions that got us where we are, and then throwing every section of pipe and all the braces and supports into the dustbin of history.

Schools for the poor—many urban and rural schools, and increasingly suburban schools as well—share striking similarities with prisons. In each site, discipline and security take precedence over knowledge or human development; in each site, people are subordinated to the will of—and forced to follow a strict routine set by—others, isolated from the larger community, and coerced to do work that they have no part in defining; in each folks are inspected, regulated, appraised, censured, ordered about, indoctrinated, sermonized, checked off, assessed, and kept under constant surveillance, at every turn to be noted, registered, counted, priced, admonished, prevented, reformed, redressed, and corrected. And on top of all this, students and prisoners alike are most often described by their minders through their aggregate statistical profiles: race and ethnicity, occupation or family income, residence, and religion. Schools for the poor are the prep schools for the prisoners of tomorrow.

But in spite of the increasing use of disciplinary techniques in schools, the prison analogy breaks down in one significant way: teachers are not prison guards, and our highest aspiration is not summed up in a single word: *control*.

Teachers are positioned as both subjects and objects of school surveillance, and uniquely, then, situated to help students develop a critical awareness of, and perhaps even some potential lines of resistance to, the technology of power in today's maximum-security schools. Teachers can take the prison and the analogy, the pipeline and the metaphor, as objects of study.

In schools shot through with mechanisms of disciplinary surveillance, the technology of power itself can constitute part of a humanizing curriculum. Students can think critically about disciplinary power, about how they are being watched, by whom, and for what purpose. They can question, and they can act. By questioning and acting ourselves, teachers can show them how it's done.

Preface

FRANK HERNANDEZ

I come from a large Latino family. Including myself, there are six siblings. In all, I have twenty-three nieces and nephews and forty great-nieces and great-nephews. Some of them are just entering school; others have graduated from high school and are now attending institutions of higher education. Several have completed their baccalaureate degree and are entering graduate programs. One great-niece in particular has had her challenges as a student in a school where police officers are present every day. And as a result of a scuffle with another student, my great-niece was handcuffed, given a citation, and placed on file at the local juvenile criminal justice center. The citation, if not paid soon after issuance, will increase over time, and must be paid in full before my great-niece can submit a driver's license application for consideration.

Recently, this same great-niece decided to skip school for a day. As a result of her decision, the administration, in collaboration with the juvenile system, equipped her with an ankle monitor to track her every move, particularly during school days. This past year, my great-niece completed the eighth grade and celebrated her 14th birthday—and she is on what some call the "school to prison pipeline." Unfortunately, the case of my great-niece is not unusual; it is all too common.

Across the United States, police habitually arrest youths and transport them to juvenile detention centers and, depending on the age of the youth, sometimes to the city or county jail. More often than not, these individuals are arrested for minor disruptions. The arrests do not take place in the early weekend morning hours nor do they take place in questionable neighborhoods. Rather, these arrests occur in PK–12 schools, a place where students should feel protected; a place that is often referred to as the "equal playing field"; a place that is often identified as the "gateway" to higher education. Unfortunately for some students, there is a significant divide between what schools should be and what schools are.

Surges in arrests among youths similar in age to my great-niece have occurred for such infractions as scuffles, truancy, cussing, and disobeying directions. And in no other state have these school-based arrests been more prevalent than in Texas, the state where I work as dean of education for a small master's degree-granting institution. According to the *New York Times*, (Eckholm, 2013) police officers based in Texas schools write more than 100,000 citations each year for students. And most often, the students receiving the citations lack access to legal counsel, amass huge fines, are required to do community service, or receive a criminal record that may weaken their prospects for future employment or service to country. De'Angelo Rollins, a 12-year-old middle school student, became a statistic in Texas's growing number of incidents between school-based police officers and students. After he and another boy scuffled, both were given citations. Specifically, Rollins pleaded no contest, paid a fine, was sentenced to twenty hours of community service, and was placed on four months of probation. Our school system is now looking a lot like our criminal justice system. And the students arrested are getting younger.

Take, for example, Salecia Johnson. According to CNN Newswire, (Campbell, 2012) when officers arrived at Creekside Elementary in Milledgeville, Georgia, Salecia was on the floor of the principal's office screaming and crying. After numerous attempts to calm Salecia down, she pulled away from the officers and resisted them when they tried to pick her up. According to the police report, Salecia was eventually handcuffed and brought to a police station.

This school to prison pipeline has been funneling more and more students over the years. The American Civil Liberties Union (ACLU) has identified several onerous factors that help clear this path to incarceration. The first factor is students' attendance at under-performing schools. Low-performing schools are usually located in impoverished communities and have high gaps in achievement when compared with other schools. These low-performing schools tend to have substandard facilities, lack up-to-date books, have high faculty turnover, and more often than not, hire unlicensed or unqualified teachers. It is not unusual for teachers to have low expectations of students, which can contribute to students' decisions to skip school or even drop out entirely.

The second factor underlying the school to prison pipeline is the rather abstract world of zero tolerance discipline policies, which are in place at many schools and which have very concrete, real-world effects. These policies leave little room for questions or for consideration of complex circumstances, and usually result in expulsion or suspension from school; that is, zero tolerance is applied across the board for a variety of infractions and circumstances. As a result, students are more likely to get pushed through the pipeline and into the juvenile justice system than would be the case if the students were exposed to tailored, thoughtful interventions.

The third factor is students' attendance at schools where police staff the hallways and deal with schoolwide discipline. Rather than rely on teachers and administrators to handle school-discipline issues, school districts are enlisting full-time police officers. This means that students are more likely to be arrested for nonviolent behaviors than in the past. The fourth factor is alternative schools where some students enroll after having been expelled or suspended from traditional schools and where the students can expect to receive a sub-par education derived from remedial curriculum. The combination of these factors can have the effect of increasing the likelihood that troubled students will wind up in a local juvenile detention facility.

This school to prison pipeline needs to be cut off and dismantled. That's exactly what this volume proposes in detail. It reviews and clarifies works by scholars and practitioners who are exploring ways to confront and overcome this dangerous mindset privileging incarceration over education. The volume is divided into five parts whose topics range from the culture of youth incarceration to recommended alternatives to youth incarceration. The writings in this volume uncover important yet subtle relationships between the targeting of youth, incarceration rates, the segregating of youth, and the need for transformation. The volume pushes us to understand not only the devastation of imprisoning our youth but also solutions to the problem.

REFERENCES

Campbell, A., (April 17, 2012). 6-year-old student handcuffed, arrested by police in Georgia. http://www.12newsnow.com/story/17516292/6-year-old0student-handcuffed-arrested-by-police-in-georgia.

Eckholm, E., (April 12, 2013). With police in schools, more children in court. *New York Times* http://www.nytimes.com/2013/04/12/education/with-police-in-schools-more-children-in-court-.html.

Acknowledgments

Anthony, Priya, and David would like to give love to our family and friends, who have supported us, challenged us, and laughed with us over the many years on this planet. We would also like to thank everyone at Peter Lang especially Phyllis Korper, Stephen Mazur, Inda Muntu, Chris Myers, Bernadette Shade, Sophie Appel, and the series editor Shirley Steinberg, a wonderful scholar and human being. We would also like to thank the brilliant and powerful contributors to this book, who allowed us to make a radical and critical tool to aid in the dismantling of the school to prison pipeline, prison industrial complex, and the academic industrial complex. We would like to give great appreciation to Bill Ayers for writing the Foreword, Frank Hernandez for writing the Preface, and Bernardine Dohrn for writing the Afterword. We would like to thank Jason Del Gandio, Peter McLaren, Barbara Madeloni, Heidi Boghosian, Mechthild Nagel, Jamie Utt, Joy James, Emery Petchauer, Paul C. Gorski, Ruth Kinna, César A. Rossatto, David Gabbard, Paul R. Carr, John Lupinacci, E. Wayne Ross, Steve Fletcher, and Joanna Lowry for reviewing this book on such a short deadline. Finally, we would like to thank each other, the editors, for the collaboration, creativity, the long talks, many e-mails, and struggle to make this important book come to life! We hope *From Education to Incarceration* will create consciousness and inspire youth, teachers, professors, community organizers, politicians, and activists to take action against high-stakes tests, standardization, cultural imperialism, normalcy, push-outs, special education, segregated education, youth detentions, police brutality, and continued police presence in schools.

Introduction

Every Day Is Like Skydiving Without a Parachute: A Revolution for Abolishing the School to Prison Pipeline

ANTHONY J. NOCELLA II, PRIYA PARMAR, AND DAVID STOVALL

Patience has its limits. Take it too far, and it's cowardice.

—GEORGE JACKSON

To Hell with Good Intentions

—IVAN ILICH

IT STILL AIN'T GOOD FOR MOST FOLKS ...

July 13, 2013: A jury of six (predominantly white) women found George Zimmerman, whose mother is Hispanic and whose father is white, not guilty of manslaughter or second-degree murder in the death of Trayvon Martin, an unarmed African-American male walking home in a gated complex in Florida after purchasing a drink and some candy. Despite the fact that Trayvon was an unarmed minor with no criminal record, a jury of Zimmerman's supposed peers concluded that Zimmerman believed his life was being threatened and was justified in shooting Trayvon through the chest. Even though law enforcement had told Zimmerman to wait in his car and not to pursue Trayvon, the jury felt that Zimmerman was justified in his pursuit of the teen. Per a law deeply rooted in Florida's "stand your ground" legislation, armed persons are allowed to use deadly force if they feel their life is in danger.

August 9, 2014: Ferguson, Missouri, 18-year-old Michael Brown was fatally shot by 28-year-old police officer, Darren Wilson. Wilson claimed he feared for his life as Brown approached him. As a result, Wilson shot the unarmed Brown twelve times. A Grand Jury failed to indict.

July 14, 2014: Staten Island, New York, 43-year-old Eric Garner died as a result of an illegal chokehold performed by 29-year-old NYPD officer, Daniel Pantaleo. Once Garner was brought to the ground, Pantaleo released his chokehold, but kept Garner's face pressed to the concrete as four other officers attempted to restrain him. As Garner was lying face down on the sidewalk, pleading with them by repeatedly (twelve times) stating "I can't breathe," officers refused to release pressure until Garner lost consciousness. Paramedics arrived seven minutes later but failed to administer CPR. Approximately one hour later, Garner was officially pronounced dead at the local hospital. The Medical Examiner ruled Garner's death a homicide as a result of the chokehold by Pantaleo. A Grand Jury failed to indict.

November 22, 2014: Cleveland, Ohio, 12-year-old Tamir Rice was fatally shot by 26-year-old police officer, Timothy Loehmann, after responding to a dispatch report of a Black male pointing a gun at people. Upon arrival to the recreational center at which Rice was playing, Loehmann, along with a fellow officer, reported that Rice reached for a gun from his waist. Within seconds, Loehmann fired two shots which resulted in Rice's death the following day. The "gun" Rice allegedly was in possession of turned out to be an airsoft gun, which is deemed safe for recreational purposes. A Grand Jury failed to indict.

April 12, 2015: Baltimore, Maryland, 25-year-old Freddie Carlos Gray, Jr. succumbed to injuries sustained during an arrest made by Baltimore police officers for allegedly possessing an illegal switch blade. While being transported to jail in a police van, he suspiciously fell into a coma and was transferred to a hospital where he died seven days later due to a spinal cord injury. The Medical Examiner ruled the death a "homicide." Gray's death sparked revolts locally and around the world demanding justice. Various charges were filed against six police officers involved with Gray's arrest. A Grand Jury issued indictments against all of the officers on most of the charges filed. However, all six officers were eventually set free. All charges were dropped for four of the officers, while the other two officers were given a "not guilty" verdict via trial-by-judge.

We could cite countless other cases that occur each year in which the lives of Black and Latino males are consistently compromised in the name of "justice" and "self-defense." We can also cite the many—unknown and unpublicized—incidents in which women of color and LGBT2-SQQIA (Lesbian, Gay, Bisexual, Transgender, Two Spirited, Queer, Questioning, Inter-sex, and Asexual) females suffer from police brutality and sexual assault from law enforcement officials. Social media movements or specifically what is known as hashtag activism has been used to shed awareness of the violence inflicted upon Black women by police officials.

A few notable examples are #BlackWomensLivesMatter, #SayHerName, and #BlackGirlsMatter. Here are a few examples:

May 16, 2010: Detroit, Michigan, 7-year-old Aiyana Stanley Jones was shot in the head while sleeping as local law enforcement raided the child's home. Officer Joseph Weekley, member of the Detroit SWAT team, was charged with involuntary manslaughter and reckless endangerment with a gun. After two mistrials, all charges were subsequently dropped in 2015.

March 21, 2012: Chicago, Illinois, 22-year-old Rekia Boyd was fatally shot in the head by off-duty Chicago police detective after responding to complaints of partying at a local park. After engaging in a verbal altercation with another person in the park, Servin shot his firearm into a crowd that resulted in Boyd being hit. Servin was initially charged with involuntary manslaughter but that charge was dismissed by the county judge in 2015.

July 10, 2015: Waller County, Texas, 28-year-old Sandra Bland was arrested by 30-year-old state trooper, Brian Encinia. Bland was pulled over for a minor traffic violation and was subsequently arrested after Encinia alleged Bland had assaulted him. Bland was found hanging in her jail cell three days later. Her death was determined to be a suicide by the County's Medical Examiner. A Grand Jury failed to indict anyone in connection with Bland's death.

The cases briefly described above confirm the affirmation of Black criminality and disposability, resulting in the intentional slaughter of those deemed to be less than human. These (and other similar) incidents have also inspired organized demonstrations and protests throughout the country and in many parts of the world demanding racial justice. Such outrage and protesting have given rise to organized social justice movements, one of the most visible ones being Black Lives Matter, created in 2012 after the acquittal of George Zimmerman in the murder case of Trayvon Martin. Black Lives Matter was formed by three queer Black women, Alicia Garza, Opal Tometi, and Patrisse Cullors, with the intent to create awareness of—act against—anti-Black racism. #BlackLivesMatter is intended to rebuild the Black liberation movement by making it more inclusive, affirming the lives of Black marginalized groups—Black queer and trans, those with disabilities, those who are incarcerated, ALL Black lives—that may have been given minimal roles in the liberation movement in the past. It is important for readers to adequately research the purpose, goals, and guiding principles of Black Lives Matter to avoid misappropriating and misrepresenting their intent. The movement as stated on the Black Lives Matter main website (www.blacklivesmatter.com) is "an ideological and political intervention in a world where Black lives are systematically and intentionally targeted for demise. It is an affirmation of Black folks' contributions to this society, our humanity, and our resilience in the face of deadly oppression." As we update our Introduction for this revised edition, we are engaged in actions and movements to fight against white supremacy, right-wing extremism, and social injustices (including environmental and economic racism). The blatant disregard for basic human rights, specifically toward indigenous and minority groups, in order to protect private industry and political interests, force us to take action, to participate in protests, to risk arrest. Whether it's the Flint, Michigan water crisis or the current attempt to create a Native American genocide in North Dakota by the petroleum and gas industry, we must fight for environmental justice and educate our youth about these racist efforts in our teachings.

We are compelled to devote a few lines to the 8,250 residents of Standing Rock, North Dakota as they have been under constant siege protecting their 3,500-square-mile reservation from attempts by private corporations to drill an oil pipeline. Starting as early as August 2016, members of the Standing Rock Sioux Tribe have stood their ground (and have taken their complaint to the U.S. District Court) against private, corporate interests, namely a corporation called Dakota Access, a subsidiary of Phillips 66 and a Texas company called Energy Transfer. Dakota Access' intentions are to construct a $3.7 billion Dakota Access oil pipeline through the protected land. The Standing Rock Sioux Tribe, now joined by other social justice groups, including Veteran groups and Black Lives Matter, have emerged as climate change heroes, or "water protectors," of their land asserting that the pipeline would pollute their water and desecrate sacred burial grounds. Water protectors are being arrested, maced, shot with rubber bullets and fire hoses in below-freezing temperatures by a militarized police force authorized by the governor of the state. The hashtag #NoDAPL—No Dakota Access Pipeline—is being used on various social media sites to plan, organize, and communicate with activists and viewers around the country and world.

As many of the examples cited above illustrate, youth and people of color are declared "at risk" for criminal behavior, implying that sole responsibility be placed on them with very little to no consideration of the economic and/or political factors that have contributed to poor social conditions. Despite the election of Barack H. Obama (from 2009 to 2017), the United States' first Black president, racial and economic progress in America has not improved as evidenced by the examples cited above as well as the record high child poverty rates, low college enrollment (particularly for Black males), and the establishment of movements such as the Tea Party and white extremist nationalist groups. Arguably the most notable and recent event of a white nationalist movement as this volume goes into press is the unexpected victory of Donald J. Trump in the 2016 presidential election. Trump's triumph can be argued as a repudiation of social justice efforts—and the legacy of President Obama—giving rise to white nationalism as evidenced by those who voted him into office: the overlooked underclass of white and working class voters—young and old—who supporters argued were disenfranchised economically. However, it must be noted that Trump garnered support from those in higher income brackets as well (with the exception of white college-educated women). Tapping into white identity politics with the slogan "Make America Great Again," Trump's unapologetic, consistent, and well-documented racist, bigoted, sexist, ableist, and xenophobic rants on the campaign trail inspired a renewed sense of hope for white extremists. His nominations of billionaire cabinet members who have spent their lives destroying the environment, exploiting workers, privatizing public education, and defending polluters reaffirm the structural disposability and systemic disregard for every person who is not white, male, straight, cisgender, able-bodied, and middle or upper class.

The (re)emergence of a political landscape favoring the top 1% is to the detriment of the majority of ameriKKKans. Most vulnerable will be marginalized youth of color who are primary targets for arrest. What are the implications? Will "Law and Order" as Trump advocates be restored? Will racial profiling and "stop and frisk" programs be reenacted as official policy? Will incarceration rates skyrocket even more than in the past, benefiting those who profit from the existence of a corporatized prison industrial complex? As we know, enslavement of another human is against the law within the United States, except if someone is convicted of a crime, as stated in the Thirteenth Amendment of the U.S. Constitution. But if we acknowledge that the approximately 2.5 million incarcerated people are paid only cents per hour for their labor, making anything from desks to computer boards for government and corporate businesses, can we not argue that the U.S. prison system imprisons slaves, and not prisoners? This corporatized prison industrial system has more slaves than any other country in the world. What's even more alarming is that we have more convicted individuals in prisons (slaves, according to the Thirteenth Amendment) than we did enslaved Africans prior to the Civil War. What is strategically happening in the United States is that the behaviors and daily experiences of youth of color are becoming criminalized, while the U.S. government continues to argue that the aforementioned processes are not emblematic of a disproportionate system of racial profiling. On the contrary, we are confident that not only is it racial profiling, but a concerted effort to push any youth who rebels against indoctrination into dominant cultural norms and values into the prison pipeline. While most youth who are targeted and pushed out are youth of color, we include and acknowledge in this 2nd edition chapters devoted to the struggles of many other marginalized youth such as those with disabilities, those who are economically disadvantaged, those who are noncitizens or undocumented, and those who identify as LGBT2-SQQIA.

ABOUT THE BOOK

As the editors of *From Education to Incarceration: Dismantling the School to Prison Pipeline*, we understand the aforementioned cases of racial discrimination not as abnormality, but as consistent and normative to life in the United States. Similar to the Rodney King verdict of 1991 and the acquittal of the murderers of Emmet Till in 1955, the cases mentioned in the previous section underscore that Black life remains worthless under the eyes of the law. Although some may feel this to be a harsh statement, white supremacy ideologies are alive and well in the United States and promoted through numerous systems of domination and structural and institutional racism, including capitalism, the criminal justice system, and the medical industrial complex. Instead of an overt, polarizing direct form of racism, its most recent iteration is located in the realm of public policy, most notably in P–12 and higher education, housing, employment, and health care. As an alternative to outright denial and a bevy of racial epithets, racism is prevalent beneath the surface in the form of school closings, racial disparities, home foreclosures, food insecurity, and disparities in health care. With these realities, we conclude that at no point in time do we exist in a postracial world. As editors, postraciality is a ridiculously bad joke intended to placate people of color and white allies with the idea that things are *actually getting better*. Instead, for many youth of color, getting through the day is like jumping out of an airplane without a parachute: some days you get where you need to be without incident, whereas on other days, your life is in dire jeopardy. Unfortunately, there is very little in between.

In solidarity with the community of scholars, activists, educators, artists, community organizers, and youth workers entrenched in the fight against racism, we are unafraid to name the realities of white supremacy, domination, and privilege that promote racism and permeate P–16 education and public policy. Armed with neoliberal policies that have switched public goods into competition-based markets, the permanent attempt to exclude people of color from access to food, clothing, shelter, and quality health care and education should be understood as a Hemisphere since the late fifteenth century. The school to prison pipeline should be included within this paradigm.

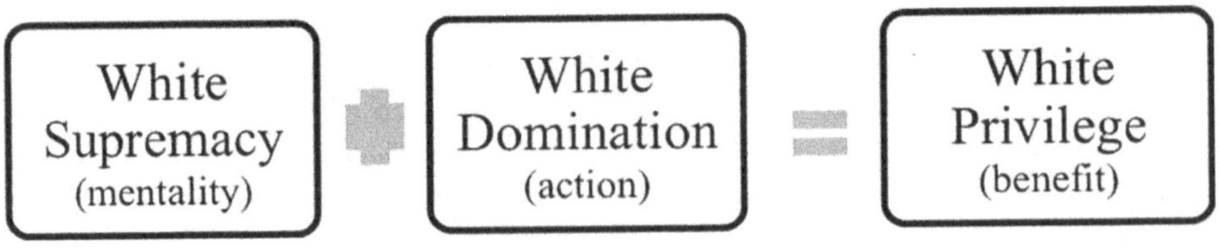

Figure 0.1. Equation of Racism (designed by Nocella II).

Expanding the late 1990s work of the Advancement Project of Washington, D.C., the Ella Baker Center for Human Rights of Oakland, California, and the Southwest Youth Collaborative of Chicago, Illinois, this 2nd edition, while including eight new chapters, seeks to challenge and reshape what is commonly known as the *school to prison pipeline.* The school to prison pipeline is a systemic process that pushes out marginalized youth from school and into the juvenile justice system through discriminating policies. As an epidemic plaguing our nation's schools, the school to prison pipeline manifests within school policies (i.e., zero tolerance, high-stakes testing) that disproportionately target and criminalize children and youth of color and those who are socially marginalized because of disability, poverty, and sexuality. These policies stem from racist theories such as the achievement gap, which argue that youth of color are not as intelligent as white students, also referred to as deficit thinking, the belief that working class students and particularly youth of color need to be "fixed" and lack social and academic skills. The assumption is they lack motivation and if they would only work "harder" (aka "pull yourself up by your bootstraps" myth) they would be successful.

According to SuspensionStories, a youth-led action research group that promotes awareness, understanding, and, ultimately, abolition of the school to prison pipeline epidemic, 1 out of 3 Black men and 1 out of 6 Latino men will be incarcerated in his lifetime; 40% of Black students are expelled from school each year; 70% of students involved in "in-school" arrests or referred to law enforcement are Black or Latino; Black and Latino students are twice as likely not to graduate from high school as white students; Black students are three and a half times more likely to be suspended than are white students; and 68% of all males in state and federal prison do not hold a high school diploma (SuspensionStories, 2013). Students are forced into the pipeline through zero tolerance policies that range from suspension or expulsion from school, to law enforcement official involvement that may lead to criminal charges, arrests, and incarceration. The establishment of such policies has opened the doors to criminalize students for even the most minor infractions (i.e., the 2013 case of two Suffolk, Virginia, second graders suspended for making shooting noises while pointing their pencils, or the 2005 case of St. Petersburg, Florida, where 5-year-old Ja'Eisha Scott was arrested for throwing a temper tantrum). As editors we are willing to join in the radical project of the abolition of the school to prison pipeline while posing viable alternatives to the abject overincarceration of Black and Latino/a youth.

This book is not a call to reform the education or criminal justice systems. We are not calling for compliance, understanding, or compromise. Instead, we must resist and abolish systems that have foundations of white supremacy and oppression. We must engage in a radically intentional, deeply concerted reimagining and rethinking of both systems of oppression that strive to institute policies and practices that tend to place the bulk of responsibility on youth themselves, aka, student accountability. For example, rather than investigate factors that result in the "pushing out" of students by school officials and policies, or lack of social justice-based programming available for diverse and vulnerable populations, marginalized youth are blamed for dropping out, for not valuing their education, or not trying hard enough. Or, rather than providing social and emotional support to the victims of oppression, or instituting programs, policies, and lesson planning on working to end and fight oppression, targets are either blamed or ignored by school officials who may view teasing as a natural phenomenon, a rite of passage, that all boys and girls endure. Rather than investigate hiring practices in which teacher recruitment efforts are in place to encourage young people from the community to pursue a career in teaching, and then hiring them, many high needs schools employ novice teachers enrolled in alternative teacher certification programs (e.g., Teach for America, NYC Teaching Fellows), which consist mainly of white able-body, able-minded, heterosexual, economically stable, Christian, cis-gender teachers. Similarly, we know that just as the Ku Klux Klan cannot be reformed to be inclusive of people of color or of marginalized religious groups, so cannot a fascist ameriKKKa and any system within it. Therefore, we are not asking you to vote, lobby, or foster progressive liberal policies, but instead to resist, rebel, and revolt against one of the most violent oppressive imperialist States that has ever existed in this world.

SUMMARY OF THE BOOK

This book is edited by three scholar-activists from differing backgrounds, all dedicated to a radical global intersectional social justice movement for the liberation of all who engage daily in street-line activism opposed to detached academics who play it safe and profit off of writing and teaching about activism. The contributors of this book come from diverse backgrounds and experiences: some are incarcerated, while others have been recently released; some are former political prisoners, while one author is a current political prisoner; some of the contributors are anarchists and youth organizers, while others are former members of the Black Panther Party; some of the contributors are Hip Hop artists and poets, while others are former gang members and hustlers. This book's diverse voices, experiences, and identities all hold to a few common goals: to end the incarceration of youth; to reject Common Core Standards, high-stakes testing, and the standardization of monolithic education found in curricula and textbooks; to denounce student push-out (see the organization Dignity in Schools); to eliminate punitive school discipline; to boycott alternative teacher certification programs; to protest police in schools; and, of course, to dismantle the school to prison pipeline.

The sections in this book are meant to encourage rich, deep conversations about incarceration and education that ultimately move readers to act. As the two systems become intimately connected, schools become the "marketplace" by which to rationalize the disposability of poor young people of color in urban spaces. As cities such as Detroit, Michigan, and Stockton, California declare bankruptcy, the public sector becomes drowned in the rhetoric of austerity without viable alternatives. In our respective homes of the Twin Cities, New York, and Chicago, the commonly shared rhetoric is that young people of color are undeserving because their families haven't capitalized on the numerous opportunities their respective locales seemingly have to offer. Missing from this equation are the realities of hyper-segregation, isolation, disenfranchisement, and marginalization that have been the norm in our respective cities because of the lack of quality public goods (i.e., schools, infrastructure, living-wage jobs). These norms create a spiral of despair that few are able to transcend. In these instances, the victims of social inequality are perpetually blamed for their circumstances, while the rich and affluent justify their lot because they are the nation's "hard workers." However, this ostensible "hard work" is done upon the backs of the disenfranchised and through budget cuts to those aforementioned dispensations that deprived communities need the most.

The book begins with a Foreword by long-time radical educator and activist Bill Ayers, who argues that one of the most important parts of revolutionizing society is defending youth and aiding in their liberation.

The ensuing Preface by Frank Hernandez, Dean of the College of Education at the University of Texas, Permian Basin, begins by sharing a story of his great-niece's experience in a junior high school that enforces harsh zero tolerance policy discipline policies. Guilty for committing a minor infraction, she was unnecessarily thrust into the school to prison pipeline. Hernandez calls for the dismantling of the school to prison pipeline and cites factors identified by The American Civil Liberties Union (ACLU) that provide practitioners strategies to do so.

Part I, The Rise of an Imprisoning Youth Culture, offers four chapters that provide a history and overview of the school to prison pipeline. In Chapter One, "Criminalizing Education: Zero Tolerance Policies, Police in the Hallways, and the School to Prison Pipeline," Nancy A. Heitzeg explains the "how, where, and why" of youth who become victims of the school to prison pipeline. Next, Annette Fuentes' "The Schoolhouse as Jailhouse" explains how the physical parameters of the school building have become so secure and controlled that it is now comparable to a prison or jail. Chapter Three, "Rethinking the School to Prison Pipeline," by David Gabbard calls for a critical reexamination—and abolition—of compulsory schooling that favors implementation of high-stakes testing/accountability standards and zero tolerance policies. Finally, Damien Soyjoyner's chapter, "Changing the Lens: Moving Away from the School to Prison Pipeline," discusses how the repression of radical groups such as the Blank Panthers of the 1960s and 1970s in ameriKKKa set the foundation for the school to prison pipeline.

Part II, Targeting Youth, moves away from the macro-analysis of Part I to investigate how certain youth cultures are more intensely repressed than others. In Chapter Five, "Punishment Creep and the Crisis of Youth in the Age of

Disposability," Henry Giroux discusses how the global and U.S. economic system—and crisis—lent itself to the rise of for-profit prisons and laws such as Stop and Frisk, both of which aid in mass incarceration. In Chapter Six, "Targets for Arrest," Jesselyn McCurdy uses case studies of Native American youth caught within the juvenile justice system to expose schools as surveillance sites with the goal of arresting youth. The last chapter of the section, "School to Prison Pipeline and Environmental and Food Justice" by Carol Mendoza Fisher investigates how ecoracist laws governed in the city of San Antonio, Texas create disadvantages for low-income communities of color to gain access to parks and recreation landscapes. Mendoza also makes the reader aware of how dangerous toxins found in air, water, soil, and food affect children's behavior, making them more susceptible to the school to prison pipeline.

Part III, Pushout Not Dropout of Marginalized Youth, focuses on some of the most vulnerable marginalized youth who often go unnoticed when examining the school to prison pipeline: Native Americans, Black girls, and LGBT2-SQQIA youth. "Red Road Lost: A Story Based on True Events," by Four Arrows, is an insightful fictional narrative documenting a case of a Native American youth caught in the juvenile justice system. Chapter Nine, "Emerging from Our Silos: Coalition Building for Black Girls," by Maisha T. Winn and Stephanie S. Franklin focuses on girls caught in the prison system and how the incarceration of female youth is increasing each year. The final chapter of the section entitled "Messy, Butch, and Queer LGBTQ Youth and the School-to-Prison Pipeline" by Shannon D. Snapp, Jennifer M. Hoenig, Amanda Fields, and Stephen T. Russel studies the often forgotten, overlooked, and vulnerable *pipeline population* of LGBT2-SQQIA youth, targeted for their actual or perceived identities. In their study, the authors examine hostile school climates, biased and differential treatment, and discipline disparities often experienced by LGBT2-SQQIA youth that could possibly lead to push-out.

Part IV, Special Education Is Segregation, argues that special education, an inherent reinforcement of so-called normalcy, aids in the marginalization and segregation of youth from nondominant cultures who behave and think differently from the status quo. In Chapter Eleven, "Warehousing, Imprisoning, and Labeling Youth 'Minorities,'" law professor Nekima Levy-Pounds exposes and critiques the social power of stigmatization and the concept of Othering. Next, in "Who Wants to Be Special? Pathologization and the Preparation of Bodies for Prison," Deanna Adams and Erica Meiners offer a comparative study of the similarities of populations within prisons and special education classes, focusing on how policies aid in this labeling that leads to the confinement and control of these populations. In the final chapter of this section, "The New Eugenics: Challenging Urban Education and Special Education and the Promise of Hip Hop Pedagogy," Anthony J. Nocella II and Kim Socha argue that special education is a repressive tool, defended by the medical industrial complex and promoted by dominant culture. This chapter argues that just as the new Jim Crow mirrors that of the old, so too is a new eugenics at play working similarly to the classic eugenics model.

Part V, Behind the Walls, offers coauthored chapters by previously and currently incarcerated people, from youth to adults. This section begins with political prisoner Mumia Abu-Jamal's chapter, "Prisons of Ignorance," which challenges the notion that academics can understand, much less relate to, the experience of being imprisoned. Abu-Jamal also demands that the oppressed, specifically people of color, educate one another and the world on nondominate histories, as the opposite remains firmly entrenched in U.S. history books of the public school system. In Chapter Fifteen, "At the End of the Pipeline: Can the Liberal Arts Liberate the Incarcerated?," Deborah Appleman, Ezekiel Caligiuri, and Jon Vang offer a paradigm for putting Abu-Jamal's argument into action via formal courses taught in prisons by volunteer professors/teachers. Rather than offering just the basic first grade to fifth grade English and Math classes, the authors argue for more radical and transformational courses and educational approaches. The final chapter in this section, "Transformative Justice and Hip Hop Activism in Action," by Anthony J. Nocella II, James, Shona, Adriana, and Donquarius, introduces Save the Kids, a national grassroots organization grounded in transformative justice and Hip Hop pedagogy. Named by youth in a New York detention facility in 2009, Save the Kids strives to build a bridge between outsiders and incarcerated youth so that the latter may be hopeful about what lies behind the prison doors.

In Part VI, Transformative Alternatives, the authors introduce alternatives to the school to prison pipeline and youth incarceration. Chapter Seventeen, "Back on the Block: Community Reentry and Reintegration of Formerly Incarcerated Youth," by Don Sawyer and Daniel White Hodge is dedicated to explaining the importance of creating communities willing to welcome and be inclusive of youth released from detention facilities, as opposed to stigmatizing them as violent criminals. This chapter also challenges the policies that hinder such individuals from obtaining an education or a job or renting an apartment. The next chapter, "Youth in Transition and School Reentry: Process, Problems, and Preparation," is by Anne Burns Thomas. Building upon ideas from the previous chapter, Burns Thomas discusses reentry with special attention to how the school system is an obstacle to those attempting to reintegrate into the community. To end this section, "A Reason to Be Angry: A Mother, Her Sons, and the School to Prison Pipeline" by Letitia Basford, Bridget Borer, and Joe Lewis echo Abu-Jamal's sentiments in a distinctive way. Borer, with two sons of color targeted by the criminal justice system, challenges the content of and engagement with cultural diversity within her course taught by Professor Letitia Basford, which Lewis aids in providing an overview of liberatory pedagogies.

Part VII, Building Alternatives to Punitive Justice, encourages readers to consider their own positionality and responsibility and challenge systemic hegemony. This section starts with the chapter, "Finding the School-to-Prison-Pipeline/ Building Abolition Futures," by Erica Meiners. Meiners encourages scholars invested in prison abolition research to reflect on their own positionality, privilege, and the in/exclusion of others, specifically, community resources and LGBT2-SQQIA and feminist voices when engaged in advocacy efforts. Is the goal of such research for professional gain or is it to participate and conquer social/educational injustices toward building transformative schools and communities? Next, Arash Daeshzadeh challenges hegemonic institutional systemic policies and practices rooted in white supremacy ideologies that objectify, criminalize, and balkanize marginalized youth in Chapter Twenty-One, "A New Choice of Weapon: Activism through Hip Hop and Restorative Justice." Readers are introduced to critical restorative justice programs (as opposed to appropriated, deficit-lens, neoliberal versions) grounded in inclusive, participatory practices in which the relationship between educators, students, parents, and community organizations is equitable. And finally, the last chapter in this section, "Youth of Color Fight Back: Transforming Our Communities," written by grassroots activists from the Youth Justice Coalition in Los Angeles, Emilio Lacques-Zapien and Leslie Mendoza, provides step-by-step strategies for dismantling the school to prison pipeline and the incarceration of youth.

Part VIII, Tactics for Abolition, comprises three chapters by the editors of this volume that offer strategies outside and inside the walls of schools to abolish the school to prison pipeline. Chapter Twenty-Three, "Tactics and Strategies to Organize for Abolishing the School to Prison Pipeline," by Anthony Nocella provides readers and community organizers with multiple strategies inspired by grassroots activists Martin L. King Jr. and Mahatma Gandhi. Chapter Twenty-Four, "Abolition Strategies for Teachers Fighting Academic Repression in the Corporate-Academic Industrial Complex," by Priya Parmar provides pedagogical philosophy and strategies for educators to consider while acknowledging the realities of the current conservative political climate pushing for the privatization of public schools. The ideas suggested are grounded in the theoretical and practical framework of Paulo Freire's critical pedagogy. And finally, the last chapter by David Stovall, "Seven Considerations for 'School' Abolition," offers strategies to eliminate the conditions that sustain and support white supremacy that has consistently and continually denigrated, marginalized, and isolated those who have historically had the least.

The Afterword, written by long-time activist-academic Bernardine Dohrn, summarizes the goals of—and analyses within—this anthology, ending with a hopeful—and radical—call to action. We also provide a list of organizations and resources for our readers to research and join in the fight to abolish the school to prison pipeline and prison industrial complex.

REFERENCE

SuspensionStories. (2013). *Graphic: School to prison pipeline.* Retrieved July 1, 2013 from http://www.suspensionstories.com/2012/06/15/graphic-school-to-prison-pipeline/

PART ONE

The Rise of an Imprisoning Youth Culture

Man that school shit is a joke
The same people who control the school system control
The prison system, and the whole social system
Ever since slavery, nawsayin?

—Dead Prez

No one is going to give you the education you need to overthrow them. Nobody is going to teach you your true history, teach you your true heroes, if they know that that knowledge will help set you free.

—Assata Shakur

CHAPTER ONE

Criminalizing Education

Zero Tolerance Policies, Police in the Hallways, and the School to Prison Pipeline[1]

NANCY A. HEITZEG

THE SCHOOL TO PRISON PIPELINE DEFINED

> *In the last decade, the punitive and overzealous tools and approaches of the modern criminal justice system have seeped into our schools, serving to remove children from mainstream educational environments and funnel them onto a one-way path toward prison. … The School-to-Prison Pipeline is one of the most urgent challenges in education today.*
>
> —NAACP (2005)

The promise of free and compulsory public education in the United States is a promise of equal opportunity and access to the "American Dream." This ideal is billed as the great democratic leveler of the proverbial playing field, and proclaims educational attainment as a source of upward social mobility, expanded occupational horizons, and an engaged, highly literate citizenry. This promise has proved to be an illusionary one, marred by a history of segregation—de jure and de facto, by class and race disparities, and by gulfs in both funding and quality. Despite some fleeting hope in the early years of the post–Civil Rights era, the promise remains elusive for many. Indeed, shifts in educational policy in the past

1 An earlier version of this chapter was published as "Education Not Incarceration: Interrupting the School to Prison Pipeline," *Forum on Public Policy*, Oxford University Press, Summer 2009, *2*.

15 years have exacerbated the inherent inequities in public education. Rather than creating an atmosphere of learning, engagement, and opportunity, current educational practices have increasingly blurred the distinction between school and jail. The school to prison pipeline refers to this growing pattern of tracking students out of educational institutions, primarily via "zero tolerance" policies, and tracking them directly and/or indirectly into the juvenile and adult criminal justice systems.

While schools have long been characterized by both formal and informal tracks that route students into various areas of the curriculum, tracking students *out* of school and into jail is a new phenomenon. Current policies have increased the risk of students being suspended, expelled, and/or arrested at school. Risk of entry into the school to prison pipeline is not random. The school to prison pipeline disproportionately impacts the poor, students with disabilities, and youth of color, especially African Americans, who are suspended and expelled at the highest rates, despite comparable rates of infraction (Brown, 2013; Witt, 2007). Youth of color in particular are at increased risk for being "pushed out" of schools—pushed out into the streets, into the juvenile justice system, and/or into adult prisons and jails. This pattern has become so pronounced that scholars, child advocates, and community activists now refer to it as "the school to prison pipeline," the "schoolhouse to jailhouse track," or, as younger and younger students are targeted, "the cradle to prison track" (Advancement Project, 2005; Children's Defense Fund, 2007; NAACP, 2005).

In part, the school to prison pipeline is a consequence of schools that criminalize minor disciplinary infractions via zero tolerance policies, have a police presence at the school, and rely on suspensions and expulsions for minor infractions. What were once disciplinary issues for school administrators are now called crimes, and students are either arrested directly at school or their infractions are reported to the police. Students are criminalized via the juvenile and/or adult criminal justice systems. The risk of later incarceration for students who are suspended or expelled and detained by police is also great. For many, going to school has become literally and figuratively synonymous with going to jail.

The school to prison pipeline is most immediately related to zero tolerance policies, their police-based enforcement, and to failing schools that are overcrowded, inadequately resourced, and highly segregated. But it is also the result of larger social and political trends. The school to prison pipeline is consistent with media-driven fears of crime and "super-predators," an increasingly harsh legal system for both juveniles and adults, and the rise of the prison industrial complex. What follows is a discussion of the factors that contribute to the school to prison pipeline, an in-depth analysis of the flaws of zero tolerance policies, and recommendations for the interruption of this growing pattern of punishing rather than educating our nation's youth.

THE SCHOOL TO PRISON PIPELINE: THE CONTEXT

The school to prison pipeline does not exist in a vacuum. It is deeply connected to a socio-political climate that is increasingly fearful and punitive. The tendency toward criminalization and incarceration has seeped into the schools, and with each year this legal net ensnares younger and younger children. The willingness of some officials to have handcuffed 5-year-olds escorted from school by uniformed police officers cannot be accounted for by educational policy alone. How have some young children come to be viewed as so dangerous? What factors account for the policy shifts that shape the school to prison pipeline? How has the line between school and legal systems become so blurred? Who benefits when a growing number of children are pushed out of education and into risk for incarceration? The answers in part can be found by a closer examination of the role of both media constructions and the ongoing push toward prisonization.

MEDIA CONSTRUCTION OF CRIME AND CRIMINALS

A substantial body of research documents the role of media—especially television—in constructing perceptions of crime and public images of the criminal, and subsequently shaping attitudes, everyday interactions, and public policy. Television reaches almost every household, and the average American consumes over 4 hours of TV viewing each day (Croteau & Hoynes, 2001, p. 5). Television shapes what issues we think about and how we think about them. This is particularly true with regard to TV news coverage of crime; "the public depends on the media for its pictures of crime" (Dorfman & Schiraldi, 2001, p. 3).

The TV world of crime and criminals, however, is an illusion. TV news does not accurately reflect reality, especially when it comes to reporting on crime. As Walker, Spohn, and DeLone (2012, p. 25) observe,

> Our perceptions of crimes are shaped to a large extent by the highly publicized crimes featured on the nightly news and sensationalized in newspapers. We read about young African American and Hispanic males who sexually assault, rob and murder whites, and we assume that these crimes are typical. We assume that the typical crime is a violent crime, that the typical victim is white, and that the typical offender is African American or Hispanic.

These assumptions are false. TV news constructs a portrait of crime, criminals, and victims that is not supported by any data. In general, the research indicates that violent crime and youth crime are dramatically over-represented, crime coverage has increased in spite of falling crime rates, African Americans and Latinos are over-represented as offenders and underrepresented as victims, and inter-racial crime, especially crimes involving white victims, is over-reported (Dorfman & Schiraldi, 2001, p. 5).

Beyond over-representation as "criminals," African American offenders are depicted in a more negative way than are their white counterparts. Blacks are most likely to be seen on TV news as criminals; they are four times more likely than whites to be seen in a mug shot; twice as likely to be shown in physical restraints; and two times less likely to be identified by name. Black suspects are also depicted as more poorly dressed and are much less likely to speak than white suspects, reinforcing the notion that they are indistinct from non-criminal blacks (Entman & Rojecki, 2000).

The media's general misrepresentation of crime and criminals certainly extends to youth; some estimates indicate that as much as two-thirds of violent crime coverage focused on youth under age 25 (Hancock, 2001). The context for the current climate of repressive youth policies was set in the late 1980s and throughout the 1990s. Media-generated hysteria inextricably linked "teen super-predators," gang violence, and the crack cocaine "epidemic," and all were unmistakably characterized as issues of race. The coverage of the youth gangs, which focused almost exclusively on African American and Latino gangs, exaggerated the extent of gang membership and gang violence, contributing to the creation of "moral panic" (McCorkle & Miethe, 1998). Headlines screamed dire warnings about the legions of teen super-predators that would come of age by 2010; of course, they were urban, they were black and brown, and they were relentlessly violent (Templeton, 1998). Given apparent legitimacy by conservative academics such as Wilson (1995) and DiLulio (1995) this super-predator script took off among both media and policy makers. Violence, gangs, crack, and youth of color became synonymous (Sheldon, Tracy, & Brown, 2001; Walker et al., 2012).

These media representations have real consequences. TV news coverage of crime reflects and reinforces what Glassner (1999) calls "the culture of fear." This is supported by decades of research. Study after study finds that heavy TV viewers (i.e., those who watch more than 4 hours a day) overestimate the crime rate, the likelihood of crime victimization, and the extent of stranger-related violence. In general, heavy TV viewers are nearly twice as likely as light viewers to report crime as the most serious problem, believe crime rates are rising, and indicate personal fear of victimization (Braxton, 1997; Farkas & Duffet, 1998; Gerbner, 1994). They have adopted what Gerbner (1994) calls "the mean-world syndrome"; they are overly fearful and mistrustful of strangers.

And, according to TV news, these "strangers" are young black or Latino males. TV news coverage of crime creates and reinforces the stereotype of the young black male, in particular, as the criminal. As Perry (2001, p. 185) observes,

"Black males historically have been presented as the 'villain.' ... The race-crime nexus is inescapable in a culture that defines black males as predators." Several studies document the impact of TV news coverage of crime on public perceptions of blacks and Latinos. The images of black males as criminals are so deeply entrenched in the public's mind that 60% of people watching a newscast without an image of the offender falsely "remembered" seeing one. Of these viewers, 70% "remembered" the perpetrator as black (Gilliam & Iyengar, 2000). In one experimental study, brief exposures to mug shots of blacks and Hispanic males increased levels of fear among viewers, reinforced racial stereotypes, and led viewers to recommend harsh penalties (Gilliam & Iyengar, 1998). Another study found that black suspects were more likely than whites to be viewed as guilty, more likely to commit violence in the future, and less likeable (Peffley, Shields, & William, 1996).

Widespread acceptance of this stereotype by the general public has implications for everyday interactions that youth of color have in public places, with employers, with teachers, with public officials, and with the police (Walker et al., 2007). Certainly, TV-driven notions of blacks and Hispanics as "predators" provide whites and others with justification for pre-judgments and negative responses. Media-based preconceptions may play a role in the school to prison pipeline. Prejudice and stereotype acceptance can lead to miscommunications between black students and white teachers; this is a possible contributor to the racial disproportionality in suspension and expulsion. Some of the highest rates of racially disproportionate discipline are found in states with the lowest minority populations, where the disconnect between white teachers and black students is potentially the greatest (Witt, 2007).

Widespread acceptance of the stereotype of youth of color as violent predators also has implications for public policy. The media script of youth of color as violent super-predators provided the backdrop for a series of policy changes as well. Juvenile justice systems across the nation were rapidly transformed in a more punitive direction with media accounts—rather than statistical evidence—driving the agenda.

> Underlying this assault on juvenile justice is the demonization of youth, particularly young people of color, who are stereotypically portrayed as roaming the streets and destroying the fabric of society. ... The media's imagery reflects confused reporting of crime statistics, at best, and forsakes the reality of crime rates in favor of sensationalized accounts of youthful offenders, at worst. (Silverstein, 1997, p. 2)

The policy shifts in juvenile justice are both consistent with and in furtherance of other significant phenomena related to the school to prison pipeline—mass incarceration and the emergence of the prison industrial complex.

THE RISE OF THE PRISON INDUSTRIAL COMPLEX

During the past 40 years there has been a dramatic escalation the U.S. prison population, a ten-fold increase since 1970. The increased rate of incarceration can be traced to the War on Drugs and the rise of lengthy mandatory minimum prison sentences for drug crimes and other felonies. These policies have proliferated, not in response to crime rates or any empirical data that indicate their effectiveness, but in response to the aforementioned media depictions of both crime and criminals and newfound sources of profit for prisons (Davis, 2003).

The United States currently has the highest incarceration rate in the world. More than 2.2 million persons are in state or federal prisons and jails—a rate of 751 out of every 100,000 (Jones & Mauer, 2013). Another 5 million are under some sort of correctional supervision such as probation or parole (Pew, 2008).

These harsh policies—mandatory minimums for drug violations, "three strikes" policies, increased use of imprisonment as a sentencing option, lengthy prison terms—disproportionately affect people of color. As Michelle Alexander (2010) observes in *The New Jim Crow*, these policies and their differential enforcement have, in effect, reinscribed a racial caste system in the United States. A brief glimpse into the statistics immediately reveals both the magnitude of these policy changes as well as their racial dynamic. Despite no statistical differences in rates of offending, the poor, the undereducated, and people of color, particularly African Americans, are over-represented in these statistics at every phase of the criminal justice system (Walker et al., 2012). While 1 in 35 adults is under correctional supervision and 1 in every 100 adults is in prison, 1 in every 36 Latino adults, 1 in every 15 black men, 1 in every 100 black women, and 1 in 9 black men ages 20 to 34 are incarcerated (Pew, 2008). Approximately 50% of all prisoners are black, 30% are white, and about 17% Latino, with blacks being imprisoned at more than 9 times the rate of whites (Bureau of Justice Statistics, 2012).

To complicate matters, punitive policies extend beyond prison time served. In addition to the direct impact of mass criminalization and incarceration, there is a plethora of what Mauer and Chesney-Lind (2002) refer to as "invisible punishments." These additional collateral consequences further decimate communities of color politically, economically, and socially. The current expansion of criminalization and mass incarceration is accompanied by legislation that further limits the political and economic opportunities of convicted felons and former inmates. "Collateral consequences" are now attached to many felony convictions and include voter disenfranchisement; denial of federal welfare, medical, housing, or educational benefits; accelerated time lines for loss of parental rights; and exclusion from any number of employment opportunities. Collateral consequences are particularly harsh for drug felons who represent the bulk of the recently incarcerated. Drug felons are permanently barred from receiving public assistance such as TANF, Medicaid, food stamps or SSI, federal financial aid for education, and federal housing assistance. These policies dramatically reduce the successful reintegration of former inmates, increasing the likelihood of recidivism and return to prison.

One of the most insidious aspects of this project in mass incarceration is its connection to the profit motive (Davis, 2003). Once solely a burden on taxpayers, the so-called prison industrial complex is now a source of corporate profit, governmental agency funding, cheap neo-slave labor, and employment for economically depressed regions. "The prison industrial complex is not a conspiracy, but a confluence of special interests that include politicians who exploit crime to win votes, private companies that make millions by running or supplying prisons and small town officials who have turned to prisons as a method of economic development" (Silverstein, 2003). This complex now includes more than 3,300 jails, more than 1,500 state prisons, and 100 federal prisons in the United States. Nearly 300 of these are private for-profit prisons (American Civil Liberties Union [ACLU], 2011). More than 30 of these institutions are super-maximum facilities, not including the super-maximum units located in most other prisons.

As Brewer and Heitzeg (2008) observe: "The prison industrial complex is a self-perpetuating machine where the vast profits and perceived political benefits to policies that are additionally designed to insure an endless supply of 'clients' for the criminal justice system." Profits are generated via corporate contracts for cheap inmate labor, private and public supply and construction contracts, job creation for criminal justice professionals, and continued media profits from exaggerated crime reporting and the use of crime/punishment as ratings-grabbing news and entertainment. The perceived political benefits include reduced unemployment rates due to both job creation and imprisonment of the poor and unemployed, "get tough on crime" and public safety rhetoric, funding increases for police as well as criminal justice system agencies and professionals.

And these policies—enhanced police presence in poor neighborhoods and communities of color; racial profiling; mandatory minimum and "three-strikes" sentencing; draconian conditions of incarceration and a reduction of prison services that contribute to the likelihood of "recidivism"; and "collateral consequences" that nearly guarantee continued participation in "crime" and return to the prison industrial complex following initial release—have major implications for youth of color.

A similarly repressive trend has emerged in the juvenile justice system. The juvenile justice system shifted sharply from its original rehabilitative, therapeutic, and reform goals. While the initial Supreme Court rulings of the 1960s—*Kent*, *in re Gault*, and *Winship*—sought to offer juveniles some legal protections in what was in fact a legal system, more recent changes have turned the juvenile justice system into a "second-class criminal court that provides youth with neither therapy or justice" (Feld, 2007).

Throughout the 1990s, nearly all states and the federal government enacted a series of legislation that criminalized a host of "gang-related activities," made it easier (and in some cases mandatory) to try juveniles as adults, lowered the age at which juveniles could be referred to adult court, and widened the net of juvenile justice with blended sentencing options that included sentences in both the juvenile and adult systems (Griffin, 2008; Heitzeg, 2009; Podkopacz & Feld, 2001; Walker et al., 2007). The super-predator youth and rampant media coverage of youth violence provided the alleged justification for this legislation as well as for additional federal legislation such as the Consequences for Juvenile Offenders Act of 2002 (first proposed in 1996) and the Gun-Free Schools Act of 1994, which provides the impetus for zero tolerance policies in schools and the school to prison pipeline, the subject of later detailed discussion.

The racial disparities are even greater for youth. African Americans, while representing 17% of the youth population, account for 45% of all juvenile arrests. (NAACP, 2005). Black youth are two times more likely than white youth to be arrested, to be referred to juvenile court, to be formally processed and adjudicated as delinquent, or to be referred to the adult criminal justice system, and they are three times more likely than white youth to be sentenced to out-of-home residential placement (Panel on Justice, 2001; Walker et al., 2012). Nationally, 1 in 3 black and 1 in 6 Latino boys born in 2001 are at risk of imprisonment during their lifetime. While boys are five times as likely as girls to be incarcerated, girls are at increasing risk. This rate of incarceration is endangering children at younger and younger ages (Children's Defense Fund, 2007).

In addition, black youth are at additional risk due to the high rates of imprisonment for African American adults. Black youth are increasingly likely to have a parent in prison—among those born in 1990, 1 in 4 black children by age 14 had a father in prison. Risk is concentrated among black children whose parents are high school dropouts; 50% of those children had a father in prison (Wildeman, 2009). African American youth are at increasing risk of out-of-home placement due to the incarceration of parents. While young black children make up about 17% of the nation's youth, they now account for more than 50% of the children in foster care. This explosion in foster care has been fueled by the destabilization of families and the mass incarceration of black men and women (Bernstein, 2005; Brewer, 2007; Roberts, 2004; Wildeman, 2009).

It is youth of color who are being tracked into the prison pipeline via media stereotyping, a punishment-oriented juvenile justice system, and educational practices such as zero tolerance. All are designed, by intent or default, to ensure an endless stream of future bodies into the prison industrial complex. As Donzinger (1996, p. 87) aptly notes,

> Companies that service the criminal justice system need sufficient quantities of raw materials to guarantee long-term growth *in the criminal justice field, the raw material is prisoners.* ... The industry will do what it must to guarantee a steady supply. For the supply of prisoners to grow, criminal justice policies must insure a sufficient number of incarcerated Americans whether crime is rising or the incarceration is necessary.

While media coverage was instrumental in creating the climate of fear, the policy shifts that resulted were consistent with larger trends in criminal justice. Critics of these policy changes charge that this is no mere coincidence. The proliferation of mandatory minimum sentences, punitive measures in juvenile justice, and attendant collateral consequences serve to incarcerate and reincarcerate current generations, but it is the school to prison pipeline and related educational policies/practices that shape the "client pool" for future generations of the incarcerated. While Advanced Placement high school courses and vocational tracks prepare students for their respective positions in the workforce, it is the "schoolhouse to jailhouse track" that prepares students for their futures as inmate neo-slave laborers in the political economy of the prison industrial complex. The age of mass incarceration and the prison industrial complex calls for the continual replenishment of the ranks of the imprisoned, and it is youth of color who are most often selected to fill that onerous role.

THE SCHOOL TO PRISON PIPELINE: ZERO TOLERANCE AND POLICING IN THE HALLWAYS

While media and the rise of the prison industrial complex create the context, shifts in educational policy provide the immediate impetus for the flow of children from school to legal systems. The school to prison pipeline is facilitated by several trends in education that most negatively impact students of color. These include growing poverty rates and declining school funding, resegregation of schools by race and class, underrepresentation of students of color in Advanced Placement courses and over-representation in special education tracks, No Child Left Behind (NCLB), high-stakes testing, and rising drop-out/push-out rates (Darling-Hammond, 2007; NAACP, 2005). All these factors are correlated with the school to prison pipeline, and each is the subject of lengthy analysis elsewhere.The focus here is increased reliance on zero tolerance policies, which play an immediate and integral role in feeding the school to prison pipeline. These policies, in combination with the aforementioned factors, provide the direct mechanism by which students are removed from school by suspension/expulsion, pushed toward dropping out, charged in juvenile court, and routed into the prison pipeline.

While there is no official definition of "zero tolerance," generally the term means that a harsh, predefined, mandatory consequence is applied to a violation of school rules without regard to the seriousness of the behavior, mitigating circumstances, or the situational context (American Psychological Association [APA], 2006). Zero tolerance policies are additionally associated with an increased police and security presence at school, metal detectors, security cameras, locker and person searches, and all the accoutrements of formal legal control. Violators—disproportionately black and Latino—are suspended, expelled, and increasingly arrested and charged in juvenile court as a result (American Bar Association [ABA], 2001).

Zero tolerance rhetoric, which was borrowed from the War on Drugs, became widespread as school officials and community leaders expressed outrage at gang shootings and the impending wave of "super-predators." Despite school crime rates that were stable or declining, related policies were implemented by the mid-1990s. The Gun-Free Schools Act of 1994 (GFSA) provided the initial impetus for zero tolerance policies. The GFSA mandates that all schools that receive federal funding must (1) have policies to expel for a calendar year any student who brings a firearm to school or to a school zone, and (2) report that student to local law enforcement, thereby blurring any distinction between disciplinary infractions at school and the law. Subsequent amendments to the GFSA and changes in many state laws and local school district regulations broadened the GFSA focus on firearms to apply to many other kinds of weapons (Birkland & Lawrence, 2009; Skiba, 2001).

Most schools have adopted zero tolerance policies for a variety of behavioral issues—largely directed toward weapons, alcohol/drugs, threatening behavior, and fighting on school premises—and, as the name implies, indicate zero tolerance for any infractions. According to the Centers for Disease Control (2006), in most cases 100% of school districts had prohibitions against weapons and fighting, nearly 80% had bans on gang activity at school, and more than 90% had implemented zero tolerance policies for alcohol, tobacco, and other drugs.

The Safe Schools Act of 1994 and a 1998 amendment to the Omnibus Crime Control and Safe Streets Act of 1968 promoted partnerships between schools and law enforcement, including the provision of funding for in-school police forces or school resource officers (Raymond, 2010). It has become routine for districts to assign staff/volunteers to monitor halls and bathrooms, equip staff with communication devices, use metal detectors and cameras, and have uniformed security guards or police present. It is less common but is now also possible for some schools to employ canine units, Tasers, and SWAT team raids for drug and weapons searches (Birkland & Lawrence, 2009). Ironically, although enhanced security measures were largely inspired by the school shootings in mostly white suburban schools, they have been most readily adopted and enforced in urban schools with low student-to-teacher ratios, high percentages of students of color, and lower test scores. Nearly 70% of these schools report a police presence (Justice Policy Institute, 2011; Na & Gottfredson, 2011; Skiba, 2001).

Zero tolerance policies have generally involved harsh disciplinary consequences such as long-term and/or permanent suspension or expulsion for violations, and often arrest and referral to juvenile or adult court. While the original intent of the GFSA was to require these punishments for serious violations involving weapons, they have frequently been applied to minor or nonviolent violations of rules such as tardiness and disorderly conduct. According to the ABA (2001), zero tolerance policies do not distinguish between serious and non-serious offenses, nor do they adequately separate intentional troublemakers from those with behavioral disorders. They cast a very wide net; students have been suspended or expelled for having nail clippers, Advil, and mouthwash. Zero tolerance policies target students for minor infractions, increasingly focus on younger elementary and preschool students, and often rely on force and arrest for relatively minor disciplinary issues. Consider the following cases:

- A 17-year-old high school junior shot a paper clip with a rubber band at a classmate, missed, and broke the skin of a cafeteria worker. The student was expelled from school.
- A 9-year-old on the way to school found a manicure kit with a 1-inch knife. The student was suspended for 1 day.
- Two 10-year-old boys from Arlington, Virginia, were suspended for 3 days for putting soapy water in a teacher's drink. The boys were charged with a felony that carried a maximum sentence of 20 years, and were formally processed through the juvenile justice system before the case was dismissed months later.
- A Pennsylvania kindergartener told her pals she was going to shoot them with a Hello Kitty toy that makes soap bubbles. The kindergartener was initially suspended for 2 days, and the incident was reclassified as "threat to harm others."
- In Massachusetts, a 5-year-old boy attending an after-school program made a gun out of Legos and pointed it at other students while "simulating the sound of gunfire," as one school official put it. He was expelled.
- A 5-year-old boy in Queens, New York, was arrested, handcuffed, and taken to a psychiatric hospital for having a tantrum and knocking papers off the principal's desk.
- In St. Petersburg, Florida, a 5-year-old girl was handcuffed, arrested, and taken into custody for having a tantrum and disrupting a classroom.
- An 11-year-old girl in Orlando, Florida, was Tasered by a police officer, arrested, and faces charges of battery on a security resource officer, disrupting a school function, and resisting with violence. She had pushed another student.
- An honors student in Houston, Texas, was forced to spend a night in jail when she missed class to go to work to support her family.

- A 13-year old from New York was handcuffed and removed from school for writing the word "okay" on her school desk. (Advancement Project, 2012; Eckholm, 2013; Justice Policy Institute, 2011)

Zero tolerance policies have proliferated without evidence that they actually improve school safety and security (Skiba, 2001). In theory, zero tolerance policies are intended to have a deterrent effect for intentionally troublesome students, that is, the mere presence of the policies is intended to thwart disruptive behavior. But, as with harsh penalties for juvenile and criminal justice, zero tolerance was adopted and expanded in lieu of data supporting either effectiveness or need.

There is, however, mounting evidence that these policies do contribute to the school to prison pipeline. According to the Advancement Project (2005),

> Zero tolerance has engendered a number of problems: denial of education through increased suspension and expulsion rates, referrals to inadequate alternative schools, lower test scores, higher dropout rates, and racial profiling of students. … Once many of these youths are in "the system," they never get back on the academic track. Sometimes, schools refuse to readmit them; and even if these students do return to school, they are often labeled and targeted for close monitoring by school staff and police. Consequently, many become demoralized, drop out, and fall deeper and deeper into the juvenile or criminal justice systems. Those who do not drop out may find that their discipline and juvenile or criminal records haunt them when they apply to college or for a scholarship or government grant, or try to enlist in the military or find employment. In some places, a criminal record may prevent them or their families from residing in publicly subsidized housing. In this era of zero tolerance, the consequences of child or adolescent behaviors may long outlive students' teenage years. (p. 12)

Several specific problems with zero tolerance policies warrant closer examination: racial disproportionality, increased rates of expulsion, elevated drop-out rates, and denial of due process and equal protection for students.

RACIAL DISPROPORTIONALITY

On the surface, zero tolerance policies are facially neutral; they are to apply equally to all regardless of race, class, and gender. A growing body of research suggests that these policies are anything but (ABA, 2001; NAACP, 2005; Skiba, 2001).

Criminalized education disproportionately impacts the poor, students with disabilities, LGBT students, and youth of color, especially African Americans, who are suspended, expelled, and arrested at the highest rates, despite comparable rates of infraction (Advancement Project, 2011; Witt, 2007). The U.S. Department of Education, Civil Rights Division, documents the disparity. Nationally, black students were three and a half times more likely to be suspended or expelled than their white peers. One in five black boys and more than 1 in 10 black girls received an out-of-school suspension (Lewin, 2012).

Black students make up only 18% of students, but they account for 35% of those suspended once, 46% of those suspended more than once, and 39% of all expulsions. In districts that reported expulsions under zero tolerance policies, Hispanic and black students represent 45% of the student body, but 56% of those expelled under such policies (Advancement Project, 2012; Lewin, 2012). In addition, black and Latino students represent more than 70% of the students arrested or referred to law enforcement at school (Eckholm, 2013). This racial over-representation then manifests itself in both higher drop-out rates for students of color (students from historically disadvantaged minority groups have little more than a fifty-fifty chance of finishing high school with a diploma) as well as the racialized dynamic of the legal system (Losen & Gillepsie, 2012; Schott Foundation for Public Education, 2012).

These racial disparities cannot be explained by differences in behavior; they must be explained by differential enforcement of zero tolerance policies. Since research has found no indication that African American youth violate rules at higher rates than do other groups (Skiba, 2001), the persistence of stereotypes of young black males and "cultural miscommunication" between students and teachers is oft cited as one key factor. Eighty-three percent of the nation's teaching ranks are filled by whites, mostly women, and stereotypes can shape the decision to suspend or expel.

> Some of the highest rates of racially disproportionate discipline are found in states with the lowest minority populations, where the disconnect between white teachers and black students is potentially the greatest. White teachers feel more threatened by boys of color. They are viewed as disruptive. (Witt, 2007, p. 6A)

The matter is further complicated by the tendency of teachers and school officials to define disruptive white youth as in need of medical intervention rather than zero tolerance consequences. One of the growth sectors of psychiatry is the diagnosis and treatment of Disorders of Infancy, Childhood and Adolescence (DICA), particularly the Disruptive Behavior Disorders of Attention-Deficit Hyperactivity Disorder and the Oppositional Defiant Disorder and Conduct Disorder (APA, 2006; Diller, 1998; Males, 1996). These psychiatric labels perfectly overlap with potential educational and legal labels, and thus offer an alternative mechanism for parents, school officials, and law enforcement to deal with disciplinary infractions and drug use by students. Indeed, research indicates that class, insurance coverage, and race are key indicators of who receives treatment (Safer & Malever, 2000). These factors play a significant role in the labeling of youth in particular; study after study shows racial disparities in the diagnosis and treatment of ADHD as well as other Disruptive Behavior Disorders, with the indication that teachers are most likely to expect and define ADHD as an issue for white boys (Currie, 2005; Safer & Malever, 2000).

This racial disproprtionality is cited as one of the key factors in the school to prison pipeline. Students who are already subject to what the Panel on Juvenile Justice (2001) calls compound and cumulative risk for legal processing have that risk magnified by zero tolerance policies that are unequally applied.

INCREASED RATES OF SUSPENSIONS AND EXPULSIONS

Not surprisingly, zero tolerance policies have led to a dramatic increase in suspensions and expulsions. Annually, there are approximately 3.3 million suspensions and more than 100,000 expulsions each year (National Center for Education Statistics [NCES], 2012). This number has nearly doubled since 1974, with rates escalating in the mid-1990s as zero tolerance policies began to be widely adopted (NAACP, 2005). These rates have risen even though school violence generally has been stable or declining (Skiba, 2001).

In addition to increased rates of suspension/expulsion for elementary and secondary students, zero tolerance policies have seeped downward to impact preschool children. Nearly 7 of every 1,000 preschoolers are expelled from state-funded preschool programs—more than three times the rate of expulsions in grades K–12 (NAACP, 2005).

This is not a climate conducive to education—not just for the suspended, certainly, but for all students. Turning schools into "secure environments"—replete with drug-sniffing dogs, searches, and school-based police—lowers morale and makes learning more difficult. It also engenders a sense of mistrust between students and teachers, and contributes to negative attitudes toward school in general (Advancement Project, 2005).

For students who are suspended or expelled, the stakes are even higher. Students are deprived of educational services and, at best, are referred to substandard, alternatives schools. Many states fail to offer any access to alternative schools. Students are left to fend for themselves, and if they are reinstated they have become even further behind their peers and more likely to be suspended again (Polakow-Suransky, 2010). In fact, rather than deterring disruptive behavior, the most likely consequence of suspension is additional suspension (National Association of School Psychologists [NASP], 2006). There has yet to be a research study identifying a direct correlation between zero tolerance policies and safe schools; a few studies have indicated that the zero tolerance policies do not result in fewer disciplinary infractions or reductions in the number of repeat offenders. The American Psychological Association (2006) reported finding no evidence that zero tolerance policies are associated with negative outcomes for youth, academically, socially, emotionally, and behaviorally; this includes a decreased commitment to education in light of perceptions of unfair treatment (Arum & Preiss, 2008).

Increasingly, suspension and expulsion occur simultaneously with arrest. Many schools are further expediting the flow of children out of the schools and into the criminal justice system by doling out a double dose of punishment for students who misbehave. In addition to being suspended or expelled, students are also increasingly finding themselves arrested or referred to law enforcement or juvenile court and prosecuted for behavior at school. Students who are suspended or expelled may also be referred to juvenile court by school officials, but in a growing number of schools, zero tolerance policies are directly enforced by police or school resource officers. There have been no national data collected on juvenile arrests that originate at school, but reports on a variety of districts indicate that school-based arrests have more than doubled. The presence of police officers at school—most of them large, urban, predominantly minority schools—adds as well to racial disparities as racial profiling practices are transferred from the streets to the hallways (Advancement Project, 2005; Dohrn, 2000). In addition, the majority of these arrests are not for weapons or drugs, but instead for minor infractions such as disorderly conduct or disruptions. This criminalization of what were once issues of school discipline is a direct conduit into the prison pipeline.

ELEVATED DROP-OUT RATES

Zero tolerance policies contribute to the already high drop-out rate for students of color. Students from historically disadvantaged minority groups (American Indian, Hispanic, and black) have little more than a fifty-fifty chance of finishing high school with a diploma. By comparison, graduation rates for whites and Asians are 75% and 77% nationally, respectively. Students in intensely segregated (90%–100%) minority schools are more than four times as likely to be in predominantly poor schools than their peers attending schools with fewer than 10% minority students (84% compared with 18%) (Orfield & Lee, 2004; Schott Foundation, 2012). And of course, these are the schools that take the most strident approaches to zero tolerance.

Increased drop-out rates are directly related to the repeated use of suspension and expulsion (NASP, 2006). Students who have been suspended or expelled are more likely to experience poor academic performance, and eventually drop out (Advancement Project, 2011). Additional suspensions increase this likelihood; the National Center for Education Statistics (2006) documents this: 31% of high school sophomores who left school had been suspended three or more times, a rate much higher than for those who left school who had not been suspended at all.

Critics have noted that zero tolerance policies have been used to "push out" low-performing students in the era of No Child Left Behind legislation. Since school funding is directly tied to test scores, NCLB gives schools an incentive to get rid of rather than remediate students with low test scores. According to the NAACP (2005),

> Ironically, some of the hallmarks of modern education reform—including demands for greater accountability, extensive testing regimes, and harsh sanctions imposed on schools and teachers—actually encourage schools to funnel out those students whom they believe are likely to drag down a school's test scores. Rather than address the systemic problems that lead to poor educational performance, harsh discipline policies provide schools with a convenient method to remove certain students and thereby mask educational deficiencies. (p. 4)

Recent studies show how schools in a number of states have raised test scores by "losing" large numbers of low-scoring students; most of these students are of color. In one Texas city, scores soared while tens of thousands of students—mostly African American and Latino—disappeared from school. Educators reported that exclusionary policies were used to hold back, suspend, expel, or counsel students to drop out in order to boost scores (Advancement Project, 2010; Darling-Hammond, 2007).

Even when well-intentioned educators wish to help these students, schools are often lacking the guidance counselors, intervention programs, and other resources to address students with special educational and behavioral needs. They may feel there is no alternative to pushing them out, even if the result may involve immediate or future incarceration. Zero tolerance policies create a venue for doing so.

LEGAL AND CONSTITUTIONAL QUESTIONS

Zero tolerance policies raise a myriad of legal issues related to statutory vagueness, inconsistent application, and lack of due process for searches/seizures and arrests that occur on school property (ABA, 2001). These policies present clear constitutional questions with regard to both definition and enforcement.

Zero tolerance mandates have come under attack for both statutory vagueness and failure to allow local school administrators discretion in determining application of these policies. Many state laws fail to clearly distinguish between serious and trivial policy violations. For example, many state laws do not define "dangerous weapon," but then require expulsion under the federal Gun-Free Schools Act. It is this lack of clarity that has allowed for the expulsion of students with scissors and nail clippers. Similar vagueness pervades other aspects of zero tolerance, including the failure to define "dangerous drugs," threatening behavior, and so on (Polakow-Suransky, 2010). Statutory vagueness makes it impossible for students to know exactly what is being prohibited, and lack of clearly defined school rules and procedures allows officials tremendous discretion to suspend and expel students for minor infractions.

This vagueness plagues due process expectations as well. Again, many states have no stated requirements or clearly published set of expectations for students and parents. Not only is there no clarity as to exactly what is prohibited, there is also no identified procedure that enumerates students' rights, procedural expectations, or processes to allow for appeal or re-instatement (Polakow-Suransky, 2010). This is a clear violation of even the rudimentary due process rights accorded to students under the Supreme Court decision of *Goss v. Lopez* (419 U.S. 565 1975), which held that students may not be suspended without a hearing. Under many state laws, students may currently be suspend and/or expelled without hearings or, in fact, without any written policy guidelines as to recourse, appeal, or request for reinstatement.

The due process concerns for students are magnified by the shrinking boundaries between school and legal systems. The requirement that school officials report certain infractions to law enforcement and the increased presence of police at schools may lead to arrest the due process protections that students may expect outside school (Feld, 2007). Evidence used to legally incriminate students may be obtained in violation of the Fourth and Fifth Amendment prohibitions against unreasonable search/seizure and self-incrimination; students' expectations of school are different from their expectations of police encounters on the street. Zero tolerance policies have led to increased student concerns over perceived rights violations at school, with African American students the most likely of any group to report discrimination in disciplinary procedures (Arum & Preiss, 2008). This result is unsurprising, given that black and Latino students represent more than 70% of the students arrested or referred to law enforcement at school (Eckholm, 2013).

In the past decade, a growing number of legal challenges to zero tolerance policies have been raised. The bulk of these suits involve policies related to drugs and weapons and raise questions regarding vagueness, interrogations in lieu of *Miranda*, and intrusive searches and seizures. Most of these cases are brought by students from wealthier, majority white schools (Arum & Preiss, 2008). Recently one of these cases made it to the U.S. Supreme Court. In *Safford Unified School District #1 et al. v. Redding*, the Court ruled that a strip search of 13-year-old Savana Redding (who was accused of bringing prescription ibuprofen to school) was, in fact, unreasonable. The decision, which barred some school strip searches for drugs, did not offer schools much guidance or students much hope for Fourth Amendment protection. The narrow ruling upheld the school's right to search Redding's backpack and outer garments. Further, the school was told only to take into account the extent of danger of the contraband in question and to question whether there would be good reason to think it had been hidden in an intimate place (Liptak, 2009). For the foreseeable future, students who are at the most risk of being pushed out of school and into the prison pipeline can expect few legal protections or due process guarantees.

INTERRUPTING THE SCHOOL TO PRISON PIPELINE

> *At issue are the values of a nation that writes off many of its poorest children in deficient urban schools starved of all the riches found in good suburban schools nearby, criminalizes those it has short-changed and cheated, and then willingly expends ten times as much to punish them as it ever spent to teach them when they were still innocent and clean.*
>
> —Kozol (2005)

The school to prison pipeline has already claimed tens of thousands of young lives. Fueled by poverty and segregation, an underfunded education system pressured by high-stakes testing and zero tolerance policies, media misrepresentation of youth crime, and an increasingly draconian justice system, this link between education and incarceration continues to threaten the future of untold prospective students. Failure to address these contributing factors is costly, certainly in terms of the funds diverted from education toward incarceration, but also in lost potential and lost lives.

> Many of these young people never reenter the mainstream educational system, and the loss to society is immeasurable. Not only do communities lose the potential talents that these students hold, but they also commit themselves to expending vast resources—far greater than the resources it would take to adequately fund public education—to deal with the problems that these students will likely pose when they grow into adults. (NAACP, 2005)

For nearly a decade, scholars and activists have organized and pushed for policy changes—particularly an end to zero tolerance policies in school—to interrupt the school to prison pipeline. Recommendations have come from scholars, non-profit advocacy organizations (such the Advancement Project, the NAACP, the Southern Poverty Law Center, the ACLU, the Consortium to Prevent School Violence, and the Children's Defense Fund), and professional associations (e.g., the National Association of School Psychologists, the American Psychological Association, the American Bar Association). The goal of all these programs is to stymie the steady flow of youth of color out of school and into legal systems.

Since zero tolerance policies represent the most immediate and direct conduit from school to legal systems, they have been the target of reform suggestions. Short of repealing zero tolerance legislation, legislatures and school districts could take steps to alleviate some of the surrounding legal issues and disparities. Recommendations include the following (ABA, 2001; Advancement Project, 2012; Hewitt & Losen, 2010; NAACP, 2005):

- State legislatures must clarify statutes pertaining to the referral of students to law enforcement agencies.
- State legislatures must protect the civil rights of all students and safeguard against discriminatory practices that lead to disproportionate expulsion of minority students.
- States should maintain compulsory attendance requirements for those under 16 and mandate and offer alternative educational services.
- State legislatures should clearly define and enforce reinstatement procedures.
- State legislatures should mandate and school districts should engage in collection of arrest/summons data and should monitor referrals to law enforcement to root out subjective, unnecessary, and discriminatory referrals.
- School districts must be sensitive to the experiences that communities of color have had with law enforcement.
- Schools should notify students and parents under what circumstances the law requires, or standard practice dictates, referral of students to law enforcement agencies and for what conduct.
- Schools should implement policies that require that parents, or an adult advocate for the student, be present for any questioning of children in cases in which it is possible that criminal charges may be filed.
- Students should be routinely advised of their *Miranda* rights in cases in which criminal charges may be filed.

Similarly, school districts and school administrations could revise their particular policies to reduce suspensions and expulsions and offer meaningful alternatives for disruptive students. Suggestions—which have been established by experience and data as effective alternatives—include the following (APA, 2006; Consortium to Prevent School Violence [CPSV], 2008; Hewitt & Losen, 2010; Justice Policy Institute, 2011; NASP, 2008):

- Schools must cease criminalizing students for trivial behaviors that can be handled by traditional, educationally sound school disciplinary measures.
- Schools should avoid incorporating harsh automatic consequences that do not consider mitigating circumstances into school codes of conduct for specific violations, or remove these restrictions if already in place.
- Schools must employ a wide variety of disciplinary consequences in student codes of conduct, and indicate that the use of these should be tailored to the specific circumstances of the student and the violation.

- Schools should specify graduated categories of inappropriate or undesirable behaviors, and align them with categories of consequences—this is more desirable than specifying punishments for each behavior.
- Schools should minimize the use of exclusionary disciplinary punishments and include an amnesty clause in which it is stipulated that nonviolent students who inadvertently bring banned objects to school or find them can give them to a school official without fear of punishment.
- Schools must instruct their mental health experts—school psychologists, counselors, and social workers—to research and develop discipline policies and positive behavior training strategies.
- In developing alternatives to zero tolerance, schools should involve families and community resources and include violence prevention, social skills training, and early intervention strategies.
- Schools should eliminate police, refrain from using law enforcement responses to student behavior, offer an officer who comes in contact with youth, supply additional training, and create graduated responses to student behavior that take into account the circumstances of the case.

Pilot projects in several school districts have achieved success in reducing suspension and expulsions by relying on alternatives to zero tolerance policies. A number of school districts and states have revised their disciplinary policies, distinguishing between minor infractions and more serious violations, offering graduated responses to discipline, reducing the amount of suspension time, and encouraging a non-punitive commonsense approach to discipline (APA, 2006; NAACP, 2005; NASP, 2006; Southern Poverty Law Center, 2008). Other districts have implemented better data collection methods to facilitate the documentation of disparities in school discipline with an eye toward remedies. Still others have offered additional training and evaluation for police officers who patrol the hallways, with a particular emphasis on dealing with students who have disabilities or mental health challenges (Advancement Project, 2012; Justice Policy Institute, 2011). Most recently, several school districts have turned away entirely from a punishment-centered approach and instead have adopted an approach with an emphasis on restorative/transformative justice models and peace circles as means to create a positive school climate and culture (Brown, 2013; Prison Culture, 2013; Urban Strategies Council, 2012).

Restorative/transformative justice methods have emerged as one of the most promising approaches to creating schools where community—not social control—is at the center. North Lawndale College Prep (NLCP) in Chicago offers an example of how students can benefit from a reliance on counselors rather than cops, and how student conflict mediators can resolve crises in school. Prison Culture (2013) describes a visit to NCLP:

> Walking the halls at NLCP, one is greeted by messages of peace and by college banners. When you talk to students, they seem happy to be at school. ... When we visited, the school was at over 100 days of peace and counting. Every month, student conflict mediators (Peace Warriors) plan incentive events for uninterrupted days of peace.
>
> "Keeping the peace" is very important at NLCP. ... What comes across clearly in the students' words is that they consider the school community to be a family. Families disagree and in the good ones, you are not cast out if you make a mistake.
>
> Restorative justice plays an important role in NLCP's culture. Peace circles are regular occurrences. The entire school has bought into the concept. You can hear it when students talk about getting second chances and teachers discuss the importance of keeping students in school rather than pushing them out through suspensions. (para. 3–5)

Comparable approaches have achieved success in Oakland, Portland, and Denver, where once high suspension and expulsion rates have been reduced dramatically (Brown, 2013; Urban Strategies Council, 2012). The work of transformative justice is often time consuming, but it is certainly less costly in both dollars and lives than the current policies that push students out of school onto a pathway to prison.

But as the school to prison pipeline exists in a larger context, so too must efforts to dismantle it. The interruption of the school to prison pipeline not only requires reforms of educational policies such as zero tolerance, but it also requires a deep examination of our lust for punishment. Current racialized fear-driven policies such as zero tolerance, mass incarceration, and mandatory minimum sentences are rooted in a socio-political climate that emphasizes punishment rather than prevention. Rather than invest in education, policy makers have chosen instead to subsidize incarceration—yes, for corporate profit and political gain, but at exorbitant social costs. While impoverished schools struggle to expend approximately $10,000 per pupil per year, it costs more than $50,000 annually to incarcerate that same child (Kozol, 2005). Different choices might be made if the youth at risk were wealthy or white, but they are not.

Ultimately, the school to prison pipeline can only be truly interrupted by uprooting the racist and classist underpinning of juvenile and criminal justice, by a return to a separate, less punitive juvenile justice system, and by the reenvisioning of a legal system guided by reparative justice rather than retribution and mass imprisonment (Justice Policy Institute, 2008; Council on Crime and Justice, 2008). The future of youth of color depends on our ability to reject the endless cycle of incarceration and recommit to the promise of education.

REFERENCES

Addington, L. A. (2009). Cops and cameras: Public school security as a policy response to Columbine. *American Behavioral Scientist, 52*(10), 1426–1446.

Advancement Project. (2005). *Education on lockdown: The school to jailhouse track.* Washington, DC: Author.

Advancement Project. (2010). *Test, punish and push-out: How "zero tolerance" and high-stakes testing funnel youth into the school-to-prison pipeline.* Washington, DC: Author.

Advancement Project. (2011). *Federal policy, ESEA reauthorization, and the school-to-prison pipeline.* Washington, DC, Author.

Advancement Project. (2012, December 12). *Testimony of Judith A. Browne Dianis Co-Director, Advancement Project Hearing on Ending the School-to-Prison Pipeline Before the Subcommittee on the Constitution, Civil Rights, and Human Rights, Senate Committee on the Judiciary.* Washington, DC, Author.

Advancement Project. (2013). *Police in school is not the answer to the Newtown shootings.* Washington, DC: Author.

Alexander, M. (2010). *The new Jim Crow: Mass incarceration in the era of colorblindness.* New York: Free Press.

American Bar Association. (2001). *Zero tolerance policy.* Washington, DC: Author.

American Civil Liberties Union. (2011). *Banking on bondage: Private prisons and mass incarceration.* New York: Author.

American Psychological Association. (2006). *Are zero tolerance policies effective in the schools? An evidentiary review and recommendations.* Washington, DC: Author.

Arum, R., & Preiss, D. (2008, October 15). *From* Brown *to bong "hits": Assessing a half century of judicial involvement in education.* Washington, DC: American Enterprise Institute for Policy Research.

Birkland, T. A., & Lawrence, R. (2009). Media framing after Columbine. *American Behavioral Scientist, 52,* 1387.

Bernstein, N. (2005). *All alone in the world: Children of the incarcerated.* New York: New Press.

Braxton, G. (1997, June 4). Ratings vs. crime rates: Putting L.A.'s changing numbers into perspective. *The Los Angeles Times.*

Brewer, R. M. (2007). Imperiled black families and the growth of the prison industrial complex in the U.S. In *Justice where art thou?* Minneapolis, MN: Council on Crime and Justice.

Brewer, R. M., & Heitzeg, N. A. (2008). The racialization of crime and punishment: Criminal justice, color-blind racism and the political economy of the prison industrial complex. *American Behavioral Scientist, 51*(5), 65.

Brown, P. L. (2013, April 3). Opening up, students transform a vicious circle. *The New York Times.*

Bureau of Justice Statistics. (2012). *Sourcebook of criminal justice statistics.* Washington, DC: U.S. Government Printing Office.

Centers for Disease Control. (2006). *School policy and school environment questionnaire.* Atlanta, GA: Author.

Children's Defense Fund. (2007). *America's cradle to prison pipeline.* Washington, DC: Author.

Conrad, P., & Schneider, J. W. (1998). *Deviance and medicalization: From badness to sickness.* Philadelphia: Temple University Press.

Consortium to Prevent School Violence. (2008). *Zero tolerance.* Muncie, IN: Author.

Croteau, D., & Hoynes, W. (2001). *The business of media: Corporate media and the public interest.* Thousand Oaks, CA: Pine Forge Press.

Darling-Hammond, L. (2007, May 21). Evaluating No Child Left Behind. *The Nation.*

Davis, A. (2003). *Are prisons obsolete?* New York: Seven Stories Press.

Diller, L. M. (1998). *Running on Ritalin.* New York: Bantam.

DiLulio, J. (1995). The coming of the super-predators. *The Weekly Standard, 1*, 11.

Dohrn, B. (2000). "Look out kid—it's something you did": The criminalizing of children. In V. Polakow, (Ed.), *The public assault on America's children: Poverty, violence and juvenile justice* (pp. 157–186). New York: Teachers College Press.

Donzinger, S. (1996). *The real war on crime: Report of the national criminal justice commission.* New York: Perennial.

Dorfman, L., & Schiraldi, V. (2001). Off balance: Youth, race and crime in the news. Retrieved from http://buldingblocksforyouth.org/media/media.htlm

Dorfman, L., Woodruff, K., Chavez, V., & Wallack, L. (1997). Youth and violence on local television news in California. *American Journal of Public Health, 87*, 1311–1316.

Eckholm, E. (2013, April 12). With police in schools, more children in court. *The New York Times.*

Entman, R. M., & Rojecki, A. (2000). *The black image in the white mind: Media and race in America.* Chicago: University of Chicago Press.

Farkas, S., & Duffet, A. (1998). *Crime, fears and videotape.* Washington, DC: Public Agenda.

Feld, B. C. (2007). Juvenile justice in Minnesota: Framework for the future. In *Justice where art thou?* Minneapolis, MN: Council on Crime and Justice.

Frymer, B. (2009). The media spectacle of Columbine: Alienated youth as an object of fear. *American Behavioral Scientist, 52*, 1387.

Gerbner, G. (1994, Spring). Reclaiming our cultural mythology. *In Context*, 34.

Gilliam, F. D., & Iyengar, S. (1998, Winter). The superpredator script. *Nieman Reports, 52*, 45–52.

Gilliam, F. D., & Iyengar, S. (2000). Prime suspects: The influence of local television news on the viewing public. *American Journal of Political Science, 44*(3), 560–573.

Gilliam, F. D., Iyengar, S., Simon, A., & Wright, O. (1996). Crime in black and white: The violent, scary world of local news. *Harvard International Journal of Press-Politics, 1*, 23.

Glassner, B. (1999). *The culture of fear: Why Americans are afraid of the wrong things.* New York: Basic Books.

Goss v. Lopez. (1975). 419 U.S. 565.

Hancock, L. (2001). Framing children in the news: The face and color of youth crime in America. In V. Polakow, (Ed.), *The public assault on America's children: Poverty, violence and juvenile justice* (pp. 78–100). New York: Teachers College Press.

Heitzeg, N. A. (2009, Winter). Race, class and legal risk in the United States: Youth of color and colluding systems of social control. *Forum on Public Policy.*

Hirschfield, P. J. (2008). Preparing for prison? The criminalization of school discipline in the USA. *Theoretical Criminology, 12*(1), 79–101.

Jones, S., & Mauer, M. (2013). *Race to incarcerate: A graphic retelling.* New York: Free Press.

Justice Policy Institute. (2008). *Disparity by design.* Washington, DC: Author.

Justice Policy Institute. (2011). *Education under arrest: The case against police in schools.* Washington, DC: Author.

Kim, C., Losen, D., & Hewit, D. (2010). *The school to prison pipeline: Structuring legal reform.* New York: NYU Press.

Kozol, J. (2005). *Shame of the nation: The restoration of apartheid schooling in America.* New York: Crown.

Lewin, T. (2012, March 6). Black students face more discipline, data suggests. *The New York Times.*

Liptak, A. (2009, June 26). Supreme Court says child's rights violated by strip search. *The New York Times.*

Losen, D. J., & Gillespie, J. (2012). *Opportunities suspended: The disparate impact of disciplinary exclusion from school.* Los Angeles: The Center for Civil Rights Remedies at the Civil Rights Project.

Mauer, M., & Chesney-Lind, M. (Eds.). (2002). *Invisible punishment: The collateral consequences of mass imprisonment.* New York: New Press.

McCorkle, R. C., & Miethe, T. D. (1998). The political and organizational response to gangs: An examination of a moral panic in Nevada. *Justice Quarterly, 15*, 41–64.

Na, C., & Gottfredson, D. C. (2011). Police officers in schools: Effects on school crime and the processing of offending behaviors. *Justice Quarterly.*

NAACP. (2005). *Interrupting the school to prison pipe-line.* Washington, DC: Author.

National Association of School Psychologists. (2006). *Zero tolerance and alternative strategies: A fact sheet for educators and policymakers.* Bethesda, MD: Author.

National Center for Education Statistics. (2012). *The condition of education.* Washington, DC: Author.

Nolan, K. (2011). *Police in the hallways: Discipline in an urban high school.* Minneapolis: University of Minnesota Press.

Orfield, G., & Lee, C. (2004). *Historic reversals, accelerating resegregation, and the need for new integration strategies.* Los Angeles: Civil Rights Project.

Panel on Justice. (2001). *Juvenile Crime, Juvenile Justice.* Washington D.C.: The National Academies.

Peffley, M., Shields, T., & William, B. (1996). The intersection of race and crime in television news stories: An experimental study. *Political Communication, 13*, 309–327.

Perry, B. (2001). *In the name of hate: Understanding hate crime.* New York: Routledge.

Pew Center on the States. (2008). *One in 100: Behind bars in America 2008.* Washington, DC: Author.

Podkopacz, M. R., & Feld, B. C. (2001). The back-door to prison: Waiver reform, blended sentencing, and the law of unintended consequences. *Journal of Criminal Law and Criminology, 91*, 997.

Polakow-Suransky, S. (2010). America's least wanted: Zero tolerance policies and the fate of expelled students. In V. Polakow (Ed.), *The public assault on America's children: Poverty, violence and juvenile justice* (pp. 101–139). New York: Teachers College Press.

Prison Culture. (2013, April 13). *A different approach to school safety: A short film.* Retrieved from http://www.usprisonculture.com/blog/2013/04/19/a-different-approach-to-school-safety-a short-film/

Raymond, B. (2010). *Assigning police officers to schools.* Problem-oriented guides for police response guides series (Guide no. 10). Washington, DC: Center for Problem-Oriented Policing.

Roberts, D. (2004). The social and moral cost of mass incarceration in African American communities. *Stanford Law Review, 56*(127), 1271–1305.

Safer, D., & Malever, M. (2000). Stimulant treatment in Maryland public schools. *Pediatrics, 106*(3), 553.

Safford Unified School District #1 et al. v. Redding. Certiorari to the United States Court of Appeals for the Ninth Circuit No. 08–479. Argued April 21, 2009—Decided June 25, 2009.

Schott Foundation for Public Education. (2012). *The urgency of now: 50 state report on black males and education.* Cambridge, MA: Author.

Sheldon, R. G., Tracy, S. K., & Brown, W. B. (2001). *Youth gangs in American Society.* Belmont, CA: Wadsworth.

Silverstein, K. (1997, June). America's private gulag. *Prison Legal News.*

Skiba, R. (2001). *Zero tolerance, zero evidence: An analysis of school disciplinary practice.* Bloomington: Indiana Education Policy Center, Indiana University.

Southern Poverty Law Center. (2008). *School to prison pipeline project.* Retrieved from http://www.splcenter.org/legal/schoolhouse.jsp

Templeton, R. (1998, January–February). Superscapegoating: Teen "superpredators" hype set stage for draconian legislation. *FAIR*. Retrieved from on November 24, 203 http://fair.org/extra online-articles/superscapegoating/.

Urban Strategies Council. (2012, May). *African American male achievement initiative: A closer look at suspensions of African American males in OUSD.* Oakland, CA: Author.

Walker, S., Spohn, C., & DeLone, M. (2012). *The color of justice: Race, ethnicity and crime in America* (6th ed.). Belmont, CA: Wadsworth.

Wildeman, C. (2009). Parental imprisonment, the prison boom, and the concentration of childhood disadvantage. *Demography, 46*, 265–280.

Wilson, J. Q. (1995). *Crime.* San Francisco: Institute for Contemporary Studies.

Witt, H. (2007, September 5). School discipline tougher on African Americans. *Chicago Tribune.*

CHAPTER TWO

The Schoolhouse as Jailhouse[1]

ANNETTE FUENTES

The Columbine Memorial is carved into a knoll in Clement Park, a vast tract of emerald lawns, sports fields, and playgrounds on Pierce Street, abutting Columbine High School in Littleton, Colorado. Past the baseball field and picnic areas, the memorial is hidden from view until you are right at its entrance. A few discreet signs around the park direct visitors to the red rock and granite environmental design, with its inner "ring of remembrance" and outer "ring of healing." The inner ring offers individual biographies of the twelve students and one teacher killed that day, spelled out on the top surface of a granite wall. On the ground, a looped ribbon and the words "Never Forgotten," the motto of those touched by the tragedy, are worked into a stone paving design. Etched onto dark tablets on the red wall of the outer ring are quotes from unnamed students, teachers, and community members, as well as one from Bill Clinton, who was president when the assault occurred. One unattributed quote asks rhetorically, yet provocatively, "It brought the nation to its knees but now that we've gotten back up how have things changed; what have we learned?"

I visited Littleton at the ninth anniversary of the Columbine tragedy as part of my two-year reporting and research project on the real nature of school violence and the hyperbolic reactions to it that have come to characterize polices

1 Adapted from *Lockdown High: When the Schoolhouse Becomes a Jailhouse* (New York: Verso, 2011).

on safety and discipline in public schools. My book, *Lockdown High: When the Schoolhouse Becomes a Jailhouse* (Verso), from which this chapter is adapted, explores the many ways students' civil liberties, educational opportunities, and genuine security have been sacrificed on the altar of political expediency and public hysteria over violent incidents, such as the shooting in one Colorado high school on April 20, 1999.

It would be difficult to overstate the impact the Columbine attack has had on popular attitudes about youth violence and school safety, and on policing and security policies in public schools. It wasn't the first public school shooting with multiple victims. There was a string of them from 1997 to 1998, including incidents in Springfield, Oregon, and Jonesboro, Arkansas. But the toll at Columbine High—fifteen dead, including the two attackers, and twenty-four wounded—was the highest, and the teens' weaponry was unprecedented. Columbine, as the incident is now known, is the yardstick by which successive school shootings have been measured. Ironically, the tragedy occurred as rates of school violence in general and shootings in particular were declining. Youth crime overall began to plummet after its apex in 1993. For youth homicides, the numbers are dramatic: From 1993 to 1998, juvenile homicide arrests dropped by 56%, reaching their lowest rate since the FBI began recording this statistic in 1964 (Brooks, Schiraldi, & Ziedenberf, 2000, p. 6). School crime echoed this trend: Between 1992 and 1998, the rate of nonfatal violent crimes for students ages 12 to 18 dropped from 48 per 1,000 students, to 43 per 1,000 (DeVoe, et al., 2002, p. 4). From 1995 to 1999, the percentage of students in that age group who reported being victims of theft or violent crime decreased from 10% to 8%, a trend most prominent among middle school students, who are often characterized as being the most difficult. Over that same time span, students were feeling safer, with 5% in 1999 saying they avoided one or more places in their school, compared with 9% in 1995 (DeVoe, 2002, pp. 8, 34). Even these small numbers suggest that the public's view of schools as dangerous was out of proportion to the reality for 90% of students during those years with higher rates of reported incidents.

As for violent deaths at schools—the boogeyman of the school-violence nightmare—there simply is no real trend at all. In the 1992–1993 school year (the first year such data were collected) there were fifty-seven "school-associated deaths," and that included thirty-four students killed by other students and six student suicides; the rest were teachers and other school employees. The total dipped over the next few years, and then reached fifty-seven again in 1997–1998. The 1998–1999 school year, the year of Columbine, would have had the lowest number of school deaths on record—twenty-five—but for the fifteen deaths in that tragic incident. According to the National Center for Education Statistics, the DOE agency that co-publishes the annual school crime and safety report,

"Between July 1, 1992, and June 30, 1999, no consistent pattern of increase or decrease was observed in the number of homicides at school" (DeVoe, 2002, p. 8). Indeed, each year's report typically begins with a summary noting that students are safer at school than away from school. The 2002 report noted that students were less than half as likely to be victims of a violent crime at school than elsewhere. And the trend continued: In the 2003–2004 school year, young people were more than *50 times* more likely to be murdered and almost *150 times* more likely to commit suicide away from school. Schools, it seems, are a much safer haven than children's homes and communities, and much safer than prevailing perceptions suggest (Baum, Cataldi, Dinkes, Kena, & Snyder, 2006, p. 6).

However, statistical realities were easily swamped by widespread public fears of school and youth violence. Polls taken after the well-publicized 1998 elementary school shooting in Jonesboro, for example, found that 71% of respondents expected a school shooting in their community; a poll conducted two days after Columbine found 80% expected more school shootings. Reporting on school shootings and Columbine in particular played no small role in bringing school violence into communities and homes around the country with coverage that created an echo chamber for simmering public panic about schools. For the news media, Columbine was a terrible tragedy but a great story. It garnered the most public interest of any story that year, with one survey finding that 68% of Americans followed it closely ("Columbine Shooting," 1999). Top newspaper and broadcast executives named Columbine the year's second most important story, right after President Bill Clinton's impeachment (Levinson, in Chyi & McCombs, 2004).

Since the September 11, 2001, terror attacks, school administrators and law enforcement officials have been even more emboldened to apply the terrorist label to students with the usual behavioral problems, as well as more serious ones. Looked at another way, the lockdown approach to school security, which views students as potential terrorists and schools as likely targets requiring heavy policing and surveillance, was in many ways the paradigm for the national security crackdown that swept the country after September 2001. Columbine, a rare act of violence at one school, became the excuse for implementing costly new security systems and disciplinary codes that curtailed students' rights to free speech, due process, and privacy. Likewise, the September 11 attacks, horrifying but rare acts of foreign terrorism on U.S. soil, have been used to justify retrenchments in civil liberties and widening surveillance by the government. In both incidents, authorities declared that "everything has changed" to justify extraordinary measures supposed to make us all safer, but which provided little evidence of that outcome (Brooks, Schiraldi, & Ziedenberg, 2000, p. 7). The Columbine scenario is terrifying, but the odds of it occurring in your hometown are about 1 in 2 million. Still, many people believe it can happen anytime, anywhere.

ZERO TOLERANCE, ZERO LOGIC

More than a decade later, the post-Columbine hysteria has not evaporated. It's been integrated into the lockdown philosophy of school safety and youth discipline. Students making threats of violence—real or make-believe—are subjected to swift and harsh prosecution, even if no crime has occurred. Witness 17-year-old Jeremie Dalin from Fox River Grove, Illinois, who was convicted in June 2008 for making a "false terrorist threat." Dalin, a senior at Barrington High School, posted a message on a Web site about Japanese anime, warning of an attack on Halloween at Adlai E. Stevenson High School. There are four schools in the country with that name and Dalin didn't specify which. The FBI traced the posting to Dalin's house hours after a student at a school named Stevenson High in a nearby town saw it on the Web site and reported it. Although Dalin had second thoughts and removed the posting and the FBI ruled it a prank, the teen was arrested and prosecuted. Odder still, Dennis Oh, the teen who reported Dalin's prank, was arrested and charged with obstructing a peace officer because he posted the phony threat on another Web site. Dalin faced up to fifteen years in prison.

Zero tolerance disciplinary policies have been a critical building block in the construction of the Lockdown High model of public schools. The term "zero tolerance" debuted during the Reagan administration's War on Drugs back in the mid-1980s, when domestic drug trafficking and its related violence were ravaging urban areas while foreign trafficking by the Reagan-backed, contras-funded civil war in Nicaragua. Reagan's education secretary William Bennett (who had also been the first U.S. drug czar) brought the War on Drugs and a zero tolerance mentality into public schools, and Congress backed him up. In 1986, it passed the Drug Free Schools Act to require that schools adopt strict rules against student possession of drugs and alcohol on campus. The Clinton administration, though, gave zero tolerance a sturdier foothold in the schools. In 1994, Congress enacted the Gun-Free Schools Act as part of a comprehensive education bill. It mandated a one-year expulsion of students who bring a gun to school and provided funding to schools for antiviolence programs. It was a time of public hysteria about youth crime, hyped by pop criminologists such as James Q. Wilson, who predicted a violent juvenile crime wave, and John DiIulio, whose "super-predator" was a new, vicious young criminal—implicitly a black or Latino urban male (DiIulio, 1995, p. 23). Racial coding and stereotypes infused such theories and fed the public's rampant fear of young minority males. The real dimensions of juvenile crime were far milder: a spike in violent offenses that began in the late 1980s, crested in the early 1990s, and has been falling ever since.

When the Columbine school incident occurred in 1999, school violence, including homicides, was at its lowest point in a decade. But by then, fear of African American and Latino "ghetto gangstas" had expanded to include youth of all demographics, whether they lived in affluent suburbs or poor inner cities. Columbine only accelerated the zero tolerance juggernaut already in motion. Federal mandates for zero tolerance policies on guns and drugs at school were kid stuff compared to those that state and local school authorities cooked up. Egged on by a fearful populace, schools have devised disciplinary codes that extend prohibitions on weapons well beyond firearms to include such things as nail clippers or files, or kitchen knives innocently packed with school lunches. Drug prohibitions have ensnared over-the-counter pain medications, such as Midol or aspirin, even herbal cough drops. But it is the zero tolerance approach to student behavior that has caused the most far-reaching damage, unleashing an epidemic of suspensions that jeopardizes hundreds of thousands of students' futures.

Although school administrators are bound to adhere to federal and state laws requiring suspension or expulsion for gun and drug violations, on student behavior they determine if a shove or a wedgie is an assault, or if talking out in class is disorderly conduct. "The zeitgeist now is zero tolerance, so that sets the tone for how we're going to handle behavior issues in schools," says Linda M. Raffaele-Mendez, professor of school psychology at the University of South Florida. "Zero tolerance says you get the kid out when there is an infraction that meets one of these criteria" (Raffaele & Knoff, 2003, p. 40). A study by Raffaele-Mendez of suspensions in Tampa public schools found that weapons and drug violations accounted for less than 1% of disciplinary actions while a huge amount were for disruptive behavior (Raffaele & Knoff, 2003, p. 40). "There is a sense among administrators that they want their school to be a certain way, and this kid is not like that, so I want him out," she says. "I don't think most administrators believe suspension will have any effect on a kid's behavior" (Raffaele, 2003).

Zero tolerance policies have maintained a tenacity and intensity in schools that defy logic, given consistently falling rates of school violence and youth crime overall. One reason, according to many educators and legal advocates, is the obsessive focus on testing and standards encouraged by the No Child Left Behind Act of 2001. From classroom teachers to principals to district superintendents, the pressure to show "AYP"—adequate yearly progress—and avoid a succession of penalties is a powerful incentive to weed out the most difficult students, who are often underachievers. "The wave of school shootings fed concerns and states went wild with zero tolerance, giving principals total discretion to kick out any student they wanted," says Mark Soler, president of the Children's Law and Policy Center in Washington, D.C. "Now, zero tolerance is fed less by fear of crime and more by high-stakes testing. Principals want to get rid of kids they perceive as trouble" (Soler, 2003).

In Texas schools, which were the guinea pigs for NCLB-style education reform during George W. Bush's tenure as governor, zero tolerance plus high-stakes testing has added up to produce astronomical suspension rates and a system of alternative detention schools that warehouse poor, minority low achievers. "We've had testing in Texas much longer, before Bush [was governor], and I've seen over the years how life on campus revolves around testing," says Augustina Reyes, education professor at the University of Houston (Reyes, 2006). Reyes researched Texas's zero tolerance practices and found, like Raffaele-Mendez, that mandatory suspensions were a tiny fraction and discretionary disciplinary actions were the lion's share, with such subjective violations as "serious and persistent misbehavior" common. "Teachers think, 'With bad kids in my class I'll have lower achievements on my tests. I'll use discretion and remove that student,'" she says. "If teachers are told, 'Your scores go down, you lose your job,' all of a sudden your values shift very quickly" (Reyes, 2003).

The explosion in school suspensions in Texas became a national story in July 2011 with the release of *Breaking Schools' Rules*, a groundbreaking report on disciplinary practices in the state's public schools (Fabelo, Thompson, Plotkin, Carmichael, Marchbanks, & Booth, 2011). The report, co-published by the Council of State Governments and the Public Policy Research Institute, was based on a longitudinal study of some one million Texas seventh-graders over three years. It found 54% of all students were suspended at least once, and nearly 75% of special education students experienced suspensions. African American males fared the worst and just 3% of all suspensions and expulsions were for conduct requiring mandatory punishment; 97% of disciplinary actions were for conduct that was deemed a violation of school codes at the discretion of teachers and administrators. Texas's policies are extreme but not unique. Every year, millions of suspensions are disrupting students' education with tens of thousands of children expelled or placed in lower-quality disciplinary schools. Getting an accurate national tally of disciplinary actions and the offenses that trigger them is difficult for several reasons. The federal Department of Education (DOE) requires states to collect data on student discipline, but those data are not compiled into a national total. And adding up state numbers is an apples-and-oranges proposition because states and localities create their own disciplinary codes. So what Texas calls "insubordination" or "terroristic threats" won't necessarily have a match in New York's statutes. Some states break down their disciplinary action data into more specific components, such as in-school or out-of-school suspensions, while others do not.

Nonetheless, it's possible to get a bead on the magnitude of the suspension epidemic. The DOE's National Center for Education Statistics provides some trend data on school disciplinary policies and actions in its School Survey on Crime and Safety (Dinkes, Kemp, and Baum, 2009). The survey is a sampling of the nation's public schools, and school administrators can opt to participate or not. The 2003–2004 survey reported that 46% of schools took serious disciplinary action against students, and the total number of such actions was 655,700. Nearly three-quarters of those actions were suspensions. About a fifth was for insubordination. The survey's definition of *insubordination* is something with which many parents of adolescents and teens are probably familiar: "deliberate and inexcusable defiance of or refusal to obey a school rule, authority, or a reasonable order. It includes but is not limited to direct defiance of school authority, failure to attend assigned detention or on-campus supervision, failure to respond to a call slip, and physical or verbal intimidation/abuse" (Dinkes, Kemp, and Baum, 2009, p. 126). In the 2007–2008 survey, the same percentage of schools reported taking a total of 767,900 disciplinary actions against students, with the same proportion for insubordination, and a slightly higher number of suspensions.

The School Survey on Crime and Safety vastly understates the suspension epidemic, however, for several reasons. First, it counts only out-of-school suspensions of five days or longer. States devise their own rules on suspensions—how long they last, whether there is a cap on the total number of days a student may be suspended, and what activity a suspended student must perform for in-school punishments. In Texas, for example, in-school suspensions can mean long-term exile. Deborah Fowler, legal director of Texas Appleseed, a public interest law center in Austin, led a team of legal and educational experts researching the state's disciplinary practices and was shocked to see the "enormous number of students being referred to ISS [in-school suspensions] every year. We became very concerned about that. And there is no cap on the number of days the student can spend there. We've heard of kids sitting in ISS for thirty days," Fowler says. "And there doesn't have to be any instruction. They may be given work, maybe not" (Fowler, 2007).

Second, the survey samples fewer than three thousand schools nationwide, so its numbers are projections. Even a quick tally of suspensions reported by a handful of states with aggressive zero tolerance policies reveals that a more realistic national total of suspensions would number in the millions annually. Let's start with California, with 6.2 million students enrolled in public schools. California has the second-highest number of suspensions of any state with 783,000 in the 2008–2009 school year. Florida's K–12 enrollment was more than 3 million in the 2008–2009 school year with 264,000 in-school plus 235,000 out-of-school suspensions. (Florida doesn't report the number of students suspended.) Nearby, Georgia's public schools have an astronomical rate of suspensions for their students, who numbered 1.75 million in 2005–2006. Their in-school suspensions were 505,000, out-of-school suspensions were 314,000 that year, and the brunt was borne by some 300,000 students facing multiple disciplinary actions. In Lockdown High, school disciplinary codes have redefined typical student actions and behaviors as prohibited and created catchall categories for violations that didn't seem to fit anywhere else. And it is those violations—not weapons possession or violent crimes—that account for the preponderance of student incidents leading to suspensions and other disciplinary actions.

Concerned youth advocates and education activists have been documenting the role of Lockdown High in feeding the nation's prison system and the disproportionate harm done to black students. National 2000 statistics from the U.S. Department of Education give a glimpse of the glaring discipline disparity: African American students were 17% of the entire public school population but accounted for 34% of all out-of-school suspensions and 30% of expulsions (Office of Civil Rights U.S. Department of Education, 1998). White students, by contrast, were 62% of the student population but accounted for 48% of out-of-school suspensions and 49% of expulsions. In almost every state, suspension, expulsion, and incarceration rates were higher for African Americans than they were for the general student population. Some state education departments have begun to acknowledge the race gap on disciplinary actions as problematic and requiring action (Office of Civil Rights U.S. Department of Education, 1998).

Russell Skiba, education professor at Indiana University and a pioneer in research on school discipline, has documented a racial disparity going back more than twenty-five years, which has been made worse by zero tolerance policies (Michael, Nardo, & Peterson, 2000). A 2000 study of race and discipline co-authored by Skiba goes beyond the general consensus that minority students are overrepresented among those suspended and expelled to explain why it occurs (Michael, Nardo, & Peterson, 2000). The authors find that the discrepancy begins with teachers' reactions to student behavior. Skiba and his colleagues found that teachers were referring African American students to the principal's office for less serious and more subjective reasons, such as disrespect, excessive noise, threats, and loitering. White students were more likely to be cited for smoking, vandalism, obscene language, and leaving school without permission—all more objectively defined violations. While some would explain that the higher rates of discipline reflect higher rates of wrongdoing by African American students, Skiba et al. cite research on the overrepresentation of blacks in the criminal justice system and on the decreased number of disciplinary actions against them in schools with greater numbers of black faculty. Taking income levels into account, too, they conclude that the discipline gap is "evidence of a pervasive and systematic bias that may very well be inherent in the use of exclusionary discipline" (Skiba, Michael, Nardo, & Peterson, 2000, p. 2). One can call it a form of profiling in our classrooms (Skiba, Michael, Nardo, & Peterson, 2000, p. i). In 2010, Skiba and Daniel Losen of UCLA's Civil Rights Project released their study of school suspensions of middle school students nationwide that confirmed the "high frequency" of the disciplinary practice and the inequitable impact on African American students (Losen & Skiba, 2010, p. 13).

Suspensions for discretionary reasons, like violating a dress code or talking back to a teacher, are more than excessive. Each punishment sidelines a student and disrupts her education and increases the risks of dropping out. The report

Breaking Schools' Rules (Fabelo, Thompson, Plotkin, Carmichael, Marchbanks III, & Booth, 2011) found that 10% of students who had been disciplined eventually dropped out. Worse, it identified the connection between zero tolerance discipline and the school to prison pipeline: Students suspended for a discretionary code violation were three times more likely than students who were not disciplined to become involved with the juvenile justice system in the following year.

The preponderance of evidence that students and academic achievement were being damaged by the continuation of punitive discipline motivated the American Psychological Association to weigh in on the issue. At its annual convention in 2006, the professional organization released a report by its Zero Tolerance Task Force that gleaned evidence from two decades of research into school climate and discipline. Called simply "Are Zero Tolerance Policies Effective in the Schools?: An Evidentiary Review and Recommendations" the report from the APA task force, which included Indiana University's Russell Skiba, answered the question with a resounding "No" (American Psychological Association Zero Tolerance Task Force, 2008, p. 852). It identifies and then rebuts the fundamental premises behind zero tolerance policies, including the idea that serious school violence is "out of control"; that suspending students for misdeeds creates a better learning climate for other students; that punitive discipline is a deterrent to future misbehavior; and that parents and communities overwhelmingly support zero tolerance. The report also highlights the lopsided impact for black students, a result it attributes to poor teacher training and lack of cultural competence with diverse student populations. And most important, the psychologists address child and adolescent development and how zero tolerance is an inappropriate, even harmful strategy for correcting behavioral problems, especially those with emotional or neurological roots. The report prescribes a series of reforms to school disciplinary policies, recommending a drastic scaling back on the most harsh punishments and adopting flexibility in disciplining individual students. In place of zero tolerance, the task force called for strategies to reconnect alienated youth within a school community that fosters connectedness among teachers, students, parents, and administrators. Improved training for teachers in classroom management and cultural competence is also vital.

THE SECURITY STATE GOES TO SCHOOL

Zero tolerance disciplinary codes are joined in many schools by security technologies more typically associated with prisons, especially since the Columbine incident, as the default strategy for maintaining a safe environment. The proliferation of high-tech security, from surveillance cameras to metal detectors to more recent forays into biometric scanners, was aided and abetted by the federal government even before Columbine. In 1998, Congress reacted to a spate of high-profile shootings over the previous year by enacting the Safe Schools Initiative, a seemingly muscular program meant to show how seriously lawmakers took school violence. The shootings were indeed shocking and came in rapid-fire succession: October 1997 in Pearl, Mississippi; December 1997 in Paducah, Kentucky; March 1998 in Jonesboro, Arkansas; and May 1998 in Springfield, Oregon. Among other things, the initiative directed the National Institute of Justice (NIJ) to develop new and appropriate weapons detection and surveillance technologies for schools. NIJ created a School Safety Program and made its National Law Enforcement and Corrections Technology Centers–Southeast the home for research into state-of-the-art policing and prison technologies that could apply to public schools. At the same time, NIJ funded Sandia National Laboratories, a Department of Energy facility in Albuquerque, New Mexico, to apply its expertise in security technologies to schools. Sandia is run by the defense and aeronautics behemoth Lockheed Martin under contract to the Department of Energy and primarily supports the U.S. nuclear weapons program.

The NIJ's National Law Enforcement and Corrections Technology Center–Southeast also works on new applications of hot security and surveillance technologies for public schools. One of a half dozen regional centers established by the NIJ, the Southeast Center was assigned the school safety portfolio as its specialty. In recent years, the Southeast Center has focused on cell phones, according to deputy director Peter Cosgrove. The effort is called Detect and Defeat: Detect the cell phone and disable it without disabling communication in an entire area. Cosgrove says the technology can apply in prisons, where cell phone use is prohibited, and schools, where it is often restricted. The two institutions, he notes, have much in common. "If you want to stretch the comparison, you have kids in school being educated in life, and in prison you have a similar situation of people being reeducated. In theory they're not far apart," Cosgrove philosophizes. "On the administrative side, you're trying to regulate and control a large group of people, so there are a lot of similarities. So if we're developing a technology, we can use it in both areas" (Cosgrove, 2007).

Technological strategies have been embraced over the past two decades by schools with rare reservations about the civil liberties or privacy of students and teachers. Nearly 6% of public schools of all levels employ random metal detector checks on students. For middle schools, it's 10%; for high schools, 13%. Slightly more than 1% use walk-through detectors daily, and that increases to 2% for middle schools and nearly 4% for high schools. Security cameras are the most prevalent technology used in 36% of all schools; nearly 64% of high, 42% of middle, and 29% of primary schools use surveillance cameras. Viewed through a different lens, 11% of all students attend schools that use metal detectors, and 58% of students attend school under the watchful eye of surveillance cameras. With a total public school population of some 26 million, simple math says that for millions of children, being scanned and monitored has become as much a part of their daily education as learning to read and write (Baum et al., 2006, 111–113). Of course, not all schools have the gadgetry of Lockdown High. But in some localities, costly high-tech security, such as the newest biometric or software system for access control, is as integral to the educational agenda as are new textbooks. In one indicator of how important security technology has become in schools, the trade magazine *Security* published its first ranking of the "biggest and the best security programs in the U.S." and gave public schools a prominent place on it (McCourt, 2006, para. 6) Called the Security 500, the list includes fourteen public school districts—six of them in Florida. Ranked 291, Houston Independent School District was tops among schools—and one step above Intel. Number one on the list was the Department of Homeland Security (McCourt, 2006).

Fear of school violence is not the only force driving security hardware into public schools. In the past decade, the U.S. security industry has increasingly targeted public schools as a vast, rich market for its hardware and software products and services. Schools still represent a small fraction of the industry's gargantuan market, estimated to approach $20 billion annually and increasing by 20% a year, according to the Security Industry Association (SIA), a trade group. But that fraction has been growing from a sliver to a meatier slice of the pie. The SIA considers school security one of its key "Industry Issues," and tracks proposed state and federal legislation related to it, offering assessments of how it will benefit or hurt business prospects of SIA members. *SDM* magazine, a security industry publication, surveyed businesses about their growth markets. The survey found that the education market, which includes grades K–12 and colleges, was the third fastest-growing market in 2007 with a 15% annual sales increase, behind commercial real estate and retail customers, at 30% and 21%, respectively. The magazine noted that a recent shooting at Virginia Tech University helped rivet attention on school security in general (Pohle, 2007).

News reporting on the rare act of school violence—particularly shootings—not only rivets attention but spurs spending by schools that might make officials feel better but won't actually make students safer. For example, a week after the April 20, 1999, Columbine tragedy, Texas-based Garrett Metal Detectors was reportedly "awash in new orders as principals and teachers across the country try to shake feelings of vulnerability in the wake of the Columbine High School massacre" (Knox, 1999, para. 1). In the previous four years, schools had become Garrett's largest single market, comprising 25% of all sales (Knox, 1999). And that was before September 11. Today, the industry promotes its technology to schools with the language of homeland security. Not only must schools protect students and faculty from the terrorists within—the bad, violent student—they must protect them from the terrorists without—whether jihadists or sex predators.

to us" (Mack, 2008). As for incidents of violence or disciplinary problems, which Mack is required to report to the city Department of Education—well, he says, there aren't any. "I've never had any kind of incident to report. If the security agents get weapons, I haven't seen them," Mack says (2008).

The Urban Academy model refutes punitive, zero tolerance strategies as the most effective approach to school safety and discipline, and ample evidence exists that shows their harmful effects on children. Authoritarian strategies have been predicated on a faulty foundation—the idea that school violence is epidemic and growing worse and demanding drastic measures at the cost of student rights and educational quality. Now, while it is true that violence and disciplinary problems have been and will always be present in schools to a greater or lesser degree, communities and administrators can choose to address them with strategies that are more appropriate to the basic mission of schools: to educate. By surrendering to the Lockdown High model, school board members, principals, and teachers have abdicated their responsibility and lost the opportunity to make safety and discipline part of the curriculum. Zero tolerance and metal detectors are often easier choices when schools face intense pressure to perform under federal testing mandates and budget cuts force out programs considered nonessential. And the political pressure behind punitive discipline policies and security fixes can be enormous. But the failure of zero tolerance, reflected in the epidemic of students suspended and pushed out of schools, is becoming harder to ignore.

One of the first and now most widely cited studies on school violence and strategies for creating safer schools was published back in 1999 by Matthew Mayer and Peter Leone. The authors, professors of education, analyzed data on school crime from the National Crime Victimization Survey, which queried public school students from 12 to 19 years old. Their findings suggested that schools with "a higher level of disorder" had more security measures, including metal detectors, locked doors, and security guards or other staff patrolling hallways, and that those very security measures may actually contribute to the school's disorder (Mayer & Leone, 1999). They called it a "cycle of disorder" in which restrictive controls in school create a "reciprocal, destructive relationship" with students, who "tend to engage in more acts of self-protection and live in a heightened state of fear" (Mayer & Leone, 1999, p. 352). Acknowledging that some might argue that the presence of high-security measures is a necessary response to the disorder and violence, Mayer and Leone suggest a different interplay: "Creating an unwelcoming, almost jail-like, heavily scrutinized environment, may foster the violence and disorder school administrators hope to avoid" Mayer & Leone, 1999, p. 349). Schools with the least disruption, they found, were those where students understood the "system of law"—the rules of conduct. The solution, Mayer and Leone state, is "for schools to focus their efforts; effective communication rather than control is the best way to establish the legitimacy of the school's system of law in the minds of students" (Mayer & Leone, 1999, p. 352).

The antithesis of that cycle of disorder, Urban Academy, had an eloquent advocate in one student, Ryan Kierstedt, who spoke about his experiences in public schools at a press conference called by the New York Civil Liberties Union in February 2007 to discuss its new report, "Criminalizing the Classroom: The Over-Policing of New York City Schools" (Mukherjee, 2007). Urban Academy's rejection of scanners was a key reason he became a student there. Kierstedt had been attending high school in East New York, Brooklyn, but was fed up with how students were treated and the poor-quality education. "Since I was thirteen years old, I've been going through scanners at school and I never thought much about it until I realized that not everyone goes through them," Kierstedt said. "They don't trust us, so we don't trust them." He quit school for a year. "I decided I wasn't going to school anymore because no one was teaching me anything. I decided to go to the bookstore and just read," he said, until a family friend told him about the Urban Academy, where "we have no metal detectors, and they actually teach me. Nobody at school is afraid of being stabbed and there's no animosity from the security agents."

REFERENCES

American Psychologist Zero Tolerance Task Force. (2008). Are zero tolerance policies effective in the schools? *American Psychologist*, 63(9), 852–862.

Associated Press. (1999, April 28). School security business booming.

Baum, K., Cataldi, E. F., Dinkes, R., Kena, G., & Snyder, T. D. (2006). *Indicators of school crime and safety: 2006* (NCJ 214262). Washington, DC: National Center for Education Statistics.

Brooks, K., Schiraldi, V., & Ziedenberg, J. (2000). *School house hype: Two years later*. Washington D.C.: Justice Policy Institute.

Chyi, I. H., & McCombs, M. (2004, Spring). Media salience and the process of framing: Coverage of the Columbine school shootings. *Journalism and Mass Communication Quarterly, 81*(1), 22–35.

Columbine shooting biggest news draw of 1999. (1999, December 28). Washington, DC: Pew Research Center for the People and the Press.

Cosgrove, Peter (August 2007). telephone interview with author.

DeVoe, J. F., Duhart, D. T., Kaufman, P., Miller, A., Peter, K., Planty, M., et al. (2002). *Indicators of school crime and safety: 2002* (NCJ 196753). Washington, DC: National Center for Education Statistics.

DiIulio, John. (November 27, 1995). "The Coming of the Super-predators." *Weekly Standard*, p. 23.

Dinkes, R., Kemp, J., and Baum, K. (2009). Indicators of School Crime and Safety: 2008 (NCES 2009–022/NCJ 226343). National Center for Education Statistics, Institute of Education Sciences, U.S. Department of Education, and Bureau of Justice Statistics, Office of Justice Programs, U.S. Department of Justice. Washington, DC, p. 126.

Fabelo, T., Thompson, M. D., Plotkin, M., Carmichael, D., Marchbanks, M. P., & Booth, E. A. (2011, July). *Breaking schools' rules: A statewide study on how school discipline relates to students' success and juvenile justice involvement.* College Station, TX: The Public Policy Research Institute, Texas A&M University, Council of State Governments Justice Center.

Fowler, Deborah (November 2007). telephone interview with author.

Kaufman, P., Chen, X., Choy, S. P., Ruddy, S. A., Miller, A. K., Fleury, J. K., Chandler, K. A., Rand M. R., Klaus, P., & Planty, M. G. (2000). *Indicators of school crime and safety: 2000* (NCJ 184176). Washington, DC: National Center for Education Statistics.

Knox, N. (April 28, 1999). *School Security business booming*, Associated Press.

Losen, Daniel J., & Skiba, Russell J. (September 13, 2010). Suspended education: Urban middle schools in crisis. Retrieved at http://civilrightsproject.ucla.edu/research/k-12-education/school-discipline/suspended-education-urban-middle-schools-in-crisis.

Mack, Herb (September 2008). telephone interview with author.

Mayer, M. J., & Leone, P. E. (1999, August). A structural analysis of school violence and disruption: Implications for creating safer schools. *Education and Treatment of Children, 22*(3), 333–356.

McCourt, M. (September 2006). Security 500 ranking: The biggest and best, *Security*.

Michael, Robert S., Nardo, Abra Carroll, & Peterson, Reece (June 2000). *The Color of Discipline Sources of Racial and Gender Disproportionality in School Punishment.* Report #SRS1. p. i.

Mukherjee, E. (March 2007). *Criminalizing the Classroom: The Over-Policing of New York City Schools.* New York Civil Liberties Union.

National School Safety Center. (2004). Safeguarding schools against terrorism. Retrieved http://www.schoolsafety.us/free-resources/schools-and terrorism/safeguarding_schools_against_terror.pdf

Office of Civil Rights, U.S. Department of Education, Fall *1998 Elementary and Secondary School Civil Rights Compliance Report: National and State Projections (2000)*. Washington, DC: Government Printing Office.

Pohle, L. (2007, June 1). An education market primer. *SDM.*

Raffaele, Linda M. (June 2003). telephone interview with author.

Raffaele, Linda M., Knoff, Howard M., Who gets suspended from school and why?: Disciplinary infractions in a large school district, *Education and Treatment of Children*, Vol. 21, No. 1, February 2003, p. 40.

Reyes, Augstina (June 2003). telephone interview with author.

Reyes, A. (2006). *Discipline, achievement, and race: Is zero tolerance the answer?* Lanham, MD: Rowman & Littlefield.

Skiba, R. J., Michael, R. S., Nardo, A. C., & Peterson, R. (2000, June). *The color of discipline: Sources of racial and gender disproportionality in school punishment* (Policy Research Report #SRS1). Bloomington: Indiana Education Policy Center.

Soler, Mark (June 2003). telephone interview with author.

CHAPTER THREE

Rethinking the School to Prison Pipeline

DAVID GABBARD

On Tuesday of this week, I had to go to D. H. Conley High School to pick up my oldest son, Jackson, at 9:00 a.m. He'd stayed up until 4:00 a.m. the night before, working on a report for his English class due that day. He wanted me to pick him up early, after he turned in the report. I wasn't happy that he'd procrastinated so badly, but I understood where he was coming from. He was dead on his feet. I saw no sense in making him sleepwalk through the rest of his classes, and he had more work to get done on his Senior Project due the next day. He needed to come home and get some sleep.

As I drove down the long road leading through the student parking lot to the front of the school and the visitor's lot, a tall middle-aged African-American man with a mouthful of chewing tobacco stepped out of a red pickup truck and waved for me to stop. "I need to know who you are and why you're here," he said. "Jesus H. Christ," I thought to myself. "They pay this guy to play parking lot *gestapo*?" But I refrained from giving him a hard time, even if he was spraying tobacco juice into my Saturn with every syllable he spat. He might be gross and remarkably inconsiderate, but he didn't make the policy to harass everyone who tried entering the school from this direction. He was just a tool of the school. He was probably happy to be getting paid for sitting on his ass, chewing his chaw, and exercising what authority had been delegated to him. "I'm here to pick up my son for a doctor's appointment," I lied. "Well, you can't go this way. You have to go back out, turn right, and take the entrance up by the tennis courts."

Elite and privileged groups have always had the financial and/or political means to pass their advantages on to their children. With this in tow, it becomes very hard to take someone like Bill Gates seriously when, in his teacher recruitment commercial for Teach.gov, he says "My success came from how lucky I was to have some great teachers" (Gates, 2010). Maybe so, but shouldn't he at least preface that with an acknowledgement that he was also "lucky" to have a father wealthy enough to pay $25,000 a year for his tuition at the Lakeside School, whose course catalog easily rivals most small private liberal arts colleges? The history and social studies curriculum at Lakeside's "Upper School" (high school) includes required courses in Modern World History, 1200–1870, Contemporary World History, 1870 to the Present, and United States History with electives in

- The Ancient Mediterranean World
- The Cold War
- After the Cold War, the World at the Turn of the 21st Century
- Introduction to Philosophy
- Introduction to World Religions
- The Holocaust and Genocide Studies
- Leadership for the Modern Era
- Comparative Government and Politics
- Freedom, Crime, and the Law
- Africa Today
- Global Village
- Music of the African Diaspora
- Natives and Strangers: American Immigration
- Microeconomics
- Developing Economies
- Issues in the Contemporary Middle East and North Africa
- Race Matters: A (Fairly) Contemporary Intellectual History of African America, and
- Gender Studies

How many of us who attended public schools had those opportunities available to us? Perhaps more people would demand such a curriculum, but few of us have any awareness of the existence of places like Lakeside or Groton, let alone any knowledge of their curricula.

Nevertheless, if only because employers, primarily since the 1950s, began requiring educational credentials from their job candidates, the meritocratic argument for schooling did develop some measure of legitimacy over the years. Looking at Table 3.1, we find a very significant difference (18.6%) between the

Table 3.1. Adapted from source by author: Center for Labor Market Studies at Northeastern University (2009).

Level of Educational Attainment	Unemployment Rate Among 16- to 24-Year-Old Out-of-School Youth in 2008 (%)
College Graduates	13.3
1–3 Years of College	21.2
H. S. Graduate	31.9
H. S. Dropouts	54

unemployment rates in 2008 for college graduates and high school graduates, and a nearly identical (17.9%) difference between those who earn a high school diploma and those who do not (Center for Labor Market Studies, 2009).

Since the 1950s, then, most Americans learned to take the rules of the game for granted. If you work hard in school and graduate, you'll be able to find a job and establish some economic security for yourself. But that myth is quickly coming unraveled.

In the words of a New Jersey man who lost his job in 2010, "I did everything right, I played by the rules, I got skills, I excelled in my job, all to no avail ... I don't know what I'm going to do," he continued. "All the years of both parties talking about free trade agreements and how we will retrain America was just a bunch of BS; it was easy to say all that when times were good" (Delany, 2011). As Arthur Delany (2011) has so accurately pointed out, Barack Obama made these changes to what we used to take for granted as the "rules of the game" official, or at least publicly acknowledgeable, in his 2011 State of the Union address:

> Many people watching tonight can probably remember a time when finding a good job meant showing up at a nearby factory or a business downtown. You didn't always need a degree, and your competition was pretty much limited to your neighbors. If you worked hard, chances are you'd have a job for life, with a decent paycheck and good benefits and the occasional promotion. Maybe you'd even have the pride of seeing your kids work at the same company. That world has changed. And for many, the change has been painful. I've seen it in the shuttered windows of once booming factories, and the vacant storefronts on once busy Main Streets. I've heard it in the frustrations of Americans who've seen their paychecks dwindle or their jobs disappear—proud men and women who feel like the rules have been changed in the middle of the game. They're right. The rules have changed. In a single generation, revolutions in technology have transformed the way we live, work and do business. Steel mills that once needed 1,000 workers can now do the same work with 100. Today, just about any company can set up shop, hire workers, and sell their products wherever there's an Internet connection. (Obama, 2011)

Lest we be duped into renewing any faith in the "change" we were told we could "believe in," Obama has pledged to the U.S. Chamber of Commerce that he would pursue even more free trade agreements—this time with Panama, Colombia, and South Korea. With the North American Free Trade Agreement (NAFTA) having eliminated nearly 900,000 U.S. jobs between 1991 and 2003 (Scott, 2003), it ought to strike us as highly unlikely that these pending new agreements will do anything but dim the economic prospects of America's youth, making it even harder for parents to point to a future economic payoff to motivate their children to stay in school.

According to an April 2011 report from the Economic Policy Institute, "the unemployment rate for workers age 16–24 was 18.4%—the worst on record in the 60 years that this data has been tracked" (Sheirholz & Edwards, 2011, p. 1). Even under the best of economic times, I couldn't honestly tell either of my sons that doing well in school and going on to earn a 4-year degree would guarantee that they'd be able to find a job in their chosen fields. In today's economy, however, a 4-year degree is even less certain to secure employment, as the unemployment rate for college grads in 2010 reached nearly 10%. With 85% of college graduates reporting that they are moving back home with mom and dad, we can expect that number for 2011 to climb even higher (Sheirholz & Edwards, 2011, p. 1).

At least I can tell them that a college degree still improves their chances, because the unemployment rate among those with only a high school diploma or GED now stands at 22.5%. For dropouts, of course, the unemployment rates are even worse at 32.9%. For those between the ages of 16 and 24, the figures are far worse. According to a study conducted by the Center for Labor Market Studies at Northeastern University (2009), the jobless rate in 2008 for those with a 4-year degree or higher was 13.3%, while it was 21.2% for those with 1–3 years of post-secondary education, 31.9% for high school graduates, and 54% for young high school dropouts. As reflected in Table 3.2, the fewer number of years of schooling that one completes strongly correlates with both risk of unemployment and risk of incarceration.

Table 3.2. Source: Center for Labor Market Studies at Northeastern University (2009).

	Unemployment Rate Among 16- to 24-Year-Old Out-of-School Youth in 2008 (%)	Incarceration Rate Among 16- to 24-Year-Old Out-of-School Youth 2006–2007 (%)
College Graduates	13.3	0.1
1–3 Years of College	21.2	0.7
H. S. Graduate	31.9	1.0
H. S. Dropouts	54	6.3

At its core, the problem is this. The continued existence of compulsory schooling perpetuates the myth that people's success or failure hinges on their performance in school. In turn, this allows the state to blame schools for the larger problems in the economy that result in shrinking opportunities for people to find work. And this multitiered game of victim blaming drives the endless calls for school reform. The truth is that schools will never be reformed as long as they are made compulsory by the state. As documented by the previously mentioned Advancement Project, the only meaningful changes we've witnessed in schools over the past thirty years since the state launched its massive *A Nation At Risk* propaganda campaign that blamed schools for the alleged inability of U.S.-based corporations to compete in the global economy have been the implementation of high-stakes testing/accountability and zero tolerance policies. Neither of those policies have changed the nature of compulsory schooling, but have only served to intensify its effects; namely, disciplining docile bodies to accept boring and monotonous work as an inevitable part of life while subjecting those who refuse to recognize the beneficence of this therapy to remedial discipline in prison.

The United States, which has less than 5% of the world's population, has 25% of the world's prisoners (Liptak, 2008). Figures range from between 2.3 and 2.5 million Americans living behind bars. As the market economy continues its collapse, we should expect to see these numbers escalate, as globalization and domestic neoliberal policies continue to create a larger surplus population of people whom the market cannot absorb. State policy makers certainly do. As the National Association for the Advancement of Colored People (NAACP) points out in its April 2011 report, *Misplaced Priorities: Over Incarcerate, Under Educate*:

> Over the last two decades, as the criminal justice system came to assume a larger proportion of state discretionary dollars nationwide, state spending on prisons grew at six times the rate of state spending on higher education. In 2009, as the nation plummeted into the deepest recession in 30 years, funding for K–12 and higher education declined; however, in that same year, 33 states spent a larger proportion of their discretionary dollars on prisons than they had the year before. (NAACP, 2011, p. 1)

Corporations and Wall Street investment firms also recognize and seek to capitalize on this same trend. The prison industry complex is one of the fastest-growing industries in the United States. Even the federal government and its defense contractors exploit the situation. "According to the Left Business Observer, the federal prison industry produces 100% of all military helmets, ammunition belts, bullet-proof vests, ID tags, shirts, pants, tents, bags, and canteens" (Pelaez, 2008, p. 1).

Sooner or later, people will have to recognize that compulsory schools are part of the problem. Eliminating them is part of the solution.

REFERENCES

Advancement Project. (2010). *Test, punish, and push out: How zero tolerance and high-stakes testing funnel youth into the school to prison pipeline*. Retrieved June 9, 2011 from http://www.advancementproject.org/digital-library/publications/test-punish-and-push-out-how-zero-tolerance-and-high-stakes-testing-fu

Alliance for Excellent Education. (n.d). *About the Crisis*. Retrieved June 9, 2011 from http://www.all4ed.org/about_the_crisis.

Beard, C. A. (1913). *An economic interpretation of the constitution of the United States*. New York, NY: Macmillan.

Cayley, D. (2005). *The rivers north of the future: The testament of Ivan Illich*. Toronto: House of Anansi Press.

Center for Labor Market Studies at Northeastern University. (2009). *Joblessness and jailing for high school dropouts and the high cost for taxpayers*. Retrieved June 9, 2011 from www.clms.neu.edu/.../The_Consequences_of_Dropping_Out_of_High_School.pdf

Delany, A. (2011, May 23). 'I Played By The Rules'—'The Rules Have Changed.' *Huffington Post*. Retrieved June 9, 2011 from http://www.huffingtonpost.com/2011/05/23/long-term-unemployment_n_864873.html

Emptywheel. (2011, March 8). They won't even create jobs in the military-industrial complex anymore. *Emptywheel*. Retrieved June 9 from http://emptywheel.firedoglake.com/2011/03/08/they-wont-even-create-jobs-in-the-military-industrial-complex-anymore/

Forbes Magazine. (2010, April 29). No. 15: Groton School, a profile of one of America's 20 best prep schools. *Forbes Online*. Retrieved June 9 from http://www.forbes.com/2010/04/29/best-prep-schools-2010-opinions-groton-school.html

Foucault, M. (1977). *Discipline and Punish: The birth of the prison*. New York, NY: Vintage Books.

Gates, B. (2010, September 29). TEACH: Government, business leaders thank their teachers. U.S Department of Education. Retrieved June 9 from http://www.ed.gov/blog/2010/09/teach-government-business-leaders-thank-their-teachers/

Hitchens, C. (2007). *God is not great*. New York, NY: Twelve Books.

Hitchens, C. (2010). Can civilization survive without God? *A Conversation with Christopher and Peter Hitchens*. Retrieved June 9, 2011 from http://pewforum.org/Belief-in-God/Can-Civilization-Survive-Without-God-.aspx

Jefferson, T. (1779/1904–5). A bill for the more general diffusion of knowledge. In *The works of Thomas Jefferson, Federal edition*. New York and London: G. P. Putnam's Sons.

Lakeside School (2011). *Academics in the Upper School*. Retrieved June 9, 2011 from http://www.lakesideschool.org/podium/default.aspx?t=122219

Liptak, A. (2008). U.S. prison population dwarfs that of other nations. *New York Times* (April 23) Retrieved June 9, 2011 from http://www.nytimes.com/2008/04/23/world/americas/23iht-23prison.12253738.html

National Association for the Advancement of Colored People. (2011, April 7). *Misplaced priorities: Over incarcerate, under educate*. Retrieved June 9, 2011 from http://www.naacp.org/pages/misplaced-priorities

Obama, B. (2011). *State of the union address*. Retrieved June 9, 2011 from http://www.npr.org/2011/01/26/133224933/transcript-obamas-state-of-union-address

Pelaez, V. (2008). The prison industry in the United States: Big business or a new form of slavery? *The global research*. The Center for Research on Globalization. Retrieved June 9, 2011 from http://www.globalresearch.ca/index.php?context=va&aid=8289

Quinn, S. (Interviewer) and Hitchens, C. (Interviewee). (2008). *Divine impulses*. Retrieved The Washington Post from http://www.washingtonpost.com/wp-dyn/content/video/2008/01/08/VI2008010802108.html?hpid=topnews.

Rohrlich, J. (2011). Why are prisoners building patriot missiles? *Minyanville*. Retrieved June 9, 2011 from http://www.minyanville.com/businessmarkets/articles/defense-industrial-base-defense-budget-defense/3/7/2011/id/33198

Scott, R. E. (2003, November 17). *The high price of 'free' trade: NAFTA's failure has cost the United States jobs across the nation*. Economic Policy Institute. Retrieved June 9, 2011 from http://www.epi.org/publication/briefingpapers_bp147/

Sheirholz, H., & Edwards, K. A. (2011, April 20). *The class of 2011: Young workers face a dire labor marker without a safety net*. Economic Policy Institute. Briefing Paper #306. Retrieved June 9, 2011 from http://www.epi.org/latest_research/

CHAPTER FOUR

Changing THE Lens

Moving Away from the School to Prison Pipeline

DAMIEN M. SOJOYNER

Over the course of the past 15 years, there has been an abundance of literature that seeks to conceptualize the school to prison pipeline (STPP) as the primary model of analysis with respect to the criminalization of youth in general and Black youth in particular. While language and work in relationship to it have been highly effective in organizing communities around discipline policies and policing of schools, the phrasing and current policy initiatives around STPP fail to dig deep and address the root causes that have led to increased surveillance, racialized and economic segregation within education, and, importantly, the enormous effect that public education has had upon institutionalizing the current prison regime. My aim through the course of this chapter is to focus on Los Angeles as a key site in order to understand what is necessary to shift our mode of analysis away from the school to prison pipeline and come up with a new vocabulary/lexicon that will allow us to understand the massive impact that education has upon society.

Los Angeles is a very important city in the context of public education, as programs such as D.A.R.E. and the criminalization of "truants" were first piloted there and then were exported across the nation. Los Angeles is also important because it is often constructed as a primary example of liberal democracy. However, historical and current realities indicate that the city is a collection of extreme racialized and economic differences. The rebellions of 1965 and 1992 are nothing if not clear indications of the city's attempt to systemically oppress both Black liberation movements and daily life in general. My analysis of Los Angeles is broken into three sections, covering from 1950 through the end of the 1960s, and situates the development of the city as both a site of extreme racial violence and the cutting edge of an attempt to diminish the effectiveness of organizing in Black communities through an assault upon the education system. The first section elucidates that Black Los Angeles was a site of intense police brutality and has to be understood as a collection of communities under constant attack. The second section addresses both the power of education as an agent for Black organizing and the determination of city and state governments to limit Black mobilization through an attack upon Black education using "soft-handed" approaches such as social work and curriculum changes. The last section asserts that by the end of the 1960s, the template for the policing of Black education had been created and that the education of Black people was engulfed by severe limits upon organizing and mobility. These three sections together demonstrate that Black Los Angeles has long been dominated by an enclosure of militarization while educational planning foregrounded the development of the current prison regime.

PART 1—BLACK LOS ANGELES, ORGANIZING, AND POLICE VIOLENCE

In 1963, Hugh R. Manes wrote a detailed analysis, "A Report on Law Enforcement and the Negro Citizen in Los Angeles" (Manes, 1963). Manes, a white attorney, had a unique perspective on the issue of police violence within Los Angeles County. Through the course of his legal practice, he had represented countless Black Angelinos who had been the victims of harassment, physical violence, and psychological terror. By 1963, Manes had seen enough and issued a scathing indictment of the Los Angeles Police Department (LAPD), the mayor of Los Angeles, and white residents of Los Angeles County and connected them to the overall oppression of Black life in Southern California.

Manes outlined a case-by-case analysis of incidents of police brutality enacted upon Black people; yet in spite of the litany of evidence and in some instances of police self-admission, there was never anything in the way of the smallest inkling of justice for Black people. From 1950 to 1960, more than 5,000 complaints were filed against the LAPD, the vast majority attributed to police brutality. In spite of these figures and even in the 36% of cases in which police officers were found to be in violation of internal protocol, only in the rarest of events was legal action brought against the offending officer(s). While the district attorney's (DA) office was very quick to bring to trial Black residents who had been accused by police officers of committing minor offenses such as resisting arrest, the DA did not possess the moral fortitude to bring to trial officers who violently attacked Black people throughout the county. Adding insult to injury, once the DA's office and the

LAPD's internal review process proved to be a failure, the only civil option left was to bring a lawsuit against the LAPD. However, such actions proved to be counterproductive, as the courts always decided against Black residents. As a result, the courts affirmed the legal position of police brutality and as a consequence Black people could not rely upon the legal process for even a modicum of civil redress.

Thus, with the courts deciding one-sidedly in favor of police repression, Black people had very little in the way of formal recourse to address the issue of police violence in their community. Greatly aware of the vast discrepancy within the courts, community organizations such as the National Association for the Advancement of Colored People (NAACP) conducted investigations of police violence and brought forth charges against the LAPD. Rather than address the validity of the NAACP's claims, the mayor of Los Angeles at the time, Sam Yorty, attempted to discredit the findings of the report as the work of people and organizations that were undermining the fabric of the United States. Issuing a formal response to the NAACP report, Yorty claimed, "The words police brutality are the invention of Communist ... people who want to break down law enforcement, and the words are parroted by people who have been fooled by the Communists. It is a very clear tactic of the Communists" (Manes, 1963, p. 14). Compounding matters, Yorty claimed that violence enacted upon Black people by the police was the result of members of the Nation of Islam, who he claimed initiated violence upon police officers. Rather than make a veiled threat, Yorty urged the attorney general of California to label Black Muslims as subversive agents against the state of California.

In reality, Yorty was attempting to stave off criticism of warrantless searches against the Nation of Islam throughout Los Angeles. As some of the most vocal and fiercest organizers in the city during the latter part of the 1950s and into the 1960s, the Black Muslim community became a target of both the LAPD and city officials. Once the Black Muslim community was placed upon the list of subversives, the LAPD no longer needed to abide by formal protocol of obtaining warrants to surveil, arrest, and physically brutalize Black Muslims. According to Yorty, the appellation of the Nation of Islam as subversive agents would "enable police to take better enforcement measures against the Muslims. Their meeting places could be closed, their literature seized, and their activities otherwise curtailed" (as cited in "School Board Plans Probe," 1962). In addition to responding against the charges levied by the NAACP, Yorty's response was set against the backdrop of two significant events. The first involved the LAPD's shooting of seven members of the Nation of Islam in March 1962. Through police propaganda disseminated by the *Los Angeles Times*, the attack was labeled as justified and depicted the men shot by the police as unruly and violent militants who had no respect for law and authority. While the police alleged that they were approached by a group of Black Muslims with guns, it was soon revealed that not only were the men unarmed, but also that the LAPD had been surveilling the group during the course of the evening. In

teach technical defense skills led to the awakening of a Black working-class base for whom radical change was the only solution.

The time was ripe for organizing, as public education in Los Angeles had become solidly segregated. Moreover, the school system had also put into practice placing the most inexperienced and malcontent teachers in Black schools. The situation had become so egregious and blatant that in 1969 the American Civil Liberties Union (ACLU) filed a lawsuit against the school district. Borrowing language from the 1954 *Brown v. Board of Education* case, the lawsuit stated that the school system had put in place a structure that was both separate and unequal. It cannot be overstated that the school system's intent was to create a two-tiered education structure whereby Black students were provided with substandard and inferior education, while at the direct expense of Black students, white students were provided intellectual resources of the highest quality.

Part of the story that is often not told is that there was an entire cadre of willing and passionate Black teachers for whom teaching in Los Angeles was not an option. Educators such as Jesse Williams, who had moved his family from Houston, Texas, to Los Angeles in 1948, were shut out of the school system. Williams, a trained educator from Prairie View A&M, a historically Black college located just outside Houston, Texas, had previously taught in segregated Black schools in Houston. Yet despite the rhetoric that described California as being a liberal, all-encompassing state, Williams found when he got to Los Angeles that his experience there was much worse than it had been in Houston. Although he had taught in a racially and economically segregated Houston, he was still able to teach (E. Schnyder & E. Bohannan, personal communication, June 7, 2010). Once in Los Angeles, he soon quickly realized that the color line for teachers was strictly enforced and despite his best intentions, there was no way of breaking its hardened barrier.

It was within this setting that Black Angelinos started making demands upon the Los Angeles school system in order to address the stark economic and educational differences based upon school racial segregation. In order to justify the stark inequalities within the school system, administrators often fell back upon the excuse of lack of money needed to improve schools. The result of the lack of money led to a reduction in courses taught coupled with the removal of effective teachers in the name of budget cuts. Citing that the school system did not have enough money to address the needs that parents demanded or tor restore the previous cuts, the school officials preached a doctrine of patience. Yet by the end of the 1960s, Black people had run out of patience. At a meeting addressing the austerity measures put forth by the school district, parents had grown tired of their calls for a better education system being consistently rebuffed. Responding to Associate Superintendent of Schools Richard Purdy and School Board President Arthur

Gardner's dismissal of their demands, parents took the floor and cut straight to the point: "Get off your ass!" "The people will take the power in their own hands!" "Do we have to burn your school down?" (Porter, 1969).

A tipping point within the Black community had been reached and in response, Los Angeles city officials initiated a plan of militarization and forced enclosures with respect to dealing with Black education. The first major event that allowed city officials to test this new theory was in response to an altercation between students that took place during a football game between Crenshaw High School and Thomas Jefferson High School in October 1969. In droves, police descended upon the campus of the 99% Black Thomas Jefferson High School and immediately began arresting students. Further, under the guise of protecting public safety, police officers were ordered to remain at the school. Irate parents, students, and members of the neighboring community immediately questioned how the city suddenly had resources to pay for the militarization of their schools, but not for the educational resources that they had been demanding for the better part of a decade. Students at Thomas Jefferson High School organized themselves and effectively went on strike, refusing to attend school until all of the police officers were removed from campus. In addition, students demanded the return of highly effective teachers who had been transferred from Jefferson during the school year (Porter, 1969).

While the school officials acquiesced to some of the demands of removing the majority of the police from the campus of Jefferson High School, the plan had been carried out and from that point forward, policing and Black education were tied together. Throughout the 1970s, city officials attempted to tighten the reins upon Black communities through a policy of strict surveillance and enclosure of Black education. The police state that slowly formed around Black life in the 1950s became whole and extended into the everyday fabric of Black communities and, importantly, into the most cherished aspect of Black resistance, renewal, and rejuvenation—education.

In light of the relationship among Black communities, city officials, police, and public education during the 1950s and 1960s there has to be a new analysis with respect to language, policy, and action pertaining to the school to prison pipeline. Not only is the concept of the pipeline invalid, it also removes the focus upon public education as the key historical agent that led to the expansion of prisons as a site of Black enclosure. We have to resituate the historical and contemporary violence within education as something that is not only influenced by prisons, but was also an important model in developing systems of repression to limit Black communal organizing. Without a reconfiguration of our analysis, we are doomed to develop ineffective solutions with regard to Black education and will betray the legacy of Black resistance that has always placed education at the center of community development.

REFERENCES

Du Bois, W. E. B. (1935/1998). *Black reconstruction in America, 1860–1880.* New York: Free Press.

Elman, D. (Interviewer). (1962, May 1). Malcolm X [Radio interview]. New York: WBAI.

Hilliard, D. (Ed.). (2008). *The Black Panther Party: Service to the People programs.* Albuquerque: University of New Mexico Press.

Kim, C. Y., Losen, D. J., & Hewitt, D. T. (2010). *The school-to-prison pipeline: Structuring legal reform.* New York: NYU Press.

Kupchik, A. (2010). *Homeroom security: School discipline in an age of fear.* New York: NYU Press.

Manes, H. R. (1963). *A report on law enforcement and the Negro citizen in Los Angeles.* Los Angeles: Author.

Meiners, E. R. (2007). *Right to be hostile: Schools, prisons, and the making of public enemies.* New York: Routledge.

Monahan, T., & Torres, R. (2009). *Schools under surveillance: Cultures of control in public education.* New Brunswick, NJ: Rutgers University Press.

Muslims stand silent at riot arraignment: Nine in court after fatal police battle; seven other accused men in hospital. (1962, May 3). *Los Angeles Times*, p. 1.

Porter, C. (1969, October 16). Tension mounts at Jeff High, school closes: Groups meet in effort to remedy problems. *Los Angeles Sentinel*, p. A1.

School board plans probe of poor school conditions. (1969, March 6). *Los Angeles Sentinel*, p. A3.

Senker, C. (2011). *Privacy and surveillance.* New York: Rosen.

Umoja, A. O. (2002). "We will shoot back": The Natchez model and paramilitary organization in the Mississippi Freedom Movement. *Journal of Black Studies, 32*(3), 271–294.

Wald, J., & Losen, D. J. (2003). *Deconstructing the school-to-prison pipeline: New directions for youth development, no. 99.* San Francisco: Jossey-Bass.

Welfare Planning Council. (1961). *Youth problems and needs in the South Central Area* (No. 1, p. 31). Los Angeles: Author.

PART TWO

Targeting Youth

The vast majority of prisoners are not imprisoned because they are "criminals," but because they've been accused of breaking one of an ever-increasing number of laws designed to exert tighter social control and State repression. They have been scapegoated and criminalized. This can be seen in the increased number of Black, Latino, Native American and Asian youth detained under youth-crime acts and "anti-gang" laws; the number of foreign nationals (excluding most Europeans) imprisoned under hate-mongering immigration laws; and of course, the "drug" war in which hundreds of thousands have been kidnapped from their communities, even from other countries.

—Marilyn Buck

When young black men reach a certain age—whether or not there is incarceration in their families—they themselves are the target of police stops, interrogations, frisks, often for no reason other than their race. And, of course, this level of harassment sends a message to them, often at an early age: No matter who you are or what you do, you're going to find yourself behind bars one way or the other. This reinforces the sense that prison is part of their destiny, rather than a choice one makes.

—Michelle Alexander

of the income growth." The degree to which the top 1% are benefiting from the obscene policies of the new Gilded Age becomes clear in the inflated and immoral bonuses handed out to CEOs who in some cases actually contributed to the economic bust of 2008. Several statistics stand out for the economic injustice they portray. For example, "the average pay for people working in U.S. investment banks is over $375,000 while senior officers at Goldman Sachs averaged $61 million each in compensation for 2007" (Ferguson, 2012, p. 8). At the same time, the United States beats out every other developing nation in producing extreme income and wealth inequalities for 2012. The top 1% now owns "about a third of the American people's total net worth, over 40 percent of America's total financial wealth ... and half of the nation's total income growth" (Ferguson, 2012, p. 8). Rarely are the social costs of casino capitalism analyzed as part of a broader attack on democratic values, non-commodified public spheres, young people, and those populations who live on the edge of survival.

Free market fundamentalism or casino capitalism working hand in hand with the rise of the punishing state increasingly exerts its influence over a vast range of public spheres extending from school and halfway houses to airports and higher education. At the same time, political illiteracy and religious fundamentalism have cornered the market on populist rage providing support for a country in which as Robert Reich (2012) points out "the very richest people get all the economic gains [and] routinely bribe politicians" in order to cut their taxes and establish policies that eliminate access to public goods such as schools, social protections, health care, and important infrastructures.

It gets worse. Everywhere we look the powerful mega-corporations and financial elite aggressively promote failed modes of governance and a "suicidal state" (Virilio, 1998). This is particularly clear in the attempts by the bankers, hedge fund operators, and their corporate cohorts to dismantle regulations meant to restrict their corrupting political and economic power while enacting policies that privilege the rich and the powerful. In this instance, casino capitalism produces an autoimmune crisis in which a society attacks the very elements of a society that allow it to reproduce itself, while at the same time killing off any sense of history, memory, and social and ethical responsibility. As social protections are dismantled, public servants denigrated, and public goods such as schools, bridges, health care services, and public transportation deteriorate, the current apostles of neoliberal orthodoxy embrace the cruel and punishing values of economic Darwinism, with its survival-of-the-fittest ethic and its winner-take-all belief system. In doing so, the major political parties now reward as their chief beneficiaries the too-big-to-fail banks, ultra-large financial industries, the defense establishment, and mega corporations. Corruption is overlooked and casino-style speculation goes unchecked. JP Morgan's recent $2 billion trading loss is the latest example of the risky trading and high-risk speculation that demand regulatory reforms, which

JP Morgan and other financial institutions aggressively oppose, in spite of the havoc these policies have wreaked on the economy as a whole (Krugman, 2012, p. A23). Fortunately, the question of what happens to democracy and politics when dominated by corporations is now being raised by young people and others in the Occupy Wall Street movement, but this collective sense of outrage has yet to connect with a broader notion of politics that challenges not only the values of neoliberalism but also the power relations that structure its most powerful political and economic institutions.

Under neoliberalism, acts of translation become utterly privatized and removed from public considerations. Public issues now collapse into private problems. One consequence is not only the undoing of the social bond, but also the endless reproduction of the narrow register of individual responsibility as a substitute for any analyses of wider social problems, making it easier to blame the poor, homeless, uninsured, jobless, and other disadvantaged groups for their problems while reïnforcing the merging of a market society with the punishing state. One consequence is that zones of social abandonment now proliferate, while ever-growing disposable populations become normalized.

The varied populations made disposable under casino capitalism occupy a globalized space of ruthless politics in which the categories of "citizen's rights," "social protections," and "democratic representation," once integral to national politics, are no longer recognized. Disposable populations are less visible, relegated to the frontier zones of relative invisibility and removed from public view, and often placed in "a state of terminal exclusion" (Biehl, 2005, p. 14). The "machinery of social death" (Biehl, 2005, p. 14) now works its way from the prison to the halls and classrooms of public education. Poor minority youth, especially, are often warehoused in schools that resemble boot camps, dispersed to dank and dangerous work places far from the enclaves of the tourist industries, incarcerated in prisons that privilege punishment over rehabilitation, and consigned to the increasing army of the permanently unemployed. Rendered redundant as a result of the collapse of the social state, a pervasive racism, a growing disparity in income and wealth, and a take-no-prisoners neoliberalism, an increasing number of individuals and groups are being demonized, criminalized, or simply abandoned either by virtue of their status as immigrants or because they are young, poor, unemployed, disabled, homeless, or confined to low-paying jobs. What Joao Biehl (2005, p. 14) has called "zones of social abandonment" now accelerate the disposability of the unwanted.

The human face of this process and the invisible others who inhabit its geography are captured in a story told by Chip Ward, a former librarian, who writes poignantly about a homeless woman named Ophelia, who retreats to the library because like many of the homeless she has nowhere else to go to use the bathroom, secure temporary relief from bad weather, or simply be able to rest. Excluded from the American dream and treated as both expendable and a threat, Ophelia, in spite of her obvious mental illness, defines her existence in terms that offer a chilling metaphor that extends far beyond her plight. Ward describes Ophelia's presence and actions in the following way:

> Ophelia sits by the fireplace and mumbles softly, smiling and gesturing at no one in particular. She gazes out the large window through the two pairs of glasses she wears, one windshield-sized pair over a smaller set perched precariously on her small nose. Perhaps four lenses help her see the invisible other she is addressing. When her "nobody there" conversation disturbs the reader seated beside her, Ophelia turns, chuckles at the woman's discomfort, and explains, *"Don't mind me, I'm dead. It's okay. I've been dead for some time now." She pauses, then adds reassuringly, "It's not so bad. You get used to it."* [Italics added] Not at all reassured, the woman gathers her belongings and moves quickly away. Ophelia shrugs. Verbal communication is tricky. She prefers telepathy, but that's hard to do since the rest of us, she informs me, "don't know the rules." (Ward, 2007)

Ophelia represents just one of the 200,000 chronically homeless who now use public libraries and any other accessible public spaces to find shelter. Many are often sick, are disoriented, suffer from substance abuse, or are mentally disabled and on the edge of sanity owing to the stress, insecurity, and danger that they face every day. And while Ophelia's comments may be dismissed as the ramblings of a mentally disturbed woman, they speak to something much deeper about the current state of American society and its desertion of entire populations that are now considered the human waste of a neoliberal social order. People who were once viewed as facing dire problems in need of state intervention and social protection are now seen as a problem threatening society. This becomes clear when the war on poverty is transformed into a war against the poor; when the plight of the homeless is defined less as a political and economic issue in need of social reform than as a matter of law and order; or when government budgets for prison construction eclipse funds for higher education. Indeed, the transformation of the social state into the corporate-controlled punishing state is made startlingly clear when young people, to paraphrase W. E. B. Du Bois, become problem people rather than people who face problems.

Already disenfranchised by virtue of their age, young people are under assault today in ways that are entirely new because they now face a world that is far more dangerous than at any other time in recent history. Not only do they live in a space of social homelessness in which precariousness and uncertainty lock them out of a secure future, they also find themselves inhabiting a society that seeks to silence them as it makes them invisible. Victims of a neoliberal regime that smashes their hopes and attempts to exclude them from the fruits of democracy, young people are now told not to expect too much. Written out of any claim to the economic and social resources of the larger society, they are increasingly told to accept the status of "stateless, faceless, and functionless" nomads, a plight for which they alone have to accept responsibility (Bauman, 2004, pp. 76–77). Like Ophelia, increasing numbers of youth suffer mental anguish and overt distress even, perhaps especially, among the college bound, debt ridden, and unemployed whose numbers are growing exponentially.

If youth were once viewed as the site where society deposited it dreams, that is no longer true. They are now viewed mostly as a public disorder and inhabit a place where society increasingly exhibits its nightmares. Many young people now live in a post-9/11 social order that views them as a prime target of its governing through crime complex. This is made obvious by the many "get tough" policies that now render young people as criminals, while depriving them of basic health care, education, and social services. Punishment and fear have replaced compassion and social responsibility as the most important modalities mediating the relationship of youth to the larger social order. When war and the criminalization of social problems become a mode of governance, youth is reduced to a target rather than a social investment. As anthropologist Alain Bertho points out, "Youth is no longer considered the world's future, but as a threat to its present" (as quoted in Durand, 2009). The only political discourse available for young people is a disciplinary one. Youth now represents the absent present in any discourse about the contemporary moment, the future, and democracy itself and increasingly inhabit a state that mimics what Michel Foucault (2003, p. 260) calls "an absolutely racist state, an absolutely murderous state and an absolutely suicidal state." How young people are represented in both historical and contemporary terms tells us a lot about "the social and political constitution of society" (Comaroff & Comaroff, 2006, p. 267). Young people have always been defined through what Jean and John Comaroff (2006, p. 280) have termed a kind of doubling in which young people are perceived ambiguously as both a threat and a promise. While this has been less true of poor minority youth, young people historically still occupied that middle ground between being seen as a nightmare and a "source of yet-to-be-imagined futures" (Comaroff & Camaroff, 2006, p. 280). Youth no longer occupy a middle ground between despair and hope, especially poor youth of color. On the contrary, young people today are largely seen as markets, commodities, or disposable populations.

Part of this transformation of young people from facing problems to being a problem can be traced to the collapse of the social state and the rise of a market-driven society. The social contract, however feeble, came crashing to the ground in the late 1970s as Margaret Thatcher in Britain and soon afterward Ronald Reagan in the United States came to power. Both of these infamous hard-line advocates of market fundamentalism announced respectively that there was no such thing as society and that government was the problem, not the solution. Democracy and the political process were soon hijacked by corporations and hope was appropriated as an advertisement for the white-washed world of the likes of Disney. At the

THE YOUTH CRIME-CONTROL COMPLEX

Against the idealistic rhetoric of a government that claims it venerates young people lies the reality of a society that increasingly views youth through the optic of law and order, a society that appears all too willing to treat youth as criminals and when necessary make them "disappear" into the farthest reaches of the carceral state. Under such circumstances, the administration of schools and social services has given way to modes of confinement whose purpose is to ensure "custody and control" (Bauman, 2004, p. 82). Hence, it is not surprising that "school officials and the criminal justice system are criminalizing children and teenagers all over the country, arresting them and throwing them in jail for behavior that in years past would never have led to the intervention of law enforcement" (Herbert, 2007, p. A29).

For instance, as the logic of the market and crime control frame a number of school policies, students are now subjected to zero tolerance rules that are used primarily to humiliate, punish, repress, and exclude them (Robbins, 2008; Saltman & Gabbard, 2003). What are we to make of a society that allows the police to come into a school and arrest, handcuff, and haul off a 12-year-old student for doodling on her desk? Or, for that matter, a school system that allows a 5-year-old kindergarten pupil to be handcuffed and sent to a hospital psychiatric ward for being unruly in a classroom? Where is the public outrage when two police officers called to a day-care center in central Indiana to handle an unruly 10-year-old decide to Taser the child and slap him in the mouth? How does one account for a school administration allowing a police officer in Arkansas to use a stun gun to control an allegedly out-of-control 10-year-old girl? The contempt that schools and the justice system have for young people was recently played out in the case of a 17-year-old high school junior and honor student, Diane Tran, who was tossed in jail for a night because she was "missing too much school" (Seltzer, 2012). What was overlooked beyond the larger issue of whether jail is the answer for any young person under the age of 18 is that Tran was not only taking advanced level classes but was also working two jobs to help support her two siblings without the help of her parents, who had moved out of town. In the face of a public uproar over the case and the elevation of Tran as "a poster-girl for both the recession and for the criminalization of youth," the judge who sentenced Tran stated, "A little stay in the jail for one night is not a death sentence" (Seltzer, 2012). What is disturbing is that this dangerous use of punitive disciplinary practices seems to exceed all notions of reason when it comes to young people. Moreover, as prison becomes a fundamental fact of American life, more and more young people are being sent to for-profit juvenile detention centers where they experience what Booth Gunter (2012) calls "unbelievable brutality."

Even more shocking is the rise of zero tolerance policies to punish students with disabilities. Instead of recognizing the need to provide services for students with special needs, there is a dangerous trend on the part of school systems to adopt policies "that end in seclusion, restraint, expulsion, and—too often—law enforcement intervention for the disabled children involved" (Smith, 2012). Sadly, this is but a small sampling of the ways in which children are being punished instead of educated in American schools, especially inner-city schools.

All of these examples point to the growing disregard American society has for young people and the number of institutions willing to employ a crime-and-punishment mentality that constitutes not only a crisis of politics, but also the emergence of new politics of educating and governing through crime (Simon, 2007, p. 5). Of course, we have seen this ruthless crime optic in previous historical periods, but the social costs of such criminalization was viewed as a social issue rather than as an individualized problem. That is, in which crime and reform were viewed as part of a broader constellation of socio-economic forces. For one example of this broader understanding of crime, I want to turn to Claude Brown, the late African American novelist, who understood something about this war on youth. Though his novel, *Manchild in the Promised Land*, takes place in Harlem in the 1960s, there is something to be learned from his work. Take, for example, the following passage from his book, written in 1965:

> If Reno was in a bad mood—if he didn't have any money and he wasn't high—he'd say, "Man, Sonny, they ain't got no kids in Harlem. I ain't never seen any. I've seen some real small people actin' like kids, but they don't have any kids in Harlem, because nobody has time for a childhood. Man, do you ever remember bein' a kid? Not me. Shit, kids are happy, kids laugh, kids are secure. They ain't scared a nothin'. You ever been a kid, Sonny? Damn, you lucky. I ain't never been a kid, man. I don't ever remember bein' happy and not scared. I don't know what happened, man, but I think I missed out on that childhood thing, because I don't ever recall bein' a kid. (Brown, 1965, p. xxxv)

In *Manchild in the Promised Land*, Claude Brown wrote about the doomed lives of his friends, families, and neighborhood acquaintances. The book is mostly remembered as a brilliant, but devastating portrait of Harlem under siege—a community ravaged and broken by drugs, poverty, unemployment, crime, and police brutality. But what Brown really made visible was that the raw violence and dead-end existence that plagued so many young people in Harlem stole not only their future but their childhood as well. In the midst of the social collapse and psychological trauma wrought by the systemic fusion of racism and class exploitation, children in Harlem were held hostage to forces that robbed them of the innocence that comes with childhood and forced them to take on the risks and burdens of daily survival that older generations were unable to shield them from. At the heart of Brown's narrative, written in the midst of the civil rights struggle in the 1960s, is a "manchild," a metaphor that indicts a society that is waging a war on those children who are black and poor and have been forced to grow up too quickly. The hybridized concept of "manchild" marked a liminal space if not a liminal drift in which innocence was lost and childhood stolen. Harlem was a well-contained, internal colony and its street life provided the conditions and the very necessity for insurrection. But the many forms of rebellion young people expressed—from the public and progressive to the interiorized and self-destructive—came with a price, which Brown reveals near the end of the book: "It seemed as though most of the cats that we'd come up with just hadn't made it. Almost everybody was dead or in jail" (1965, p. 419).

Childhood stolen was not a plea for self-help—that short-sighted and mendacious appeal that would define the reactionary reform efforts of the 1980s and 1990s, from Reagan's hatred of government to Clinton's attack on welfare reform. It was a clarion call for condemning a social order that denied children a viable and life-enhancing future. While Brown approached everyday life in Harlem more as a poet than as a political revolutionary, politics was embedded in every sentence of the book—not a politics marked by demagoguery, hatred, and orthodoxy, but one that made visible the damage done by a social system characterized by massive inequalities and a rigid racial divide. *Manchild* created the image of a society without children in order to raise questions about the future of a country that had turned its back on its most vulnerable population. Like the great critical theorist, C. Wright Mills, Claude Brown's lasting contribution was to reconfigure the boundaries between public issues and private sufferings. For Brown, racism was about power and oppression and could not be separated from broader social, economic, and political considerations. Rather than denying systemic causes of injustice (as did the discourses of individual pathology and self-help), Brown insisted that social forces had to be factored into any understanding of both group suffering and individual despair. Brown explored the suffering of the young in Harlem, but he did so by utterly refusing to privatize it, or to dramatize and spectacularize private life over public dysfunction, or to separate individual hopes, desires, and agency from the realm of politics and public life.

Nearly fifty years later, Brown's metaphor of the "manchild" is more relevant today than when he wrote the book, and "the Promised Land" more mythic than ever as his revelation about the sorry plight of poor and minority children takes on a more expansive meaning in light of the current economic meltdown and the dashed hopes of an entire generation now viewed as a generation without hope for a decent future. Youth today are forced to inhabit a rough world where childhood is nonexistent, crushed under the heavy material and existential burdens they are forced to bear.

What is horrifying about the plight of youth today is not just the severity of deprivations and violence they experience daily, but also how they have been forced to view the world and redefine the nature of their own childhood within the borders of hopelessness, cruelty, and despair. There is little sense of a hopeful future lying just beyond highly policed spaces of commodification and containment. An entire generation of youth will not have access to decent jobs, the material comforts, or the security available to previous generations. These children are a new generation of youth who have to think, act, and talk like adults; worry about their families, which may be headed by a single parent or two out of work and searching for a job; wonder how they are going to get the money to buy food and how long it will take to see a doctor in case of illness. These children are no longer confined to so-called ghettoes. As the burgeoning landscapes of poverty and despair increasingly find expression in our cities, suburbs, and rural areas, these children make their presence felt—they are too many to ignore or hide away in the usually sequestered and invisible spaces of disposability. They constitute a new and more unsettling scene of suffering, one that reveals not only the vast and destabilizing inequalities in our economic landscape but also portends a future that has no purchase on the hope that characterizes a vibrant democracy.

DEFENDING YOUTH AND DEMOCRACY IN THE TWENTY-FIRST CENTURY

One way of addressing collapsing intellectual and moral visions regarding young people is to imagine those institutions, policies, values, opportunities, and social relations that both invoke adult responsibility and reinforce the ethical imperative to provide young people, especially those marginalized by race and class, with the economic, social, and educational conditions that make life livable and the future sustainable. Clearly the rudiments of such a vision, one that moves beyond what Alain Badiou has called the "crisis of negation" (interview with Van Houdt, 2011), which is a crisis of imagination, historical possibility, and an aversion to new ideas, can be found in the emerging global protests of the Occupy movement in North America and other youth resistance movements around the globe. What is evident in this worldwide movement is a bold attempt to imagine the possibility of another world, a rejection of the current moment of historical one-dimensionality, a refusal to settle for reforms that are purely incremental.

The Occupy Wall Street movement suggests that the young people are once again a source of creativity, possibility, and political struggle. Moreover, the movement points to a crucial political project in which new questions are being raised by many young people about emerging anti-democratic forces in the United States that threaten the collective survival of vast numbers of people, not exclusively through overt physical injury or worse, but also through an aggressive assault on social provisions on which millions of Americans depend. What is partly evident in the Occupy Wall Street movement is both a cry of collective indignation over economic and social injustices that pose a threat to humankind, and a critical expression of how young people and others can use new technologies, develop democratic social formations, and enact forms of critical pedagogy and civil disobedience necessary for addressing the diverse anti-democratic forces that have been poisoning American politics since the 1970s.

The protesters are making a claim for a sense of collective agency in which their voices must be heard as part of a concerted effort to shape the future that they will inherit. This effort is part of a new form of politics that offers resistance to the frontal assault being waged by casino capitalism against the social good, economic justice, immigrants, unions, worker rights, public servants, democratic public spheres, the notion of the common good, and human dignity itself. And it does so by delineating the contours, values, sensibilities, and hidden politics that now shape the commanding institutions of power and everyday relations of the 99%, who are increasingly viewed as excess, disposable, and unworthy of living a life of dignity, shared responsibility, and hope. This task of delineation is not easy: the conditions of domination are layered, complex, and deeply flexible. Yet while the forms of oppression are diverse, there is a promising tendency within the Occupy Wall Street movement to refocus these diverse struggles into new forms of collective endeavor and modes of solidarity built around social and shared rather than individualized and competitive values.

The current protests make clear that this is not—indeed, *cannot be*—only a short-term project for reform, but a political movement that needs to intensify, accompanied by the reclaiming of public spaces, the progressive use of digital technologies, the development of public spheres, new modes of education, and the safeguarding of places where democratic expression, new identities, and collective hope can be nurtured and mobilized. America is losing its claim to democracy, prompting a new urgency for a collective politics and social movements capable of both negating the established order and imagining a new one. Until we address what Stanley Aronowitz (2012) has brilliantly analysed as our "Winter of Discontent" American society will continue to engage in autoimmune practices that attack the very values, institutions, social relations, and struggles that keep the ideal of democracy alive. At the very least, the American public owes it to its children and future generations, if not the future of democracy itself, to begin to dismantle this machinery of violence and reclaim the democratic spirit of a future that works for life, justice, and human dignity rather than support the registers of social and ethical morbidity dressed up in the spectacles of consumerism and celebrity culture. It is time for the 99% to connect the dots, educate themselves, and develop social movements that can rewrite the language of democracy and put into place the institutions and formative cultures that make it possible. It is also time for such movements to acknowledge that while condemning corruption and greed is not unimportant, the path to real democracy must go beyond such moralism and address the systemic forces at work that produce corruption, massive levels of inequality, greed, and the rise of a form of economic Darwinism.

Such a project suggests making evident not only how casino capitalism intensifies the pathologies of racism, student debt, war, inequality, sexism, xenophobia, poverty, unemployment, and violence, but also how to take up the challenge of developing a politics and pedagogy that can actualize a democratic notion of the social—that is, further understand and collectively organize for a politics whose hope lies with defending the shared values, spaces, and public spheres that enable an emergent radical democracy. There is no room for failure here because failure would cast us back into the clutches of an authoritarianism that while different from previous historical periods, shares nonetheless the imperative to proliferate violent social formations and to deal a death-blow to the promise of a democracy to come.

REFERENCES

Aronowitz, S. (2012, Spring). The winter of our discontent. *Situations, 4*(2), 37–76.

Bauman, Z. (1999). Introduction and in search of public space. *In Search of Politics* (p. 8). Stanford, CA: Stanford University Press.

Bauman, Z. (2004). *Wasted lives* (pp. 76–77). London: Polity Press.

Biehl, J. (2005). *Vita: Life in a zone of social abandonment* (p. 14). Berkeley: University of California Press.

Brown, C. (1965). *Manchild in the promised land.* New York: Signet Books.

Christine, C. (2010, January 21). Kaiser study: Kids 8 to 18 spend more than seven hours a day with media. *Spotlight on Digital Media and Learning: MacArthur Foundation.* Retrieved from http://spotlight.macfound.org/blog/entry/kaiser_study_kids_age_8_to_18_spend_more_than_seven_hours_a_day_with_media/

Comaroff, J., & Comaroff, J. (2006). Reflections of youth, from the past to the postcolony. In M. S. Fisher & G. Downey (Eds.), *Frontiers of capital: Ethnographic reflections on the new economy* (p. 267). Durham, NC: Duke University Press.

Durand, J-M. (2009, November 15). For youth: A disciplinary discourse only (L. Thatcher, Trans.). *TruthOut.* Retrieved from http://www.truthout.org/11190911

Ferguson, C. H. (2012). *Predator nation* (p. 21). New York: Crown.

Foucault, M. (2003). *Society must be defended: Lectures at the College de France, 1975–1976* (p. 260). New York: Picador.

Giroux, H. A. (2010). *Youth in a suspect society: Democracy or disposability?* New York: Palgrave Macmillan.

Giroux, H. A. (2012). *Disposable youth: Racialized memories, and the culture of cruelty.* New York: Routledge.

Goode, E. (2011, December 19). Many in U.S. are arrested by age 23, study finds. *The New York Times.* Retrieved from http://www.nytimes.com/2011/12/19/us/nearly-a-third-of-americans-are-arrested-by-23-study-says.html?_r=1&pagewanted=print

Gunter, B. (2012, May 11). The unbelievable brutality unleashed on kids in for-profit prisons. *AlterNet*. Retrieved from http://www.alternet.org/story/155326/the_unbelievable_brutality_unleashed_on_kids_in_for-profit_prisons

Herbert, B. (2007, June 9). School to prison pipeline. *The New York Times*, p. A29.

Kimberly, M. (2012, May 9). Jail for sending their kid to school? How America treats black women and children like criminals. *AlterNet*. Retrieved from http://www.alternet.org/story/155330/jail_for_sending_their_kid_to_school_how_america_treats_black_women_and_children_like_criminals/

Krugman, P. (2012, May14). Why we regulate. *The New York Times*, p. A23.

Lewin, T. (2010, January 20). If your kids are awake, they're probably online. *The New York Times*, p. A1.

Reich, R. (2012, April 6). The fable of the century [Weblog post]. *Robert Reich's Blog*. Retrieved from http://robertreich.org/post/20538393444

Reuters. (2011, November 22). 45% struggle in US to make ends meet. *MSNBC: Business Stocks and Economy*. Retrieved from http://www.msnbc.msn.com/id/45407937/ns/business-stocks_and_economy/#.T3SxhDEgd8E

Robbins, C. (2008). *Expelling hope: The assault on youth and the militarization of schooling*. Albany, NY: SUNY Press.

Saltman, K., & Gabbard, D. (Eds.). (2003). *Education as enforcement: The militarization and corporatization of schools*. New York: Routledge.

Seltzer, S. (2012, June 5). What does it say about America that we jail teens for having sex or being late to school? *AlterNet*. Retrieved from http://www.alternet.org/story/155747/what_does_it_say_about_america_that_we_jail_teens_for_having_sex_or_being_late_to_school_/?page=entire

Simon, J. (2007). *Governing through crime: How the war on crime transformed American democracy and created a culture of fear* (p. 5). New York: Oxford University Press.

Smith, S. E. (2012, May 22). Police handcuffing 7-year-olds? The brutality unleashed on kids with disabilities in our school systems. *AlterNet*. Retrieved from http://www.alternet.org/story/155526/police_handcuffing_7-year-olds_the_brutality_unleashed_on_kids_with_disabilities_in_our_school_systems?page=entire

Staff, *Rethinking Schools*. (2012, January 15). Stop the school-to-prison pipeline. *TruthOut*. Retrieved from http://truth-out.org/index.php?option=com_k2&view=item&id=6106:stop-the-schooltoprison-pipeline

Stiglitz, J. E. (2012, June 5). The price of inequality. *Project Syndicate*. Retrieved from http://www.project-syndicate.org/commentary/the-price-of-inequality

Tanner, L. (2009, November 2). Half of US kids will get food stamps, study says. *Chicago Tribune*. Retrieved from http://www.chicagotribune.com/news/chi-ap-us-med-children-food,0,6055934.story

Van Houdt, J. (2011). The crisis of negation: An interview with Alain Badiou. *Continent*, 1.4. Retrieved from http://continentcontinent.cc/index.php/continent/article/viewArticle

Virilio, P. (1998). The suicidal state. In J. DerDerian (Ed.), *The Virilio reader* (pp. 29–45). New York: Oxford University Press.

Ward, C. (2007, April 2). America gone wrong: A slashed safety net turns libraries into homeless shelters. *TomDispatch.com*. Retrieved from www.alternet.org/story/50023

CHAPTER SIX

Targets for Arrest

JESSELYN McCURDY

Some say that we have created a system that funnels poor children of color into the juvenile and, more disturbingly, criminal justice systems from the day they are born (Children's Defense Fund, 2007). Others say that from these children's first day of school, the education system is looking for ways to push them out of the classroom. In 2009, as the country fell into its most recent economic recession, states slashed funding for K through 12 and higher education, but thirty-three states increased funding for prisons. Over the past twenty years, state spending for prisons has grown to six times the rate of state spending for higher education (NAACP, 2011). All of these realities add up to the fact that in this country putting people in prison is a higher priority than keeping children in school. Since our priority seems to be to fill jails and prisons and not classrooms, many say that we have created what is called either the "cradle to prison" or "school to prison" pipeline. This simply means that children, specifically children of color, are being pushed into the criminal justice system directly from the educational system.

A generation ago it was unheard of for a child to be arrested at school; now, however, in some schools it is a weekly and sometimes daily occurrence. For the most part these arrests are for non-violent offenses such as "disruptive conduct" or "disturbance of the peace" (Advancement Project, 2005, p. 18). An increase in youth violence is not the reason for the increasing numbers of could be arrested, possibly in violation of his Fifth and Sixth Amendments rights.

J.D.B v. North Carolina

The Supreme Court recently confronted this issue in *J.D.B v. North Carolina*, 131 S.Ct. 2394 (2011). The case involved a middle school student from Chapel Hill, North Carolina, who was identified by the court as J.D.B. Without contacting his grandmother who was his legal guardian, he was called out of class and questioned for more than thirty minutes by two law enforcement officers and two school administrators about breaking into two homes. Before beginning questioning, they did not give J.D.B. any *Miranda* warnings nor tell him he was free to leave the room.

The officials encouraged the middle school student to "help yourself by making it right" and threatened him with juvenile detention. After first denying any involvement in two recent home break-ins, he confessed to his role in the break-ins. He then was told he could refuse to answer more questions and was free to leave, but he continued to provide details to the school and police officials, including the location of items stolen in the break-ins. He also wrote a statement at one of the police officer's request.

J.D.B's attorney later argued that his confession should not be admissible in court as evidence. But the North Carolina Supreme Court held that the boy was not in custody at the time of his statements and that it would not "extend the test for custody to include consideration of the age" of the questioned individual.

However, the United States Supreme Court ruled that police must factor in the age of young suspects whom they intend to question into their decisions about whether to give *Miranda* warnings. The 5–4 decision by the Supreme Court stressed that children are more vulnerable to pressure than are adults and emphasized using common sense in such situations. Nevertheless, it did not give specific guidelines on how to consider a young person's age.

As troubling as police officers coercing confessions out of middle school students is, the fact that SROs are more prevalent in schools in low income–high poverty communities is even more troubling. The increased SRO presence in these communities results in more children of color being subjected to daily contact with the police. This in turn creates more possible contact with the juvenile and criminal justice systems (Majd, 2011).

With the increasing presence of police officers, began the disintegration of our schools from positive learning environments providing a high-quality education to institutions more focused on punishing students for typical adolescent behavior and minor violations of the rules. The more police officers there are in schools, whether their background or prior experience is as school resource officers, local police, or former prison guards, the more their presence alters a school's mission to educate its students. The fear is that many schools are no longer preparing children to graduate from high school and go on to college, but are instead preparing children to graduate and go on to prison. The more our schools resemble prisons, the easier it is for children to transition from high school to the state penitentiary.

Studies indicate that an increased presence of police officers in schools results in more student arrests and more arrests for behavior that traditionally has been handled by school officials and parents (Dahlberg, 2012). The more school police officers a school district employs per student, the higher the number of arrests that district will have compared with districts that do not deploy law enforcement officers in schools. Many of these young people are arrested for offenses such as "disorderly conduct," "disturbing lawful assembly," "violating codes of conduct," or assaults that were the result of a fight on school grounds (Dahlberg, 2012).

While behavior such as that which resulted in school shootings in the late 1990s deserves student exclusion from the classroom, more frequently students are removed from school for typical adolescent behavior such as fighting, throwing food, cursing, or disobeying a teacher. Arrest, expulsion, and suspension policies affect children as young as 5 years old, and there are several cases of schools calling the police to arrest kindergartners after they threw temper tantrums.

ARRESTING DEVELOPMENT

School systems are increasingly relying on juvenile and criminal justice officials to punish and discipline students. Instead of dealing with misbehavior internally by giving students detention or calling their parents, some teachers' first instinct is to call 911 to deal with the child. School officials are also calling the police to deal with children who are increasingly younger. There have been recent cases of police officers taking children as young as 5 years old out of kindergarten in handcuffs and having them arrested, booked, fingerprinted, and charged with felonies for behavior that is equivalent to a temper tantrum. Not only are young children subjected to arrest, but also middle and high school students are routinely taken from school and faced with the very adult consequences of arrest for very childish behavior. Below are some stories that illustrate how school officials have given up on internal discipline of students and how commonplace it is for children of all ages to be led from school in handcuffs. These are just a few stories taken from media accounts of highly publicized incidents.

KINDERGARTENERS IN HANDCUFFS

Chaquita Doman (1998)

Chaquita Doman, a 5-year-old kindergartener, was arrested in Tallahassee, Florida. Chaquita was accused of biting and scratching a support teacher; she was arrested, booked, and fingerprinted, and her mug shots were taken. Barbara Frye, a spokesperson for the Escambia County School District in Tallahassee, explained, "We had a child who went into a rage. … She was supposed to be in line for lunch and, in doing so, was throwing some furniture and turning some over" (as quoted in Gilberti, 1998).

At the time, the 5-year-old faced a felony charge of battery of an educator or elected official. The support teacher Chaquita was accused of battering, Linda Green, said she sought the child's arrest so that she could receive mandatory counseling.

St. Petersburg, Florida, Kindergartner (2005)

On March 14, 2005, videotape captured a 5-year-old girl being hauled off in handcuffs following an extended tantrum at Fairmount Park Elementary School, St. Petersburg, Florida, in teacher Christina Ottersbach's classroom. Ottersbach ended up recording nearly a half an hour of video showing the girl alternately lashing out and quietly ignoring her teachers' instructions.

The footage starts in Ottersbach's classroom, where assistant principal Nicole Dibenedetto and teacher Patti Tsaousis are trying to calm the girl down and get her to clean up a mess that she had made. Ottersbach is not in the room, having pulled her other students out of the classroom because of the girl's unseen outburst, leaving just the three. Eventually, the girl does start cleaning up the mess, but then she refuses to leave the room. Only when Dibenedetto and Tsaousis ask her to make a choice before they count to five does she finally leave the room with them.

The tape cuts to Dibenedetto's office and the kindergartener is seen ripping papers off the wall and refusing Dibenedetto's requests that she stay seated in a chair. The girl then begins to swing at the assistant principal, who puts her hands up to block the girl's punches.

Next voices can be heard saying that police have arrived. The girl sits down in the chair and remains there as three uniformed St. Petersburg police officers walk in. "Do you remember me?" one of them asks the girl. "I'm the one who told your mom I'd put handcuffs on you" (as quoted in "ABC News," 2005).

The officers immediately pull the girl from the chair and handcuff her hands behind her back. The tape cuts off just seconds later after the little girl has started screaming. No charges were filed against the girl.

Desre'e Watson (2007)

Desre'e Watson was a 6-year-old kindergarten student at Avon Elementary in Highlands County, Florida, in 2007. On the morning of March 28 at Avon Elementary, according to the police report, Desre'e "was upset and crying and wailing and would not leave the classroom to let them [students] study, causing a disruption of the normal class activities" (Herbert, 2007).

After a few minutes, Desre'e was taken to another room and isolated. But she would not calm down. She flailed away at the teachers who tried to control her. She pulled one woman's hair. She was kicking. After twenty minutes of this behavior, the police were called and, according to their account, at the sight of the two officers Desre'e "tried to take flight" (Herbert, 2007). She ducked under a table. One of the police officers went after her. Each time the officer tried to grab her to drag her out, Desre'e would pull her legs away.

Ultimately, the police officer pulled her from under the table and handcuffed her. However, the handcuffs were not made for kindergarteners; her wrists were too small. Since her wrists were too small to handcuff, the police officers handcuffed her biceps. Then Desre'e was put in the back of a patrol car and driven to the police station where she was fingerprinted and a mug shot taken. She was later charged with battery on a school official, which is a felony, and two misdemeanors: disruption of a school function and resisting a law enforcement officer. After a brief stay at the county jail, she was released to the custody of her mother.

Salecia Johnson (2012)

A 6-year-old kindergartner, Salecia Johnson, was handcuffed by police in Milledgeville, Georgia, after she threw a tantrum. On April 13, 2012, Salecia was accused of tearing items off the walls and throwing furniture in an outburst at Creekside Elementary School. Police said the girl knocked over a shelf that injured the principal.

The school called police and the police report says that when an officer tried to calm the child down in the principal's office, she resisted and was handcuffed. The 6-year-old was charged with simple assault and damage to property. The kindergartner's family said the child was shaken up by being put in a cell at the police station. When the girl's aunt and mother arrived at the police station, Salecia was alone in a holding cell and complained about the handcuffs being really tight and hurting her wrists ("Police handcuff Ga. kindergartner for tantrum," 2012).

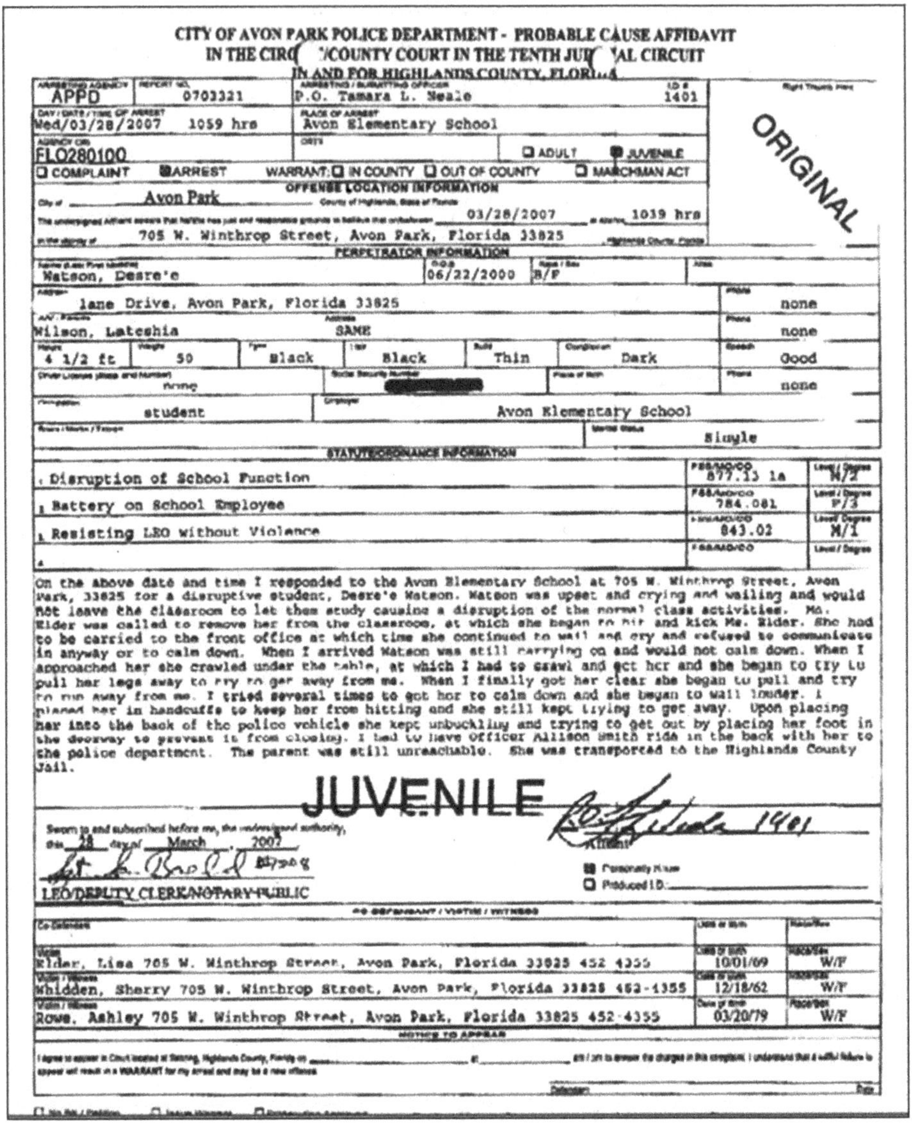

CITY OF AVON PARK POLICE DEPARTMENT - PROBABLE CAUSE AFFIDAVIT
IN THE CIRC /COUNTY COURT IN THE TENTH JU AL CIRCUIT
IN AND FOR HIGHLANDS COUNTY, FLORI A

APPD | 0703321 | P.O. Tamara L. Neale | ID # 1401

Wed/03/28/2007 1059 hrs | Place of Arrest: Avon Elementary School

ORIGINAL

FLO280100 | ADULT | JUVENILE (checked)

COMPLAINT | ARREST (checked) | WARRANT: IN COUNTY | OUT OF COUNTY | MARCHMAN ACT

OFFENSE LOCATION INFORMATION

City of Avon Park | 03/28/2007 | 1039 hrs

705 W. Winthrop Street, Avon Park, Florida 33825

PERPETRATOR INFORMATION

Watson, Desre'e | DOB 06/22/2000 | B/F

lane Drive, Avon Park, Florida 33825 | none

Wilson, Lateshia | SAME | none

4 1/2 ft | 50 | Black | Black | Thin | Dark | Good

none | [redacted] | | none

student | Avon Elementary School

Single

STATUTE/ORDINANCE INFORMATION

	FSS/MO/CO	Level / Degree
1. Disruption of School Function	877.13 1a	M/2
2. Battery on School Employee	784.081	F/3
3. Resisting LEO without Violence	843.02	M/1
4.		

On the above date and time I responded to the Avon Elementary School at 705 W. Winthrop Street, Avon Park, 33825 for a disruptive student, Desre'e Watson. Watson was upset and crying and wailing and would not leave the classroom to let them study causing a disruption of the normal class activities. Ms. Elder was called to remove her from the classroom, at which she began to hit and kick Ms. Elder. She had to be carried to the front office at which time she continued to wail and cry and refused to communicate in anyway or to calm down. When I arrived Watson was still carrying on and would not calm down. When I approached her she crawled under the table, at which I had to crawl and get her and she began to try to pull her legs away to try to get away from me. When I finally got her clear she began to pull and try to run away from me. I tried several times to get her to calm down and she began to wail louder. I placed her in handcuffs to keep her from hitting and she still kept trying to get away. Upon placing her into the back of the police vehicle she kept unbuckling and trying to get out by placing her foot in the doorway to prevent it from closing. I had to have Officer Allison Smith ride in the back with her to the police department. The parent was still unreachable. She was transported to the Highlands County Jail.

JUVENILE

Affiant 1401

Sworn to and subscribed before me, the undersigned authority, this 28 day of March, 2007

LEO/DEPUTY CLERK/NOTARY PUBLIC

Personally Known (checked)
Produced I.D.

CO-DEFENDANT / VICTIM / WITNESS

	Date of Birth	Race/Sex
Co-Defendant		
Elder, Lisa 705 W. Winthrop Street, Avon Park, Florida 33825 452 4355	10/01/69	W/F
Whidden, Sherry 705 W. Winthrop Street, Avon Park, Florida 33825 452-4355	12/18/62	W/F
Rowe, Ashley 705 W. Winthrop Street, Avon Park, Florida 33825 452-4355	03/20/79	W/F

NOTICE TO APPEAR

STORIES OF OLDER YOUTH

Student Arrested for Texting (2009)

A 14-year-old girl was arrested in school in Wauwatosa, Wisconsin, after refusing to stop texting on her cell phone in class. A school resource officer's report says the student refused to stop texting during class after a teacher told her to stop and the student told the resource officer she didn't have a phone after she was pulled out of the classroom. She continued denying she had a phone, forcing the resource officer to return to the classroom twice and find other students who saw her using it, according to the report. The male school resource officer called for a female officer to conduct a search, the report says. The student laughed as the female officer explained that she found the Samsung phone in the student's clothes, hidden near her buttocks. The officer notes that the student "is known to me and the administration based on prior negative contacts" (Durhams, 2009).

The officer gave the student a $298 ticket for disorderly conduct and kept her Samsung phone. A police spokesperson said that she was arrested more for her behavior than for the texting; "all she had to do was put the phone away and that would have been that" (as quoted in Durhams, 2009). After the arrest, the student was suspended for a week.

Tyell Morton: Senior Prank Gone Horribly Wrong (2011)

A high school prank gone wrong left 18-year-old Rushville, Indiana, high school senior Tyell Morton in jail and facing serious criminal charges. Morton was arrested after school surveillance cameras captured a picture of a man dressed in a hooded sweatshirt and wearing latex gloves entering the school concealing a package and leaving without it.

Believing it contained explosives, officials had the school evacuated and the Indiana State Police bomb squad was called. Actually, the package contained a blow-up doll that was placed in the girls' restroom. Tyell admitted to putting the package there as a prank, and he was charged with felony criminal mischief.

School officials said that the practical joke cost them more than $8,000. One of Rush County's prosecutors, Phil Caviness, said, "In this post-Columbine world, that's what you get when these kinds of things happen" (WGRZ, 2011).

If Tyell had been convicted he would have faced up to eight years in prison. School officials also wanted to exclude him from his high school graduation ceremony and barred him from school property. He was a good student and had previously never been in trouble with the law.

After national publicity about the case, in August 2011, prosecutors in the case announced that they would drop charges against Tyell if he stayed out of trouble for a year and performed community service.

Jacob Fleener: Principal Did Not See the Humor in a Facebook Parody (2011)

Benjamin Drati, the Clovis West High School principal, was upset after Jacob Fleener, a student, repeatedly throughout the school day logged on to a Facebook page that parodied the school official. The consequence was Jacob was arrested by police in the middle of taking an English exam. Jacob said he didn't create the satirical site, nor did he use school computers to log on to the Facebook page (Sherbert, May 10, 2011).

However, police interrogated him and a school's resource employee confiscated Jacob's cell phone. The student was read his *Miranda* rights and then released to his father. Although Jacob later apologized to the principal, he was arrested and suspended for participating in identity theft because the Facebook page lifted the principal's photo from the school's Web site. In a letter to Jacob's parents, the school stated that after serving his suspension he would be transferred to an alternative education program.

After Jacob served his suspension, the principal dropped him from his classes and continued to pursue the transfer, telling him he had to enroll elsewhere. Later the school district abruptly reversed its decision and informed Jacob that he could return to Clovis, make up his classwork, and his arrest record would be expunged. However, Jacob's family said the records were not erased and he was unable to make up all of his missed schoolwork.

The district attorney's office stated that no crime had been committed and so it declined to prosecute the case. Nonetheless, the principal continues to insist that Jacob committed identity theft and was a cyber bully. Jacob and his family are currently suing the school district, seeking damages for slander, infliction of emotional distress, and negligence.

Seventh-Grader Arrested for Burping in Class (2011)

In Albuquerque, New Mexico, a 13-year-old student was arrested for burping during class. According to a civil lawsuit, after the student "burped audibly" in class a teacher called the school resource officer, who in turn called the authorities to have him arrested for "interfering with public education" (Solove, 2011).

The lawsuit also claims that school authorities transported the boy from the school to the detention facility without notifying his parents. In addition, it describes an incident that took place in early November in which the same boy was allegedly strip searched on suspicion of selling marijuana, but was never charged.

The attorney for the seventh-grader said the City of Albuquerque is using petty misdemeanor charges to arrest children. The same attorney settled a class action lawsuit against the City of Albuquerque Police Department for arresting children for nonviolent crimes. The attorney said that the class action was initiated after a girl was arrested for not wanting to sit next to a "stinky" boy in class.

Consequences of Being a Target for Arrest

The failures of the public education system in this country are pushing students out of school and into the criminal justice system. The school system has become a gateway into the juvenile justice system through disciplinary policies that mandate school suspension, expulsion, and arrest for a growing number of common student behaviors and rule violations. One arrest during high school almost doubles the chances that a young person will drop out of school; if the child ends up in court, that nearly quadruples the chances of that child dropping out of school (Majd, 2011).

Without educational opportunities and high school graduation, the future life prospects for youth of obtaining employment and staying out of the criminal justice system are dismal. When a student drops out of school he or she is three and half times more likely than high school graduates to be incarcerated in a lifetime (Martin & Halperin, 2006). For example, in North Carolina and New York all 16- and 17-year-olds and in Massachusetts all 17-year-olds are treated as adults; therefore, an arrest can result in a permanent adult criminal record and incarceration in jail or prison alongside adult offenders (U.S. Department of Justice, National Institute of Corrections, 2012). The cost of incarcerating a person is nearly three times more than the cost of a public school education (Dahlberg, 2012).

When school administrators and teachers have low expectations for students, children are more than willing to meet those low expectations. Thus, when authorities label students as delinquent, difficult, or criminals, and do not expect children to be productive or successful in life, it becomes a self-fulfilling prophecy for these young people (Majd, 2011). These young people sometimes are stigmatized and experience embarrassment and emotional trauma as a result of being arrested at school in front of their classmates (Advancement Project, 2005). Youth who no longer see themselves as having the potential to be successful because they have been arrested, adjudicated delinquent, or convicted of a crime will often see themselves as failures without any motivation to follow the rules.

The Data Do Not Lie, But They Do Confirm Our Fears

A recent survey of the U.S. Department of Education's Civil Rights Office found that African American students in large school systems are arrested far more often at school than are white students. In March 2012, United States Department of Education data were released and they provide the most in-depth study of how public schools across the country increasingly call on police to handle problematic student behavior (St. George, 2012).

The Department of Education collected data from 72,000 schools across the country during the 2009–2010 school year. The data showed that 96,000 students were arrested while on campus and 242,000 were "referred" to law enforcement by school officials. This means that students may have come in contact with police officers but were not necessarily arrested or cited (St. George, 2012).

The Civil Rights Office's analysis also focused on larger school districts with more than 50,000 students enrolled and the data showed that African American students represented 24% of enrollment but 35% of arrests. White students represented 31% of the students enrolled but only 21% of arrests. There was less of a disparity in arrests for Hispanic students; they accounted for 34% of enrollment and 37% of arrests (St. George, 2012).

This is the first time that these types of data about student contact with law enforcement have been collected on this level and with this specificity. However, no data were collected about the types of offenses involved. These data are important in revealing that the behavior that is landing children in jail would have been, in years past, handled with calls to parents and visits to the principal's office. Even the Secretary of Education, Arne Duncan, when he was schools chief in Chicago, acknowledges that he was shocked that the vast majority of arrests of young people originated in schools (St. George, 2012.).

Schools have begun to incorporate some of the bad qualities of our juvenile and criminal justice systems. Teachers and administrators are using some of the same failed policies of criminal justice systems such as mandatory sentences, three strikes and you're out laws, and aggressive policing for minor infractions (Majd, 2011). In the school systems, these policies translate into mandatory punishments, exclusion from school after three rule violations, and arrest for typical teenage behavior. They result in the same inequities and racial disparities that exist in the criminal justice system. Black students are 3.5 times, Latino students are 2 times, and Native American students are 1.5 times more likely to be expelled from school than are white students (Dignity in Schools Campaign, Who's Getting Pushed Out, Factsheet 2009).

If you ever are in any American jail or prison, you will see the striking similarities between penal institutions and schools in this country today. Whenever you enter a prison, you are required to go through a metal detector, submit to a search of your body and belongings, and be escorted at all times. Today, many students have these same experiences every day at school. Students are required to walk through metal detectors, are subjected to searches by police officers, and are under constant surveillance as they move from class to class. Schools have police officers standing at the ready to take young people from their classrooms directly to their jail cells.

Just why would the education system in this country mimic the criminal justice system that by many if not most accounts is a dismal failure? America represents about 5% of the world's population, but has 25% of the world's prisoners (NAACP, 2011). In this country, the criminal justice system incarcerates approximately 2.3 million people in prisons and jails at any given time (Warren, 2008). We operate the world's largest prison system and have the world's highest incarceration rate (i.e., 754 per 100,000 people) (NAACP, 2011). We are the world leader in prisoners, but rank 26th in high school graduates among the world's richest nations (Associated Press, 2010).

Many people in prison for nonviolent crimes are serving very long sentences. The federal and state governments spend approximately $68 billion each year to incarcerate people in prisons and jails and juvenile detention centers, not to mention the cost of monitoring the more than 7.3 million people who are on parole or probation in our communities (Pew Center on States, 2009). Two-thirds of those incarcerated are rearrested for a new offense within three years of being released (Langan & Levin, 2002).

Just as a decline was starting to occur in the presence of law enforcement in schools around the country, on December 21, 2012, twenty children and six adults were tragically killed in a mass shooting at the Sandy Hook Elementary School in Newtown, Connecticut. Some of the first responses to the tragedy were to increase the number of police officers (and some are advocating for more armed officers) in schools. We must resist this knee-jerk reaction of resorting to policies that we already know have failed to keep schools safe. For example, armed security guards were present at Columbine on the day of that school shooting in 1999 (Terkel, 2012).

Approaches to addressing school violence that have worked include making schools safe by creating welcoming and nurturing environments for all students. Alternatives to posting police officers in schools have been developed that balance the need for security with the need for students to be nurtured. For instance, Denver, Colorado, a community that understands school violence, located as it is just a short distance from Columbine, recently reduced the heavy presence of school policing. Denver instituted a plan that limits police involvement in schools by promoting restorative justice principles over suspensions and expulsions for typical school offenses like wandering the halls or talking back to teachers (St. George, 2013). Since this collaborative effort between community leaders, school officials, students, and police was taken, suspensions have been cut in half and expulsions are down by two-thirds (St. George, 2013).

In Atlanta, Georgia, and Montgomery, Alabama, students are allowed to be arrested only on third strikes for minor offenses like fights, disorderly conduct, and disruption (St. George, 2011). As a result of this approach being used in Atlanta, school referrals to juvenile courts have fallen by 70%, weapons incidents on campus are down 90%, and graduation rates are up more than 20% since 2003 (St. George, 2011).

Finally, in Connecticut, the communities of Manchester, Stamford, and Windham have been working closely with the Connecticut Juvenile Justice Alliance to support students and reduce student arrests (Connecticut Juvenile Justice Alliance, 2013). In its first year, this program has produced significant results with Manchester's high school arrest rate down 78% in 2011–2012, and expulsions down 63% district-wide. The Windham school district reduced arrests by 34% and reduced in-school suspensions as well (Connecticut Juvenile Justice Alliance, 2013).

CONCLUSION

The criminal justice system is not a model of success that the education system in this country should emulate. Pushing children out of schools into a criminal justice system that proves time and time again that it does not work is insanity in its purest form. As Albert Einstein once wrote, "Insanity: doing the same thing over and over again and expecting different results" and this is exactly what we are doing to our children. We must expect and require more for our children than a cell in the state penitentiary, if for no other reason than we cannot morally or fiscally afford to incarcerate another generation of children. Current estimates indicate that it costs more than $34,000 a year on average to incarcerate a prisoner (American Civil Liberties Union, 2012). It is in the best interest of children, educators, and American citizens to keep our young people in school and not march them off to their prison cell.

REFERENCES

ABC News (April 22, 2005). *Police handcuff 5-year-old after tantrum.* Retrieved from http://abcnews.go.com/US/story?id=694504&page=1 http://news.yahoo.com/police-handcuff-ga-kindergartner-tantrum-112459850.html

Advancement Project. (2005). *Education on lockdown: The schoolhouse to jailhouse track.* Washington, DC: Author.

American Civil Liberties Union. (2012). *At America's expense: The mass incarceration of the elderly.* New York: Author.

Associated Press. (2010, December 7). In ranking,. U.S. students trail global leaders. *USA Today.* Retrieved from http://usatoday30.usatoday.com/news/education/2010–12–07-us-students-international-ranking_N.htm

Children's Defense Fund. (2007). *Cradle to prison pipeline.* Washington, DC: Author. Retrieved from http://www.childrensdefense.org/child-research-data-publications/data/cradle-prison-pipeline-report-2007-full-highres.html

Connecticut Juvenile Justice Alliance (2013, January). *Adult decisions: Connecticut rethinks student arrests.* Bridgeport, CT: Author. Retrieved from http://www.ctjja.org/resources/pdf/CTJJA-AdultDecisions-WhitePaper.pdf

Dahlberg, R. (2012, Spring). *Arrested futures: The criminalization of school discipline in Massachusetts' three largest school districts.* Boston, MA: ACLU. Retrieved from http://aclum.org/arrested_futures

Dignity in Schools Campaign, Who's Getting Pushed Out, Factsheet (2009). http://dignityinschools.org/document/whos-getting-pushed-out-fact-sheet

Donahue, E., Schiraldi, V., & Ziedenberg, J. (1998). *School house hype: School shootings and the real risks kids face in America.* Washington, DC: Justice Policy Institute. Retrieved from http://www.justicepolicy.org/uploads/justicepolicy/documents/98–07_rep_schoolhousehype_jj.pdf

Durhams, S. (2009, February 19). Tosa East student arrested, fined for repeated texting. *Journal Sentinel Online* [Milwaukee, WI]. Retrieved from http://www.jsonline.com/news/milwaukee/39711222.html

Finn, P., McDevitt, J., Lassiter, W., Shively, M., & Rich, T. (2005, March). *Comparison of program activities and lessons learned among 19 school resource officer programs* (Doc. No. 209272). Washington, DC: U.S. Department of Justice. Retrieved from https://www.ncjrs.gov/pdffiles1/nij/grants/209272.pdf

Gilberti, W. (1998, February 25). Five-year-old arrested in Florida on felony charges. *World Socialist.* Retrieved from http://www.wsws.org/en/articles/1998/02/yrfe-f25.html

Herbert, B. (2007, April 9). 6-year-olds under arrest. *The New York Times.* Retrieved from http://select.nytimes.com/2007/04/09/opinion/09herbert.html?_r=2&hp&

Langan, P., & Levin, D. (2002). *Recidivism of prisoners released in 1994.* Washington, DC: U.S. Department of Justice, Bureau of Justice Statistics. Retrieved from http://www.bjs.gov/index.cfm?ty=pbdetail&iid=1134

Majd, K. (2011, Winter). Students of the mass incarceration nation. *Howard Law Journal.* Retrieved from http://www.law.howard.edu/dictator/media/229/how_54_2.pdf

Martin, N., & Halperin, S. (2006). *Whatever it takes: How twelve communities are reconnecting out-of-school youth.* Washington, DC: American Youth Policy Forum. Retrieved from http://www.aypf.org/publications/WhateverItTakes/WITfull.pdf

Mukherjee, E. (2007). *Criminalizing the classroom: The over-policing of New York City schools.* New York: New York Civil Liberties Union. Retrieved from http://www.nyclu.org/pdfs/criminalizing_the_classroom_report.pdf

NAACP. (2011). *Misplaced priorities: Under educate, over incarcerate.* Baltimore, MD: Author. Retrieved from http://www.naacp.org/pages/misplaced-priorities

Petteruti, A. (2011, November 15). *Education under arrest: The case against police in schools.* Washington, DC: Justice Policy Institute. Retrieved from http://www.justicepolicy.org/research/3177

Pew Center on the States. (2009, March 2). *One in 31: The long reach of American corrections.* Washington, DC: Author. Retrieved from http://www.pewstates.org/research/reports/one-in-31–85899371887

Police handcuff Ga. kindergartner for tantrum (2012, Apr 17). Associated Press. Retrieved from http://www.advancementproject.org/resources/entry/education-on-lockdown-the-school house-to-jailhouse-track

Sherbert, E. (May 10, 2011). "High School Principal Upset Over Facebook Parody, Has Student Arrested at School". Retrieved from http://blogs.sfweekly.com/thesnitch/2011/05/clovis_west_facebook_parody.php

St. George, D. (2011, October 17). Judge Steve Teske seeks to keep kids with minor problems out of court. *The Washington Post.* Retrieved from http://www.washingtonpost.com/lifestyle/style/judge-steve-teske-seeks-to-keep-kidswith-minor-problems-out-of-court/2011/09/21/gIQA-1y8ZsL_story.html.

St. George, D. (2012, March 6). Federal data shows racial gaps in school arrests. *The Washington Post.* Retrieved from http://articles.washingtonpost.com/2012–03–06/national/35446604_1_school-arrests-national-education-policy-center-enrollment

St. George, D. (2013, February 18). A shift in Denver: Limits on police in schools. *The Washington Post.* Retrieved from http://www.washingtonpost.com/local/education/a-shift-in-denver-limits-on-police-inschools/

Solove, K. (December 2, 2011). *Student arrested for burping in class.* Retrieved from http://abcnews.go.com/blogs/headlines/2011/12/student-arrested-for-burping-during-class/)

Terkel, A. (2012, December 23). Columbine High School had armed guard during massacre in 1999. *The Huffington Post.* Retrieved from http://www.huffingtonpost.com/2012/12/21/columbine-armed-guards_n_2347096.html

2. Voting exclusion—after the White Primary was abolished in 1946, San Antonio required property ownership to vote in elections both bond and tax, there was a poll tax, residency requirements, and voting registration materials printed exclusively in English as methods of exclusion. The city of San Antonio annexed 66 square miles of suburban communities and created an even larger dominant white voting block and this resulted in the federal government intervening and at large elections were then changed to district elections in 1977.

   Because of these racist penalties the numbers of voters from communities of color were kept low and this further put amenities such as green space and parks out of reach.
3. Appropriation of funding—taxes collected were distributed to white schools and infrastructure at a higher rate than for minority urban schools and neighborhoods (Booth et al. 1983, pp. 133–156).
4. Court judgments—decisions by State and Supreme Courts refused in instances and/or have backtracked on the elements of race and poverty caused a 30-year struggle in the court system to even the inequalities. Yet the inner city schools remain underfunded as compared to their suburban counterparts. *Edgewood ISD v. Kirby* and *Orange Cove v. Neely* were two such cases.
   Currently, divestment in the public education by the Texas Legislature is ongoing and the school finance system has been ruled unconstitutional by District Court Judge John Dietz. The case has been appealed by the Attorney General Abbott and is expected to be decided in 2016 by the Texas Supreme Court.
5. Federally subsidized segregation through the location of housing projects continues to reinforce segregation, both economic and racial.
6. Suburban City Development also gained traction through transportation projects that facilitated white flight to the suburbs and this shifted the focus for funding. Highway projects, the placement of the medical center and the University of Texas at San Antonio are included in this (Booth et al., 1983; Wood, 1982).
7. Local planning decision made by city leaders who were predominantly white dictated tax investments be spent on the Northside to the neglect of the urban core (Mason, 1998; Rogers, 1990; Wood, 1982).
8. Local control given to cities to run school boards and districts created a multitude of districts using property taxes as the base for funding schools. White-only school districts did not want to share tax dollars and resisted integration (Mason, 1998).

The intersection of racially determined policies created the geography of communities of color in San Antonio today. This partitioning of the city into racially segregated areas reinforces limits to access of green space.

Further enabling this lack of access are the policies of the City of San Antonio's Housing Authority. This persists after research shows that economically integrated housing advances academic performance (Schwartz, 2010) and racially integrated housing increases chances at opportunity (Briggs, 2005). Statistics from SAHA's demographic report of 2012 shows low-income housing concentrated primarily in the urban core in high-poverty areas:

> Less than 11% (2,095) of SAHA households are living in low poverty neighborhoods while 3% (180) of Public Housing households 14% (1,915) of Voucher households live in similar low-poverty neighborhoods. (http://www.saha.org/pdf/Demographic-Report.pdf)
>
> Over 24% (7,072) of SAHA children are living in high poverty neighborhoods
> 66% (4,791) of Public Housing children
> 12% (2,281) of Voucher children. (SAHA, 2013)

GENERAL DEMOGRAPHICS OF SAN ANTONIO

Map 7.1 of San Antonio is divided into city council districts. The urban core is made up of parts or all of districts 1, 2, 3, 5, and 7. The suburbs are made up of districts 8, 9, and 10.

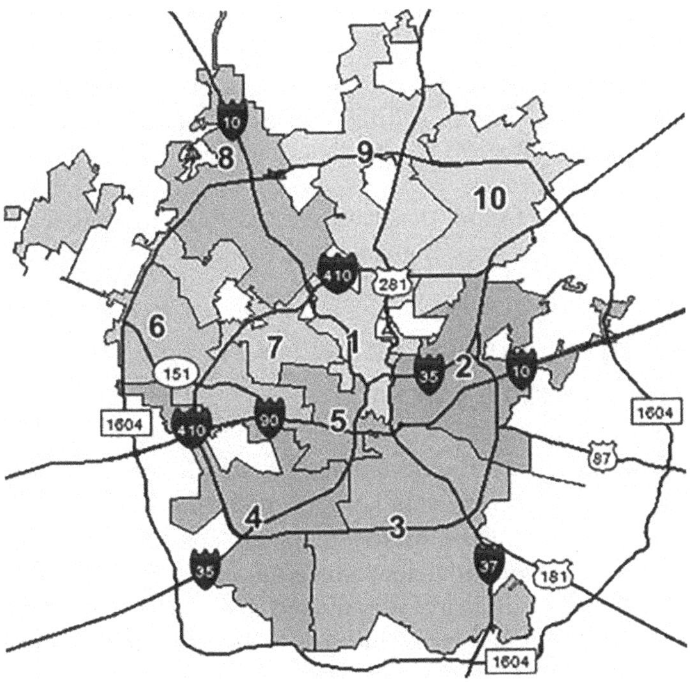

Map 7.1. Source city of San Antonio.

Demographic data on poverty, income, education, and ethnicity of the neighborhoods for the urban core and the suburbs are in Table 7.1. The table outlines that people of color live predominantly in the urban core, have a higher level of poverty, have less education and a lower median household income than their white suburban counterparts.

Table 7.1. Demographics of urban and suburban zip codes in San Antonio.

	Zip	Population							Below Poverty Level				Income & Education		
		Total	African American		Hispanic		White		Total	African American	Hispanic	White	Median Household Income	% with Bachelors Degrees	% W HS Diploma
Urban Zip Codes	78201	45,307	800	2%	38,850	86%	5,139	11%	20%	28%	21%	17%	$ 35,282	14%	69%
	78202	11,691	3,424	29%	7,675	66%	624	5%	44%	38%	47%	40%	$ 24,639	9%	61%
	78203	6,099	1,527	25%	4,294	70%	307	5%	42%	44%	40%	50%	$ 24,846	9%	61%
	78204	11,125	62	1%	10,052	90%	923	8%	30%	21%	30%	25%	$ 30,800	12%	64%
	78205	1,453	166	11%	706	49%	529	36%	36%	100%	40%	22%	$ 25,903	30%	68%
	78207	55,514	1,823	3%	50,435	91%	2,870	5%	42%	74%	42%	44%	$ 22,605	4%	53%
	78208	3,736	286	8%	2,967	79%	393	11%	36%	68%	35%	27%	$ 22,866	8%	58%
	78209	39,197	1,194	3%	11,285	29%	25,438	65%	13%	30%	18%	9%	$ 62,525	29%	95%
	78210	36,865	2,018	6%	30,956	84%	3,489	10%	30%	45%	30%	18%	$ 32,676	12%	69%
	78212	28,415	641	2%	17,552	62%	9,477	33%	20%	41%	16%	7%	$ 36,613	31%	77%
Suburban Zip Codes	78248	13,638	234	2%	3,401	25%	9,320	68%	4%	9%	10%	2%	$ 105,987	64%	97%
	78249	49,951	2,739	6%	21,356	43%	21,384	43%	16%	35%	19%	10%	$ 70,689	36%	85%
	78250	54,903	2,976	5%	32,480	59%	16,995	31%	9%	4%	10%	7%	$ 60,726	25%	91%
	78255	10,826	207	2%	3,562	33%	6,327	58%	3%	0	2%	3%	$ 111,307	59%	99%
	78256	6,855	369	5%	2,105	31%	3,410	50%	20%	57%	28%	11%	$ 69,649	72%	98%
	78257	3,950	54	1%	1,410	36%	2,292	58%	10%	13%	20%	4%	$ 112,202	66%	96%
	78258	40,586	1,670	4%	12,221	30%	22,733	56%	4%	3%	9%	1%	$ 107,479	62%	97%
	78260	24,844	857	3%	7,294	29%	15,134	61%	5%	6%	12%	3%	$ 106,182	51%	96%
	78261	13,513	741	6%	4,152	31%	7,661	57%	1%	4%	2%	1%	$ 98,729	56%	97%
	78266	5,591	437	8%	3,731	67%	1,162	21%	4%	3%	5%	4%	$ 105,536	48%	94%

Source: American Census 2010.

The same systemic factors that have created these barriers for urban youth have a symmetry in lower rates of green space.

ENVIRONMENTAL RISKS AND REGULATORY ENVIRONMENT

The Texas Commission on Environmental Quality is the agency charged with issuing permits and enforcing standards on polluting industries. The City of San Antonio enabled to make stricter regulations within its boundaries. The current paradigm of regulation does not issue permits with consideration to cumulative impact. Each industry is evaluated solely on its own emissions without including other pollutants in the area; it is as if each one operated in a vacuum.

Some environmental risks children face are citywide but the restricted mobility of urban children of color makes them subject to the high polluting factors in close proximity.

Water Quality Degradation

The water supply is based on the Edwards Aquifer and has been designated by United States Environmental Protection Agency (EPA) as the sole source, meaning it is the water supply for 1.5 million residents. The Edwards Aquifer has no filtration and only receives chlorine and fluoride. Reports from the Edwards Aquifer Authority show contaminants ranging from pharmaceuticals, to dry cleaning solvents and nitrite. Twenty-eight parameters exceeded Protective Concentration Levels in one or multiple samples. Environmental injustice surrounded water in a new 3.4 billion dollar pipeline bought for the increased population growth but paid for in higher rates by everyone including communities of color regardless of economics. This regressive growth tax burdens people of color who live in the high-poverty inner city in order to buy privately owned water from rural areas to supply the suburbs. San Antonio Water System, the local water purveyor initiated the plan and negotiated it without public input. Coalitions of rural residents, environmental advocates, and social justice urban groups were completely ignored by city council who voted unanimously to approve it.

Ozone

San Antonio is the last top ten largest cities to be within the EPA's compliance level but high seasonal ozone levels persist and the expectation is to be in Non-Attainment, the point at which Federal law intervenes for public health and safety, in the near future. The Eagle Ford Shale which is south and west of the city is affecting the city's air negatively and has associated increases in rail traffic. Fracking is adding contaminants to the air from San Antonio to Austin (AACOG, 2014). Ozone has health effects that can result in respiratory problems, skin cancer, and immune system suppression.

Coal Burning Plants

Texas is the highest producer of coal in the nation. For San Antonio a complex of coal burning power plants contribute mercury, arsenic, nickel, chromium, ozone precursors and dioxin to San Antonio's air (EPA, Mercury and Air Toxics Standards).

In addition, all of the coal burning plants are on the southeast edge of the city in much closer proximity to the urban core and communities of color, approximately 10 miles from downtown as opposed to a range of 20 to 30 miles for suburbs. Studies show that health impacts diminish with greater distance (MacIntosh & Spengler, 2011).

Rail Traffic

Railroad lines were one of the first to be established in San Antonio and the lines were laid in areas where communities of color were closest to. Now rail transport through the inner city includes toxics and coal. Derailments are higher than the national average and prompted communities to be organized.

A report by a local group called Southwest Workers Union details the toll of running toxics on neglected rail lines in the inner city.

> 2004 has brought an unprecedented rash of disasters for the communities inside Bexar County. Since the start of this year Union Pacific has amassed 21 derailments in San Antonio, the majority concentrated in Southern part of the city. The deadly year of Union Pacific started with several trains plunging off a bridge behind a high school spilling almost 6 thousand gallons of diesel fuel into the San Antonio River in May. In a short 7 months, the unconscionable negligence of Union Pacific and lax action of elected officials have caused 10 derailments, have taken 5 lives of Bexar County residents, have left over 50 people suffering from injuries and have recklessly placed thousands more at risk. In June, two trains collided causing the deadliest rail accident in more than a decade in the United States as over 90 tons of chlorine gas ruptured, killing 3 people. The chlorine cloud sent over 50 people to nearby hospitals. Months later another man died from exposure to chlorine and the health of many more residents is severely compromised. On several occasions, toxic cars were one or two away from those derailed. In November, 3 the reckless behavior of Union Pacific crushed a young worker as he sat at his desk as a train car plunged into a commercial building. While tracks are fixed immediately, neither the railroad nor the City have yet to repair the sidewalks or bridge from the derailment in May, leaving hundreds of students without a safe path to walk. (Southwest Workers Union, 2004)

Children in the San Antonio area must contend with outdoor air quality pollution and there is a gap in studies allowing for the entire range and depth of the pollutants to which they are exposed. But we do know children take up higher rates of pollutants due to their growth rates and time spent outside (Ritz & Wilhelm, 2008).

Children also spend a substantial amount of their time at school, they travel back and forth to their school and often have to spend additional time in after school care programs. Their neighborhoods are disproportionately exposed to pollutants, but if they could leave and spend most of their days in a school located in an area of town with less pollution this could help ameliorate some of the pollutant load; however, neither the State of Texas nor its cities have ordinances about school siting criteria, which take into account the health-damaging effects of being next to industry, rail, highways, and the mixing and adding of these emissions or the benefits of green space. Therefore, even the suburban schools are placed within air pollution from quarries. Suburban schools are not exempt from polluting industries, yet they have much more green space to provide for attenuation.

Table 7.4 contains representative elementary schools in the zip codes that made up the historical urban core and from suburban zip codes directly north of the city where the original suburban development began. The children who attend schools in the urban core are primarily children of color. With the exception of Alamo Heights, Terrell Hills, Olmos Park, all of whose students attend the Alamo Heights independent school district shown in Table 7.5, the schools in these zip codes belong to the San Antonio Independent School District, the Northeast Independent School District, and Northside Independent School District. Pollution sources in the same zip code as the elementary schools were examined to get a picture of the differences in environment quality.

URBAN COMPARED TO SUBURBAN POLLUTION SOURCES

The following pollution data are from the Texas Commission on Environmental Quality using the Central Registry database of permits and the EPA Enforcement and Compliance History Online (ECHO) database to develop a count of facilities located within the selected urban and suburban zip codes.

The facilities listed for Small Source can hold permits under the Clean Air Act (CAA), the Resource Conservation Recovery Act (RCRA), and/or the Clean Water Act (CWA). The CAA of 1970 regulates emissions to air. The RCRA of 1976 regulates the disposal of hazardous waste and solid waste. The CWA of 1972 regulates discharges to water.

- The Large Source emitters are large level permittees who must analyze and quantify their emissions.
- Industrial Hazardous Waste consists of waste that is generally a threat to the environment or human health.
- Leaking Petroleum Tanks are typically gas stations that have leaked gas and/or diesel.

Table 7.2. Urban pollutant sources by zip code.

Urban Zip Codes	Large Source Air Pollutant Emission facilities	Small Source Multimedia Pollutant Facilities	Industrial Hazardous Waste facilities/emitters	Leaking Petroleum Storage Tanks
78201	23	35	7	81
78202	0	3	4	17
78203	0	0	3	15
78204	2	9	14	37
78205	3	15	14	35
78206	0	1	0	0
78207	0	12	15	67
78208	0	3	3	14
78209	0	27	5	39
78210	3	9	10	59
78212	1	22	6	64
Totals	**32**	**136**	**81**	**438**

Source: EPA ECHO (2014), TCEQ Central Registry (2014).

- some smaller source air pollutant facilities are not required to submit Air Pollutant Inventory Numbers to TCEQ or EPA, industrial sources such as dry cleaners, auto body centers do.

The inner city zip codes listed in Table 7.2 had 15 Emergency Response episodes indicative of spills or incidents that involved authorities and/or fire suppression.

The suburban zip codes listed in Table 7.3 had 7 Emergency Response episodes.

These tables do not capture any unpermitted facilities, violations, or non-compliance. Texan regulatory agencies' budgets are often cut in the name of pro-business lobbying and low taxation and it leaves a situation where industry has a lot of loopholes. Many industries are relied on to self-report emission data. Often

Table 7.3. Suburban pollutant sources by zip code.

Suburban Zip Codes	Large Source Air Pollutant Emission Facilities	Small Source Air Pollutant Facilities	Industrial Hazardous Waste Facilities	Leaking Petroleum Storage Tanks
78248	0	2	0	1
78249	6	20	4	16
78255	0	2	0	1
78256	0	2	10	0
78257	8	12	2	6
78258	5	18	0	1
78259	2	6	1	0
78260	2	2	0	2
78261	0	2	0	4
78266	3	8	4	
Totals	**25**	**76**	**21**	**31**

Source: EPA ECHO (2015).

there are no onsite field investigations due to staffing shortages. Unless there is a complaint there is no guarantee an investigator will ever visit a site. Investigators have even been blocked from entering by hostile businesses and must return with law enforcement in the worst cases. Combined with lobbying from industry this system is in what Environmental and Consumer Advocate Ralph Nader calls "Regulatory Capture," providing a lot of benefit to businesses and socializing the costs to the public in terms of pollution.

The quantity of facilities in the urban core is larger and the sources more diverse, translating into a broader range of chemicals. Without proper green space the concentration is left to dissipate slower, reaches higher levels, and has fewer paths of bio-remediation.

Children attending schools in the urban core are subject to the same pollutants as their neighborhoods are (Tables 7.4 and 7.5).

Table 7.4. Representative urban and suburban elementary schools.

Urban Elementary	Address	Zip	ISD
Baskin	630 Crestview Dr.	78201	SAISD
Beacon	1411 West Ashby Place	78201	SAISD
Franklin	1915 W. Olmos. Dr.	78201	SAISD
Maverick	107 Raleigh St.	78201	SAISD
Neal	3407 Capitol Ave.	78201	SAISD
Nelson	1014 Waverly Ave.	78201	SAISD
Wilson	1421 Clower Street	78201	SAISD
Bowden	515 Willow Street	78202	SAISD
Washington	1823 Nolan Street	78202	SAISD
Douglass	318 Martin Luther King Drive	78203	SAISD
Smith	823 South Gevers Street	78203	SAISD
Briscoe	2015 South Flores Street	78204	SAISD
Collins Garden	167 Harriman Place	78204	SAISD
Barkley-Ruiz	1111 S. Navidad St.	78207	SAISD
JT Brackenridge	1214 Guadalupe	78207	SAISD
Brewer	906 Merida St.	78207	SAISD
Crockett	2215 Morales Street	78207	SAISD
De Zavala	2311 San Luis St.	78207	SAISD
King	1001 Ceralvo St.	78207	SAISD
Margil	1000 Perez Street	78207	SAISD
Ogden	2215 Leal Street	78207	SAISD
Rodriguez	3626 W. Cesar E. Chavez Blvd.	78207	SAISD
Storm	435 Brady Blvd.	78207	SAISD
Pershing	600 Sandmeyer St.	78208	SAISD
Lamar	201 Parland Place	78209	SAISD
Northwood	519 Pike Road	78209	NEISD
Green	122 W. Whittier St.	78210	SAISD
Herff	996 South Hackberry	78210	SAISD
Highland Park	635 Rigsby Ave.	78210	SAISD
Japhet	314 Astor Street	78210	SAISD
Riverside Park	202 School St.	78210	SAISD
Steele	722 Haggin St.	78210	SAISD
Stewart	1950 Rigsby Ave.	78210	SAISD
Cotton	1616 Blanco Rd.	78212	SAISD
Rogers	620 Mcllvaine Street	78212	SAISD

Suburban Elementary	Address	Zip	ISD
Huebner	16311 Huebner Road	78248	NEISD
Boone	6614 Spring Time Dr	78249	NISD
Carnahan	6839 Babcock Rd	78249	NISD
Locke Hill	5050 De Zavala Rd	78249	NISD
Scobee	11223 Cedar Park	78249	NISD
Steubing	11655 Braefield	78249	NISD
Wanke	10419 Old Prue Rd	78249	NISD
Aue	24750 Baywater Stage	78255	NISD
Ellison	7132 Oak Drive	78256	NISD
May	15707 Chase Hill Blvd	78256	NISD
Leon Springs	23881 IH 10 W	78257	NISD
Canyon Ridge	20522 Stone Oak Parkway	78258	NEISD
Hardy Oak	22900 Hardy Oak Blvd.	78258	NEISD
Las Lomas	20303 Hardy Oak Blvd.	78258	NEISD
Stone Oak	21045 Crescent Oak	78258	NEISD
Vineyard Ranch	16818 Huebner	78258	NEISD
Wilderness Oak	21019 Wilderness Oak	78258	NEISD
Bulverde Creek	3839 Canyon Parkway	78259	NEISD
Encino Park	2550 Encino Rio	78259	NEISD
Roan Forest	22710 Roan Park	78259	NEISD
Tuscany Heights	25001 Wilderness Oak	78260	NEISD
Cibolo Green	24315 Bulverde Green	78261	NEISD

Table 7.5. Alamo Heights school district encompassed within urban core.

Alamo Heights Independent School district	Elementary School	
	Howard	78209
	Cambridge	78209
	Woodridge	78209

Source: Alamo Heights Independent School District (2014).

INTERSECTION OF SCHOOL TO PRISON AND ECO-RACISM

Schooling of low-income children of color in San Antonio is highly segregated by geography, income, and race and is underfunded. Attendance in a highly populated dense inner city school raises the risk of children of color to be involved with law enforcement (Carmichael, Whitten, & Voloudakis, 2005). With the No Child Left Behind Act of 2001 there began a Zero Tolerance Policy in schools that exacerbated the school to prison pipeline effect (Fabelo et al., 2011; Heitzeg, 2009). And all of the above effects show up in San Antonio's three examined districts' discipline data (The Public Education Information Management System Discipline Data 2013). National disproportionality is detailed below:

National disproportionality

U.S. Department of Education Office for Civil Rights, CIVIL RIGHTS DATA COLLECTION Data Snapshot: School Discipline
Issue Brief No. 1 (March 2014)

- Disproportionately high suspension/expulsion rates for students of color: Black students are suspended and expelled at a rate three times greater than white students. On average, 5% of white students are suspended, compared to 16% of black students.
- Arrests and referrals to law enforcement, by race and disability status: While black students represent 16% of student enrollment, they represent 27% of students referred to law enforcement and 31% of students subjected to a school-related arrest. In comparison, white students represent 51% of enrollment, 41% of students referred to law enforcement, and 39% of those arrested. Students with disabilities (served by IDEA) represent a quarter of students arrested and referred to law enforcement, even though they are only 12% of the overall student population.

While boys and girls each represent about half of the student population, boys represent nearly three out of four of those suspended multiple times out of school and expelled.

Racial disparities in out-of-school suspensions also start early; black children represent 18% of preschool enrollment, but 42% of the preschool children suspended once, and 48% of the preschool children suspended more than once.

Risk factors that may affect funneling to the school to prison pipeline include: history of delinquency, male, academically at-risk, economically disadvantaged, or mentally or emotionally disabled, urbanicity.

Graphs 7.1–7.9 and Tables 7.6–7.11 do not address risk factors but do include a varying degree of urbanicity from the denser urban core to the less dense suburbs, and the disproportionality of discipline across racial lines is shown. In every case African-American numbers in relation to the population in the district show to be the most impacted by racial bias.

Table 7.8. Juveniles disposed to probation in zip codes: urban core, San Antonio Fiscal Year 2013.

	White	Black	Hispanic	Total	SR	Schools Referral as % of totals
78201	*	*	36	39	12	31
78202	2	9	17	28	8	29
78203	*	*	*	6	*	
78204	*	*	8	8	2	25
78207	*	*	59	64	20	31
78208	*	*	*	*	*	
78209	*	*	*	6	0	0
78210	*	*	35	38	19	50
78212	*	*	9	9	*	
Totals	N/A	N/A	164	198	61	31

Source: Texas Juvenile Justice Department 2015.

Table 7.9. Juveniles disposed to probation in suburban zip codes: San Antonio.

	White	Black	Hispanic	Total	SR	Schools Referral as % of Totals
78248						
78249	*	*	6	10	4	40
78250	*	*	16	23	6	26
78255	*	*	*	*	*	
78256	*	*	*	*	*	
78257	*	*	*	*	*	
78258	*	*	*	*	*	
78259	*	*	*	*	*	
78260	*	*	*	*	*	
78261	*	*	*	*	*	
78266						
Totals			22	33	10	30

Source: Texas Juvenile Justice Department.

Table 7.10. Juveniles placed in detention in urban core zip codes.

	White	Black	Hispanic	Total	SR	Schools Referral as % of Totals
78201	*	*	53	57	16	28
78202	2	10	25	37	12	32
78203	*	*	7	13	3	23
78204	*	*	13	13	4	31
78207	*	*	76	81	28	35
78208	*	*	*	6	*	
78209	*	*	7	13	2	15
78210	*	*	53	59	30	51
78212	*	*	13	13	4	31
Totals		10	247	292	99	34

Source: Texas Juvenile Justice Department (2015).

Table 7.11. Juveniles placed in detention in suburban zip codes.

	White	Black	Hispanic	Total	Yes	Schools Referral as % of Totals
78248	*	*	*	*	*	
78249	6	4	12	22	7	32
78250	*	*	21	31	9	29
78255	*	*	*	*	*	
78256	*	*	*	*	*	
78257	*	*	*	*	*	
78258	7	*	*	9	2	22
78259	*	*	*	*	*	
78260	*	*	*	*	*	
78261	*	*	*	6	*	
78266						
Totals	13	4	33	68	18	26

Source: Texas Juvenile Justice Department (2015).

GREEN SPACE

Eco-racism and Green Space

Texas lags behind the nation in parks for all residents as does Bexar County, the county in which San Antonio is located.

"The proportion of Bexar County residents with access to parks is 33%, the same as for Texas as a whole. Bexar County had 119 recreational facilities in 2010. In 2010, there were 7 recreational facilities per 100,000 population in Bexar County, the same as for the state of Texas. This is far lower than the national benchmark of 16.11" (Bexar County Health Assessment, 2013). General outdoor space is also eroded. Community concerns noted in the same 2013 health assessment in San Antonio include poor quality of streets and lighting which makes walking difficult, rules that ban basketball hoops on streets limiting exercise opportunities, thus making the space in closest proximity to communities of color restricted and reducing walking score rank of San Antonio to 40 among large cities.

Parks, green space, natural landscape funding disparities due to racism are not just a San Antonio issue. Since racist policies were applied nationally, inequity in green space can be seen in other parts of the country. These policies result in varying levels of green space in metropolitan areas, as studied in California, in national parks and is distorted toward diminished green spaces in communities of color (Downey, 2007; Pulido, 2000; Sister, Wolch, & Wilson, 2010). First looking at the broad area of urban to suburban green space in San Antonio and then specifically at parks shows disparities at both ends of the spectrum.

Green space provides several benefits that privilege the suburban area of San Antonio. The benefit of air filtration is one of those.

For green space to provide ecological functions it should meet minimum criteria. Table 7.12 shows that the suburbs have three times the amount of green space in acreage as the urban core.

Table 7.12. Green space in acreage: urban and suburban totals.

2007	Urban Residential	Suburban Residential
Total land area in acres	107,484	259,310
Green space	66584 (61.9%)	200900 (77.5%)
Trees/open space	34576 (32.2%)	85434 (32.9%)
Grass	32008 (29.8%)	115466 (44.5%)

Water quality protection is another benefit of green space. Since clean air and water are basic human needs, this arena of eco-racism literally threatens the health of communities of color and urban youth.

The amount of impervious cover is a marker of water quality degradation as it is made up of asphalt and impenetrable surfaces that carry pollutants. The United States Geological Survey in their National Water Quality Assessment program reports the higher the impervious cover, the more degradation is occurring (Table 7.13).

Table 7.13. Impervious cover in acres.

2007 Acreage Breakdown	Urban Residential	Suburban Residential
Impervious cover	38,687 or 34% of total acreage	45,481 or 18% of total acreage

Source: Adapted from American Forests Study.

American forests calculated that in 2007 San Antonio's urban trees removed 12.7 million pounds of air pollutants annually and that water pollutants that are absorbed by tree roots include:

- Cadmium
- Chromium
- Copper
- Lead
- Nitrogen
- Phosphorous
- Zinc

The Edwards Aquifer has no filtration system; these and other contaminants are to be taken in by the water supply in levels surpassing those safe for people if the suburban forests were to be overdeveloped. These suburban changes may provide housing and commercial opportunities for the area but will affect the entire city negatively. Yet the urban community does not gain the benefits of living there, but still bears the costs, both of degraded water quality and higher water costs that in turn provide infrastructure subsidies to development.

Parks

Parks in San Antonio are not funded equally and are very different in quality. The total acreage of suburban parks is 3771 acres. The total acre for urban parks is 1690.

Figure 7.2 is a detailed breakdown of parks.

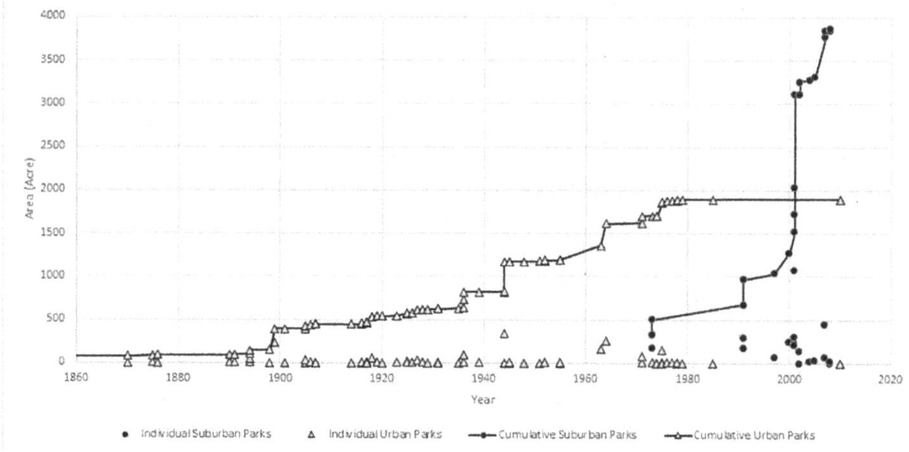

Figure 7.2. San Antonio park area in urban and suburban zip codes.
Source: City of San Antonio Parks Inventory (2014).

Urban parks were primarily built before 1960 and parks that were created and augmented after were largely funded by the Federal Government and through pressure applied by Communities Organized for Public Services (COPS) on the city council after discovering many bond projects simply had not been built. COPS studied and learned the inequities in funding applied by the City of San Antonio's various departments up through the city council that was governed by white businessmen called the Good Government League (GGL). The GGL favored money going to suburbia and used their political power to funnel money unequally (Booth et al., 1983; Mason, 1998).

San Antonio installed a majority Mexican American city council for the first time ever in the mid-1970s. This council presented a city master plan that sought to address the neglect and inequality of funding that had been perpetuated through racist policies. The plan included equalizing funding for parks and was summarily rejected by the next majority white city council (Booth et al., 1983). This reflects the plateau in funding and park creation we see in Figure 7.2 and continues today as seen in the funding of Bond Projects (Graphs 7.10 and 7.11).

The disinvestment post-1980 in the urban core can be seen when Parks Departments focused more on suburban parks. These policies interact with Bond and Credit Rating Agencies to reinforce that cities cut budgets to the Parks and Recreation Departments for efficiency. Outsourcing and privatization sparked the park conservancy, the park redevelopment corporation, and managements by nonprofits.

The suburban parks in San Antonio are either entirely city run or in unison with Friends of the Parks groups. The urban parks are city run, conservancy run, and planned out by redevelopment corporations.

- Conservancies are public partnerships enhanced by private money
- Redevelopment corporations are local government corporations to do the business of contracting, bidding, purchasing
- Friends of the Park are volunteer groups organized to help the city run a park working with the parks department to ensure proper management.

All of these entities have been formed to reduce the distribution and payment by city government for providing these formerly 100% public services.

Rules in place at parks run by Development Corporations, be they nonprofits or not, may prove risky for urban youth who are perceived as criminals to be spending their time in.

Urban youth of color may not roam as freely due to racist perceptions. They are seen as less innocent than other children their same age (Allison et al., 2014).

These management corporations share rules or events that typify restrictions on use. The following list does not apply to everyone but is inclusive of the most common:

- opening and closing times
- no skateboarding
- no public speaking
- fees for public protest, for insurance, security
- no loitering
- no feeding of wildlife
- no pets
- pets on leashes only
- no videotaping
- Incompatible facets of privatized parks
- special events
- space for hire
- programming
- retail

What Does Green Space Provide for Children?

Green space provides stress relief for children in economically disadvantaged communities (Aspinall & Thompson, 2011; Aspinall et al., 2012) And also stress reduction (Berdel et al., 2014; Evans, 2006; Louv, 2005; Strife & Downey, 2009).

These benefits increase as the diversity of fauna increases also (Fuller, Irvine, Devine-Wright, Warren, & Gaston, 2007). Playing in green space in nature increases resilience to negative events (Flouri, Joshi, & Midouhas, 2014), and most importantly for children, their avoidance of the school to prison pipeline aids in reducing attention deficits (Faber Taylor, Kuo, & Sullivan, 2001; Faber Taylor & Kuo, 2004, 2009; Schmiedeler & Schneider, 2013). Self-control is increased (Faber Taylor, Kuo, & Sullivan, 2002). Since lack of self-discipline and attention deficit have a destructive effect on school performance and may provoke infractions and a response based on race that escalates into interaction with the court system, access to green space is vital. In the urban area the parks are:

- small
- not very bio-diverse
- not considered as safe
- the large ones are more privatized, run by public/private partnerships with commerce involved
- often part of drainage correction projects
- commoditized, catering to the tourism industry
- full of prescriptive programming

In the suburban area the parks are:

- large
- many are still run by private/public partnerships that include an influx of higher donations due to proximity to population with more disposable income
- for the enjoyment of nature
- to protect the underlying Edwards Aquifer
- have no retail

The suburbs have a lot more land mass, the density of housing is not as high as in the urban core but the urban core needs higher green space to mitigate the high pollutant output of industrial, car, and rail emissions. Yet, when planning and budget decisions are made the distribution of parks do not reflect this need. A Bond election results from COSA (1978) reflects the preferences of urban whites not to spend taxes on parks in the inner city. Proposition 5 which was to provide money for parks in the urban core only had 17% of the predominantly white precinct's vote, while precincts that were more than 50% Latino or Black voted 80% more and above for it (Booth et al., 1983).

In a review of Bond Projects from 2007 and 2012 disparity is seen in the quantity of appropriations made to the parks and to parks chosen to receive funding.

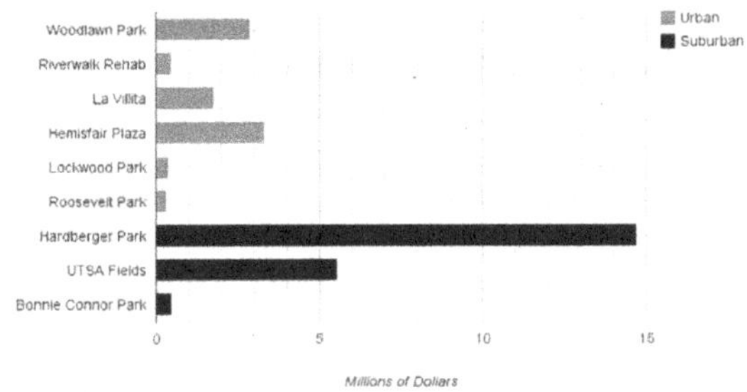

Graph 7.10. Park Bond Project Funding, 2007.

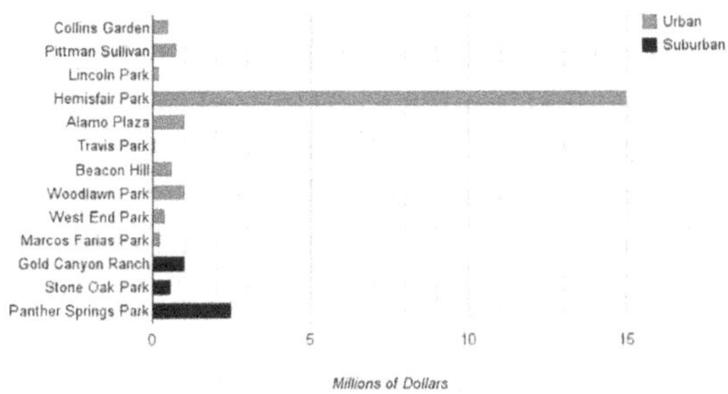

Graph 7.11. Park Bond Project Funding, 2012.

The oldest parks were given to the city as part of the Spanish Land Grant; some were federally funded through the defunct Model Cities program or other noncity money. A total of 46 acres of park land off the City Parks directory are actually cemeteries, 39 acres is the San Antonio Botanical Garden which costs 24 dollars for a child and 1 adult to enter. After subtracting those, the number of acreage and parks in the urban core was reduced to 1690 acres.

The missions of suburban parks to urban parks are different and cater to the feeling of nature as an escape from the city while providing interactions with the flora and fauna or provide for nature as teacher. For example, below is a stated mission from the suburban Friedrich Park:

> Our mission:
> 1) Preserve and manage San Antonio's Natural Areas to protect natural ecosystems,
> 2) Promote inclusive and transformative relationships between people and natural systems.
> Source: Friends of Friedrich Park

Even though Phil Hardberger Park is not inner city it is considered by the conservancy to be an urban park and prescribes an inclusionary and educational quality.

Faber Taylor, A., Kuo, F. E., & Sullivan, W. C. (2001). Coping with ADD: The surprising connection to green play settings. *Environment and Behavior, 33*(1), 54–77.

Faber Taylor, A., Kuo, F. E., & Sullivan, W. C. (2002). Views of nature and self-discipline: evidence from inner city children. *Journal of Environmental Psychology, 22*, 49–63.

Flouri, E., Joshi, H., & Midouhas, E. (2014). The role of urban neighbourhood green space in children's emotional and behavioural resilience. *Journal of Environmental Psychology, 40*, 179–186. DOI: 10.1016/j.jenvp.2014.06.007.

Fry, R. (2012). *The rise of residential segregation by income*. Washington, DC. Retrieved from http://www.pewsocialtrends.org/files/2012/08/Rise-of-Residential-Income-Segregation-2012.2.pdf

Fuller, R. A., Irvine, K. N., Devine-Wright, P., Warren, P. H., & Gaston, K. J. (2007). Psychological benefits of green space increase with biodiversity. *Biology Letters. Royal Society*. DOI: 10.1098/rsbl.2007.0149. Published 22 August 2007.

Heitzeg, N. A. (2009). Education or incarceration: Zero tolerance policies and the school to prison pipeline. Professor of Sociology and Program Director, Critical Studies of Race/Ethnicity, St. Catherine University, St. Paul, MN. Forum on Public Policy.

Louv, J. R. (2005). *Last child in the woods: Saving our children from nature-deficit disorder*. Chapel Hill, NC: Algonquin.

MacIntosh, D., & Spengler, J. (2011, March 7). Emission s of hazardous air pollutants from coal fired power plants. *Environmental Health and Engineering*. Retrieved from http://www.lung.org/assets/documents/healthy-air/coal-fired-plant-hazards.pdf

Mason, K. (1998). *African Americans and race relations in San Antonio, Texas, 1867–1937*. New York, NY: Garland Pub.

Miller, C. (2005). On the border: An environmental history of San Antonio. San Antonio, TX: Trinity University Press.

Pulido, L. (2000). Rethinking environmental racism: White privilege and urban development in Southern California. *Annals of the Association of American Geographers, 90*(1), 12–40.

Ramo, C. (2001). The educational legacy of racially restrictive covenants: Their long term impact on Mexican Americans, 4 Scholar: St. Mary's Law Reveon Race and Social Justice. 149–184, 159–166.

Ritz, B., & Wilhelm, M. (2008). Air pollution impacts on infants and children. UCLA Institute of Environment and Sustainability. Retrieved November 15, 2014 from http://www.environment.ucla.edu/reportcard/article1700.html

Rogers, M. B. (1990). *Cold anger a story of faith and politics* (p. 120). Denton, TX: University of North Texas Press.

Schmiedeler, S., & Schneider, W. (2013). Attention-deficit hyperacticity disorder (ADHD) in the early years: Diagnostic issues and educational relevance. *Clinical Child Psychology and Psychiatry*. DOI:10.1177/1359104513489979.

Schwartz, H. (2010). Housing policy is school policy. Economically integrative housing promotes academic success in Montgomery county, Maryland. The Century Foundation, October 15. Rucker C. Johnson. 2001.

Sister, C., Wolch, J., & Wislon, J. (2010). Got green? Addressing environmental justice in park provision. *Geojournal, 75*(3), 229–248.

Strife, S., & Downey, L. (2009). A new direction for environmental inequality research. *Childhood Development and Access to Nature: Organization and Environment, 22*(1), 99–122. DOI:10.1177/1060266093333340.

Wood, J. (1982, January). The model cities program in perspective: The San Antonio, Texas experience. Subcommittee on Housing and community Development of the Committee on Banking, finance and Urban Affairs House of Representatives.

Websites

AACOG Air Quality Report for TCEQ. (2014). Retrieved from http://www.aacog.com/index.aspx?NID=98

AACOG Closed Landfill Inventory. (n.d.). Retrieved October 15, 2014, from http://arcserver.aacog.com/flexviewers/ClosedLandFills/index.html

Alamo Area Council of Governments. (2014). Ozone status EPA/non-attainment. Retrieved from http://www.aacog.com/index.aspx?NID=98

Bexar County Health Assessment Report. (2013). Health Collaborative Bexar County's Community Health Leadership. Retrieved November 15, 2014 from https://iims.uthscsa.edu/sites/iims/files/Newsletters/bexar%20CHA%202013%20final.pdf

Environmental Protection Agency Enforcement and Compliance History Online. (2014). Retrieved from http://echo.epa.gov/?redirect=echo Zip code search

Issue Brief No. 1. (2014 March). Retrieved from http://www2.ed.gov/about/offices/list/ocr/docs/crdc-discipline-snapshot.pdf

National Oceanic Atmospheric Association (NOAA), Southern Region Headquarters (2010, February 12). Retrieved from http://www.srh.noaa.gov/images/ewx/climate/satclisum.pdf

SAISD.net. List of schools. 20 October 2014. Retrieved from http://www.saisd.net/main/index.php?option=com_content&view=article&id=4106&Itemid=333

San Antonio Housing Authority. (2013). DEMOGRAPHIC REPORT 2013 Policy, Planning, and Public Affairs Reporting Period: January 2012 to December 2012 April 1, 2013. Retrieved from http://www.saha.org/pdf/Demographic-Report.pdf

Southwest Workers Union. (2004). Rails of Disaster: Union Pacific's Toxic Tracks in San Antonio, TX. Retrieved from http://www.swunion.org/EJ/corporate/Toxic%20Tracks%20of%20Union%20Pacific.pdf

Texas Commission on Environmental Quality Central Registry Database. (2014). Retrieved from http://www15.tceq.texas.gov/crpub/. Search for facilities in San Antonio zip codes.

Texas Commission on Environmental Quality List and maps of Bexar County Superfund sites in Bexar County. Retrieved from https://www.tceq.texas.gov/remediation/superfund/sites/county/bexar.html

Texas Education Agency. PEIMS Discipline Data for 2013–2014, District Level Annual Discipline Summary. Texas Education Agency. Retrieved from http://ritter.tea.state.tx.us/adhocrpt/Disciplinary_Data_Products/Disciplinary_Data_Products.html

Texas Juvenile Justice Department. (2015). Public information request for disposition by schools to law enforcement per zip code for fiscal year ending 2013.

U.S. Department of Education Office for Civil Rights, CIVIL RIGHTS DATA COLLECTION Data Snapshot: School Discipline.

United States Department of Commerce and American Fact Finder. Census. (2010). Quick Facts for San Antonio. Retrieved from http://quickfacts.census.gov/qfd/states/48/4865000.html

Urban Ecosystem Analysis: San Antonio, Texas—Calculating the Value of Nature. American Forest. (2009 May). Retrieved from www.americanforests.org; https://webapps1.sanantonio.gov/rfcadocs/R_5633_20091015095327.pdf

and relatives who lived in much older trailer homes on the reservation miles away. She remembered when she was younger and lived in one that used only cardboard for windows. Having no stove, her father lit wood fires on a sheet of metal placed on the floor. The roof was so full of leaks that the heat would melt the snow that had collected there, causing the water to drip into strategically placed pots. Fortunately, the breaks in the roof filtered out just enough smoke to prevent everyone from asphyxiating. Years later her father had been the recipient of a grant-funded project that "loaned" him a new trailer home equipped with a real stove. This was the home she still occupied.

Reluctantly, she answered the phone. The caller was Rick Two Bears. He said he had bad news for her and that he would be at her place in five minutes. She got dressed slowly, lit the newspapers she had placed carefully under the wood the night before, and put a pot of water on top of the stove. By the time Rick knocked on the door, the coffee was made. He apologized for being a little late, explaining that his truck had slid off the road and he had to wait for some buddies to pull it back out. Mary sat quietly, sipping and nodding, waiting for him to say what he had come to say.

All she heard was "Tommy is no longer with us." She blanked out the rest of the details. Rick watched as she went to the kitchen and took a small steak knife off the table. She began cutting her graying hair and chanting a song he had heard too many times before. He knew too well how many young Indian youth killed themselves on and off reservations across the country. He had read that boys committed suicide ten times more often than the national average for children of all races in the United States and girls were double that figure, but it was not the statistics he considered. Rather, he was counting the number of children whose funerals he had attended in the past few months. He thought how he himself had considered suicide often throughout his school days and later when he scavenged garbage cans for remnants of alcohol lurking in the bottom of bottles. Saved by a commitment to his Sun Dance vows, he had tried several times to get Tommy to join him in this sacred ritual. But Tommy, like many others his age, laughed at the traditional ways. After all, school had convinced him long ago to dismiss such traditions. What frightened Rick the most was how the idea of suicide somehow seemed a normal option for his people.

Tommy's suicide could not be a surprise to his mother. She sang louder as she sliced her long hair to avoid any chance that she would picture him choked to death by his own belt, rigged as high as he could reach on the cell bars. Rick had described it, with a comment that the jailors hardly ever took the belts away from the boys. Mary pushed out such thoughts and she smiled at the memory of Tommy when he was just 2 years old.

For the first two years after his birth, Mary, reared traditionally herself, young and unmarried, carried Tommy in a back cradle. As a result, he spent much time observing his natural environment. Surrounded by wilderness, he spent hours listening to the bird and animal sounds while his mom shucked corn outside their dilapidated trailer several miles from the dirt road that wound through the pine-strewn hills for another six miles before hitting the paved road that was still twenty more miles from the closest elementary school. Mary had never been to school herself. Her father, who had suffered through the horrors of boarding school, used all of his skills and influences to keep her away from the "white man's education." She earned money to help cover basic expenses on weekends by selling her remarkable artistry and beadwork to tourists who passed by where the dirt road met the paved road.

By the time Tommy was 7 years old, he could mimic almost every bird and animal in the woods and on the plains. He spoke his Native language beautifully and possessed the patience, honesty, and humility that his grandparents' animal stories cultivated in him. He knew how to hunt and could run like the wind. His grandfather, wanting to follow the traditional ways he had acquired, encouraged Mary to do the same. He convinced his daughter to keep Tommy away from the school and did his best to keep Tommy's existence a secret. Word got out about Tommy, however, and one warm spring morning Mary and her family received a visit from a woman who introduced herself as a child protection specialist who had been assigned "the case" under the auspices of the Indian Child Welfare Act (ICWA). She respectfully interviewed Mary and her parents and talked with Tommy as well. She told them Tommy was the subject of a neglect proceeding and a determination was to be made about whether the state court had jurisdiction over the tribal court. The fact that Mary herself had never gone to school had some significant bearing on outcomes, as did the remoteness of their home and the lack of community, and the criminal record of her grandfather who had been arrested several times in his early days for disorderly conduct. To complicate matters, reservation borderlines had been changed during the past year and the land on which the family lived was no longer legally on the reservation, but now belonged to the state. Because Tommy was no longer technically "domiciled" on the reservation, the state court claimed jurisdiction.

Mary recalled the look of grief in her father's eyes a week later when he received word from his cousin that the state was mandating involuntary foster care placement and termination of parental rights. Tommy was to be taken away from his family. The next Monday after Mary learned this tragic news, she and Tommy walked and hitchhiked the twenty-six miles to the school and enrolled him. Mary believed enrolling Tommy, even against her father's wishes, would prevent him from being taken away. Apparently a school bus came right past where her dirt road met the paved road, so each day they would have only six miles to walk to and from the bus stop. Moreover, Mary was offered a part-time job helping teach art classes for the children. School began and curiously the state representative never appeared to take Tommy away. Several months went by and even Mary's father was starting to admit he had been wrong about keeping Tommy away from school. Tommy seemed to be enjoying himself, at least at first. Because he had not learned to read, however, Tommy had entered the first grade with a "special education" label. In addition to being unable to keep up with children his own age in first grade academic requirements, he was constantly looking out the window and "talking to the birds," as one teacher reported. A psychologist was called in, who recommended Ritalin for Tommy. Mary refused to allow it, however; now she was starting to admit her father had been right!

In the fourth month of school, an unhappy Tommy, made fun of by the students and humiliated and punished by the non-Indian teachers from a border town, was called to the director's office along with Mary. An officer from the state's child welfare services was waiting. This person was not as friendly as the one who had visited their home. She said that although the ICWA laws were intended to keep Indian families together, the state court was using a judicial exception to the law, quoting an "Existing Indian Family" doctrine from the Adoption and Safe Families Act of 1997. She showed Mary some papers, explaining all of this as well as documentation regarding her grandfather's previous arrest record.

Tommy was taken away immediately after the meeting. Mary pleaded in vain. He was not even allowed to return to his home to gather his things or say goodbye to his grandfather and grandmother. Mary called her friend Rick Two Bears. Rick worked for the reservation police department and had made a few visits to Mary's weathered trailer home "in the middle of nowhere" with an eye on courtship. Rick drove to the school and found Mary distraught with grief. Her child had been taken away. Rick was not unfamiliar with stories such as this. Foster care had become an economic boon for private group home providers who brought in millions of dollars in state contracts. One in particular, the Evergreen Home for Children, had close connections with the state's governor. The home had received much of its funding through no-bid contracts as a result. It seemed as though the schools were making a living off the Indian children. Less than 12% of the state's population was Native but they represented more than 65% of the foster home population (Sullivan & Walters, 2011). Rick could not give solace to Mary but his own anger transformed her sense of helplessness into a battle cry.

Within a week of being taken away, Tommy was placed in one of the Evergreen homes located in a mostly white city about 250 miles from the reservation. Mary did everything she could to get Tommy back, but even an attorney Rick managed to have visit her could do nothing. Mary continued to work at the school but never regained her joyful way of being in the world. Two years later, when the new federal NCLB laws came down from the Bush administration requiring all classroom workers in state contract schools to have at least an Associate degree, Mary was let go (New Jersey Teachers Union, 2004). She returned to her efforts at selling her art but only once did she manage to take a bus into the city to visit Tommy before Rick told her he had been moved to a detention center even further away.

By the time Tommy was 11, he had been punished and suspended numerous times from the city schools he attended. Usually the only Indian student in his classes, he fought back against constant teasing. Each time he was singled out as being the instigator of fights and soon branded as "a violent child." When he was 13, a Mormon couple adopted him. Responding negatively to their strict discipline, he ran away several times and the discipline intensified. One day the sister and brother-in-law of the husband visited Tommy's new home along with their 11-year-old daughter. While the adults were playing cards in the evening, one of them discovered Tommy "playing doctor" with the little girl in his bedroom. Within an hour the police took Tommy to jail to wait for a court date. He was to be tried as a violent sexual offender. While awaiting his court appearance, he spent four days in an adult cell with three white men. The three men raped him the first night and told him if he said anything they would find him and kill him.

At the hearing the judge asked Tommy whether he had "explored the private parts" of the girl who was the "victim" of his sexual offences. Tommy, who had been taught early on never to tell a lie, nodded his head. It did not matter and was not brought up that the two children were mutually engaged in "playing doctor" and that such "exploration" was no more than the most innocent "peek" at the girl's breasts when she herself lifted up her shirt. Nor were any culturally relevant understandings offered by the judge, a common problem in Indian youth incarceration (American Indian Development, n.d.).

With his extensive referral history of behaviors, which if he had not been Indian would have been ignored or dealt with informally, Tommy was sentenced and sent to a private out-of-state "treatment" facility for youth who were thought not to be suitable for juvenile correctional institutions. With costs of more than $250 per day charged to the state, these transfers were an economic boon for the service provider. It took three years for Mary to receive a letter from the state, which was sent to her via the facility, asking for her to sign a form giving her permission for Tommy's medical treatment if he should need it. She signed it and asked the principal if he could send it back but she never learned where her son had actually been placed.

It was 1999. Tommy was almost 16. This was the year a bill called the Violent and Repeat Juvenile Offender Accountability and Rehabilitation Act was passed in the Senate by a vote of 73–25 (S-254, 1999). Senator Paul Wellstone was a member of the Senate minority who opposed the bill because it would eliminate the federal requirement that allows states to address disproportionate minority confinement in the juvenile justice systems. Wellstone argued that minority youth in every state are proportionately overrepresented at every stage of the process, from arrest to and especially at the level of confinement. In a series of questions put to Republican supporters of the bill, Wellstone asked whether race was a factor when police on the streets decide which kids are searched and which kids are not.

> You don't think that has anything to do with race? When we get to the question of which kids are arrested and which kids are not, you don't think that has anything to do with race today in America? When we get to the question of the evaluation of youth by probation officers, you don't think that has anything to do with race? When we get to the question of the decision whether to release or detain by a judge, based upon who has the money and who does not have the money to put up a bond, you don't think that has anything to do with race? And when we get to the question of sentencing, you don't think that has anything to do with race, Senators? You are sleepwalking through history. (Farrell, 1999)

Three years later Senator Wellstone, after speaking against the Iraq war resolution, died in a plane crash (Four Arrows & Fetzer, 2003).

The staff at the correctional facility where Tommy now resided were young, underpaid, and mostly white. Although the laws in the state required reporting physical "take downs," Tommy had been wrestled to the ground by several hefty counselors a number of times for his fighting with other youth and for his belligerent attitude. Nevertheless, reports were seldom filed. The second week of his stay, he began schooling. When he walked into the classroom, the other children began making fun of his Indian-ness. When one boy asked him where his tomahawk was and another asked whether his squaw mother was a prostitute, Tommy jumped both boys at the same time. Within minutes counselors again had him pinned to the floor. Later he was taken to a small three-by-five-foot concrete room with an iron door and a small window and forced to wear a pink jumpsuit. He spent the night in this solitary confinement with a "suicide watch" staff looking in on him. The next morning Tommy was back in the classroom but still in his jumpsuit. The social studies lesson this day was about "the first Americans," a phrase written on the top of a multiple choice quiz that identified the first Americans as Kit Carson, Davy Crockett, and other non-Indian pioneers who made a living exterminating Indians (although this fact was masked by the teacher referring to them only as "Indian fighters").

The next morning Tommy was taken to the facility's weekly sexual offender meeting. Staffed by local psychiatrists and psychologists, some from the state and others on the school's payroll, the facility used the traditional Alcoholics Anonymous model. Tommy followed older, seriously harmful sexual offenders in standing before the intimidating group and saying his coached and memorized statement, "My name is Tommy Red Plume and I am a sexual offender." For the next year, Tommy suffered an education not all that dissimilar from the one his grandfather had suffered in boarding school. Like most Indian prisoners, he was denied release time or home visitations two times more often than his white counterparts. Where the other boys would be merely reprimanded for their offenses, he received the harshest punishments for lesser offenses that he committed.

Placed in housing with the other boys undergoing sexual offender counseling and fearful he would get raped again, Tommy managed an escape. Runaways were common at the facility and boys, half-frozen by the cold night air, by morning were usually picked up several miles down the road or hiding in crops in the local fields. It was more than sixty miles to the nearest town. Tommy's endurance and athletic ability, however, as well as his early days of tolerating cold weather allowed him to persevere. He made it to town and fell in with a gang of Indian teenagers.

Most of the children in the gang were 15 to 17 years of age. Some were escaped foster children but others had run away from abusive homes on the reservation. Often they were arrested for "just being Indian." When this happened, the teenagers would appear in court without parents and without attorneys, but the judges would take their pleas and sentence them anyway. A number of them had been placed in holding cells at one time or another and a few had experienced the same insult that Tommy had suffered. Most of their parents had no idea where their children were. One of the gang members was a beautiful, but not to be taken advantage of, Indian girl around 17 years of age. Remarkably, she had managed to get to high school graduation without experiencing the juvenile justice system. However, when she was not allowed to wear her traditional buckskin dress during the ceremony, she wore it underneath her black robes. Just before she went on stage to get her diploma, she took off the robe. Before she made it to the stage, the principal pulled her aside, reprimanded her, and prevented her from further participation in the ceremony. She knew her brother was in the city gang and decided to chuck it all and join him. In effect, she had become one of the gang's leaders.

By the time Tommy was 17, he had lived more than a year in the streets. He had been locked up several times and then let go because of overcrowded conditions and political opposition to adult holding cells for youth. In one instance, he made his way back to the reservation to see his mother. His grandmother had passed on and his grandfather was still mourning her loss. Tommy knew he could not stay and Rick Two Bears drove him back to his gang's hideout in an abandoned factory. The next week Tommy got drunk in public, was arrested, and was sent to a new private detention facility located only two hours from his reservation. This one, however, was quite different from the others.

The Beaver Trail Youth Ranch was a staff-secured (no fences or guards) detention facility for youth convicted of various infractions, including drive-by shooters from New York and a number of American Indian youths arrested for significantly lesser offences. This one was different from the others. Its new director implemented an educational/rehabilitation model based on American Indian values and learning paths. The new program was guided largely by a booklet written by Larry Brendtro, Martin Brokenleg, and Steve Van Bockern, *Reclaiming Youth at Risk*, published in 1990 by the National Educational Service. Based on the belief that American Indian philosophies concerning child management represent the most effective system of positive discipline ever developed and on the empowerment of children, it followed a balanced approach that recognized independence, belonging, mastery, and generosity depicted in a "Circle of Courage" medicine wheel. The program director, part Indian himself, had fired more than half the original staff and replaced them with more like-minded and qualified people. He managed to take all the children off their drugs, such as Ritalin, replacing them with "obecalp" pills. (These were actually sugar pills, whose name is "placebo" spelled backwards.) Soft drink machines were removed from the facility and all students took daily exercise walks. Peer culture meetings took control of behavioral issues, with staff sitting outside the youth circles, monitoring and offering help when needed. Horses, cows, and pigs were assigned to different youth who took full responsibility for their care. Instead of being locked up or denied exercise opportunities for infractions, students were given chances to "make things right" with logically deduced natural consequences. Within fifteen months of taking over the facility, the director and his new team had managed to reduce physical restraints from 122 per quarter to fewer than 20 per quarter. Escape attempts had decreased from 100 per year to only one.

Tommy thrived in the new environment. Word got out that he was there and Rick Two Bears brought Mary to see Tommy as often as possible, averaging two or three visits per month. Tommy's early childhood skills made him a natural leader and the culturally relevant curriculum and traditional Indigenous approaches to classroom learning brought his reading skills rapidly to grade level by the end of the second year. He participated in traditional ceremonies led by a reservation elder and before his 18th birthday, he had begun preparing for junior college and had submitted two applications for a scholarship. His grandfather passed away and he was allowed to leave campus with Rick to attend the traditional services. He stayed two nights with his mother, who now lived alone in the trailer, and the two caught up on their relationship.

Rick Two Bears had heard about the facility's radical changes even before he knew Tommy was there. All the Indians were talking about it, it seemed. He also knew its existence was at risk. A number of the conservative and religious right members of the community had written letters of complaint to the juvenile justice administrators. These were the same groups of people who had been responsible for replacing the word "youth," with the word "juvenile" in the original legislation because "juvenile" was more detached from possibilities for compassion. They worried that without the more stringent disciplines of the past decade, the community would be at risk. The detention facility was only "staff-secured," they wrote, and they worried the "inmates" would run away and sneak into their homes and do "God knows what" while the homeowners were sleeping. There was also political pressure from a few owners of other facilities who felt the new model was a bad example. After all, if it worked, as it was obviously doing, this might reduce recidivism and thus reduce profitability, although this was not their argument, of course.

True to the prediction, after 18 months of operation, the director of the youth facility was fired. His dismissal came about because he had been ordered to start receiving out-of-state youth even if medical releases from parents or guardians were not yet on hand. According to the state, too many youth were being sent to other states with more lenient policies. The Youth Ranch was losing money as a result. The director, after consulting with his physicians, learned that this would put the youth at risk if there were ever a need for a serious operation. Additionally, his staff did not have time to find parents or guardians and secure signatures on consent forms, as he was being asked to do. If he could not get these signatures, he would have to continue to require medical release for all new admittances. The next day the head of the larger corporation arrived with apologies, a two-week severance check, and a replacement for the director. Within a month, all of the innovations were replaced with the standard educational and disciplinary approaches. The children, who were managing well without drugs, were placed back on their medication regimen.

Two weeks into the "new" program, Tommy overheard one of the newly hired staffers refer to him as a "fucking Indian" in a private conversation with another staffer who laughed and ridiculed the previous director's affinity for the "savages." Tommy burst through their office door and jumped both of them. They wrestled him to the ground and called for reinforcements, and Tommy was placed in the concrete solitary room until state police officers arrived. He was taken to the city's crowded holding facility, placed in an adult cell, again with several drunken Caucasians. At approximately 4:20 a.m., according to the coroner, Tommy managed to choke himself to death with his belt. It is unknown whether he had been abused by the other inmates, as had happened years before.

Epilogue: There are approximately 26,000 American Indians in U.S. jails and prisons. This is a rate almost 40% higher than that of the general population. However, if African Americans, who constitute about half of all prisoners, are excluded from the calculation, the disproportionality is far greater. The role of "education" and anti-Indianism in all of this is fundamental (Four Arrows, 2013). Too many Indian youth tormented by the hegemony of Western education, then caught in the undercurrents of the social welfare system experience, and further discouraged in youth detention centers will continue to face what "Tommy" experienced. In his review of my text, *Teaching Truly: A Curriculum to Indigenize Mainstream Education*, William Ayers speaks to the problem of anti-Indianism with which we must all come to terms when he says that a "spiritual and material collapse" is upon us as a result of a "techno/imperial/capitalist juggernaut" (as quoted on book jacket, Four Arrows, 2013). In referring to the goal of incorporating Indigenous value systems and knowledge into our contemporary schooling, Noam Chomsky's review of the book offers that we must do a better job of taking care of our Indian youth as well as all children, before it is too late: "We must nurture and preserve our common possession, the traditional commons, for future generations, and this must be one of our highest values, or we are all doomed" (as quoted on book jacket, Four Arrows, 2013).

REFERENCES

American Indian Development (AIDA). (n.d.). Mentoring program. Retrieved from http://www.aidainc.net/Products_Services/mentoring.htm

Farrell, J. (1999). Senate passes juvenile crime bill S. 254; Wellstone opposed measure over disproportionate minority confinement issue [Press release]. *Common Dreams.* Retrieved from http://www.commondreams.org/pressreleases/may99/052199a.htm

Four Arrows. (2013). *Teaching truly: A curriculum to indigenize mainstream education.* New York: Peter Lang.

Four Arrows & Fetzer, J. (2003). *American assassination: The strange death of Senator Paul Wellstone.* New York: Vox.

New Jersey Teachers Union. (2004). Highly qualified teachers need not apply. *Free Republic.* Retrieved from http://www.freerepublic.com/focus/f-news/1087288/posts

Sullivan, L., & Walters, A. (2011, October 25). Native foster care: Lost children, shattered families. Washington, DC: National Public Radio. Retrieved from http://www.npr.org/2011/10/25/141672992/native-foster-care-lost-children-shattered-families

S. 254, 106th Cong. (1999). Retrieved from http://thomas.loc.gov/cgi-bin/query/z?c106:S.254

Wagner, P. (2004, December 14). Importing constituents. Prisoners of the Census. Retrieved from http://www.prisonersofthecensus.org/montana/importing.html

CHAPTER NINE

Emerging FROM OUR Silos

Coalition Building for Black Girls

MAISHA T. WINN AND STEPHANIE S. FRANKLIN[1]

While taking a stroll through the "museum" of radical Black women, James (2012) argues that one will encounter the names, faces, and stories of women who "remain on the fringe of consciousness due to denied access to 'Black respectability.'" These women, James argues, "need to be liberated from the museum" where they have been forgotten. James argues that Claudette Colvin is one example of a woman whose story was left behind in exchange for a more respectable story found in Rosa Parks. In a biography of Claudette Colvin, Hoose (2009) captures the story of a 15-year-old girl who had the tenacity to refuse to give up her seat on a segregated Montgomery bus in 1956 to a white woman prior to the high-profile story of Rosa Parks. When Colvin became pregnant, she was no longer a candidate for marking this movement. According to Colvin, "There was a time when I thought I would be the centerpiece of the bus case. I was eager to keep going in court. … I had enough self-confidence to keep going. … But what I did know is that they all turned their backs on me, especially after I got pregnant. It really, really hurt" (Hoose, 2009, p. 61). Colvin at the time of her resistance was armed with a new knowledge of self after learning about Sojourner Truth and Harriet Tubman during "Negro History Month" at her segregated school. "I felt like Sojourner Truth was on one side pushing me down,"

1 The co-authors of this chapter would like to thank Stacy D. Copeland, Esq., Legislative/Policy Attorney at Mecca's Place, Inc., for her research assistance with this chapter.

explained Colvin, "and Harriet Tubman was on the other side pushing me down. I couldn't get up."[2] We open with the story of Claudette Colvin in our efforts to draw attention to African American girls in the juvenile justice and child welfare systems who have been forgotten and abandoned, especially when they have been marked as delinquent, troubled, and undeserving, thus pushing them further from the possibilities of respectability. Elsewhere, Winn asserts that the focus on African American girls is in no way a competition of who suffers more between African American girls and African American boys (Winn, 2011). This is not a race to the bottom, and we are taking a participatory/advocacy stance in order to disrupt the school/prison/child welfare nexus for African American girls.[3]

Through our involvement with Behind the Cycle: Integrative Approaches to Criminal Justice Reform (BTC),[4] we decided it was time to emerge from our silos and take on BTC's challenge to make a "collective impact" on the lives of girls entangled in the juvenile justice and child welfare systems (Kania & Kramer, 2011). As an educational researcher and teacher educator (Maisha) and a child welfare attorney (Stephanie), we have become increasingly concerned with the policing of girls, and Black girls in particular, and their consequent entanglement with the juvenile justice system. In our work as youth advocates we have collected the stories of girls who experience mis-education, socio-economic and political disenfranchisement, and an overall sense of "dispossession" (Fine & Ruglis, 2009). In her work with a woman-focused theater company introducing incarcerated and formerly incarcerated girls to process, product, and playmaking, Maisha became keenly interested in the racing, classing, and gendering of the school/prison nexus (Fisher, 2008; Fisher, Purcell, & May, 2009; Winn, 2010a, 2010b, 2011, 2012; Winn & Behizadeh, 2011; Winn & Jackson, 2011). As a child welfare attorney with a practice that has served more than 3,300 children, Stephanie encountered many children whose lives were impacted by detention centers, jails, and prisons

---

2 This quote is from Margot Adler's (2009) story "Before Rosa Parks, There was Claudette Colvin." Retrieved from http://www.npr.org/templates/story/story.php?storyId=101719889 on December 2, 2013.

3 In a Minnesota Public Radio segment, "Why don't we talk about young Black females?," scholars discussed the invisibility of Black girls against the backdrop of the Trayvon Martin case. Retrieved from http://minnesota.publicradio.org/display/web/2013/09/25/daily-circuit-black-female-youth on December 2, 2013).

4 Behind the Cycle was funded by the Open Society and developed by Catherine Beane. In December 2008 we met at a Behind the Cycle conference in Bethesda, Maryland, that hosted the formerly incarcerated, lawyers, judges, scholars, artists, youth advocates, and a host of stakeholders interested in disrupting and dismantling the school to prison pipeline as well as challenging policies and practices that led to unequal imprisonment of Blacks and Latinos.

and started to witness larger numbers of girls—and Black girls in particular—who had juvenile records. We have learned that we can no longer afford to work independently in our silos. Education and legal discourses have much to offer each other. The purpose of this chapter, then, is to illuminate the threads of resilience and possibility in the lives of girls who experience confinement in schools, in social service institutions, and as devalued citizens. This chapter explores, in part, the ways in which girls can be best served through both an education and legal services. It highlights the collective voices of Black girls across the United States and how girls find their power to produce, transform, heal, and reintroduce themselves to the world.

This cross-disciplinary work is critical. Dialogue and action across disciplines are necessary to initiate and support existing justice movements that seek to humanize the faces of the incarcerated, particularly Black girls. Speaking from the disciplines of education and law, we discovered commonalities in our work and acknowledge the importance of creating a dialogue and space that illuminated Black girls' genius, gifts, and talents. We understand the fragility of Black girls in spite of the ways in which their identities have been constructed through media as loud, bossy, sassy, hypersexualized, and in some cases the antithesis of feminine. Throughout our work together we "historicize" the lives of Black girls while identifying the current trend of incarcerating and undereducating Black girls, silencing and dismissing them as irrelevant, immaterial, and insignificant (Gutiérrez, 2008). Throughout this chapter we propose to:

- Discuss the importance of collaboration and multidisciplinary conversations about the juvenile justice system and efforts toward reform.
- Provide a historical educational and legal analysis on the silencing and dismissal of Black girls.
- Introduce cross-disciplinary work and pedagogical practices that regenerate and uplift Black girls prior to any involvement with the child welfare and juvenile justice systems.
- Amplify the stories of Black girls entangled in the juvenile and criminal justice systems.
- Initiate a national dialogue that focuses on the needs of Black girls.

WHY COLLABORATION? WHY NOW?

As we continued to work in our respective silos we had not imagined the possibilities that might emerge through collaboration. It was through our experiences at the aforementioned December 2008 Behind the Cycle Summit that brought together youth advocates from numerous fields including educators, health and mental

Although the UDHR and CRC are international documents that have provided guidelines to care for and assist children globally, the United States has not ratified the CRC and does not have a constitutional mandate domestically to ensure a constitutional *"right to education"* for children in the United States. The *"right to education"* is not explicitly stated in the U.S. Constitution, but unfolds as a "liberty" interest under the Fourteenth Amendment of the U.S. Constitution in the *Meyer v. Nebraska* (1923) case. In *Meyer* (1923) the Court held that liberty:

> *without doubt, it denotes not merely freedom from bodily restraint but also the right of the individual to ...* ***acquire useful knowledge*** *... and enjoy those privileges long recognized at common law as essential to the orderly pursuit of happiness by free men.* (p. 399)

Recognizing the importance of education, the famous landmark case that "desegregated schools," *Brown v. Board of Education* (1954), set out its findings, stating the importance of government to educate children and to do so equally. Specifically, the Supreme Court stated:

> Today, education is perhaps the most important function of state and local governments. Compulsory school attendance laws and the great expenditures for education both demonstrate our recognition of the importance of education to our democratic society. It is required in the performance of our most basic public responsibilities, even service in the armed forces. It is the very foundation of good citizenship. Today it is a principal instrument in awakening the child to cultural values, in preparing him for later professional training, and in helping him to adjust normally to his environment. In these days, it is doubtful that any child may reasonably be expected to succeed in life if he is denied the opportunity of an education. Such an opportunity, where the state has undertaken to provide it, is a right which must be made available to all on equal terms. (p. 493)

Brown (1954), through legal precedent, set an environment that children should be afforded the right to education to reach their fullest human potential, regardless of race. Moreover, national policy reinforces *Brown* (1954), reaffirming the importance of equal education opportunity. The General Education Provisions Act, 20 USCS 1221-1 (2005), states:

> Recognizing that the Nation's economic, political, and social security require a well-educated citizenry, the Congress (1) reaffirms, as a matter of high priority, the Nation's goal of equal educational opportunity, and (2) declares it to be the policy of the United States of America that every citizen is entitled to an education to meet his or her full potential without financial barriers. (Para. 1)

However, fast-forwarding close to sixty years later, we still see the persistence of racism, sexism, and classism. These "isms," by their very root, undermine and retard the ability of an individual, namely, a young Black girl, to reach her highest human potential.

Although constitutional protections, federal case law, and national policies underscore the importance of education, realities tell us something different. With school zero tolerance policies that suspend children of color, particularly African American children, loss of instructional time is detrimental and has long-term consequences (Dillon, 2010; Losen & Skiba, 2010; M. Morris, 2012; Southern Poverty Law Center, 2012). In *Suspended Education* (Losen & Skiba, 2010), a report that highlighted suspension patterns and trends by middle schools in eighteen of the largest school districts in the nation, the researchers found that of middle school Black children, 28.3% of Black males and 18% of Black females were suspended (p. 6). In fact, the Black female suspension rate was higher than any other race, ethnicity, or gender outside of Black males (Latin males, 16.3%; Native American males, 15.9%; white males, 10%; Asian/Pacific Islander males, 6%; Native American females; 9.6%, Latin females, 8.5%; white females, 4%; and Asian/Pacific Islander females, 2.1% [Losen & Skiba, 2010, p. 5]). Although the study found that Black girls were suspended a little over ten points less than Black boys, it found that Black girls were trending at a higher rate of suspension (5.3 percentage points) than Black boys (1.7 percentage points [Losen & Skiba, 201, p. 8]).

Black girls bear the brunt of school zero tolerance policies and there is very little discussion about it. They are suspended or expelled for issues oftentimes that center on disrespect and lack of cooperation or what Monique Morris (2012) refers to as "subjectively determined as worthy of reprimand" (p. 5). Loss of instructional time can lead to a number of future social problems for Black girls that solidify them as part of the permanent underclass, thwarting their possibility of reaching the *American Dream* built on the belief of having *opportunity* that leads to the ability to ascend in class in U.S. culture.

A black girl feels others' disdain and discomfort. She understands, on an intuitive level, that the expression of who she is, as a young woman, is controversial to the *accepted* norms of femininity in this culture. Or, as M. Morris (2010) states, that her behaviors are viewed as "a deviation from the social norms that define female behavior according to a narrow, white middle-class definition of femininity." (p. 5). Because she is often viewed as "inherently criminal and hyper-sexual" (Guevara, Herz, & Spohn, 2006, p. 264), her actions and behaviors are often criminalized. The focused attention on her "attitude" and her general "oppositional defiance to authority," she knows on a deeper level, is rooted in the devaluation of who she is as a human being.

ZERO TOLERANCE POLICIES: AN ATTEMPT TO DESTROY THE BLACK GIRL

Losen and Skiba (2010) stated in their report that "there is no evidence that frequent reliance on removing misbehaving students improves school safety or student behavior" (p. 2). However, the research suggests that there is evidence that loss of instructional time leads to increased incarceration in juvenile detention and adult prison systems (Advancement Project, 2010, pp. 4–5), increased dropout rates (National Women's Law Center, 2007, p. 12), and teen pregnancy, welfare dependency, and low-paying jobs (pp. 8–10). When a child is not engaged in meaningful educational activities that build her literacy competence and prepare her for a world where she is expected to contribute and care for herself, she will find that her opportunities for advancement in a "class-obsessed" culture are expelled. She will find herself where our ancestors were in the seventeenth, eighteenth, and nineteenth centuries, subject to the Slave Codes (2013) modified for the twenty-first century, with an inability to read and write, indirectly sanctioned through zero tolerance policies (U.S. Department of Education, 2007).

With disproportionate numbers of African American girls entering the juvenile justice system (M. Morris, 2012, p. 3) and the "herstory" of oppression of Black women and their constant invisibility that extends to Black girls, accessing education and the importance of literacy and the value that it brings to the human experience cannot be granted solely to the privileged few, but to all ("Slave Code," 2013). Consistent marginalization of Black girls leads to illiterate Black girls who live in a capitalist society where they are unable to enjoy the privilege of their right to reach their fullest human potential and joy. Endemic in the structure of capitalism is the perpetuation of class hierarchies that, more often than not, suffocate the potential of the most vulnerable in our culture or the ones who are deemed disposable and unworthy. Generally, the face of the vulnerable and disposable is women and girls, especially those of us who are of color, evidenced by unequal pay for work in an article by Strasser (2012) and in a lecture by Rahman at the Social Justice Feminism Conference (2012). Furthermore, arguments concerning the "disposability" of Black women have been well documented in the work of Black feminists such as Audre Lorde, bell hooks, and many others.

Through international recognition, treaties such as the Convention on the Elimination of All Forms of Racial Discrimination (CERD) was ratified, but the Convention on the Elimination of All Forms of Discrimination against Women (CEDAW) was not. The United States, in its endemic structural racism, sexism, and classism, has continued to fail Black girls. Silencing and dismissing their needs through continued policies and practices such as the policing of Black girls and families, from Stephanie's experience and opinion as the intentional and sometimes unjustified oversight and intrusion of Child Protective Services in the lives of Black families (Brunson & Miller, 2008, p. 533; Children's Bureau, 2010); placing disproportionate numbers of Black children in foster care and the juvenile justice system (Children's Bureau, 2012; Children's Defense Fund, 2011; Puzzanchera, Sladky, & Kang, 2012); and incarcerating increased numbers of Black women, all perpetuate their marginal existence (Pfeffer, 2013).

WHERE SHE FINDS HER POWER

Despite the continued and pervasive attempts to destroy her, she can prevail. Finding her voice in literature and writing, and understanding the power of story and lived experience as an educational guide to literacy and power, she ultimately transforms these experiences into personal and political empowerment. She is writing her way to freedom, dismantling the chains that bind her mind, her heart, her soul and recognizing and digesting the power of her existence and the promise she holds for the future.

Without the works of bell hooks, Angela Davis, Alice Walker, Toni Morrison, Toni Cade Bambara, Barbara Smith, June Jordan, Audre Lorde, Barbara Christian, and many more, Black girls cannot exist. These women paved the way for us to write, feel, and politically empower ourselves to our own freedom of consciousness and political relevance through their various works. We stand on their shoulders and the shoulders of so many powerful Black women who preceded them, including our mothers and grandmothers, Sojourner Truth, Harriet Tubman, Anna Julia Cooper, Fannie Lou Hamer, and many unnamed sisters we do not know, but feel the strength of their intellect and genius that's rooted in our DNA. The path has been laid for Black women to walk into the power of our foremothers, to carry the torch of liberation of our mind, body, and spirit that rejuvenates and uplifts our souls, making us center, making us priority, moving into the center of consciousness, and understanding our connection within leads to our liberation without!

She will find power in voice, power in her ability to find herself in the midst of muckiness that leaves her breathless and unable to exhale. Choking the life from her soul is where she will make her most powerful and ardent discovery, the discovery of her voice, her self. The discovery in the power to heal and transform herself, to understand her own worth and contribution to the world that no one else can make but her. It is rooted in the disgust, the pain, the herstory, the knowing of self that will liberate and empower her to move beyond her unintended trajectory to widen her vision that supports her, revolutionizes her, and moves her to empowerment of herself and her ability to transform all. It is the rootedness of her power that politically empowers her to change things for those who look like her, understanding that in doing so, she will change things for everyone because she lives on the fringe. Living on the fringe is her power. It is her incubation. It allows her to see things that only those who have endured deep pain can see and moves her to revolutionizing her consciousness which liberates us all! She finds this in her voice, through literacy, and the understanding of the lived experience which will break the school to prison pipeline. As bell hooks states in *Sisters of the Yam* (1993, p. 5), quoting Toni Cade Bambara in her anthology *The Black Woman* (1970), "Revolution begins in the self and with the self!"

WHO AM I? BLACK GIRLS' STORIES OF TRIUMPH AND RESILIENCE

Stephanie has the privilege of providing legal representation to a small case assignment of teenaged (ages 17–21), deep-end Black girls. "Deep-end girls," defined by Stephanie for her selective case assignment, are young women who: a) are in the custody of the local departments of social services (hereinafter referred to as the "Department") for a minimum of four years; b) have or had involvement with the juvenile justice and/or adult criminal justice system; c) have been sexually abused; d) diagnosed with mental health issues, namely Oppositional Defiant Disorder; e) are prescribed psychotropic medications; f) are having educational issues (i.e.,: academic, behavioral and/or truancy) and/or are in special education classes; g) have been in a minimum of five foster care placements since the commencement of the case; and h) are chronic runaways (chronic runaway is defined by Stephanie as an individual that leaves a foster care placement, a minimum of five times, without permission, and fails to return for a minimum of two days). These are the girls that Stephanie seeks, the girls whom she feels called to represent and support as they walk their journey to self-discovery, empowerment, and the importance of their existence, despite the externalities that make them feel unworthy and undervalued.

Below are the stories of two remarkable young women who are symbols of triumph, resilience, and self-discovery through the eyes of Stephanie.

The first young woman is Dusty. She has been in foster care since 2007. Her recent diagnoses included Attention Deficit Hyperactivity Disorder (ADHD), Bi-Polar Disorder, Depression, Schizo-Affective Disorder, Post-Traumatic Stress Disorder, and Oppositional Defiant Disorder. She was sexually abused in her mother's home before being removed by the Department. She is 18 years old and does not like being in foster care. She resides in a residential treatment facility (secured facility for children with intense mental health needs) and attends school at the facility.

She's been in ten placements while in the custody of the Department and has been in and out of several mental health institutions and is on several psychotropic medications. She fights, pulls knives on others, and cuts herself. She was recently arraigned for pulling a knife on her foster care provider and is viewed as having a "bad attitude."

Life is hard for her for many reasons; she does not live with her family, her father is incarcerated and has been so for approximately four years, and she does not know whether she will ever go home. She admitted to Stephanie that she does not like to get attached to people because people leave her.

While her story may be disheartening to many, Stephanie would like to share the strength of who she is. When things are tough, which they are right now, she finds moments of strength. In her desperation in deciding whether to injure herself, she more recently, unlike in the past, has turned to adults with whom she finds comfort and solace, explaining to them the pain and anger that she is experiencing at that moment and candidly asserting that she would like to harm herself. This is progress for Dusty, marking her internal power to reach for help when she is in immense pain. She has also turned to journaling, expressing that it helps her get the rage and pain out so that she can settle and find peace within herself.

This story marks Dusty's triumph and resilience in a life that is particularly hard and painful.

The next young woman is Bianca. Bianca is 19 years old and has been in the custody of the Department since 2007. She has been in eleven foster care placements and in the past had been a chronic runaway. She is diagnosed with ADHD, Bi-Polar Disorder, and Oppositional Defiant Disorder.[5] *She is prescribed psychotropic medication, attended an alternative school, and is seen as a young woman with "an attitude problem." In the past, she has had juvenile delinquency involvement for assault and theft.*

Bianca's mother had been incarcerated for approximately a year while she's been in care. She has a poor relationship with her father. Although she visits her mother regularly and they have a wonderful relationship, she does not live with her. Bianca has been in her current placement for two years. This is a testament to Bianca's growth. She has had a history of running away and multiple disrupted placements. Bianca graduated from high school in the spring of 2013 and wants to continue her studies on the collegiate level.

---

5 Attention Deficit Hyperactivity Disorder (ADHD) involves inattentiveness, over-activity, impulsivity, or a combination. For these problems to be diagnosed as ADHD, they must be out of the normal range for a child's age and development. http://www.nlm.nih.gov/medlineplus/ency/article/001551.htm

Bi-Polar Disorder is a serious mental illness in which common emotions become intensely and often unpredictably magnified. Individuals with Bi-Polar Disorder can quickly swing from extremes of happiness, energy, and clarity to sadness, fatigue, and confusion. http://www.apa.org/topics/bipolar/index.aspx

Depression is a medical illness that causes a persistent feeling of sadness and loss of interest. Depression can manifest as physical symptoms, too. Also called Major Depression, Major Depressive Disorder, and Clinical Depression, it affects how you feel, think, and behave. Depression can lead to a variety of emotional and physical problems. You may have trouble doing normal day-to-day activities, and Depression may make you feel as though life isn't worth living. http://www.mayoclinic.com/health/depression/DS00175

Schizo-Affective Disorder is a mental condition that causes both a loss of contact with reality (psychosis) and mood problems. http://www.ncbi.nlm.nih.gov/pubmedhealth/PMH0001927/

Post-Traumatic Stress Disorder is an anxiety problem that develops in some people after extremely traumatic events, such as combat, crime, an accident, or natural disaster. http://www.apa.org/topics/ptsd/index.aspx

Oppositional Defiant Disorder is a pattern of disobedient, hostile, and defiant behavior toward authority figures. http://www.ncbi.nlm.nih.gov/pubmedhealth/PMH0002504/

This is a story of triumph and resilience for Bianca. When Bianca was asked what helped her settle down and stay in her current placement and continue in school, she stated that feeling "wanted" in her current placement helped her and that music and reading assisted her in working through difficult things.

YOU DON'T SEE US BUT WE SEE YOU

We cannot ignore the obvious. We have a responsibility as educated, middle-class Black women on the other side of Black girlhood to use our critical lenses and personal histories while engaging in this dialogue. As youth cultural workers, we are mindful that the way we view ourselves is not always how the youth we work with view us. We experience a form of double consciousness we refer to as mirrored selves; we know that as girls we experienced struggles that are endemic to Black girlhood including being silenced, policed, and stereotyped and as Black women we have developed coping skills to endure these continued assaults on our character. However, the girls we work with cannot see this—and why should they? They see professionals who move differently throughout the world. For these reasons we argue that it is imperative for Black women on the other side of Black girlhood to make themselves visible while engaging in this work.

Emerging scholarship focusing on Black girls and learning is setting the stage for the inclusion of Black girls' voices and humanity in learning communities. The session "You're Who We've Been Waiting For: Empowering Black Girls Within and Beyond the English Classroom" at the National Council of Teachers of English Annual Convention in 2011 featured the scholarship of Delicia Greene, Gholdy Muhammad, and LaToya Sawyer. During that session, Muhammad introduced the "Sister Authors" who know the power of literacy and affirm each other and their literate identities by reading and writing together. One of the "Sister Authors" in Muhammad's study, Iris, posits, "I feel like I am a part of something bigger than myself. It's not just about me, my voice is not just representative of me. What I say is representative of everyone who looks like me. … I was able to travel outside of the realm of myself. To become something more than what I am."

INITIATING A DIALOGUE THAT FOCUSES ON THE NEEDS OF BLACK GIRLS

It is the authors' intention in this chapter to highlight the need for attention to be paid to Black girls. Their stories are painful, the research devastating. These authors are recommending that coalition building for Black girls that reach across disciplines is imperative to providing support and resources to allow them to reach their fullest potential. We need more research, more stories, more documented lived experiences, more ground-centered work that engages Black girls on their path to self-discovery, self-determination, and transformative resistance. Pushing paradigms to include ground-centered work beyond theory and white papers is imperative to their growth and support as young women.

By emerging from our silos, we build a platform to do this work. It allows us to transcend our limited understanding of the plight of Black girls through our narrow lenses of discipline, and gives us an opportunity to garner an understanding in a global way that broadens our vision for the work and what we all have to offer to support Black girls.

The famous words of the U.S. Declaration of Independence in 1776 stated that we have the right to "life, liberty and the pursuit of happiness." At the time the Declaration was written, this belief, did not extend to Black people because of our enslavement status. However, through consistent resistance and powerful movements initiated by our ancestors, the right to "life, liberty and the pursuit of happiness" extends to all people today, regardless of color or gender.

We need to ensure that every Black girl is afforded this right and this begins with her right to an education, her literacy, which is a building block to solidifying her opportunity to reach what is supposed to be intended for all people of the United States, "life, liberty and the pursuit of happiness." It is her human right. And it is our responsibility to ensure that she reaches it.

REFERENCES

Adler, M. (March 15, 2009). Before Rosa Parks, There was Claudette Colvin. Retrieved from http://www.npr.org/templates/story/story.php?storyId=101719889 on December 2, 2013.

Advancement Project. (2010, March). *Test, punish and push out: How "zero tolerance" and high-stakes testing funnel youth into the school-to-prison pipeline.* Washington, DC, Advancement Project.

Bambara, T. (1970). *The Black woman.* New York: Washington Square Press.

Beane, C. (2012, October). *America at the crossroads: Charting a new course toward an integrative justice paradigm.* Washington, DC: American Constitution Society.

Brown, R. N. (2008). *Black girlhood celebration: Toward a hip-hop feminist pedagogy.* New York: Peter Lang.

Brown v. Board of Education. 347 U.S. 483 (1954).

Brunson, R. K., & Miller, J. (2006). Gender, race, and urban policing: The experience of African-American youths. *Gender & Society, 20*(4), 531–552.

Burnham, L. (2012). *New women's movement initiative.* Paper presented at the Social Justice Feminism Conference, University of Cincinnati College of Law, Center for Race, Gender and Social Justice. Cincinnati, OH.

Children's Bureau. (2010). *Child maltreatment.* Washington, DC: Author. Retrieved from http://archive.acf.hhs.gov/programs/cb/pubs/cm10/cm10.pdf.

Children's Defense Fund. (2011). *Portrait of inequality: Black children in America*. Washington, DC: Author. Retrieved from http://www.childrensdefense.org/programs–campaigns/Black–community–crusade–for–children–II/bccc–assets/portraitofinequality.pdf.

Dillon, S. (2010, September 14). Racial disparity in school suspensions. *The New York Times*, p. A16.

Fine, M., & Ruglis, J. (2009). Circuits and consequences of dispossession: The racialized realignment of the public sphere for U.S. youth. *Transforming Anthropology, 17*(1), 20–33.

Fisher, M. T. (2008). Catching butterflies. *English Education, 40*(2), 94–100.

Fisher, M. T., Purcell, S. S., & May, R. (2009). Process, product, and playmaking. *English Education, 41*(4), 337–355.

General Education Provisions Act, 20 U.S.C. § 1221–1 (2005).

Guevara, L., Herz, D., & Spohn, C. (2006). Gender and juvenile justice decision making: What role does race play? *Feminist Criminology, 1*(4), 258–282.

Gutiérrez, K. (2008). Language and literacies as civil rights. In S. Greene (Ed.), *Literacy as a civil right: Reclaiming social justice in literacy teaching and learning* (pp. 169–184). New York: Peter Lang.

hooks, b. (1993). *Sisters of the yam* (p. 5). Cambridge, MA: South End Press.

Hoose, P. M. (2009). *Claudette Colvin: Twice toward justice*. New York: Farrar, Straus & Giroux.

James, J. (2012, September 20). *Women and political imprisonment: From Rosa Parks to Ramona Africa*. Paper presented at the University of Wisconsin, Madison.

Kania, J., & Kramer, M. (2011, Winter). Collective impact. *Stanford Social Innovation Review*. Retrieved from http://www.ssireview.org/articles/entry/collective_impact.

Lewin, T. (2012, March 6). Black students face more discipline, data suggests. *The New York Times*, p. A11.

Losen, D., & Skiba, R. (2010). *Suspended education: Urban middle schools in crisis*. Montgomery, AL: Southern Poverty Law Center.

Meyer v. Nebraska, 262 U.S. 390, 399 (1923).

Morris, E. W. (2007, June). "Ladies" or "loudies"? Perceptions and experiences of Black girls in classrooms. *Youth and Society, 38*(4), 490–515.

Morris, M. (2012). *Race, gender, and the school-to-prison pipeline: Expanding our discussion to include Black girls*. New York: African American Policy Forum.

National Women's Law Center. (2007). *When girls don't graduate we all fail: A call to improve high school graduation rates for girls*. Washington, DC: Greenberger, M., Samuels, J., Chaudhry, N., et al.

Open Society Institute (February 2008). Moving toward a more integrative approach to criminal justice reform. Washington D.C., Open Society. Retrieved from http://bobbyscott.house.gov/uploads/justice_reform_080228.pdf on December 2, 2013.

Pfeffer, R. (2013, May 27). Growing incarceration of young African-American women a cause for concern. *Oakland Local*. Retrieved from http://archive.oaklandlocal.com/posts/2011/05/growing-incarceration-young-african-american-women-cause-concern.

Puzzanchera, C., Sladky, A., & Kang, W. (2012). *Easy access to juvenile populations: 1990–2011*. Washington, DC: Office of Juvenile Justice and Delinquency Prevention. Retrieved from http://www.ojjdp.gov/ojstatbb/ezapop/.

Rahman, A. (2012). *Social justice feminism*. Presentation at the Social Justice Feminism Conference, University of Cincinnati College of Law, Center for Race, Gender and Social Justice. Cincinnati, OH (October 26, 2012).

Slave code. (2013.). *Encyclopedia Britannica's guide to Black history*. Retrieved from http://www.britannica.com/blackhistory/article-9399807.

Smith, B. (1983). The Combahee River Collective statement. In *Home girls, a Black feminist anthology*. New York: Kitchen Table.

Southern Poverty Law Center. (2012, October). *SPLC: DOJ lawsuit a "wake-up call" to end Mississippi's school-to-prison pipeline*. Montgomery, AL: Southern Poverty Law Center. Retrieved from http://www.splcenter.org/get-informed/news/splc-doj-lawsuit-a-wake-up-call-toend-mississippi-s-school-to-prison-pipeline#.UbxXdtzD_cs.

Strasser, A. R. (2012, April 12). Charts: How unequal pay is even more unequal for some women. *Think Progress*. Retrieved from http://thinkprogress.org/economy/2012/04/17/465806/charts-how-unequal-pay-is-even-more-unequal-for-some-women/.

Taifa, N., & Beane, C. (2009). Integrative solutions to interrelated issues: A multidisciplinary look behind the cycle of incarceration. *Harvard Law and Policy Review, 3*(2), 283–306.

United Nations. (1948). Universal declaration of human rights. Retrieved from http://www.jus.uio.no/lm/un.universal.declaration.of.human.rights.1948/portrait.a4.pdf.

United Nations. (1969). Convention to eliminate all forms of racial discrimination. Retrieved from http://www.ohchr.org/EN/ProfessionalInterest/Pages/CERD.aspx.

United Nations. (1979). Convention to eliminate all forms of discrimination against women. Retrieved from http://www.un.org/womenwatch/daw/cedaw/text/econvention.htm.

United Nations. (1990). Convention on the rights of the child. Retrieved from http://www.ohchr.org/EN/ProfessionalInterest/Pages/CRC.aspx.

U.S. Department of Education. (2007). *A first look at the literacy of America's adults in the 21st century*. Washington, DC: National Center for Education Statistics. Retrieved from http://www.eric.ed.gov/PDFS/ED489066.pdf.

U.S. Department of Health and Human Services. (2012). AFCARS report. *Administration of Children, Youth and Families*. Retrieved from http://www.acf.hhs.gov/programs/cb.

Wenger, E. (1998). *Communities of practice: Learning, meaning, and identity*. New York: Cambridge University Press.

Winn, M. T. (2010a, December). "Betwixt and between": Literacy, liminality, and the "celling" of Black girls. *Race, Ethnicity, and Education, 13*(4), 425–447.

Winn, M. T. (2010b, September). "Our side of the story": Moving incarcerated youth voices from margin to center. *Race, Ethnicity, and Education, 13*(3), 313–326.

Winn, M. T. (2011). Girl Time: Literacy, justice and the school-to-prison pipeline. New York: Teachers College Press.

Winn, M. T. (2012). The politics of desire and possibility in urban playwriting: (Re)reading and (re)writing the script. *Pedagogies: An International Journal*.

Winn, M. T., & Behizadeh, N. (2011). The right to be literate: Literacy, education, and the school-to-prison pipeline. *Review of Research in Education, 35*(1), 147–173.

Winn, M. T., & Jackson, C. A. (2011, September–October). Toward a performance of possibilities: Resisting gendered (in)justice. *International Journal of Qualitative Studies in Education, 24*(5), 615–620.

CHAPTER TEN

Messy, Butch, AND Queer

LGBTQ Youth and the School to Prison Pipeline

SHANNON D. SNAPP, JENNIFER M. HOEING, AMANDA FIELDS, AND STEPHEN T. RUSSELL

In January 2014, the U.S. Departments of Education and Justice released a historic federal discipline guidance package, which recognized how punitive discipline disproportionately affects underrepresented youth, outlined strategies to reduce punitive discipline, and encouraged positive approaches to keep students in school (U.S. Department of Education, 2014). Automatic and punitive discipline policies and practices often result in student entrance into the juvenile justice system, a process referred to as the "school to-prison pipeline." These steps by the federal government respond to consistent media attention on the ineffectiveness of zero-tolerance discipline and grassroots efforts aimed at altering school policies and practices that punish youth for minor and often vague infractions (e.g., willful deviance; Dignity in Schools Campaign, 2014). A solid and growing body of research supports these efforts and has provided substantial evidence regarding how the school to prison pipeline disproportionately affects youth of color, specifically African-American and Latino males (e.g., Skiba, Shure, & Williams, 2011, for review; Wallace, Goodkind, Wallace, & Bachman, 2008) and youth with disabilities (APA, 2008). In addition to these disparities, new evidence has emerged that indicates how other marginalized youth, referred to as the *pipeline population* (Snapp & Licona, in revision), are pushed out of school and into the criminal justice system, including lesbian, gay, bisexual, transgender, queer, and questioning (LGBTQ) and gender nonconforming youth[1] (Himmelstein & Bruckner, 2011).

1 Some research has suggested that gender nonconforming youth, who may not necessarily identify as L, G, B, T, or Q, are also part of the pipeline population; however, most research

Far less is known about the school discipline experiences of LGBTQ youth as compared to other youth within the pipeline population. This missing component is likely due to the lack of federal data about LGBTQ youth's school experiences (with the exception of bullying; Mitchum & Moodie-Mills, 2014). Only one study to date has documented that LGBTQ youth, particularly, girls and youth of color, are more likely to be expelled from school than heterosexual youth for similar infractions (Himmelstein & Bruckner, 2011). Evidence that LGBTQ youth constitute the pipeline population is supported by the overrepresentation of LGBTQ youth in juvenile detention facilities. For example, LGBTQ youth are twice as likely as their heterosexual peers to be detained for nonviolent offenses such as running away, prostitution, and truancy (Garnette, Irvine, Reyes, & Wilber, 2011). This emerging evidence points to the necessity of understanding how the school experiences of LGBTQ students may lead to disparities in punitive punishment, exclusionary discipline, or representation in juvenile justice systems (Hunt & Moodie-Mills, 2012; Snapp & Licona, in revision).

It may be that the stigma and prejudice associated with homosexuality is at the root of differential treatment in school discipline: In some ways, the processes associated with disparities for LGBTQ youth may be similar to processes experienced by marginalized racial/ethnic groups. For example, Fine's (1986, 1991) research with inner city youth troubled the way we view "dropouts," suggesting that the majority of youth rarely drop out of school but are pushed out due to a number of systemic barriers. Fine's work demonstrated through youth's stories that school policies, practices, and climates made it difficult for youth to learn and excel. Some youth, for instance, were disciplined for being truant when family needs demanded their attention; others were discharged despite their desire to stay in school. In short, poor school conditions offered little hope to youth that education was meaningful or necessary (Fine, 1991). Similar conclusions about failed school policies are drawn by critical educational theorists who point to polices such as zero-tolerance approaches to discipline that make youth "disposable" (Giroux, 2003) and encourage underperforming youth to find alternative routes to education (e.g., GED; Tuck, 2012). Related systemic barriers such as familial and housing concerns likely challenge LGBTQ youth's ability to learn and successfully complete school as well, and may increase the likelihood that youth will be encouraged to seek out nontraditional educational pathways.

However, there may be additional processes that lead to disciplinary disparities for LGBTQ youth. In particular, several media stories about school discipline demonstrate that LGBTQ students who try to protect themselves against

has focused on LGBTQ youth. In the chapter, we highlight the experiences of gender nonconforming youth when distinguished by participants.

homophobic bullying may be punished and excluded from school in the process (e.g., Eng, 2012; Golgowki, 2014). One state-wide study revealed that LGBTQ youth were three times more likely to be injured or threatened with a weapon and two times more likely to get in a physical fight at school compared to their heterosexual peers (Massachusetts Department of Elementary and Secondary Education (MDESE), 2006). Further, when students are **bullied** based on sexual orientation, teachers seldom intervene (Peters, 2003). In this context, studies show that students who are bullied due to actual or perceived sexual orientation are more likely to bring a weapon to school and skip school (MDESE, 2006; Russell, Sinclair, Poteat, & Koenig, 2012). These experiences of discriminatory harassment make LGBTQ youth more susceptible to truancy, assault, and disorderly conduct charges (Majd, Marksamer, & Reyes, 2009). Thus, higher rates of victimization from bullying for LGBTQ youth may lead to disparate rates of suspension or expulsion (Russell et al., 2006). In effect, LGBTQ youth may be blamed, ignored, or even punished for behaviors that should elicit support rather than punishment from school staff.

In an effort to better understand these disciplinary disparities and the pathways that may push LGBTQ youth out of school and into the juvenile justice system or alternative education, we conducted an exploratory study with LGBTQ youth and adult advocates to document experiences of discipline at school, perceived reasons for LGBTQ discipline disparities, and pathways LGBTQ youth experience through the school to prison pipeline. While our particular focus for this research is on understanding the narratives and pathways of LGBTQ youth, we also pay close attention to the intersections of youths' identities to understand how youth with multiple underrepresented identities may experience exacerbated discipline disparities in school.

METHOD

In collaboration with the Gay Straight Alliance (GSA) Network and local community organizations, we designed a study to address experiences and observations about LGBTQ youth and discipline in schools. Youth and adult advocates were recruited for the study and consented or assented prior to participation. Participants could skip any question and end the focus group or interview at any time. The study protocol for both youth and adults was approved by our university's institutional review board.

PROCEDURE AND PARTICIPANTS

Our research team (including GSA Network and local collaborators) helped generate a list of adult advocates (educators, including school administrators, teachers, counselors, policy makers, staff at youth serving organizations, and activists) that have knowledge or direct experience with LGBTQ youth and school discipline. Adult advocates from across the United States, including Arizona, California, Colorado, D.C., Georgia, Illinois, and Louisiana (n = 19), participated in hour-long phone interviews. Participants answered eight open-ended questions about LGBTQ youth and school discipline (e.g., "What is your perspective on LGBTQ youth and their treatment in terms of school discipline?"; "What are the trajectories for youth who are suspended, expelled, or 'pushed out'?"; "Do you know if any LGBTQ youth or gender nonconforming youth considered transferring or 'dropping out' of school?"). Adult interviews were conducted between December 2012 and March 2013. Adults were not remunerated for their time but were offered a copy of research findings following the completion of the study.

Youth focus group participants were identified through an online or paper survey developed and administered through GSA Network and local CBOs from August 2012 to August 2013. GSA Network sent out the survey to their e-mail listserv and also recruited youth at the GSA Youth Empowerment Summit (YES). Over 300 youth (n = 322) youth completed the survey. The research team then selected youth from the survey to participate in focus groups based on the following criteria: (a) youth had indicated they had experienced school discipline, (b) they agreed to be contacted and provided contact information (either phone or e-mail), (c) they were LGBTQ identified, and (d) they were currently in grades 9–12. Given that GSA Network has a large constituency of straight allies, several youth were ineligible for the study based on these criteria. However, an exception was made for the inclusion of straight youth based on their write-in responses on the survey. For example, while they themselves were not LGBTQ identified, their role as an ally had been related to their own discipline experience or they had witnessed discipline of their LGBTQ friends. Our aim was to recruit 40 youth to participate in the focus groups as well as to select youth from multiple underrepresented groups within the remaining eligible sample. All LGBTQ youth of color who remained were contacted in order to maximize our potential to speak to the experiences of youth with intersecting identities. In sum, 31 youth agreed to participate in follow-up focus groups. Youth identified their demographic characteristics on the survey by checking boxes that most accurately represented their race/ethnicity, gender, and sexual orientation. Write-in options were also available. Youth participants were diverse, approximately 48% had underrepresented racial/ethnic identities, 19% identified as bisexual, 19% as gay, 16% as queer, 16% as straight, nearly 13% as questioning, 10% as lesbian, and 6% as pansexual. Nearly half identified as female (45.16%). Additional demographic information can be found in Table 10.1.

Books From California
51 W. Easy St
Simi Valley, CA 93065
UNITED STATES
customerservice@booksfromca.com

Books From California
51 W. Easy St
Simi Valley, CA 93065
UNITED STATES

To: Alibris APEX DC 76902014-10 - APEX
800 Avondale Ave.

Grandview Heights, OH 43212-3473
UNITED STATES

If this order is shipping from the US to an international buyer, remember to attach proper documentation. Complete and attach USPS Form CN-22 for all Priority Mail International Envelopes or First-Class Mail International shipments (available at your post office).

Order Number:	33959002
Ship Method:	Standard
Customer Name:	Alibris APEX DC 76902014-10 - APEX
Order Date:	9/10/2026
Alibris Order #:	76902014-10
Email:	

Items:

Table 10.1. Demographic Information of Youth Participants (n = 31) (Adapted from author's research).

Race/Ethnicity	CA	GA	AZ	Total	%
Caucasian	4	3	9	16	51.61
Hispanic	3	2	2	7	22.58
Multiracial	1	0	3	4	12.9
African-American	1	1	0	2	6.45
Asian American	1	0	0	1	3.23
Native American	0	0	1	1	3.23
n	**10**	**6**	**15**	**31**	**100**
Sexual orientation					
Bisexual	1	1	4	6	19.35
Gay	3	0	3	6	19.35
Queer	0	2	3	5	16.13
Straight	2	1	2	5	16.13
Questioning	2	1	1	4	12.9
Lesbian	1	1	1	3	9.68
Pansexual	1	0	1	2	6.45
n	**10**	**6**	**15**	**31**	**100**
Gender					
Female	6	4	4	14	45.16
Male	3	2	4	9	29.03
Transgender	0	0	4	4	12.9
Gender Queer	1	0	2	3	9.68
Two Spirit	0	0	1	1	3.23
n	**10**	**6**	**15**	**31**	**100**

Focus groups were conducted between February and September 2013, and participants received a $20 gift card. Eight focus groups were conducted via phone or in-person with youth (n = 31): four were conducted in person in Arizona, two via phone in California, and two via phone in Georgia. Phone focus groups were conducted via teleconference. Youth dialed in to a toll-free number and were greeted by an interviewer from the research team who asked each youth to state their name and provide verbal consent. The focus group questions were the same for in-person and phone focus groups, though for phone focus groups, the interviewer provided several prompts to ensure that all participants on the call had a

Further, these terms for "problem" youth can be used to justify bullying. A Louisiana adult stated: "Kids are like, 'well, you know they're punks.' It's what they call gay kids down here. 'Oh, he's a punk,' like that explains it [bullying], and there's no other explanation." Youth who have been bullied for their sexual or gender identity also recount terms they were called in school by faculty and students alike: "The administration did say pretty homophobic slurs. They're kind of like, 'Oh, it wasn't meant to be like that,' and 'you're just being a princess'" (Youth, Arizona).

Adults and youth also identified moments when the name-calling escalated and youth were forced to respond, resulting, in some cases, in further negative attention from other students and staff. For instance: "I got bullied, so I, like, started dressing like a boy and got this thug mentality. They looked at me like I was the bad Chola, the Mexican lesbian bitch. So no one messed with me any more at school, but the administration, they were always watching me" (Youth, Arizona). For this youth, gender expression may have helped fend off additional attention from youth but not from the administration.

Participants named several terms that have been used to identify LGBTQ youth who disrupt gender and sexual identity norms. These words are used covertly and overtly by school administrators, teachers, security officers, and students. They problematize LGBTQ youth for behaviors that often go unpunished when enacted by straight or gender-conforming youth. As one adult from Georgia explains: "LGBTQ youth are being either chastised or disciplined for their gender expression, for their appearance, for their behavior, for their mannerisms, or for some sort of affection towards same gender youth. We don't necessarily see that with students who are straight or are assumed to be straight."

YOUTH ARE PUNISHED FOR PDA AND SELF-EXPRESSION

Several narratives from youth and adults illustrate that LGBTQ youth get into trouble for public displays of affection (PDA). Punishment for PDA varies from disproportionate attention from school administrators to punitive discipline. An adult advocate from California said: "What you will definitely find is that there's gonna be a more rigorous, more shame-based response to same-sex coupling and sexualized behavior as there is with heterosexual kids." A Colorado adult shared a similar story: "Same sex couples at one school were being punished for holding hands in the hallway when opposite sex couples were not." Policies against PDA are believed to be disproportionately enforced for queer youth:

> Folks get in trouble because they kiss or express some kind of affection, and it goes against policy, but they don't enforce that for straight youth, and it'll happen for queer youth

> because that stands out to an administrator. That'll, you know, be something that catches someone's eye versus another heteronormative display. (Adult, California)

Youth participants also noticed this discrepancy: "It's kind of annoying that they tell my two [same sex] friends no PDA, and there's another couple who's full blown making out and it's okay because they're different sex" (Youth, California). Another youth describes the higher risk of punishment for LGBTQ youth: "I do believe that there is more of a chance for same-sex couples using PDA getting in more trouble. It's not that they do get in more trouble, it's just that there's the possibility for them to get in more trouble" (Youth, California). Such a possibility became a reality according to this youth:

> I have some friends, they're dating, two girls, and they were holding hands in the hallway after lunch period and I guess they kissed just once. It wasn't anything prolonged and in a place near a lot of heterosexual couples doing the same thing. Our school police officer specifically targeted them and gave them this lecture on how it's against school policy and student conduct and no public displays of affection and it was really terrible. (Youth, California)

According to participants, PDA by LGBTQ youth not only gets more attention from school staff but often results in harsh forms of punishment that can be detrimental for youth in multiple ways:

> One young woman was caught by campus security holding hands with her girlfriend at the edge of campus. They called the parents, and in this case she was out to her family already, but, had she not been, the system could have outed the student to her parents and that could have resulted in the whole process of coming out when the timing wasn't right, which could have resulted in getting kicked out of the house. (Adult, California)

Another example of disproportionate punishment for PDA did not end as well:

> A principal rolled up on two girls who were holding hands, took them to the principal's office, and put labels on them. I don't know if the students identified as being lesbian, but he called them that and he threatened to suspend them. And he called both of their parents and outed the students. (Adult, Georgia)

One youth relayed a similar story about a bisexual couple in her school:

> I befriended these two bisexual girls, and later in the year they got into a relationship and our vice principal was a little older than the other staff members, and I think he grew up in a time where homosexuality was really looked down upon. He would always see the straight kids holding hands and making out in the halls, and one day after school they were holding hands and the vice principal dragged them into his office and suspended my friend Elisabeth for a week and gave my friend Jenna detention for three days and later called their parents and outed them. (Youth, California)

In these cases, LGBTQ youth were punished for displays of affection witnessed by school administrators; however, some students may not be "caught in the act" but are punished based on false accusations or rumor. One student describes how an act of friendship was taken out of context and resulted in punishment: "A friend of mine that was a girl … it turned into this huge rumor where apparently I was in the bathroom making out with her. I had to go to the office and that had never happened. I hugged her in the hallway. It was just things like that. They were just accusing me of kissing her, and they gave me in-school suspension" (Youth, California).

Disparate punishment was not only documented for PDA but also for youth's self-expression and appearance. Several participants indicated that youth who do not conform to gender norms are treated differently in school:

> I've seen a great deal of students who have been pushed out because they are perceived to be LGBT or are. I've noticed that [for] the gender non-conforming females who may want to dress in more male gender based clothing. The level of punishment may be much more severe than a gender conforming student who can have just as much of a strong temperament. But this [gender non-conforming] person makes other people uncomfortable, and level of suspension may come at a faster rate and at a higher rate. (Adult, District of Columbia)

Based on this quote it appears that girls who do not conform to gender norms may be unfairly perceived as threatening and harshly punished as a result. Another participant explained why some youth are likely to experience disproportionate punishment:

> I think it's specifically going to be the gender non-conforming kid because these types of biases, the assumptions about who is an aggressor in an altercation, for example, tends to be a gut instinct that is based off of what these people look like. (Adult, District of Columbia)

Even in circumstances in which an altercation is absent, gender nonconforming youth may be at risk of being labeled by administrators. One example from an Arizona youth illustrates this point:

> The teachers … they thought we were selling weed in school, they thought that me and her were both selling weed 'cause like, the way we were dressing, 'cause we were the only girls at that middle school that dressed like boys. So it was like "now we're bad."

Other youth may not have been subject to the same level of search and seizure as the previous example but are not able to express themselves fully in school and feel safe. Administrators were often the ones to question youths' choice in clothing, for example, which places the burden on youth to change in order to be accepted. An adult advocate in Arizona stated:

> I remember being in touch with trans youth that would express themselves in ways that were not their [assigned] gender and they would complain a lot, or the students would be

> told to not wear a dress you know from teachers, or [asked] "why are you dressed like a guy?" not understanding that it was insulting them directly.

Youth whose gender identity contrasts with their biological sex are often questioned about their gender expression, which may feel like an affront. A youth in Arizona confirms this observation:

> I identify as genderqueer. So I wear gender-expressive clothes and sometimes I'd be uncomfortable to go in certain classes, because of the way students would treat me. I got talked to by the administrators and they were like, "So you don't want to go to class because of what you choose to wear, so why don't you just choose to wear different things?" I was like, "I should be able to wear whatever I want to wear, you know, and feel comfortable."

When youth try to express themselves, they run the risk of being unfairly interpreted or punished, and, again, the onus to change is placed on the youth. One participant articulates the rationale concerning "choice" that may arise when youth are blamed for their own mistreatment:

> I'm thinking of a young black woman who identifies as gay, but has a really short haircut, like people would see on a boy, what you would call a fade. That's in people's face, and I think it's almost okay to discriminate or talk about or relegate to a different status because it's like "well she chose to put that in my face", you know and "she didn't have to." So if there's a woman who identifies as gay or bisexual and you know she has long hair and she looks feminine, then it doesn't challenge anyone's beliefs. (Adult, Louisiana)

In this case, when young people choose to express themselves, particularly if it confronts gender norms, mistreatment or discrimination becomes "okay"; in essence it becomes normalized. Youth have been punished for their self-expression when it challenges other's beliefs and social codes. One Georgia adult recounts a story that made headlines: "A student named Nathaniel Williams out of Louisiana was suspended for a week for wearing hair extensions … lots of the girls have colorful hair extensions, and it's disproportionate because none of the other girls are getting suspended for having hair weaves." In this example, discipline in the form of suspension was disproportionate not only to the "offense" (wearing hair extensions) but also because it reflected a double standard. Another youth tells a story about the threats of punishment he received for applying makeup in school:

> I put on make-up during class, and I'm not supposed to do that in class, and I do have huge gestures. It's my way of expressing myself. One of the teachers was like, "if you're going to do all this in my class then I'm going to have to put your desk outside for the rest of the year" and I was like, "oh, where did this come from?" He just told me this two weeks ago. I'm like "school's about to end, so what's the point?" I mean everyone does it [puts makeup on], but I guess I'm the only one who's not supposed to. (Youth, California)

Because the threat of ridicule, victim blame, and punishment is real, some students purposely avoid self-expression that may generate attention. One Arizona youth said,

> Just seeing the type of attention that people put on anybody who didn't seem like they were the same as anybody else ... that made me want to avoid expressing myself in any way, because I didn't want the same attention they were receiving.

Another Arizona youth echoed this concern and tried to mask self-expression that might reveal his sexual orientation: "I guess I just avoid that whole situation in general, like I really just focus on how I dress, just so that I wouldn't give off that idea that you know, I was gay." These youth attempt to secure safety by managing their image and identity, and while effective, may have implications for their overall wellness (Legate, Ryan, & Weinstein, 2012).

The stories shared by participants illustrate that youth who violated gender norms (regardless of their sexual identity) experienced differential treatment in school. Often, as highlighted by some of the previous quotes, youth were read as aggressive or problematic. Additionally, stories about youths' resistance to victimization highlights another pathway that pushes youth out of school and may lead them into the juvenile justice system.

YOUTH WHO PROTECT THEMSELVES ARE PUNISHED

When LGBTQ youth respond to bullying by fighting back, they are often blamed and punished for their own victimization. The narratives from our study indicate the ineffectiveness of school policies and practices meant to protect youth and prevent violence. Failure to support youth and create hospitable school climates is an additional pathway toward school push-out. Some youth respond with defensive violence, while others use preemptive violence. One adult from Arizona reported the following regarding a particular youth:

> She told me "yes I do beat people up when people piss me off," and after talking to her it's like, ok, "you're being provoked constantly, and people are constantly calling you names, constantly trying to fight you and so you're fighting back," or you're like, "I know this person's gonna come at me so you try to get to them first."

It appears that fighting back or picking fights with others is a defense mechanism that can be useful to fend off threat from other students; however, this behavior is likely to result in punishment. In another narrative, fighting became a collective strategy: "We even had our own LGBT gang who was beating up other kids ... the LGBTQ youth were grouping together to provide support for each other the same way other gangs do" (Adult, District of Columbia). When victimization is not addressed in school policy or practice or by the adults who enforce those policies, youth may take singular or collective measures to protect themselves.

Zero tolerance policies mean that, for many youth, acts of self-protection were met with harsh discipline, leading to suspensions, detentions, and expulsions as a pathway out of school. In some cases, students who did not react with violence were suspended anyway:

> He said he wasn't trying to fight back or anything. It didn't get to that point. He was literally just putting his hands up over his head to keep the guy from—and when the teacher saw the incident, she basically took both of them to the principal's office, and they both got suspended for fighting. (Adult, California)

Another student was also suspended for fighting, but, in this example, as in others, the fighting was a result of continued harassment:

> When she finally blew up, she got the most severe [punishment] because this has been months and months of harassment, and she blew up and really hurt another student. And you know, she ended up getting extended suspension, so she just dropped out. She was 16 at the time and just didn't see the point of being out of school for 45 days and then coming back … And she just felt like she wasn't going to be supported in the school. (Adult, District of Columbia)

One Arizona adult explains a possible chain of events for some LGBTQ youth who are regularly harassed in school: "It's pushing them to this point where 'you're not protecting me,' 'you're not listening to me,' and so 'I have to fight back on my own.' And when they fight back, 'boom, now you did something so we can kick you out.'" These quotes illustrate the point that some youth seek support when harassed, but when school staff fail to intervene, youth may feel they "have to fight back." Further, failure to support students can be viewed as a "setup" of sorts in which "problem youth" are positioned to fail. A similar pathway plays out very clearly for one young person who is transgender and presents as male at school but identifies as female:

> We have one classic kind of story of like a trans, young person … She was having difficulty with, with just not even like a lot of kids, but just a handful of young people who were bullying her and it went on and on. She reported it every single time that it happened, but for whatever reason, the report site—what I guess is supposed to happen, with their anti-bullying policy, is that you make a report and then whoever you report to, that person is supposed to write up some piece of paper that is supposed to then go directly to the social worker. And she reported it, every single day. This piece of paper, that's supposed to be generated, never made it to the social worker. She told people at school that she was going to bring a knife to school the next day, and they still didn't do anything. And then she brought a knife. Now, granted, it was a butter knife. She was arrested at school for that, and she went to juvenile bureau here and was released later that day, but then was put automatically in expulsion proceedings, and she's also special ed … she has an IEP … she's ADHD. So it's just stuff like where the admin weren't in the mood to ask what was going on. I mean, she ended up being bounced around from one house to another because of juvenile court proceedings and family rejection. (Adult, Louisiana)

Despite numerous attempts to get help from adults in her school, this student was left with few options, and though she was the one regularly harassed, she was punished for an act of self-protection. Another youth who experienced push-out recounted:

> I fought a boy because he was calling me names … I got in trouble for hitting him because he was a good kid at the school, but he was a jerk. He was all popular in a different area than I was. So yeah, obviously I was already the bad kid. We got in a fight and he didn't get in trouble. (Youth, Arizona)

This youth highlights the injustice when "good" youth escape punishment for victimization but "bad" (perhaps code for nondominant) youth are punished. These inequities result in frustration with school administration:

> I'm always getting kicked out of school like, and I would tell them, "She hit me first because she called me a dyke." I mean, "that's self-defense and you're kicking me out?" They don't kick her out. I got expelled … because I was fighting with the girl. They thought it was a lesbian moment … they thought I was hitting on her. (Youth, Arizona)

This student's story reveals the bias in some school administrators toward heterosexual youth, as well as a refusal to consider the background and experiences of LGBTQ youth. Stories of victim blame and punishment were so common that one youth wondered, "Why would you punish the victim for fighting back?" (Youth, California). This young person raises an important question that adults have trouble articulating, as evidenced by the following quote:

> When I was in middle school … I did not go to school very often, or I was always late. I was bullied a lot. Some of it was because people thought I was a lesbian, and everyone found out that I had issues with self-harm and anorexia, and I got targeted for that too. When I went to the administration … my parents had to go several times … they kinda said a lot of things like "oh well that's just how kids are" or … "boys will be boys" or they would say "oh girls are mean" or … they would tell me "if you didn't dress the way you did, they wouldn't bother you". (Youth, Georgia)

Platitudes such as "boys will be boys," coupled with victim blame are ineffective solutions that breed mistrust and confusion. Another youth shares a conceptually distinct story about how her mistrust of school administrators was cause for punishment:

> They started telling me that they were going to expel me or suspend me just because I didn't want to tell them any of the information. They wanted to find out if I was gay, and I told them, "I don't trust you guys' and they were like, 'we don't care if you don't trust us, you gotta tell us." I was going to get suspended because I wouldn't tell them who was bullying me. (Youth, California)

In this example, it appeared as though the school administrators were concerned about the youth's safety. However, threatening a young person with suspension and disrespecting this student's boundary hardly warrants trust.

In addition to being disciplined, youth who fight back may be sent to alternative schools or leave school altogether. One youth from Georgia explained that options were limited when youth fight: "You get like two instances of bullying, [then] you get sent to an alternative school." In this case, being sent to an alternative school may operate similarly as zero tolerance. There are a set number of "offenses" and then youth are sent away. Some youth made the decision to leave: "I felt like I just wanted to leave, like I didn't—I couldn't even imagine finishing high school. So, I transferred" (Youth, Arizona). Another youth describes a similar situation in which victimization led to truancy and eventually a move:

> She had to move away because some of the kids at our school was making fun of her because she was a lesbian … and there were some people who were making fun of her and calling her names, and she went to the administrator and talked with them. So they got suspended for three days … but when they came back they kept it up, and so she went to tell her mom … and she [mom] said "ok we won't let you go to school for a couple of days." So she comes back, but it's still happening. So the mom is like' ok, well let's move' "cause I don't want to see my daughter getting yelled at because of who she is." (Youth, Arizona)

This story reveals the range of solutions (from staying home from school to moving) that young people and their parents may take to address bias-based victimization. It also reveals the failure of exclusionary discipline to prevent future victimization. Taken together with other narratives, it creates a clear portrait of the ways that school policies and the adults that enforce them often fail to protect students. The onus to intervene fell on the shoulders of youth, and, when fought to protect themselves, they were punished and pushed out of school. Youth may also be forced to transfer, drop out, or attend an alternative school when their current school fails to support them.

MULTIPLE FACTORS THAT PROPEL PUSH-OUT

While participants indicate that school-based victimization leads to push-out, their stories also reflect a number of intersecting factors that sometimes contribute to their pathways out of school: compromised mental health (sometimes as a result of school experiences); learning challenges; and family problems or homelessness. First, for some youth, emotional trauma is a result of feeling unwelcome in school. One youth reports: "One girl she got bullied really bad … and she ended up having like a really bad nervous breakdown and like attempted suicide at school … she didn't come to school anymore after that" (Youth, Georgia). Push-out may also lead to encounters with the justice system:

> So I think that both the emotional and mental effect of being excluded from school and being criminalized for minor misbehavior … makes you fall behind in school. You may

> either drop out or you may be put on some sort of academic probation ... where it's easier for schools to push you out or expel you. Or you may be spending some time at home while you're expelled or on the streets, which may be getting you into other like illicit activities ... that end you up in jail (Adult, Colorado).

One adult in Louisiana illustrates how the pipeline works:

> The more you're out of school, very specifically if you're a young, black male with special education ... the more disengaged you get in school, the more disenfranchised you get about your opportunities in schools, and so then you drop out. While you are out, you get picked up 'cause you're standing outside or your friends who don't go to school say "come on let's go somewhere," and you know all manner of bad decisions happen.

Once youth have been detained, the school to prison pipeline becomes more of a reality, especially when probation requirements conflict with students' ability to attend school. One adult from California explained the dilemma of probation: probation requires youth to go to school, but, if it is not safe, they end up violating their probation in order to protect themselves.

This cycle disproportionately affects youth with multiple underrepresented identities:

> I think that when you're talking about the school-to-jail push out, you do need to consider every piece of someone's identity. So if you're a youth of color and you're also LGBT, you are at a higher risk of being pushed out of school because of your identities and because of the racism ... and homophobia within our school system. (Adult, Colorado)

Another adult describes how systemic oppression multiplies for youth: "For gender non—conforming youth and LGBT youth of color, [it] is really a multiplying effect of the different types of institutional barriers that are impacting their ability to succeed" (Adult, California).

In addition to school, many youth face rejection at home. This rejection can have profound implications for youth that do encounter the police. One California adult explains:

> So then if they do end up getting citations or ending up in the police department ... and if they're queer and have issues with ... their parents and they don't get claimed, then they end up staying one or two nights in jail just because they don't have a supportive parent. Once they do engage with law enforcement as juveniles, the parents and their relationships to their guardian plays a much more impactful role than if they were straight.

When neither schools nor families claim youth, they may be held for longer than necessary and end up in detention centers:

> A lot of LGBTQ youth that I work with have been placed in detention centers for non-violent crimes or status offenses, so for truancy, being put out of home, being held in contempt

> for court, for not going to meetings for families in need of services … a lot of them end up in jail for pretty much not even committing a crime. (Adult, Colorado)

Another adult notes that just being homeless could be grounds for arrest: "They were on the streets because they'd been kicked out of their homes … they were getting picked up for hustling, but more often than not they were just getting picked up because they were homeless youth on the street" (Adult, District of Colombia).

Homelessness is considered the "crux of the pipeline" and, according to one participant, "the number one indicator of whether a young person will get connected to the juvenile justice system" (Adult, District of Colombia.). Homelessness is critical for LGBTQ youth because, once youth are on the street, they must find ways to survive and prioritize survival over school.

> A lot of our trans youth are homeless, so when they drop out of school, it's not necessarily just due to discrimination at school, it's also to survive so as a trans youth. … they're not able to work to support themselves, so they engage in alternative ways of getting income. (Adult, Louisiana)

One adult advocate describes a youth who dropped out of a GED program: "She actually was straight up, like, 'I'm homeless' and 'I can't satisfy school and my education right now, it's just so far from, that's just not my top my concern at all'" (Adult, Louisiana). Many LGBTQ youth would rather stay on the streets than return to families that are "… not affirming."

These narratives from youth and adults identify the multiple barriers that make it difficult to impossible for youth to complete their education. While some youth are sent to alternative schools, others may find themselves on the streets due to school push-out, family rejection, or both. When schools "out" youth to unsupportive families, those youth often end up homeless because their families have either kicked them out or it becomes too traumatic to live with rejecting families. Time on the street and homelessness place immeasurable burdens on youth to fend for themselves to survive; they are vulnerable to arrest whether or not they are engaged in illicit activities. The lack of family support and financial means may result in more time spent in detention than is warranted. These factors, along with a lack of support for LGBTQ youth's self-expression and self-protection, work individually and collectively to create multiple pathways that lead youth through the school to prison pipeline.

DISCUSSION AND CONCLUSION

This study adds to the limited research on LGBTQ youth and the school to prison pipeline by using narratives to identify several pathways that push LGBTQ youth out of school. While participants spanned several states across the United States, all representing different sociopolitical and cultural contexts, similar stories emerged from both youth and adults. Based on participant knowledge and experience, our findings indicate that actual or perceived sexual and/or gender identity impacts discipline experiences in school. The narratives reveal that LGBTQ and gender nonconforming youth are under particular scrutiny in schools; their presence and actions, especially when not conforming to gender norms, often result in punishment and victimization which may be ignored or even encouraged by educators and administrators.

Educators and administrators also tend to enforce school policies unequally in the case of LGBTQ youth. For instance, the threat of punitive punishment for PDA is real for LGBTQ youth. Sometimes youth in the study had expressed affection toward their partner; other times, they were considered guilty despite the evidence. Rumors regarding LGBTQ youth may be disproportionately attended to and believed by school administration. Similarly, youth who did not follow traditional gender norms were punished for dress code violations. Youth in these situations were often viewed as or targeted for being problematic or aggressive. Within this study, multiple examples were given to document the use of exclusionary discipline (e.g., suspension, expulsion) for PDA and self-expression that was clearly biased toward LGBTQ youth. Surveillance, "shame-based" responses, and punitive punishment facilitate push-out and entry into the pipeline.

While youth reported frequent school-based victimization, they also expressed a lack of support from teachers, staff, and administration. In effect, LGBTQ youth who are mistreated learn to mistrust school administration and staff, leading some youth to keep their backgrounds and experiences to themselves even when requested to tell their side of the story. Without this support, youth reported fighting back to protect themselves and/or becoming truant to escape victimization, making them susceptible to exclusionary punishment. Disparate treatment in school can also create problems for youth at home, especially if students are outed by school administrators. The failure of school policies and practices (and the adults that enforce them) to support LGBTQ youth and the problematizing of LGBTQ youth in schools mimics Fine's (1986; 1991) framework of school push-out and Giroux's (2003) characterization of disposable youth. Youth that are viewed as problems and not "worth saving" become disposable. Once disposable, it is likely that youth will transfer (typically to alternative schools), drop out, get their GED, or end up involved in the justice system. These pathways are similar to that of urban youth who may be encouraged to drop out and obtain their GEDs, a process that is often misrepresented as an easier track than high school completion (Fine, 1991; Tuck, 2012).

In this process, some youth get caught in the juvenile justice system. Though few of these narratives emerged in this study, in part due to the focus on youths' school experiences, other studies have found that, while LGBTQ youth represent only 5–7% of the youth population, they represent 13–15% of the juvenile justice population (Majd et al., 2009). Disproportionate rates as these require further investigation into how the school system facilitates entry to prison (Mitchum & Moodie-Mills, 2014) in spite of "good intentions" by school administrators and teachers to provide equal access to education (Fine, 1991). While it is clear that discipline varies for LGBTQ youth, it is also clear that when school discipline is exclusionary, youth are vulnerable to the pipeline. This vulnerability is exacerbated by family rejection, homelessness, and other forms of discrimination youth may encounter. Because LGBTQ youth experience discipline disparities (Himmelstein & Bruckner, 2011) and are overrepresented in the homeless population (Cochran, Stewart, Ginzler, & Cauce, 2002) as well as the juvenile justice system (Majd et al., 2009), a strong case is made for the need of coalitional efforts to reduce disparities and intervene in the production of the pipeline (Snapp & Licona, in revision). We argue, however, that schools can serve as a "firewall" that stops the flow of the pipeline for youth who may face multiple forms of oppression and marginalization. This does not mean all school discipline is treated equally, but it does draw attention to the harm done by exclusionary and punitive discipline, particularly for nonmajority youth. It also highlights the need for additional research regarding other forms of discipline that may not exclude but still punish youth. For instance, detention, suspension, and expulsion (all forms of exclusionary discipline) likely have varying effects on young people's ability to learn and succeed in school. However, other forms of discipline may be less obvious but still have lasting effects, such as being regularly sent out of class for self-expression. It is clear that while this form of punishment is less severe, it also constrains youth's ability to learn. Future research is needed to disentangle how varying forms of discipline may be differentially associated with pathways through the pipeline.

This study is one of the first to illustrate how LGBTQ youth experience discipline disparities, establishing that LGBTQ youth are part of the *pipeline population*. Our chapter recounts the ways in which LGBTQ youth experience differential treatment that can lead to school push-out. A major limitation is the study's sample size, which included LGBTQ youth from three states that were connected to GSAs or other youth-serving organizations, and adults from seven states with diverse knowledge about the school to prison pipeline. Having participants from markedly different locations gave us a range of responses in which to understand the school to prison pipeline. For instance, youth and adults represented diverse contexts and settings (e.g., urban vs. rural) in which school discipline policies and practices vary widely. However, given we did not have a nationally representative sample, we are limited in our capability to generalize these findings to youth across the United States. Further, critiques have been made regarding sampling of LGBTQ people from GSAs such that these organizations may attract youth with more severe experiences of discrimination (Savin-Williams, 2001). Upon concluding our research on this topic, we suspect that students in GSAs may actually fend better than their non-GSA peers as GSAs provide strong sources of support and advocacy, particularly around school discipline (GSA Network, 2013). Given the multiple pathways of the school to prison pipeline, we acknowledge that our scope of the harshness students may experience is limited by the narratives we drew regarding youths' in-school experiences. Had we recruited youth who were already in juvenile detention or homeless, it is likely the complexities to these pathways would have emerged. Future research could broaden the sample by recruiting youth from the general public (see McCormack, 2014). Relatedly, youth have intersecting and fluid identities and contexts influence the variety of their experiences. The focus of this study was on LGBTQ youth, but it is important to remember that other youth also constitute the pipeline, such as pregnant and parenting teens (Fine & McClelland, 2006) and undocumented youth (Snapp & Licona, in revision).

Others have noted the importance of adding sexuality and gender to research on the school to prison pipeline (Mitchum & Moodie-Mills, 2014), as it remains underground in work on educational justice (Meiners, 2011) and absent from the Department of Education's data collection on school discipline (Hunt & Moodie-Mills, 2012). Narratives that delineate the experiences of LGBTQ youth help further this goal, illuminating disciplinary disparities that are often undocumented and highlighting new opportunities to challenge inequity in schools. Future work could include a broader range of youths' narratives and link those to specific discipline policies and practices in specific schools/regions, as culture and context most certainly have varied implications for youth. This would allow for a greater understanding of the critical moments in which youth may enter various pathways through the school to prison pipeline.

Narratives arising from our interviews and focus groups support the claim that LGBTQ youth are vulnerable to disproportionate punishment in schools. Frequently targeted for their actual or perceived identities, LGBTQ youth often experience hostile school climates and biased treatment. Further investigation of the discipline experiences of LGBTQ youth is necessary to understand ways schools can disrupt inequitable educational outcomes, move beyond "good intentions" of schools (Fine, 1991), and prevent youth from ever entering the pipeline.

REFERENCES

American Psychological Association Zero Tolerance Task Force. (2008). Are zero tolerance policies effective in the schools?: An evidentiary review and recommendations. *American Psychologist, 63*, 852–862. doi: 10.1037/0003-066X.63.9.852

Charmaz, K. (2000). Grounded theory: Objectivist and constructivist methods. In: N. K. Denzin & Y. S. Lincoln (Eds.), *Handbook of qualitative research* (2nd ed., pp. 509–535). Thousand Oaks, CA: Sage.

Cochran, B. N., Stewart, A. J., Ginzler, J. A., & Cauce, A. M. (2002). Challenges faced by homeless sexual minorities: Comparison of gay, lesbian, bisexual, and transgender homeless adolescents with their heterosexual counterparts. *American Journal of Public Health, 92*(5), 773–777.

Dignity in Schools Campaign. (2014). *Student, parent and teacher groups speak out on federal school discipline guidance released today.* Retrieved from http://www.dignityinschools.org/press-release/student-parent-and-teacher-groups-speak-out-federal-school-discipline-guidance-release

Eng, J. (2012, September 4). Dynasty Young, gay teen expelled for filing stun gun at school, sues Indianapolis district. *NBC News.* Retrieved from http://usnews.nbcnews.com/_news/2012/09/04/13661434-dynasty-young-gay-teen-expelled-for-firing-stun-gun-at-school-sues-indianapolis-district

Fine, M. (1986). Why urban adolescents drop into and out of public high school. *The Teachers College Record, 87*, 393–409.

Fine, M. (1991). *Framing dropouts: Notes on the politics of an urban high school.* New York, NY: SUNY Press.

Fine, M., & McClelland, S. I. (2006). Sexuality education and desire: Still missing after all these years. *Harvard Educational Review, 76*, 297–338.

Garnette, L., Irvine, A., Reyes, C., & Wilber, S. (2011). Lesbian, gay, bisexual, and transgender (LGBT) youth and the juvenile justice system. In F. T. Sherman & F. H. Jacobs (Eds.), *Juvenile justice: Advancing research, policy, and practice* (pp. 156–173). Hoboken, NJ: John Wiley & Sons.

Gay Straight Alliance Network. (2013). *GSA network statement in support of restorative approaches to school discipline.* Retrieved from http://www.gsanetwork.org/news/gsa-network-statement-support-restorative-approaches-school-discipline/100213

Giroux, H. (2003). Racial injustice and disposable youth in the age of zero tolerance. *International Journal of Qualitative Studies in Education, 16*, 553–565. doi: 10.1080/0951839032000099543

Golgowki, N. (2014, January 9). Transgender teen bullied at school faces criminal charges for fight which only suspended other girls. *The New York Daily News.* Retrieved from http://www.nydailynews.com/news/national/bullied-transgender-teen-faces-criminal-charges-fight-article-1.1571349

Himmelstein, K., & Bruckner, H. (2011). Criminal justice and school sanctions against nonheterosexual youth: A national longitudinal study. *Pediatrics, 127*, 49–57. doi: 10.1542/peds.2009–2306

Hunt, J., & Moodie-Mills, A. (2012). *The unfair criminalization of gay and transgender youth.* Washington, DC: Center for American Progress.

LeCompte, M. D. (2000). Analyzing qualitative data. *Theory into Practice, 39*, 146–154. doi: 10.1207/s15430421tip3903_5

Legate, N., Ryan, R. M., & Weinstein, N. (2012). Is coming out always a "good thing"? Exploring the relations of autonomy support, outness, and wellness for lesbian, gay, and bisexual individuals. *Social Psychological and Personality Science, 3*, 145–152. doi: 10.1177/1948550611411929

Majd, K., Marksamer, J., & Reyes, C. (2009). *Hidden injustice: Lesbian, gay, bisexual, and transgender youth in juvenile courts.* San Francisco, CA: Legal Services for Children, National Juvenile Defender Center, and National Center for Lesbian Rights.

Massachusetts Department of Elementary and Secondary Education (2006). *Massachusetts youth risk behavior survey results.* Retrieved from http://www.doe.mass.edu/cnp/hprograms/yrbs/05/default.html.

CHAPTER ELEVEN

Warehousing, Imprisoning, AND Labeling Youth "Minorities"

NEKIMA LEVY-POUNDS

INTRODUCTION

As the 2012 presidential election made clear, America is a nation divided by issues of race and class. Although media pundits characterized this division as a new phenomenon, the reality is that while America has grown more diverse in recent decades, it has never fully come to terms with its complex and painful racial history. This racial history is one in which Native Americans and African Americans, among other racial and ethnic groups, have long suffered under the weight of oppression, degradation, legally enforced segregation, violence, and inequitable access to economic opportunity and high-quality education. While many laws have been enacted to address some of the myriad harms and injustices that these groups have experienced, there remains significant work to be done in the fight for racial justice and equality.

In spite of the tremendous gains that were realized during the Civil Rights movement of the 1950s and 1960s, African Americans continue to lag behind whites in key quality of life indicators such as annual household income, net worth, rates of home ownership, and educational attainment, to name a few (Bowman, 2010). African Americans are much more likely to live in poverty than their white counterparts and are over-represented in the criminal justice system, with black males making up nearly 40% of the more than two million people who are currently incarcerated in the United States (Carson & William, 2012). The high rate of poverty experienced by African Americans, coupled with high rates of involvement in the criminal justice system, has served to cripple and destabilize the African American community and has caused a major shift in family structure and household composition. The mass incarceration of African American males has led to erosion within the African American family. As large numbers of African American men began entering the prison system in droves in the mid-1980s as a result of the war on drugs, African American women and children were left behind, which created a significant imbalance within families and communities (Levy-Pounds, 2010). This imbalance has led to tens, if not hundreds, of thousands of black children without access to a male role model or father figure.

Recent statistics show that 1 in 3 African American households is being headed by single women, the highest rate of any racial group (Bowman, 2010). The historical injustices and discrimination they have experienced, coupled with the current imbalance in black household composition, has resulted in higher rates of child poverty among African American children. According to the Children's Defense Fund (2012), "The 4.4 million Black children (more than one in three) living in poverty in 2010 represented an increase of over 329,000 since 2009 and over 780,000 since 2000." They also report that African American children under age 5 have the highest rate of child poverty, with 45.5% of them being poor compared with a rate of poverty of 14.6% for white children. Overall, roughly 40% of African American children are born into poverty, in comparison with 8% of white children (Children's Defense Fund, 2010). Further complicating this scenario is the fact that the majority of these families are concentrated in poor, marginalized communities in inner cities across America, where there is limited opportunity to interface with mainstream society in a productive manner (Levy-Pounds, 2007).

The lack of opportunity to navigate and network within mainstream society results in perpetual marginalization, with little hope of obtaining upward economic mobility and social acceptance, while fostering a greater likelihood of coming into contact with the criminal justice system (Levy-Pounds, 2010). Contrary to popular belief, the multifaceted and long-standing challenges that African Americans face do not merely disappear when African American children enroll in and attend public schools. In fact, the social and economic problems faced by African American children and families are often magnified when they come into contact with the public school system and are actually exacerbated in many circumstances. This occurs in part owing to the current structure and models upon which traditional public school systems are based, which often fail to take into account the unique historical and contemporary circumstances that African American children face. Without a proper framework that is organized and developed with a sensitivity toward the unique circumstances of poor children of color, public schools may unwittingly fall into the trap of improperly punishing children who do not easily fit within the mainstream model of public education and pushing them out of the public school system and into the criminal justice system (Darensbourg, Perez, & Blake, 2010).

The dangerous combination of the public school system's practices of disproportionately suspending, expelling, warehousing, labeling, and imprisoning youth of color has led to a crisis in public education, more commonly known as the school to prison pipeline (NAACP Legal Defense and Educational Fund, 2005). This chapter argues that a paradigm shift in public education is urgently needed to dismantle the school to prison pipeline and to ensure equity for all children, especially poor children of color.

THE SCHOOL TO PRISON PIPELINE IS ALIVE AND WELL IN AMERICA

In 1954, Thurgood Marshall argued vigorously before the United States Supreme Court that separate schools for black children and white children were inherently unequal and in violation of the Equal Protection clause of the Fourteenth Amendment of the U.S. Constitution. The Supreme Court's holding in the famous case, known as *Brown vs. the Board of Education* (*Brown v. Board*, 1954), upended decades of legally enforced segregation in the United States and helped pave the way for the great gains of the Civil Rights movement that further rang the death knell of Jim Crow segregation throughout the South and parts of the North (Firelight Media, 2004).

What followed this unprecedented decision was upheaval, racial violence directed toward African Americans, federal intervention in school desegregation attempts, massive protests, and ultimately busing of black children into white public school districts. While many saw school desegregation as a major cause célèbre in light of its potential to place blacks and whites on equal educational footing, some were concerned that local black schools bore the brunt of this racial experiment, as many of these schools were forced to close down and black teachers lost their jobs en masse. Regardless of how one views the decision and resulting outcomes of *Brown v. Board*, it is important to examine whether the spirit of *Brown v. Board* and its potential for racial progress in public education continues to exist or whether the discrimination and unequal treatment brought to light in *Brown v. Board* has merely taken on a different form within our public education system. Recent statistics and trends support the latter conclusion (Bell, 1997; Douglass Horsford, 2011).

In examining the current state of public education in the United States, there is certainly cause for concern with respect to the lower levels of educational attainment being obtained by poor children of color. This includes higher dropout rates among African American, Latino, and Native American children, higher rates of referrals to special education for African American males in particular, and high rates of referrals to the juvenile justice system for children of color by public school officials and school resource officers (SROs). It appears that poor children of color are in danger of failing within the public school system, which in turn limits their opportunities to obtain a college education and achieve upward social and economic mobility (Knaus, 2007).

To make matters worse, poor children of color are more likely to attend under-performing and under-resourced schools that are largely segregated along race and class lines (Biddle & Berliner, 2002). These children are also less likely to have high-caliber teachers and educational experiences that will enhance the learning environment and educational outcomes (Children's Defense Fund, 2010, p. 6). The curriculum is often outdated and out of synch with the cultural backgrounds and frames of reference in which the students can relate, and they are often viewed and labeled as "minorities," a term that bespeaks of being less than or inferior to mainstream white society.

In arguing the case of *Brown v. Board*, Thurgood Marshall worked tirelessly to demonstrate that segregated black schools that were concentrated in poor, inner-city neighborhoods were inherently unequal in comparison with segregated white schools in more affluent communities that seemed to be able to provide the best of everything to their pupils. Although the Court in *Brown v. Board* struck down legally sanctioned racial segregation in public education, it appears that a new system of segregation was constructed in its place—this time based on race, class, and geography, as opposed to race alone, and yet the results have had similar effects within the public school system ("Is Segregation Back," 2012). It is difficult to fathom that in the more than five decades since *Brown v. Board* was decided public schools continue to be racially segregated, with tremendous consequences to boot. Sadly, poor children of color who attend public schools are still obtaining an education that is both separate and unequal in comparison with their white counterparts (Knaus, 2007). As American society continues to increase in diversity, the lack of equality in public education will have a powerful ripple effect throughout our society and may threaten our nation's ability to compete on a global scale in the near future.

Although the public school system should serve as an institution that works to assist our nation's youths in becoming successful, contributing members of society, in its current form it has at times facilitated the warehousing, imprisoning, and marginalizing of youth of color. These children are disproportionately placed or "warehoused" in lower quality, alternative learning centers (ALCs) or positioned on a special education track that may result in increased marginalization and educational inequality (Center for Civil Rights Remedies, 2013). As stated by a 20-year-old African American man named Sidiq during a recent conversation: "I was referred to an ALC because the public school [I previously attended] wanted to keep a reputation about their [high] graduation rates. Since I was locked up during my junior year and my sophomore year, I barely did any work. I had to make up a year of credits, plus my senior year. I sought help from a guidance counselor who told me that I was on track to graduate, but then as the year went on, I realized that I could not make up my credits in time. So I switched out and went to an alternative school" (S. Abdullah, personal communication, November 20, 2012).

In reflecting upon his experience, Sidiq lamented, "ALCs do things to keep people in there. They wanted to put me in one ALC over the other, even though I would not have received the correct number of credits, which would have delayed my progress." Sidiq shared that after being enrolled for a short period of time, he found that it was in his best interest to withdraw from the ALC and attend a local charter school instead. One of the things that Sidiq noted about the ALC was that although there were much smaller class sizes in comparison to his previous school, most of the students in the ALC were youth who had been expelled from other schools and/or had entanglements with the juvenile justice system. Sidiq noticed that all of the students in the ALC he attended were African American and most were young men. However, none of his teachers was a person of color. Fortunately, with the help of supportive adults in the community, Sidiq was able to make up his credits over a two-year period of time and graduate from the charter school that he attended. He is now enrolled in college to pursue his Associate's degree in Business Management, a feat that he had not previously believed he could accomplish, given the challenges that he faced in school and in the juvenile justice system (S. Abdullah, personal communication, November 20, 2012).

In light of the public school system's shrinking resources and the high-stakes testing environment that currently exists (largely owing to the policies of No Child Left Behind), public schools have a built-in incentive to intentionally exclude youth who are perceived as underperforming, or who have underlying mental health issues, learning disabilities, and/or behavioral concerns. The negative perceptions about such youth tend to weigh more heavily against African American children in general and African American males in particular (Knaus, 2007).

Youth of color experience marginalization and exclusion through the public school system's disproportionate use of disciplinary measures such as suspensions and expulsions, often for behavior that is nonviolent and not serious enough to warrant such punitive responses. A disproportionate number of these children are labeled as juvenile delinquents and offenders for behavior that is in many cases consistent with typical youthful indiscretions. To put this into perspective, a policy statement of the American Academy of Pediatrics notes, "In 1997, of the 3.1 million students who were suspended, only 10% had been suspended for possession of a weapon. Most of the offenses for which students were expelled were nonviolent, noncriminal acts" (as cited by Committee on School Health, 2003). As one might imagine, the stakes are much higher for youth of color who are perceived as being defiant and anti-social, or who exhibit behaviors that are viewed as negative. Rather than being placed on a pathway to college, many of these children wind up in a pipeline to prison instead. The NAACP Legal Defense and Educational Fund (LDF) describes the situation in this manner:

> In the last decade, the punitive and overzealous tools and approaches of the modern criminal justice system have seeped into our schools, serving to remove children from mainstream educational environments and funnel them onto a one-way path toward prison. These various policies, collectively referred to as the School-to-Prison Pipeline, push children out of school and hasten their entry into the juvenile, and eventually the criminal, justice system, where prison is the end of the road. (NAACP LDF, 2005)

NAACP LDF goes on to say, "Historical inequities, such as segregated education, concentrated poverty, and racial disparities in law enforcement, all feed the pipeline. The School-to-Prison Pipeline is one of the most urgent challenges in education today." The school to prison pipeline occurs in large part as a result of the adoption of zero tolerance policies by many public schools and other policies that harshly penalize typical childlike behavior. When students violate these policies, they can be suspended, expelled, or referred to SROs, who are an increasing presence in inner-city high schools and who have the full force and authority of the law behind them to make arrests when a youth is perceived to have broken the law (NAACP LDF, 2005). Even some middle schools now increasingly employ the services of SROs, who have the authority to remove children from school grounds for behavioral concerns. SROs also have the power to issue citations and may ultimately arrest youths and transport them to juvenile detention facilities, where they may be detained until their first court appearance. It is not uncommon to hear of SROs pepper-spraying students in certain circumstances, and there have also been cases in which SROs have used Tasers on unarmed students (Chute & Smydo, 2009; Geronimo & Kim, 2009). When discussing whether he witnessed any impacts from having SROs in his public school, Sidiq responded by saying, "During my time at a public high school, I saw at least two students—a boy and a young lady—being led away in handcuffs by police officers. It didn't really seem unusual because we had at least one or two officers in the school" (S. Abdullah, personal communication, November 20, 2012).

The increasing use of SROs on public school grounds over the past two decades represents a fundamental shift in how public schools handle school misconduct issues. Occurrences such as school fights and other behavioral matters are now often handled through an SRO rather than solely as a school administrative matter, as in previous years. These policies tend to weigh more heavily against children of color (Geronimo & Kim, 2009).

While research shows that children's brains do not fully develop until they reach early adulthood, in many ways children are held to an adult standard of conduct and are harshly punished or labeled if they fail to meet this standard. As the use of SROs in public schools continues to increase, more and more poor children of color will end up in the juvenile justice system based on school referrals. According to the New York Civil Liberties Union:

> The School to Prison Pipeline (STPP) is a nationwide system of local, state, and federal education and public safety policies that pushes students out of school and into the criminal justice system. The system disproportionately targets youth of color and youth with disabilities. Inequities in areas such as school discipline, policing practices, high-stakes testing, wealth and healthcare distribution, school "grading" systems, and the prison-industrial complex all contribute to the Pipeline. (*School to Prison Pipeline*, 2009)

School disciplinary and referral policies arguably play the greatest role in determining which children will be suspended, expelled, and referred to the justice system, and often for minor infractions. Unfortunately, such policies tend to weigh against children of color and children with learning disabilities (Children's Defense Fund, 2010). When recounting his experience of facing discipline as a public school student, Sidiq recalled: "If you got detention and didn't go, then you would be assigned Saturday school. If you didn't go to Saturday school, you would be assigned to in-school suspension the whole day, which means you would sit in detention and miss a whole day of classes. This happened lots of times. I always thought it was dumb. The school was mad at me for being late to class and then I'm being pulled out of class for a whole day. During in-school suspension, most of the people would just sit there doing nothing. About 95% of the kids were African American. I went there a couple of times and then I said forget it. Anytime I would get caught, I would just walk the hallways all day" (S. Abdullah, personal communication, November 20, 2012). Sidiq's experience illustrates the disconnect that sometimes occurs between a school's disciplinary policy, the disproportionate application of said policy on African Americans, and the potentially negative impacts such policies have on a student's desire to remain engaged in the educational process for the long haul. In reflecting upon his experience, Sidiq also shared how the school would arbitrarily impose punitive responses to issues such as student tardiness without ever really identifying the root causes of a student's misbehavior or failure to abide by a school policy or rule.

For example, in Sidiq's situation, the challenges that he faced in school stemmed largely from the underlying impacts that living in poverty had on his life and the life of his family members. As Sidiq illustrated, "I always came to school with a lot of stuff on my mind. I came to school at times where we had no electricity for weeks. I did not care about talking to any of the teachers about it, because I really didn't have a connection to any of them. There were times when I would have to wake up early and iron my clothes with a large pot (by putting hot water in it and running it across my clothes) so that I wouldn't have to wear wrinkled clothes to school. I was embarrassed about my circumstances and didn't want anyone to know what I was going through" (S. Abdullah, personal communication,

November 20, 2012). For Sidiq, being disciplined for coming to school late under such circumstances made him feel as though the school did not really care about him or what he was facing, which eventually led to him become disengaged from the learning environment at school. Sidiq went on to say, "I didn't feel like the stuff that I was being taught in school mattered, so I lost interest in school. The material did not seem relevant to the things that were happening in our lives. Some of the classes were boring. I had several friends who dropped out of high school. They may have felt the same way that I felt. That school was not really relevant to their lives" (S. Abdullah, personal communication, November 20, 2012).

Although Sidiq's story is personal and based upon his unique circumstances, his story provides a clear example of how the traditional public school model is not designed to address some of the underlying social issues that students who grow up in poverty experience on a regular basis. It is clear from Sidiq's story that rushing to judgment and attempting to provide a punitive response to nonviolent student behavior is not the most effective way to keep young people engaged in and enthused about school. His story also demonstrates the importance of having teachers and counselors from diverse backgrounds who understand poverty-related issues and challenges being faced by the communities in which the students reside (S. Abdullah, personal communication, November 20, 2012).

Another important issue that deserves special attention relates to the disparate treatment experienced by those who have disabilities and underlying mental health issues in public school settings. A recent study showed that although just 8% of public school students were enrolled in special education in 2000, at the same time this group made up a whopping 32% of those in juvenile detention (NAACP LDF, 2005, p. 5). Disturbingly, racial patterns are apparent in examining the disparate treatment between different racial groups with learning disabilities. For example, the study found that African American students with learning disabilities were three times more likely to be suspended than their white counterparts. These students are also four times more likely to end up in the criminal justice system (*School to Prison*, 2009). Sadly, in many public schools, children may be suspended, expelled, or brought into the juvenile justice system for behavior that is consistent with an underlying disability (Miller et al., 2011, pp. 20–22).

An equally compelling concern that children of color face is being placed on a special education track that may relegate them to feeling that they have a second or even third class status within the public school system. Once children are placed on a special education track, it may be difficult for them to gain access to mainstream classes and opportunities to learn more advanced material in school. In recent years, scores of African American men have come forward to share their feelings of embarrassment and humiliation about being placed on a special education track, in spite of their capacity to learn and excel in public school classes.

As Christian, a 19-year-old African American male, illustrated during a recent discussion:

> I was in a "pass class." In a pass class, you have people who might have mental health issues and others that are disruptive. Students may fight each other. We don't do much. A lot of the time, we get to watch television if we are behaving correctly as an incentive. At my school, they used to buy us big bags of hot Cheetos to be on our best behavior. One hundred percent of my classmates were African American. Most of my teachers were white. I feel like I didn't learn anything. I still have challenges with things like writing, typing, and doing paperwork. I still have trouble with my penmanship. I have a hard time spelling and a hard time asking for help. (C. Bonner, personal communication, November 20, 2012)

Unfortunately, Christian's circumstances of being placed on a special education track are not unique. This is a scenario that plays itself out all too often within the public school setting in which white children are more likely to be referred to gifted and talented programs and advanced placement opportunities, while black children and other children of color are more likely to be referred to special education where they are relegated to what some consider an inferior status. This can be especially damaging in situations in which a misdiagnosis has occurred and a child is inappropriately placed in special education. From Christian's perspective, "The public school system tosses children into the pass class or special ed. where children are not being taught what they need to be taught. Some of the kids have behavioral issues, but not learning disabilities, yet they are still being sent to the pass class. It does children a disservice and does not push them to work according to their full abilities" (C. Bonner, personal communication, November 20, 2012).

PUBLIC PERCEPTION OF YOUNG BLACK MEN AS CRIMINALS

It is difficult in today's society to watch the nightly news or to read the crime section of a newspaper without seeing young black men portrayed as criminals. The image of young black men as criminal is deeply embedded in the American psyche and, whether consciously or unconsciously, it seeps its way into public school policies and practices. The problem is exacerbated by the fact that school resource officers are often placed at public schools in inner-city communities in the name of protecting children and the public safety. This agenda often weighs against young black men, who are often the recipients of harsher punishment within public schools for nonviolent infractions such as talking back to a teacher, and are referred more often to school resource officers, who in turn make referrals to the juvenile detention center for matters that are many times best handled administratively within the schools system.

AFRICAN AMERICAN MALES ARE IN NEED OF EQUITABLE ENFORCEMENT OF CURRENT PROTECTIONS IN PUBLIC SCHOOLS

As demonstrated above, young African American males face unique circumstances and challenges within society, and therefore should be entitled to equitable enforcement of current protections within the public school system. Too often, young African American males are viewed as a threat to public safety, rather than as a group that disproportionately experiences negative outcomes on an ongoing basis. Young black men are frequently labeled as gang members because of their style of dress, the neighborhoods in which they reside, and their affiliations. These stereotypes are also manifested in public schools, where teachers and staff may be hypervigilant in labeling young men as gang members and advocating for their removal from the school district.

Recent statistics show that young African American males ages 16 to 24 have one of the highest rates of unemployment in the nation (Haynes, 2009). Experiencing higher rates of poverty and social isolation may account for part of the reason this group is substantially over-represented within the criminal justice system, as they may be more susceptible to committing survival crimes than their white counterparts. In addition, the occurrences of over-policing in inner-city communities as well as higher incidences of racial profiling contribute to greater rates of criminal justice involvement for this segment of the population. According to Bureau of Justice Statistics, African American prisoners were generally younger and imprisoned at higher rates than their white counterparts (Carson & Sabol, 2012). Young black men are also at greater risk of dying from homicide than natural causes compared with the general population, and they experience poverty at a disproportionate and alarming rate. In addition, according to the Children's Defense Fund, while a white boy born in 2001 has a 1 in 17 chance of going to prison in his lifetime, a black boy born in 2001 has an unfavorable 1 in 3 chance of going to prison in his lifetime (Children's Defense Fund, 2012). Further exacerbating the situation is the fact that 1 in 15 African American children currently has at least one parent who is incarcerated. Not surprisingly, as the prison population in the United States continues to expand, it is easy to predict that a growing number of black children will grow up with not one but both parents incarcerated. Sadly, the higher rates of poverty among African Americans coupled with lower rates of educational attainment play a tremendous role in fueling the pipeline to prison that currently exists for this segment of the population.

More than half of all African American men without a high school diploma go to prison at some point in their lives, further underscoring the importance of ensuring that the learning environment is engaging and not overly punitive or limiting to those who need access to education most (Gopnik, 2012). To illustrate the important link between education and incarceration, some states use fourth grade reading scores to predict the number of prison beds that they will need ten years into the future (Cohen, 2010). All of these factors taken together produce a great deal of stress and anxiety for young African American men, which plays a role in whether and how well they will be able to engage in the learning processes within the public school system (Darensbourg et al., 2010).

CONCLUSION

The statistical outlook for the future of young black men supports the conclusion that drastic action must be taken to break the debilitating cycles that these young men face and to reinvigorate the spirit and meaning behind the Supreme Court's decision in *Brown v. Board*, which declared that segregated schools were inherently unequal, in large part because of the widely disparate treatment that children of color experienced. When public schools unfairly label, exclude, and punish poor African American male students, they may be unwittingly opening the door to criminal justice involvement for this segment of the population and reinforcing the notion of racial inferiority that the ruling in *Brown v. Board* worked to dismantle (Knaus, 2007).

Thus, in order to properly contextualize the plight of young African American men in public schools today, it is important to examine the larger and more comprehensive societal picture that contributes to the negative outcomes these men experience and why a narrowly tailored approach within public school systems should be developed for ensuring not only their survival, but, more important, their success. Although schools do not bear full responsibility to correct the social conditions and the legacy of racial discrimination that has contributed to these challenges, schools are in a unique position to help break the cycles that these young men face that are directly linked to their academic success. At the very least, public school systems should be more discerning in their use of disciplinary measures and referrals to special education and the juvenile justice system in circumstances that do not warrant such harsh and inequitable responses.

REFERENCES

Bell, D. (1997). *Gospel choirs: Psalms of survival in an alien land called home*. New York: Basic Books.

Biddle, B., & Berliner, D. (2002, May). Beyond instructional leadership: A research synthesis/unequal school funding in the United States. *Educational Leadership, 59*(8). Retrieved from http://www.ascd.org/publications/educational-leadership/may02/vol59/num08/Unequal-School-Funding-in-the-United-States.aspx

Bowman, B. (2010, February 10). A portrait of black America on the eve of the 2010 Census. *The Root*. Retrieved from http://www.theroot.com/views/portrait-black-america-eve-2010-census

Brown v. Board of Education, 347 U.S. 483 (1954).

Carson, E., & Sabol, W. (2012, December). *Prisoners in 2011*. Washington, DC: Bureau of Justice Statistics. Retrieved from http://www.bjs.gov/content/pub/pdf/p11.pdf

Center for Civil Rights Remedies. (2013, April 6). *Closing the school discipline gap: Research to practice*. Los Angeles, CA: The Civil Rights Project. Retrieved from http://civilrightsproject.ucla.edu/events/2013/closing-the-school-discipline-gap-conference-research-papers/copy_of_closing-the-school-discipline-gap-agenda

Children's Defense Fund. (2012). *Portrait of inequality, 2012*. Washington, DC: Author. Retrieved from data-publications/data/portrait-of-inequality-2011.html

Chute, E., & Smydo, J. (2009, June 14). Districts differ on police using Tasers in schools. *Pittsburgh Post-Gazette*. Retrieved from http://www.post-gazette.com/stories/news/education/districts-differ-on-police-using-tasers-in-schools-345762/

Cohen, S. (2010, December). A $5 children's book vs. a $47,000 jail cell—choose one. *Forbes*. Retrieved from http://www.forbes.com/sites/stevecohen/2010/12/25/a-5-childrens-book-vs-a-47000-jail-cell-choose-one/

Committee on School Health. (2003, November). Out-of-school suspension and expulsion. *Pediatrics, 112*(5), 1206–1209. Retrieved from http://pediatrics.aappublications.org/content/112/5/1206.full.pdf

Darensbourg, A., Perez, E., & Blake, J. (2010). Overrepresentation of African American males in exclusionary discipline: The role of school-based mental health professionals in dismantling the school to prison pipeline. *Journal of African American Males, 1*(3). Retrieved from http://journalofafricanamericanmales.com/wp-content/uploads/downloads/2010/09/Overrepresentation-of-African-American-Males-Alicia-Darensbourg-.pdf

Douglass Horsford, S. (2011). *Learning in a burning house: Educational inequality, ideology, and (dis) integration*. New York: Teachers College Press.

Firelight Media (Producer). (2004). *Beyond* Brown*: Pursuing the promise* [Film]. New York. Retrieved from http://www.pbs.org/beyondbrown/history/fullhistory.html

Geronimo, I., & Kim, C. (2009, August). *Policing in schools: Developing a governance document for schools resource officers in K–12 schools* [White paper]. New York: ACLU. Retrieved from https://www.aclu.org/pdfs/racialjustice/whitepaper_policinginschools.pdf

Gopnik, A. (2012, January 30). The caging of America: Why do we lock up so many people? *The New Yorker*. Retrieved from http://www.newyorker.com/arts/critics/atlarge/2012/01/30/120130crat_atlarge_gopnik

Haynes, V. (2009, November 24). Blacks hit hard by economy's punch. *The Washington Post*. Retrieved from http://articles.washingtonpost.com/2009–11–24/news/36811560_1_young-black-men-unemployment-rate-jobless-rate

Is segregation back in U.S. public schools? (2012, May 20). *The New York Times*. Room for Debate. Retrieved from http://www.nytimes.com/roomfordebate/2012/05/20/is-segregation-back-in-us-public-schools

Knaus, C. (2007, March). Still segregated, still unequal: Analyzing the impact of No Child Left Behind for African American students. *State of Black America*. National Urban League. Retrieved from http://www.berkeleyrep.org/school/images/Knaus.pdf

Levy-Pounds, N. (2007). From the frying pan into the fire: How poor women of color and children are affected by the sentencing guidelines and mandatory minimums. *Santa Clara Law Journal, 7*(2). Retrieved from http://digitalcommons.law.scu.edu/lawreview/vol47/iss2/2

Levy-Pounds, N. (2010, Summer). Can these bones live? A look at the impacts of the war on drugs on African American children and families. *Hastings Race and Poverty Law Journal, 7*(2), 353.

Losen, D., & Martinez, T. (2013, April 8). *Out of school and off track: The overuse of suspensions in middle and high schools.* Los Angeles, CA: The Civil Rights Project. Retrieved from http://civilrightsproject.ucla.edu/events/2013/closing-the-school-discipline-gap-conference-research-papers/copy_of_closing-the-school-discipline-gap-agenda

Miller, J., Ofer, U., Artz, A., Bahl, B., Foster, T., Phenix, T., et al. (2011). *Education interrupted: The growing use of suspensions in New York City's public schools.* New York Civil Liberties Union. Retrieved from http://www.nyclu.org/files/publications/Suspension_Report_FINAL_noSpreads.pdf

NAACP Legal Defense and Educational Fund. (2005, October 5). *Dismantling the school-to-prison pipeline.* New York: Author. Retrieved from http://www.naacpldf.org/files/case_issue/Dismantling_the_School_to_Prison_Pipeline.pdf

Roberts, A., & Springer, D. (2007). *Social work in juvenile and criminal justice settings.* Springfield, IL: Charles C. Thomas.

School to prison pipeline [Fact sheet]. (2009). New York Civil Liberties Union. Retrieved from http://www.nyclu.org/issues/youth-and-student-rights/school-prison-pipeline

Skiba, R. (2002, February 4). Special education and school discipline: A precarious balance. *Behavioral Disorders, 27*(2), 81–97. Retrieved from http://www.indiana.edu/~equity/docs/discipline_a_precarious_balance.pdf

St. George, D. (2012, March 6). Federal data shows racial gaps in school arrest. *The Washington Post.* Retrieved from http://articles.washingtonpost.com/2012–03–06/national/35446604_1_school-arrests-national-education-policy-center-enrollment

Warren, J., Gelb, A., Horowitz, J., & Riordan, J. (2012). *Pew report on the states.* Washington, DC: The Pew Charitable Trusts. Retrieved from http://www.pewstates.org/issues/public-safety-328137

CHAPTER TWELVE

Who Wants to Be Special?

Pathologization and the Preparation of Bodies for Prison

DEAN L. ADAMS AND ERICA R. MEINERS[1]

We come to writing and thinking through the tangled inter-relationships between schools, special education, and prisons from two different locations. Deanna has worked as a special education teacher, in a range of settings, for more than ten years and has taught in teacher education programs as well. For more than fifteen years Erica has taught people coming out of prisons and jails, participated in anti-prison movements, and also worked with teachers and people who are studying to become teachers. These experiences moved us to pay close attention to who is captured by "special education" discourses and the impact of these classifications.

Deanna: During my career as a special education teacher I have worked with many young people who were labeled as emotionally disturbed, "mentally retarded," mentally ill, at-risk, and juvenile offenders. Of these students 90% were African American or Latino, male, and of low socio-economic status. For example, from 1999 to 2003 I worked as a special education teacher in a juvenile detention center in central New York for boys ages 13 to 21 years old. There were twenty-five residents housed there and the residents were split into two teams based on educational records and psychological reports indicating their perceived intellectual functioning and academic abilities. Even though I was a special education teacher I taught history and health classes to all of the students, not just those on the

1 Deep thanks to the communities that support and challenge us and make this work and analysis possible.

"lower level" team. I noticed that all my students struggled academically but were motivated to do well. More than half of the students had been in special education prior to being incarcerated and 98% were African American and Latino from New York City and surrounding areas. Many of the students I worked with were labeled as emotionally disturbed or learning disabled, although I did have a few students who were labeled as having cognitive disabilities. Their school records, when we were able to get them, came in thick binders listing repeated behavioral offenses, such as disrespect for authority figures, physical altercations, as well as skipping school, which led to multiple suspensions. I began to question—why are so many black and brown students from special education classes in lockup?

In addition, as a special education teacher for homebound students, I worked with several kindergarten and first grade students who had been suspended from school for such things as being disrespectful to the teacher, refusing to comply with requests, throwing blocks, and injuring a teacher during an unwarranted restraint. The students would spend months at home waiting for an "outside evaluation" to take place or spaces in alternative programs to open up for them. During this time elementary students are entitled to five hours of instruction per week by a certified teacher and if they are in middle or high school they are entitled to ten hours per week. School districts are denying the students an equal educational opportunity when they fall further and further behind academically, are no longer able to perform at grade level, and are placed in segregated settings that focus on compliance rather than academics. From the beginning of their compulsory education, these students are judged, labeled, and sentenced to a segregated placement, one in which they will most likely remain throughout their school careers.

Erica: Two sets of experiences shaped my questions. First, as someone who teaches at a university and is responsible for working with teachers and folks interested in becoming teachers, I began to notice how the students in my classes naturalized special education classifications and these categories seemed timeless and impermeable to adjustment. Students spoke of these categories as static and as medical conditions that conferred a range of differential engagements. While we read about the problems with diagnosis of these categories, the racialized history of eugenics intimately linked to "special education," and the grotesquely disproportionate number of students of color in select educational disability categories, the belief in these classifications as "real" persisted. Of course, once I started noticing this in my classes, I realized that this adherence to the "realness" of any of these categories—Learning Disability or Behavior Disorder—was hardly exclusive to students in my classes. Mainstream media, people in my social circles, my family all generally understood these to be "real" scientific categories. There was a normal and also an abnormal.

Second, after teaching for twelve years in a high school for students who were formerly incarcerated, I have lost count of the number of people in this program who have told me, with boldness or shame, that they "can't learn" or "have a disability." Yet, throughout this program, these very same students would reveal that they were not unlike other groups of people—some had an ease for numbers and were excellent at calculations, others could produce a rhyme a minute, and a few could debate and engage the relevancy of the Three-Fifths Compromise as a lasting foundational frame for understandings of racialized U.S. citizenship. In short, their ability to learn has been undoubtedly harmed by years of isolation and forced exclusion from our public school systems, in part facilitated through a schooling system that shunted them from special education programs to school push-out, to under- or uneducation, and to our prisons system. Yet they, like many of us, were far more than the labels that they internalized, which always seem negative, broken, a failure. While it might seem too glib to construct this pathway, in order to be able to learn in this program many of the students have to actively unlearn their association of themselves with the categories of stupid, not smart, or not normal. Most of the time this task is not achievable during the course of a year.

Both of these experiences continue to push me to radically interrogate the construction of these categories and to continually ask, Who benefits from these classifications? Who does not, and why? And what are the costs of this state apparatus of normal?

THE SCHOOL TO PRISON PIPELINE

A significant body of literature in the United States has tracked the school to prison pipeline (STPP) (Browne, 2003; Duncan, 2000; Meiners, 2007; Simmons, 2009; Winn, 2010). The conception of the term "school to prison pipeline" aims to highlight a complex network of relations that naturalize the movement of youth of color from our schools and communities into under- or unemployment and permanent detention. The targeted undereducation of particular populations is nothing new. The United States has always tracked poor, non-white, non-able-bodied, non-citizens, and/or those non-gender-conforming or non-heterosexual toward under- or uneducation. The consequence of these educational policies resulted in access to non-living-wage work, participation in a permanent war economy, and/or permanent detention. White supremacy has always been central to our nation's public education system and to our carceral state. Educational scholar and activist Garrett Albert Duncan (2000) writes, "Far from being novel, today's prison industrial system is a variation on past educational and legal measures aimed at subjugating people of color in the U.S." (p. 36). While the educational outcomes are not new, the expansion of our prison nation in the United States over the past three decades has strengthened policy, practice, and ideological linkages between schools and prisons.

Organizing and research on the STPP typically identifies several key areas: disciplinary sanctions, criminalization of youth in schools, and problematic special education classifications. Research consistently demonstrates that disciplinary sanctions in schools disproportionately target youth of color who are routinely meted out for non-violent incidents. As summarized by Gregory, Skiba, and Noguera (2010), who surveyed available national research on disciplinary sanctions, schools actively target men of color: Males of all racial and ethnic groups are more likely than females to receive disciplinary sanctions. In 2004, only 1% of Asian Pacific Islander females were suspended compared with 11% of Asian Pacific Islander males. Expulsion data from that same year showed that white females were half as likely to be expelled as white males ($p < .001$), and similarly, Black females were half as likely to be expelled as Black males ($p < .05$) (Gregory et al., 2010, p. 60). Black males are especially at risk for receiving discipline sanctions, with one study showing that Black males were 16 times as likely as white females to be suspended (Gregory et al., 2010, p. 60). These gendered and racialized practices of removing students from an educational setting, the most dramatic educational sanction available, start before preschool. Important to note is that all the available data on suspensions indicate that suspensions do not improve academic achievement or students' behavior, and suspensions are not usually meted out for acts of violence. In one statewide study, "only 5% of all out-of-school suspensions were issued for disciplinary incidents that are typically considered serious or dangerous, such as possession of weapons or drugs. The remaining 95% of suspensions fell into two categories: disruptive behavior and other" (Losen & Skiba, 2010, p. 9).

Perhaps the most highly visible manifestation of the school to prison nexus is the criminalization of youth "misconduct" in schools. Most urban public schools have on-site police detachments that conduct drug tests and searches at schools, and the naturalization of this police presence creates a seamless and interlocking relationship between the school and the juvenile justice system. In Chicago public schools in 2010 there were 5,574 school-based arrests of juveniles under 18 years old on school property. Unsurprisingly, Black youth accounted for 74% of school-based juvenile arrests in 2010; Latino youth represented 22.5% of arrests (Kaba & Edwards, 2012). The New York Police Department released data in 2012 acknowledging that in the last three months of 2011, five students were arrested in New York schools every day, and these students were, again, disproportionately Black and Latino. Again, the majority of these students were arrested for "disorderly conduct" (New York Civil Liberties Union, 2012). Asserting and affirmatively challenging police conduct in schools is particularly salient when research demonstrates that one of the most popular reasons students are referred to juvenile courts is, again, subjective: "disorderly conduct" (Florida 2007–2008) and "disrupting schools" (South Carolina 2007–2008) (Hewitt, Losen, & Kim, 2010, p. 112).

Finally, as this chapter explores in more detail, the construction of the category of special education, plus the flexibility and circulation of special education classifications, continues to function to funnel youth of color toward under- and uneducation, and potential relationships with prisons and detention. Research highlights how students of color are overrepresented in "soft" disability categories (Harry & Klingner, 2006; McNally, 2003; Smith & Erevelles, 2004), warranting two formal investigations (1982, 2002) by the National Academy of Sciences. Classification as special education masks segregation, and pathologizing "students of color as disabled allows their continued segregation under a seemingly natural and justifiable label" (Reid & Knight, 2006, p. 19). Students labeled with these disabilities receive differential access to high-quality education, are not tracked toward college, experience higher rates of suspension and expulsion, and are disproportionately represented in juvenile justice prisons (Harry & Klingner, 2006; McNally, 2003). Not unlike the subjectivity of school-based disciplinary actions, in which disrespect or acting out moves children into the category of a disciplinary problem, a number of subjective factors are responsible for placing largely male youth of color in these soft disability categories (Harry & Klingner, 2006).

Racial "disproportionality" is threaded through all of these interlocking categories: school discipline, criminalization of youth, and special education. For example African American, Latino, and First Nations students are overrepresented in select "soft" disability categories and are subsequently targeted for suspension and expulsion. These same students are often pushed into alternative schools (because they have been suspended or expelled) or have been caught up in schools that are hyper-policed.

This chapter, grounded in our histories of working within and alongside the field of special education and our linkages and commitments to anti-prison and prison justice movements, offers a summary of the history of the development of the category of special education. This discussion includes an analysis of the flexibility of the category and how categories and classification systems for special education cannot be disentangled from ongoing ideologies of White supremacy. Second, we briefly outline the impact of this history and how it is intertwined with our carceral state. Students of color are not only misidentified in categories that do not fully support their academic and economic futures and track these youth toward the STPP, but the categories themselves are also deeply linked to racialized forms of capture completely intertwined with our prison nation. We close by highlighting national and local organizations working for change.

NEW FRAMES AND OLD STORIES OF THE SEGREGATION OF STUDENTS OF COLOR

African American, Latino, and First Nations youth are consistently overrepresented in special education, and classifications are malleable and have been manipulated to harm youth of color. While books have been written on this topic (for example, Winfield, 2007), we start by sketching an abbreviated history of the intersections of race, segregation, and disability in education.

In the late 1800s, researchers and scientists were using bodily measurements and skin color to determine where people from various cultures were placed on a hierarchical human ladder (Winfield, 2007). These ideas, eugenics, provided "science" for white supremacists to "prove" that non-white people were inferior. In 1892, Fredrick Hoffman published an article in which he had gathered vital statistics, including the infant mortality rate, death rate from disease caused by pauperism, criminality, and sexual immorality of African Americans and compared them with those of whites. Hoffman concluded that non-white people were not only inherently inferior, but were degenerating at a rapid pace and therefore putting a lot of effort or resources into social programs would not be beneficial because non-white people would eventually become extinct (Boeckmann, 2000). "Research" from Hoffmann's article was used in an essay published in 1900 in the *North American Review*, "Will Education Solve the Race Problem?" by John Straton, a professor at Mercer University in Macon, Georgia. Straton stated that the statistics from Hoffman were "so decisive; and judging from them, the educational work for the [N]egroes does not seem to be realizing the expectations based upon it" (cited in Boeckmann, 2000, pp. 17–18).

From 1920 through 1940, eugenicists striving for a racially and genetically "pure" society published propaganda in the form of films, literature, and state fair displays (Mitchell & Snyder, 2006). They were able to bring their propaganda into educational conferences and classrooms as scientifically based information that advanced the health and well-being of white children. This literature routinely justified segregation in schools as necessary to prevent the mixing of the races, as well as keeping "social degenerates" from preying on unsuspecting white children. Under the legitimating mantle of science, white supremacy moved into schools, curriculum, and, in particular, assessment tools. "Eugenics provided scientific legitimacy to racism by affiliating with and influencing the developing field of mental measurement" (Ferri & Connor, 2004, p. 67). These tests were used to measure intelligence, to prove racial superiority, and to identify people considered defective in some way. Intelligence tests validated "the eugenics idea that mental ability was innate and distributed along racial hierarchies" (Ferri & Connor, 2004, pp. 67–68). Specialists were trained and began working with schools to identify children who were "unfit" and to segregate them into ungraded classes (Ferri & Connor, 2004, p. 68). This was the beginning of special education, and the term "feeblemindedness" would encompass African Americans, immigrants, and the poor, who would be disproportionately represented in these special classes and schools (Ferri & Connor, 2004, pp. 66, 68). This prevailing framework of eugenics, or the belief in racial inferiority and the genetic basis of certain disabilities, particularly those that were seen as either intellectual or emotional disabilities, led to sorting children into specific educational settings, further justified by the use of intelligence testing.

Although the 1954 U.S. Supreme Court case *Brown v. Board of Education* is popularly thought to have ended racial segregation in schools, the white majority was able to keep students of color segregated through specialized instruction for students of color classified as having a deficit (Ferri & Connor, 2005). The sorting of students through tracking systems was set up by school districts after the 1954 *Brown* decision. That decision was supposedly made to improve educational opportunities for African American students, many of whom were reportedly experiencing a high rate of academic achievement problems compared with white students. However, ability tracking, based on standardized testing, resulted in the overrepresentation of African American students in the lower ability tracks (Reschly & Bersoff, 1999) and in special education classes, a practice that continues to this day. In 1955, schools in Washington, D.C., placed more than 24% of African American students in special education classrooms as opposed to white students, who made up only 3% of those classrooms (Ferri & Connor, 2005, p. 108).

The overrepresentation of African American students in particular special education categories did not go unnoticed. Starting in the 1960s, as civil action and grassroots advocacy increased, mainstream media covered the overrepresentation of African Americans in particular disability categories, and Congress became increasingly aware of the problem (Danforth & Smith, 2005; Garda, 2005). As the Office of Civil Rights (OCR) was charged with monitoring and enforcing Title VI, part of the Civil Rights Act of 1964, which "prohibits discrimination on the basis of race, color, and national origin in programs and activities receiving federal financial assistance" (42 U.S.C. § 2000d et seq.), the OCR collected data on school enrollment and student placement and was later given authority to monitor and enforce Section 504 of the Rehabilitation Act of 1973 (Russo & Talbert-Johnson, 1997). Section 504 states that

> no otherwise qualified individual with disabilities in the United States … shall solely by reason of his disabilities, be excluded from participation in, be denied the benefits of, or be subjected to discrimination under any program, or activity receiving Federal financial assistance. (29 U.S.C. 794 § 504)

Section 504 should have aided the OCR's efforts in addressing discrimination of minorities in school settings; however, through 1975 overrepresentation of minorities in segregated programs continued (Garda, 2005).

While the OCR had moderate success in enforcing de jure desegregation in southern schools, with the percentage of African American students in segregated settings being reduced from 98% in 1964 to 8.7% in 1972, the OCR was less successful in dealing with segregation taking place within schools (Glennon, 2002). The OCR was sued in 1970 by civil rights advocates for not enforcing Title VI in schools that were resistant to desegregation. In particular, segregation within schools flourished because the apparatus of special education, born in the waning era of de jure segregation in the United States, provided a "race neutral" cover for the reproduction of racialized and hetero-gendered ideologies of achievement and intelligence within schools. As Harry and Klingner (2006) state, "Sometime in the early 1970s, the special education movement and the desegregation movement officially collided. Those whom the society rejected, and excluded from its public schools, would meet in the special education setting" (p. 11). Most of the lawsuits for desegregation in the 1970s were brought under Title VI of the Civil Rights Act as cases of racial discrimination in education; however, the use of Title VI began to decline as disability laws took effect and grew in strength (Losen & Welner, 2002).

In 1975 Congress passed the Education of All Handicapped Children Act (EAHCA) when wrongful identification of minority students was thought to be "the major controversy in special education" (Russo & Talbert-Johnson, 1997, p. 140).[2]

According to Danforth and Smith (2005),

> The federal government estimated in 1975, at the time of the passage of the landmark Education for All Handicapped Children Act (Public Law 94-142) mandating special education across the nation, that 1.75 million children were being excluded from public education because of disability. (p. 27)

In order for students to access services in a public school setting, a classification was required. According to a study done by the National Rural Research and Personal Preparation Research Project in 1980, after P.L. 94–142 was enacted, there was a "478% increase in the number of students labeled emotionally disturbed (ED) in American public schools in less than 5 years" (as cited in Danforth & Smith, 2005, p. 27). Before this, a majority of these students were labeled as mentally retarded.

Between 1974 and 1978, the OCR documented overrepresentation of African Americans in "educable mentally retarded" classes. In 1979 the OCR established the Panel on Selection and Placement of Students in Programs

2 We use the term "minority" throughout this chapter, as this is a term that circulates throughout research within education to refer in particular to students of color. We recognize that this is a misleading and problematic term. In most urban U.S. school districts students of color, specifically Latino, African American, and Asian American students, constitute the overwhelming majority.

for the Mentally Retarded and found that the disproportionality could be attributed to test bias, although no single factor could be identified (Danforth & Smith, 2005). Tracking systems were set up by school districts after *Brown* to supposedly improve educational opportunities for African American students, many of whom were reportedly experiencing a high rate of achievement problems. Yet these practices of ability tracking, based on standardized testing, resulted in increasing the number of African American students placed in the categories that denote lower ability (Reschly & Bersoff, 1999); these practices continue to this day. Testing continues to justify placing students of color in segregated educational settings. Garda (2005) writes that "cultural discontent" is evident in the way white teachers refer African American students for more special education evaluations than do non-white teachers and that before school even begins, white teachers believe that they will refer an African American student for special education services (Garda, 2005, p. 1092). Research has shown that African Americans are referred to special education and labeled as "mentally retarded" (MR) 2.23 times more frequently than are white students, and 1.28 times more frequently for evaluation related to "severely emotionally disturbed" (SED) than are white students (Garda, 2005). Garda writes that "the statistics are so compelling that even the National Research Council concludes that that referral bias is 'a crucial influence in disproportionate minority representation'" (p. 1092).

These discriminatory practices of classification did not go unresisted. One of the best-known challenges to the use of IQ tests and overrepresentation of African Americans in special education classes happened in California. *Larry P. v. Riles* (1972, 1979, 1984, 1986) began as a class action suit in 1971 against the San Francisco Unified School District when it was discovered that African Americans made up 28.5% of the total student population, but 66% of those students were placed in classes for the educable mentally retarded (EMR) (Russo & Talbert-Johnson, 1997, p. 139). The case finally went to trial in 1977 before Judge Robert Peckham, who subsequently ruled that standardized intelligence tests

> are racially and culturally biased, have a discriminatory impact against black children, and have not been validated for the purpose of essentially permanent placements of black children into educationally dead-end, isolated, and stigmatizing classes for the so-called educable mentally retarded. (C-71–2270, FRP. Dis. Ct. [1979])

The case set the legal precedent against cultural bias in testing, indicating that tests taken by minority children must be norm-referenced and validated for use with that population.

Beyond the lawsuits, Congress did not fully acknowledge overrepresentation of African Americans in educational disability categories until the Individuals with Disabilities Education Act (IDEA) was reauthorized and amended in 1997. Congress amended the IDEA; Chapter 33 addressed specifically the problem of overrepresentation:

(A) Greater efforts are needed to prevent the intensification of problems connected with mislabeling and high dropout rates among minority children with disabilities.
(B) More minority children continue to be served in special education than would be expected from the percentage of minority students in the general school population.
(C) African-American children are identified as having intellectual disabilities and emotional disturbance at rates greater than their white counterparts.
(D) In the 1998–1999 school year, African-American children represented just 14.8 percent of the population aged 6 through 21, but comprised 20.2 percent of all children with disabilities.
(E) Studies have found that schools with predominately white students and teachers have placed disproportionately high numbers of their minority students into special education. (20 USC § 1400)

Yet despite this acknowledgment by Congress, the reauthorization of IDEA had little effect on the problem of racial disproportionality, and in a 2002 study conducted by the National Research Council researchers again confirmed that African Americans were overrepresented in special education programs (as cited in Garda, 2005, p. 1077).

In the 2004 reauthorization, IDEA was again amended and re-titled the Individuals with Disabilities Education Improvement Act (IDEIA) to align with No Child Left Behind (NCLB). At the time, President Bush stated,

> The Individuals with Disabilities Education Improvement Act of 2004 will help children learn better by promoting accountability for results, enhancing parent involvement, using proven practices and materials, providing more flexibility, and reducing paperwork burdens for teachers, states and local school districts. (New York State Education Department [NYSED], 2011)

The new IDEIA and the NCLB have provisions to specifically address overrepresentation of minorities in special education and to hold school districts accountable not only for overrepresentation but also for exclusionary practices such as suspensions and expulsions that lead to high drop-out rates (Losen, 2011). While schools are held to punishing accountability standards for standardized testing outcomes or teacher qualifications, the overrepresentation of kids of color in special education persists.

WHO BENEFITS? ASSESSING THE IMPACT OF SPECIAL EDUCATION CLASSIFICATION

As with any category under special education, there are complex consequences to the labeling. Particularly for the categories of emotional disturbance and other cognitive disabilities, the consequences are not positive. Students labeled with these disabilities are typically not tracked toward graduation or post-secondary education, are suspended and expelled at higher rates than students without these disabilities, and are disproportionately overrepresented in juvenile justice systems and prisons (Harry & Klingner, 2006; Losen & Orfield, 2002; McNally, 2003).

Merrell and Walker (2004) documented that students with emotional disturbance are more likely to be placed in restrictive settings; have a high drop-out rate; and within three years of leaving school, 50% of people who were formerly students identified as having an emotional disturbance have at least one arrest. Despite these data, the vast majority of research on overrepresentation of students of color in special educational categories does not address emotional disturbance or analyze various disabilities as distinct categories, including on the district and federal levels. As a consequence of the difficulty of acquiring these data, we highlight wider relationships between education, special education, and the forces of referral and suspensions that push some kids (but not others) out of school.

Of course, as previously highlighted, these classifications of emotional disturbance and cognitive and intellectual disabilities are not a ticket to academic or economic success. There is strong correlation between special education placement and school push-out and/or dropout. Kim and Losen (2010) say the following:

> Although only approximately 9 percent of students aged six to twenty-one have been identified as having disabilities that impact their ability to learn, a survey of correctional facilities found that nationally approximately 34 percent of youth in juvenile corrections had been previously identified as eligible for special education pursuant to the Individuals with Disabilities Education Act (IDEA). (p. 51)

Students of color placed with special education programs in schools are also sanctioned with greater frequency, and with harsher measures, by school discipline policies. Losen and Gillespie (2012) from the Civil Rights Project at the University of California at Los Angeles reported that even though every racial group was represented in the data on suspensions, none is as significant as the number of African American students: 1 out of every 6 Black students, as opposed to 1 out of 20 white students. In addition, their research further highlights that "students with disabilities are suspended about twice as often as their non-disabled peers. The rates for all racial groups combined are 13% for students with disabilities and 7% for those without disabilities" (p. 14) and the risk for African American students with disabilities being suspended "is a full 16 percentage points higher than for white students with disabilities" (Losen & Gillispie, 2012, p. 16). In any given school, students of color with disabilities are the most likely to receive the harshest school sanctions. According to the New York Civil Liberties Union (NYCLU, 2012), the Student Safety Act Report for 2011–2012 for New York City showed that 52.8% of Black students were suspended, and they made up 31% of the school population; likewise, 36% of

Latino/a students were suspended and they made up 40% of the population; and 32.3% of students with disabilities were suspended and they made up 12% of the population. Number one on the list of reasons for suspension was altercations/ physically aggressive behavior, followed by insubordination, horseplay, and percent level one behavior, which could be chewing gum or getting out of the seat without permission (NYCLU, 2012).

These statistics indicate that even with the protections given to students with disabilities under federal legislation such as Individuals with Disabilities Education Act (IDEA) and Section 504 of the Rehabilitation Act of 1973, schools struggle to support all students. Districts continue to push students with disabilities, especially those of color, out of school and deny them the right to a free and appropriate education. This push-out of students with disabilities transpires on a school terrain where youth of color are already disproportionately targeted for school disciplinary actions. As identified earlier, school suspension rates for African American male students are significantly higher than they are for their white counterparts (Skiba, Michael, Nardo, & Peterson, 2002). Students of color identified with disabilities are the most at risk for disciplinary proceedings such as suspension or expulsion. In their review of the research, Losen and Skiba (2010) identified great discrepancies among the reasons students were suspended nationwide and found overwhelmingly that suspensions were not the result of violence or serious misbehavior. In one statewide study "only 5% of all out-of-school suspensions were issued for disciplinary incidents that are typically considered serious or dangerous, such as possession of weapons or drugs. The remaining 95% of suspensions fell into two categories: disruptive behavior and other" (Losen & Skiba, 2010, p. 9).

Often the intervention strategies districts have developed to try to address disproportionality end up reproducing the very problems these strategies seek to transform. For example, high-stakes testing and new oppressive accountability measures play a key role in referring students to special education and continue to work to disqualify young people. The use of the model "Response to Intervention" (RtI) as a method to reduce the number of referrals to special education for learning disabilities, in addition to "School-Wide Positive Behavioral Supports" (SW-PBS), can function as a tool to push kids into special education. Urban school districts often do not have the adequate funds for professional development to properly train educators on what RtI and SW-PBS are or how they should be implemented. RtI is an intervention for students having difficulty with the general way a teacher is implementing the curriculum and the general recommendation is that there should only be 15% of the school population receiving RtI small group interventions. Fieldwork by Adams (n.d.) suggests that in urban schools approximately 60% to 80% of students are in RtI classes and this is especially true for schools with a high population of English language learners. In these schools, many times the special education teacher provides these interventions, already labeling students with academic problems. The students receiving RtI services do not respond to prescriptive reading or math programs and become frustrated. Instead of re-evaluating the plan to help the student learn, the student is now a behavior problem and needs more intensive interventions that can be found only in the special education classroom (Adams, n.d.).

Generally, SW-PBS are set up in the same manner as RtI, except that they are behavioral-based instead of academic. SW-PBS target students who receive an office referral and/or are suspended. Schools identify "offenders" who have committed infractions or "offenses." Without an intervention that also focuses on teaching students needed skills or an intervention that prioritizes identifying underlying causes of the behavior, many students end up as repeat "offenders." One study showed that after a year of implementation Black, Latino, and students with disabilities showed an increase in the number of referrals for minor behavioral infractions and received harsher punishment (Losen, 2012). The result of a failed SW-PBS is that a student is eventually placed in a segregated classroom where the focus is on compliance and not academics. As students fall further behind academically, the chances of "push-out" increase.

The gendered and racialized practices of removing students from an educational setting, the most dramatic educational sanction available, starts in preschools. As a 2005 survey of forty state pre-kindergarten programs indicates:

> Boys were expelled at a rate over 4.5 times that of girls. African-Americans attending state-funded prekindergarten were about twice as likely to be expelled as Latino and Caucasian children, and over five times as likely to be expelled as Asian-American children. (Gilliam, 2005, p. 3)

Head Start programs and public schools had the lowest rates of expulsions for this age group, with faith-based organizations having the highest. The rate of preschool expulsion, in all states but three in the forty-state survey, exceeds the rate of expulsion in K–12 classrooms (Gilliam, 2005). These push-out practices become more evident in elementary school when students unable to comply with the behavioral expectations of their teachers are suspended and even placed on homebound instruction while the schools try to find alternative placements for them. Students are being removed from elementary schools in handcuffs and taken to jail, as exemplified by the case of 6-year-old Salecia Johnson, who, on April 18, 2012, following a tantrum in school, was handcuffed and taken from her kindergarten class at Creekside Elementary School in Milledgeville, Georgia, to jail by a police officer (Jefferson, 2012).

Urban schools are subjected to the guidelines developed by those in power, which are based on white middle-class values and perceptions of people of color, culture, poverty, and family dynamics. A student's success in school is determined

materials for mainstream audiences. Nationally some of the more visible organizations include:

> Advancement Project (http://www.advancementproject.org http://www.stopschoolstojails.org/)
>
> Civil Rights Project/Proyecto Derechos Civiles (http://www.civilrightsproject.ucla.edu/)
>
> At the state level, advocacy organizations that work on juvenile and educational justice issues in many states have developed initiatives. For example, the Juvenile Justice Project of Louisiana's Schools First! Project (http://jjpl.org/new/?page_id=19) centers on the school to prison pipeline as an organizational focus. We are particularly excited by the creation of legal clinics across the United States, such as the Education Advocacy Clinic at the University of California at Los Angeles, a joint project between the UCLA Law School and the Learning Rights Center, that trains law students through providing advocacy services for young people and the adults in their lives to negotiate special education services in schools (http://www.learningrights.org/collaborative-projects/ucla-education-advocacy-clinic/).

In addition to national and state-level organizing and initiatives, across the United States many grassroots organizations that are youth or parent led organize to interrupt harsh disciplinary practices and address the intersection of disability and discipline. Examples of such organizations include Padres y Jovenes Unidos (Denver), Voices of Youth in Chicago Education (Chicago), and Parents Organized to Win, Educate and Renew—Policy Action Council (Chicago). These organizations impact school policies by bringing media attention to high suspension rates of students of color. Disproportionality in school discipline and the overlapping institutions of criminal justice and public education are generally central lenses of this work. For example, many of the above organizations shaped amazing projects such as the Dignity in Schools 2012 Campaign's "A Model Code on Education and Dignity" that included a Senate hearing in December 2012 on ending the STPP. Unfortunately, many of the related bills introduced in the House and Senate end up dying on the floor (such as the H.R. 5628 [111th]: Ending Corporal Punishment in Schools Act [2010] or H.R.415 [112th]: Restorative Justice in Schools Act of 2011). These bills would have allowed local educational agencies to use Title II sub-grants from the Elementary and Secondary Education Act (now called the No Child Left Behind Act) to train school personnel in restorative justice and conflict resolution.

Beyond a central focus on discipline, increasingly under focus are disability classification practices and the services young people receive, or not, through the application of these labels. This is particularly acute and relevant, as this chapter outlines, because students in "special education" categories are often those caught up in school disciplinary proceedings and are the youth who are building intimate relationships with the carceral state rather than having accessible pathways to academic attainment. As successful as they are, many of the organizations listed above have not focused on special education, but have given recognition to overrepresentation of Black students in special education and the higher rate of discipline for these students. Organizations that advocate for students with disabilities are often based in the legal realm consisting of law centers that litigate lawsuits against school districts on behalf of students. What is needed is a grassroots approach that has a focus aimed at targeting the STPP and its connection to special education and segregated educational settings. Such an intersectional approach can do much to disrupt the pathologization of, mostly, disabled students of color who are being targeted for carceral futures.

REFERENCES

Adams, D. L. (n.d.). *Positive is positive behavior support? An investigation into the implementation process of a school-wide positive behavior support system.* Doctoral dissertation in progress. Syracuse University, Syracuse, NY.

Blanchette, W. J., Mumford, V., & Beachum, F. (2005). Urban school failure and disproportionality in a post-*Brown* era: Benign neglect of the constitutional rights of students of color. *Remedial and Special Education, 26*, 70–81. doi:10.1177/07419325050260020201

Boeckmann, C. (2000). *A question of character: Scientific racism and the genres of American fiction, 1892–1912.* Tuscaloosa: University of Alabama Press.

Browne, J. A. (2003). *Derailed: The school to jailhouse track.* Washington, DC: The Advancement Project.

Crenshaw, K. W. (1994). Mapping the margins: Intersectionality, identity politics, and violence against women of color. In M. A. Fineman & R. Mykituk (Eds.), *The public nature of private violence* (pp. 93–118). New York: Routledge.

Danforth, S., & Smith, T. J. (2005). *Engaging troubling students: A constructivist approach.* Thousand Oaks, CA: Corwin.

Delpit, L. (1995). *Other people's children: Cultural conflict in the classroom.* New York: New Press.

Duncan, G. A. (2000). Urban pedagogies and the celling of adolescents of color. *Social Justice, 27*, 29–42.

Ferri, B. A., & Connor, D. J. (2004). Special education and the subverting of *Brown*. *Journal of Gender, Race, and Justice, 8*(1), 57–74.

Ferri, B. A., & Connor, D. J. (2005). Integration and exclusion—a troubling nexus: Race, disability, and special education. *Journal of African American History, 90*(1/2), 107–127.

Garda, R. A., Jr. (2005). The new IDEA: Shifting educational paradigms to achieve racial equality in special education. *Alabama Law Review, 56*, 1071.

Gilliam, W. S. (2005, May). *Prekindergarteners left behind: Expulsion rates in state prekindergarten programs* (FCD Brief Series No. 3). New York: Foundation for Child Development. Retrieved from http://www.fcd-us.org/PDFs/ExpulsionFinalProof.pdf

Glennon, T. (2002). Evaluating the Office for Civil Rights' Minority and Special Education Project. In D. J. Losen & G. Orfield (Eds.), *Racial inequality in special education* (pp. 195–218). Cambridge, MA: Harvard Education Press.

Gregory, A., Skiba, R. J., & Nogurea, P. A. (2010). The achievement gap and the discipline gap: Two sides of the same coin? *Educational Researcher, 39*(1), 59–68.

Harry, B., & Klingner, J. (2006). *Why are so many minority students in special education? Understanding race and disability in schools.* New York: Teachers College Press.

Hewitt, D., Kim, C., & Losen, D. (2010). *The school to prison pipeline: Structuring legal reform.* New York: NYU Press.

Himmelstein, K., & Bruckner, H. (2011). Criminal-justice and school sanctions against non-heterosexual youth: A national longitudinal study. *Pediatrics, 127*(1), 48–57.

Individuals with Disabilities Education Act, 20 USC § 1400. (1990). Retrieved from http://uscode.house.gov/download/pls/20C33.txt

Jefferson, A. (2012, April 20). Salecia Johnson's parents want answers. *The Root.* Retrieved from http://www.theroot.com/views/salecia-johnsons-parents-still-want-answers

Kaba, M., & Edwards, F. (2012). *Policing Chicago public schools: A gateway to the school-to-prison pipeline.* Project NIA. Retrieved from http://www.project-nia.org/policing-chicago-schools.php

Kim, C. Y., Losen, D. J., & Hewitt, D. T. (2010). *The school-to-prison pipeline: Structuring legal reform* [E-book]. New York: NYU Press.

Larry P. v. Riles, C-71–2270 R F P (N.D. Cal., October 16, 1979), 793 F. 2d. 969 (9th Cir. 1984).

Losen, D. J. (2011). *Discipline policies, successful schools, and racial justice.* Boulder, CO: National Education Policy Center. Retrieved from http://nepc.colorado.edu/publication/discipline-policies.

Losen, D. J. (2012). Sound discipline policy for successful schools: How redressing racial disparities can make a positive impact. In S. Bahena, N. Cooc, R. Currie-Rubin, P. Kuttner, & M. Ng (Eds.), *Disrupting the school-to-prison pipeline* (pp. 45–72). Cambridge, MA: Harvard Education Press.

Losen, D. J., & Gillespie, J. (2012). *Opportunities suspended: The disparate impact of disciplinary exclusion from school.* Los Angeles, CA: The Civil Rights Project. Retrieved from http://civilrightsproject.ucla.edu/resources/projects/center-for-civil-rights-remedies/school-to-prison-folder/federal-reports/upcoming-ccrr-research

Losen, D. J., & Skiba, R. J. (2010). *Suspended education: Urban middle schools in crisis.* Los Angeles, CA: The Civil Rights Project. Retrieved from http://civilrightsproject.ucla.edu/research/k-12-education/school-discipline/suspended-education-urban-middle-schools-in-crisis

Losen, D. J., & Welner, K. G. (2002). Legal challenges to an inappropriate and inadequate special education for minority children. In D. J. Losen & G. Orfield (Eds.), *Racial inequality in special education* (pp. 167–194). Cambridge, MA: Harvard Education Press.

McNally, J. (2003). A ghetto within a ghetto. *Rethinking Schools Online, 17*(3). Retrieved from http://www.rethinkingschools.org/restrict.asp?path=archive/17_03/ghet173.shtml

Meiners, E. (2007). *Right to be hostile: Schools, prisons and the making of public enemies.* New York: Routledge.

Merrell, K. W., & Walker, H. M. (2004). Deconstructing a definition: Social maladjustment versus emotional disturbance and moving the EBD field forward. *Psychology in the Schools, 41*(8), 899–910. doi:10.1002/pits.20046

Mitchell, D., & Snyder, S. (2006). *Cultural locations of disability.* Chicago: University of Chicago Press.

New York Civil Liberties Union. (2012). *Student Safety Act reporting on suspensions: 2011–2012* [Fact sheet]. New York: Author. Retrieved from http://www.nyclu.org/files/releases/SSA_Fact-Sheet_2011-2012.pdf

New York State Education Department (NYSED). (2011). Special education: Individuals with Disabilities Education Improvement Act 2004. Retrieved from http://www.p12.nysed.gov/specialed/idea/

No Child Left Behind Act of 2001, 20 U.S.C. § 6319. (2008).
Reid, D. K., & Knight, M. G. (2006). Disability justifies exclusion of minority students: A critical history grounded in disability studies. *Educational Researcher, 35*(6), 18–33. doi:10.3102/0013189X035006018
Reschly, D. J., & Bersoff, D. N. (1999). Law and school psychology. In C. R. Reynolds & T. B. Gutkin (Eds.), *The handbook of school psychology*. New York: John Wiley & Sons.
Russo, C. J., & Talbert-Johnson, C. (1997). The overrepresentation of African American children in special education: The resegregation of educational programming? *Education and Urban Society, 9*(2), 136–147.
Simkins, S., Hirsh, A., Horvat, E., & Moss, M. (2004). The school to prison pipeline for girls: The role of physical and sexual abuse. *Children's Legal Rights Journal, 24*(4), 56–72.
Simmons, L. (2009). End of the line: Tracing racial inequality from school to prison. *Race/Ethnicity: Multidisciplinary Global Perspectives, 2*(2), 215–241.
Skiba, R. J., Michael, R. S., Nardo, A. C., & Peterson, R. L. (2002). The color of discipline: Sources of racial and gender disproportionality in school punishment. *The Urban Review, 34*(2), 317–342.
Smith, R. M., & Erevelles, N. (2004). Toward an enabling education: The difference that disability makes. *Educational Researcher, 23*(8), 31–36.
Tisdale, K. C. (2003). *An archeology of emotional disturbance*. Unpublished doctoral dissertation. University of Georgia, Athens.
Winfield, A. G. (2007). *Eugenics and education in America*. New York: Peter Lang.
Winn, M. (2010). *Girl time: Literacy, justice, and the school-to-prison pipeline*. New York: Teachers College Press.

CHAPTER THIRTEEN

The New Eugenics

Challenging Urban Education and Special Education and the Promise of Hip Hop Pedagogy

ANTHONY J. NOCELLA II AND KIM SOCHA

I'm an artist from the start, Hip hop got in my heart, Graffiti on the wall, coulda ended in [laughs] Juvenile Delinquent

—NAS, FROM "BRIDGING THE GAP"

INTRODUCTION

School is often seen as synonymous with education. *This is a fallacy.* Education is the attainment of knowledge. School, unlike education, is an institutional stronghold of oppression, repression, domination, and authoritarianism, and it has been since its inception as a social institution. Schools, as institutions, are by definition based on structures and systems that promote normalcy and control. The U.S. school system arose in the seventeenth century, governed and established by Christian religious orders to serve the wealthy. The system began in Boston and developed throughout the first thirteen colonies. About a hundred years later, finishing schools were developed for elite white women to train as wives, mothers, and domestic workers. As Packard (1866) clearly stated in the *The Daily Public School in the United States*, the school system should be "fitting our boys and girls to be useful, intelligent (*not learned*), practical, well, *patriotic godly* men and women" (n.p., emphasis added). Of course, Packard was referring to white "boys and girls," and his commentary demonstrates that schools were established to maintain order in and loyalty to the burgeoning United States and its Christian foundation. Schooling was meant to turn children into upstanding citizens, not to educate them (i.e., Packard's comment that students "not [be] learned"). Fast-forward almost 150 years, and the system that Packard promoted continues today, and its racism has only flourished, albeit in a different guise.

On the surface, schools are places where students and teachers interact, but that is hardly the whole range of discourses. Teachers work directly with students, while administrators at varying hierarchical levels manage the teachers, systems, and the overall institution. With little effort, one can see the similarities between youth detention facilities and the school system in the United States. This should not be surprising. They are designed by the same system, government, and elite group of white, able-bodied, outwardly heterosexual, wealthy, Christian males—the undisputed "norm" of mainstream America.

From a critical race and disability studies perspective, this chapter challenges the cultural imperialist epidemic of placing students of color from economically oppressed communities into special education classes and/or the juvenile justice system because they are stigmatized through the socially constructed label of "abnormal." As Ferri and Connor explain (2006), the current system puts such individuals into an untenable situation:

> Schools have functioned as key sites for the policing of normalcy, creating and maintaining students who look and act in accordance with established norms. The removal or exclusion of students who deviate from these norms has been seen as necessary to maintain the classroom as a normalized space. Thus, American education has an ongoing history of openly excluding and/or segregating students by race and disability. ... Black and disabled citizens, positioned as the antithesis of the traditional American ideal, are nonetheless defined in relation to—or invariably against—this ideal. Thus, their very existence excludes them from, while simultaneously demanding their conformity to, this ideal. (pp. 128, 130)

For urban youth of color, this manifests through their categorization as "disabled." Our use of Nas at the start of this chapter explains why so many social justice educators (Ayers, Ladson-Billings, Michie, & Noguera, 2008) argue for using Hip Hop in the classroom to understand urban youth and their everyday experiences (Hill, 2009; Parmar, 2009). Unfortunately, these recommendations supporting Hip Hop pedagogy go largely unheeded and the educational system continues to fail youth of color.

Since 1968, starting with the research of L. M. Dunn, the disproportionate number of African American students in special education courses has been noted, and the placement continues to be standard in U.S. schools (Harry & Klingner, 2006, p. 2). Currently, the educational system defines students of color as "urban learners" and students with dis-abilities as having "special needs." These two groups of students—and, of course, those who straddle both categorizations—and those living in poverty are the most highly targeted youth demographic to enter the school to prison pipeline, the steps of which can be visualized as follows: (1) A student is placed into intellectually segregated classes, behaves "inappropriately," and is sent to school detention; (2) after amassing too many detentions, he is kicked out of school; (3) he spends his days on the streets, illegally hustling to make money, and gets arrested; (4) he winds up in a juvenile detention facility. This chapter explores the why and how of what appears to be a Herculean task: to end this cycle of oppression by dismantling the current school system and abolishing youth detention facilities.

We have already introduced the covert mission and strategy of the U.S. school system, which is to promote a Euro-centric concept of normalcy. We next demonstrate that urban education is the new special education, with youth of color targeted with the diagnosis of "disabled." The third section exposes how the U.S. school system is founded on white supremacist pedagogy. We then explain why special education is a form of segregation that is ineffective and needs to be abolished. Finally, in the last section of this chapter, we champion social justice educational approaches and pedagogies that are inclusive, equitable, and respectful of difference and diversity for all students.

In sum, we believe that the constructions of special education and urban education reinforce socially contrived binaries by marginalizing and oppressing youth. Thus, as they grow into adulthood, U.S. culture is prepping these children for one of three futures: homelessness; death by community, institution, self, or domestic violence; or incarceration in a mental hospital or prison. The highest percentage of incarcerated youth includes those of color and with supposed dis-abilities (which are often the same group of children). Moreover, while the data are not recorded by juvenile detention facilities, most incarcerated youth come from economically disadvantaged backgrounds. Thus, the school to prison pipeline is not targeting *all* youth in schools, but rather those who are part of the special education and urban education systems.

There is a crisis in schools grounded in cultural incompetency among teachers and administrators. This is a harsh reality, but rather than just assign blame, we need to address the primary source of this incompetency, which is government and higher education bureaucracies that make policies and teach these administrators and educators. In *The Culture of Incompetence*, Cartaina (2009), begins by stating that incompetence is now seen as normal, and thus expected, in inner-city schools (p. 1). As he continues to explain:

> The culture of incompetence incestuously breeds itself. It gives grossly inefficient teachers an excuse to continue working in the same way. Why? Initiatives for change are either ill conceived or inadequately implemented or funded. So when they fail, incompetent teachers can smugly say, "I told you so." They continue to teach poorly … and the community has a new pool of illiterate adults who help perpetuate a culture of crime in the city. (p. 3)

This incompetency is masked by identifying youth of color as having learning disabilities and providing them with Individualized Education Programs (IEPs).

In actuality, these youth are rarely disabled; rather, they are in many cases taking classes from culturally incompetent teachers and culturally biased standardized tests, such as I.Q. and other academic achievement tests. The overrepresentation of youth of color in special education today signifies that systemic racism has remained constant, although embodying a new configuration in schools that specifically targets youth. We should consider this indicative of a "new eugenics" movement via IEPs determined by inept (predominately white) teachers and administrators bolstered by school systems and university education departments that foster white supremacy. The three-step process of oppressing youth of color comes through stigmatization, segregation, and incarceration. Stigmatization is carried out by identifying students with learning disabilities; next, these students are segregated by placement into special education and alternative schools; finally, if these students do not conform to the rules, they are kicked out of school and typically into a career of street hustling that lands them in jail.

Special education classes are typically designed for students with learning disabilities, while alternative schools are established for students with Emotional and Behavioral Disorders (EBD). However, neither of these models is efficient for addressing students' needs, as they overlook the reasons students may appear, from a traditional perspective, to have a learning or emotional disability, for

> while it may be true that many students of color and of poor backgrounds lack interest in school learning, such behavior should not automatically be seen as a sign of laziness or lack of motivation. There are good reasons for this lack of interest. Poor, racial/ethnic, and language minority students bear the brunt of biased school practices. For example, they are overrepresented in low-track remedial classes, which are notoriously unchallenging and stigmatizing. (Villegas & Lucas, 2002, p. 41)

These low-track, remedial, unchallenging classes, held in overpopulated and underresourced public schools, are often staffed by culturally unaware teachers. Part of this problem can be traced back to Euro-centric conceptions of what is meant by "good teaching." As Delpit (2006) explains, effective teaching can differ depending upon both region and student demographics. Thus, although good teaching has traditionally meant that the instructor begins with a strong grasp of the academic material and how to disseminate that knowledge, she found something different within communities of color: "I have learned from interviews and personal experiences with communities of color that many of these individuals believe teaching begins instead with the establishment of relationships between themselves and their students" (Delpit, 2006, p. 139). As Harry and Klingner (2006) found in the case study of an African American student named Kanita, who was initially labeled as "emotionally handicapped," once Kanita found a "solid, structured teacher who challenged her strong intellect," (p. 134) she flourished in a program for academically *gifted* students. The problem, therefore, is not with the students themselves, but with a culture that labels and stigmatizes based on race and outdated conceptions of what "ability" even means. Hence, a new eugenics.

In explaining how eugenics promotes and defends racism, Kelves, author of *In the Name of Eugenics: Genetics and the Uses of Human Heredity* (1995), writes,

> Human genetics as a program of research originated with the eugenics idea that physical, mental, and behavioral qualities of the human race could be improved by suitable management and manipulation of its hereditary essences. During the heyday of eugenics—much of the first half of the twentieth century—social prejudice often overwhelmed scientific objectivity in the investigation of human genetics. (p. vii)

The philosophical science of eugenics is only as powerful as the tools developed to prove its racist arguments. Currently, the eugenicist strategies in schools are standardized tests via state high school proficiency examinations, I.Q. tests, cumulative course examinations, the General Educational Development (GED) test, and the Scholastic Assessment Test (SAT). Moreover, the cultural deficit theory is designed to view students of color and the economically marginalized and isolated as unintelligent because of the aforementioned testing methods. Researchers have long noted that "IQ tests do not measure important features of intelligence and are culturally biased" (Villegas & Lucas, 2002, p. 40). To further explain this cultural bias, Kelves (1995) writes of eugenics as a system of social control:

> They have been heightened once again by a renewal of assertions that black Americans as a group are genetically less intelligent than white Americans because they score on average fifteen points lower on I.Q. tests. Genes are held to place blacks, along with whites of comparable test performance, disproportionately in poverty, in prison, on the welfare rolls, and in the statistics of illegitimate births. (p. viii)

From its establishment, the U.S. school system has determined what is and is not the truth from a Christian, formalist educational foundation. Therefore, schools were not established to foster critical thought and an engaged educated citizenry, but rather submissive, fearful, and conformist members of society. Lest one think such accusations to be sensationalistic, recently the Republican Party of Texas included the following in its 2012 platform about its education plans, as cited in Strauss's (2012) "The GOP Reject 'Critical Thinking Skills.' Really" from the *Washington Post*:

> Knowledge-Based Education—We oppose the teaching of Higher Order Thinking Skills (HOTS) (values clarification), *critical thinking skills* and similar programs that are simply a relabeling of Outcome-Based Education (OBE) (mastery learning) which focus on behavior modification and have the purpose of challenging the student's fixed beliefs and undermining parental authority. (emphasis added)

As Strauss opines, this is from the "you-can't-make-up-this-stuff department."

URBAN EDUCATION: THE NEW SPECIAL EDUCATION

Urban education was changed by white migration from urban areas to the suburbs in 1950s and 1960s America. Simultaneously, the urban community became ghettoized. Urban education today is reformist at best, with Ferri and Connor (2006) arguing that the high number of students of color in special education classes connotes a failure of "incremental approaches" to school reform (p. 43); at worst, urban education, as a reformist institution, perpetuates oppression. Moreover, urban education as an academic discipline has been co-opted by scholars, organizations, universities, colleges, nonprofits, corporations, and the government, who argue that schools and teachers lack the skills to teach students in urban communities, hence the achievement gap between students of color and white students. These agencies and institutions have created many local, regional, and national initiatives to train teachers with the skills to combat this proposed achievement gap by providing after school, summer, life skills, job readiness, anger management, conflict transformation, and etiquette programs (Howard, 2010). The achievement gap is nothing more than a gap between the oppressor and the oppressed; in this case, this means white people and people of color. White-dominant schooling argues for people of color to adopt a white colonial imperialist culture and a sense of inferiority to the oppressor to be successful in society. Oppressors often feel uncomfortable speaking about oppression because it leads to an expectation of accountability; therefore, they put the blame on the oppressed.

One way the governmental education system has attempted to "fix" the problems of urban learners and those with disabilities is through Individualized Education Programs (IEPs). IEPs sound like educational programs catered to fit individual students' needs. In reality, an IEP is an active file documenting which disabilities a student has. On December 3, 2004, the Individuals with Disabilities Education Act (IDEA) was reauthorized and signed into law by President George W. Bush. In the late 1990s and early 2000s, scholars and researchers saw a new identity emerging in special education classrooms. The classrooms were filling up with African American boys, while affluent white students with mental and learning disabilities with IEPs were moving to expensive private schools that cater to students with disabilities, charter schools, or home schooling.

To prove this new segregation, in an article "Reviving the Goal of an Integrated Society: A 21st Century Challenge," by Gary Orfield (2009), he reports that schools in the U.S. are more racially segregated today than they were in the 1950s. Rena Hawkins, Melissa Robinson, and Sangeeta Sinha publicize Orfield's argument by writing their chapter "US Schools are More Segregated Today than in the 1950s" in Project Censored's annual book "Censored 2010: The Top Censored Stories of 2008–09" (Phillips, Huff, & Project Censored, 2009), the second most censored story in 2008 and 2009. Hawkins, Robinson, and Sinha (2009) write the following in defense of Orfield's argument:.

> According to a new Civil Rights report published at the University of California, Los Angeles, schools in the US are 44 percent non-white, and minorities are rapidly emerging as the majority of public school students in the US. Latinos and blacks, the two largest minority groups, attend schools more segregated today than during the civil rights movement forty years ago. In Latino and African American populations, two of every five students attend intensely segregated schools. For Latinos this increase in segregation reflects growing residential segregation. For blacks a significant part of the reversal reflects the ending of desegregation plans in public schools throughout the nation. In the 1954 case *Brown v. Board of Education*, the US Supreme Court concluded that the Southern standard of "separate but equal" was "inherently unequal," and did "irreversible" harm to black students. It later extended that ruling to Latinos. (p. 17)

Students within this new era of segregation often fail to meet school standards. Thus, they are removed, by force or by choice, from the school system only to find themselves in trouble with the law, where they end up in a juvenile hall, jail, or prison. The legal cessation of segregated schools marked a pivotal point in the civil rights struggle. Today, the same needs to be done for the disability rights movement.

Just as there was once clear racial segregation in schools, there is now a clear segregation constructed by normalcy, standardization, and conformity, which is carried out beginning with governmental educational programs, then school districts, and then the teachers themselves. And quite often, this new segregation based on ability is still racially motivated. Once again noting Orfield's study, Bigg (2009) reports: "Blacks and Hispanics are more separate from white students than at any time since the civil rights movement and many of the schools they attend are struggling." Thus, the problem is not just segregation, but a style of racial disparity that does not give Blacks and Hispanics the same level of education that white children receive, and they often wind up labeled "disabled" and/or are incarcerated. The Council for Exceptional Children (CEC) (n.d.) reports on its website:

> More than 130,000 youth with disabilities are incarcerated in juvenile justice facilities in the U.S.—an over-representation compared to other youth nationally. While just 10 to 12 percent of students in public schools have disabilities, 30 to 50 percent of the students in correctional facilities receive special education. A disproportionate number are male, black, Native American, or Latino and come from economically disadvantaged backgrounds. (para. 1)

CEC explains four reasons there is an overrepresentation of incarcerated youth with disabilities; they include differential treatment theory, metacognitive deficits theory, school failure theory, and susceptibility theory. While school failure theory addresses how a student can internalize an inferiority complex after being labeled with a learning disability, it does not address issues of race within this self-identity. If a student from another culture were placed in a traditional American school, s/he would likely not be as successful as a student from the culture that the school is founded upon. The issue that the school and criminal justice systems do not want to address is that youths of color are, by default, positioned as persons with disabilities because they are from a different culture than that on which the school system is founded. Therefore, the academic achievement gap has very little to do with one's intellectual capabilities and has mostly to do with one's cultural background.

The terms "urban students," "special students," and "students with disabilities" and IEPs are all methods to stigmatize those that are not identified as "normal" by systems of cultural domination. Stigmatization is the negative labeling/branding/marking, demonizing, vilifying, defaming, smearing, slandering, or disgracing of a group, individual, theory, belief, or object. Goffman (1963) writes, "The term stigma, then, will be used to refer to an attribute that is deeply discrediting, but it should be seen that a language of relationships, not attributes, is really needed" (p. 3). This discrediting is a form of victimization of ideas, theories, groups, individuals, and objects that depart from accepted norms (Goffman, 1963, p. 5). Further, "[s]tigma means an impaired collective identity, where connection with the group is a source of discredit and devaluation because that is how the group as a whole is viewed, whether or not anyone makes an issue of it through name-calling or other forms of ridicule" (Linden & Klandermans, 2006, p. 214). The purpose of stigmatization as a tactic of political repression is to diminish and show that the person and/or group is socially and/or politically flawed. As disability is a social construction, anyone can have a disability if targeted as being different from the norm. In this case, we argue that youth of color are always already stigmatized by a Euro-American educational system as having disabilities.

CHALLENGING WHITE SUPREMACY[1]

White teachers, mainly female, dominate America's current school system (Epstein, 2005). Landsman and Lewis (2011) make a direct correlation between this deficit of Black teachers and the achievement gap among Black students. Nationwide, Black students make up about "20% of the total school enrollment"; concurrently, 70% of public school teachers are white, 8% Black (with only 1% of those being male), and 9.8% of principals are Black (p. 137). As the authors conclude from these data: "Consequently, many Black students could go through their

1 This section is adapted from Nocella and Socha's "Old School, New School, No School: Hip Hop's Dismantling of School and Prison-Industrial Complexes," to be published in the *International Journal of Critical Pedagogy.*

entire school experience without having a principal or teacher who understands their diverse needs" (p. 137).

We are not contending that white teachers have absolutely nothing of value to teach students of color. However, many white teachers trained in urban education are not prepared for the diverse needs of their students, causing some to flee the environments in which they are supposedly qualified to teach. Jorissen (2003) reports that many teachers trained in urban education face difficulties in the inner-city setting that cause them to leave and either teach in the suburbs or change careers altogether (p. 41). The result is a lack of people who are willing to teach in urban schools; consequently, inner-city schools have opened their doors to deliver the most oppressed groups of students in the United States to nonprofits such as Teach For America (TFA).

TFA recruits predominately white young adults, about 70% white (Toppo, 2009, para. 35), the majority of whom are from middle- to upper-class communities and universities. These young teachers are unlicensed, and, despite their desire to do good work, they have no formal educational background in urban teaching, but they are "willing to teach for two years in some of the USA's toughest public schools" (Toppo, 2009, para. 4). At the same time, because TFAers are cheap labor, they are forcing older teachers into early retirement—these are the educators who have *not* fled to the suburbs, but have decided to stay and teach urban youth, despite the challenges therein. As many union leaders have complained, TFAers do not have the staying power of those dedicated to teaching:

> 4% eventually go into business, according to a 2008 survey. About two-thirds remain in education—mostly in administrative or political jobs or working with policy or charitable groups—though overall only 29% of alumni are still in the classroom. That's a bit lower than the USA's overall teaching force. (Toppo, 2009, para. 22)

For children who need stability and educators with expertise, TFA does not provide the ideal solution. White teachers, especially those from TFA, are less likely to intellectually reach Black students as effectively as would those who understand their culture more intimately and directly. Another study reports that "[p]reservice students of color bring a richer multicultural knowledge base to teacher education than do white students" (Sleeter, 2001, p. 95). This problem should be of special interest in higher education as colleges and universities recruit students for their educational degree programs. Recruiting students of color for these programs should be a nationwide priority. In "African-American Male Teacher a Vanishing Phenomenon, Experts Say" (2012), it is noted that "only 2 percent of the nation's 4.8 million teachers are black men." This article cites a 2006 Colorado State University study showing that African American male teachers appear to positively affect behavior and test scores among young Black males. In that same article, Vera Triplet, CEO of a charter school network, says that "the black male educator also has a positive influence on African-American female students." Some colleges and universities have taken note and are attempting to attract more Black males to their education programs. It is hoped that others will follow suit.

Another problem with urban education is that its teachers do not live in urban communities, and urban schools are provided with the least amount of educational resources. Consequently, frustrated teachers may kick urban youth out of their classes and/or discouraged youth often decide not to attend school at all. Giroux (2009) emphasizes this dilemma by noting that

> [p]unishment and fear have replaced compassion and social responsibility as the most important modalities mediating the relationship of youth to the larger social order. Youth within the last two decades have come to be seen as a source of trouble rather than as a resource for investing in the future, and in the case of poor black and Hispanic youth are increasingly treated as either a disposable population, cannon fodder for barbaric wars abroad, or the source of most of society's problems. (p. 18)

With some teachers buying into this perspective, the school to prison pipeline becomes an inevitability. While frustrated teachers will likely retain their jobs when they dismiss students from their classes, the discouraged youth removed from his/her school is left to the streets to join the military or to be drawn into illegal activities that will integrate him/her into the criminal "justice" system for life. As long as students and teachers cannot relate to each other in terms of daily experiences, culture, and history, there will be a breakdown in educational process.

With so many youth of color incarcerated, one would assume there are university courses dedicated to ending the school to prison pipeline. Unfortunately, many urban education programs do not address this issue. Instead, they focus on reformist initiatives on topics such as the academic achievement gap, digital equity, cultural competency, and after school programs that cater to schools, teachers, students, and parents. Indeed, it has been noted that "[m]ost educators have little knowledge of, or experience with, the juvenile justice system. Pre-service training focuses on curricula and teaching methodologies for use in the typical school classroom" (Special Education Policy Issues Project, 2006).

The CEC reports that it is now mandatory that incarcerated youth with disabilities are given an IEP. However, many detention facilities are not testing all youth to determine whether they have a disability or not. The facilities often do not have qualified individuals conducting the tests that determine one's intellectual capacity. More important, after the incarcerated youth leave a detention facility, they have two folders detailing their deviant behavior: one with their criminal history and one with their learning disability diagnosis and allied IEP. Many youth with IEPs will also leave with prescriptions for potent drugs to counteract their criminal behavior and supposed disabilities. While diagnoses and IEPs are supposed to aid students, they become mere tools of stigmatization. Consequently, the youth may develop a complex about their mental acuity while schools, teachers, and courts can label such individuals as threats to society.

As detention facilities close because of national community-based alternatives to incarceration, funding to keep them open is depleting as well. The closing of facilities means profit losses. Therefore, facility administrators seek grants and federal funding by claiming a need for special education programs that are possible only if youth have IEPs. Thus, more youth with IEPs means more funding. In other words, juvenile detention facilities have a financial stake in labeling students as disabled. It would not be surprising if, in the near future, all incarcerated youth will have an IEP before or soon after incarceration.

ABOLISHING SPECIAL EDUCATION AND SEGREGATION[2]

Challenges to "special education" are not meant to disregard that people do have physical and mental differences for which they may require inclusive assistance. However, meeting the needs of such students is not possible within American schools because of their founding dualistic philosophies based upon the idea that there are always going to be winners and losers, achievers and underachievers, the intelligent and the unintelligent. The current U.S. educational system is not meant to be collaborative, but instead individualistic and competitive, wherein only the "normal" succeed (Kohn, 1992). It is not meant to be inclusive, but instead a place with rigid standards that, if not met, means failure for society's "losers." Thankfully, there have been some positive responses to this broken system.

Inclusive education arose out of the "social changes since the end of the Second World War and which include the end of colonialism, the increase of labor-force mobility, and the tension between global and local cultures," while also challenging the division between mainstream and special education (Armstrong, Armstrong, & Spandagou, 2010, p. 4). Most recently, inclusive education has evolved as an intersectional philosophy and a revolutionary concept for promotion and inclusion of all identities. It is respectful toward and supportive of diversity and difference. Despite the optimistic goals of inclusive education, Ferri and Connor (2006) note that the public backlash among community "stakeholders" against inclusive education indicates "fear that an increase of students with disabilities in general education classrooms [and again, this often means students of color] makes teaching and learning difficult, if not impossible" (p. 46). Thus, inclusive education is not without its obstacles. Further, inclusive education is becoming an umbrella movement and/or ideology that scholars are consistently defining and

---

2 Some of this section is adapted from Anthony J. Nocella (2008), "Emergence of Disability Pedagogy," *The Journal for Critical Education Policy Studies*, *6*(2).

re-defining, so there is the danger of co-optation that could lead to more rigid restrictions on what "inclusivity" means. Therefore, a specific pedagogy that advocates and provides a platform for people with disabilities needs to be maintained. Special education, which began as the first advocacy and liberatory pedagogy for students with disabilities in the early 1800s, is now thought of as reformist at best; at worst, it reinforces the status quo of a segregated educational system (Osgood, 2005). Special education promotes students with "special needs" (an offensive term critiqued by disability studies scholars because all people have special needs) to be segregated from standard classes and if they are wealthy enough, they may attend private segregated schools. The essence of disability pedagogy is the experience of being marginalized, stigmatized, and oppressed, while disability simply means the inability to perform. Society has thus far not proved itself to be inclusive. Throughout modern history, groups labeled as minorities—women, people of color, the non-heteronormative—have been diagnosed and categorized as disabled or less than human (Nocella, 2008). Disability pedagogy's overall goals are to challenge all systems of domination, deconstruct disability and explain it as a social construction, and promote an inclusive social justice education that is equitable and respectful of difference and diversity (Applebaum, 2001; Nocella, 2008).

Educational professionals today have degrees in special education; however, special education is the antithesis of both disability studies and inclusive education. Special education and segregated education, which cater to students who learn differently, are the result of a larger, systematic marco-problem of the illusion of normalcy within the school system. Dyson (1999) concisely explains what special education really is; he charges special education with serving "the interests of the advantaged members of society by maintaining and rationalizing the further marginalization of those whom it claims to help" (p. 40). Special education was created to segregate children who were labeled as "deviant" and a challenge to the "established order of regular schooling" (Dyson, 1999, p. 40). Professionals were established and authorized as those who had privileged "knowledge" about these children and discouraged any interrogation of the system that constructs such difference as deviant. Special education encourages society to ignore the distinctive characteristics that students different from the so-called norm may contribute to the classroom. Special education is separate education that is inherently unjust. As Dyson concludes, "It follows, therefore, that only inclusive education can deliver social justice" (1999, p. 40).

Len Barton, author of "The Politics of Special Education: A Necessary or Irrelevant Approach?" (2004), notes problematic assumptions within the concept of special education: "disabled children and young people" need protection from reality and the "real world"; so-called normal children need protection from the "disabled"; and there are educators with "special qualities" making them most able to work with the "disabled" (p. 68). Barton sums up his critique by stating: "Such developments have been depicted as being in the best interests of the child, peers, and society generally" (p. 68). In contrast, segregation is not for the benefit of the child; it is for, as stressed above, the safety of society and the "normal" students. The International Movement of Disabled People and the British Council of Disabled People are critical of special education. Indeed, increasing numbers of people with disabilities, including those who are reflecting on their experiences in such schools, are advocating the closure of such institutions in favor of an inclusive approach to education.

There is strong reason to support inclusive education and disability pedagogy over special education, but we believe that all pedagogies must be rooted in a critical and radical collaborative social justice education, pedagogy, and activist commitment. Moreover, inclusive education on its own will not challenge the larger system from which disability is constructed. Disability pedagogy critiques repressive systems such as capitalism, corporate media, and "normalcy" and also provides space for the experience of having disabilities in an educational setting to be heard and acknowledged. Effective education is not only about access to educational tools or, in recent years, "considering ways of challenging and intellectually engage learners with disabilities" (Kluth, Straut, & Biklen 2003, p. 1). Inclusive education and disability pedagogy must work together to end segregation of those stigmatized as "abnormal," "special," and "gifted." To end segregation, we must dismantle stigmatization (which constructs binaries and categories), which is the first repressive tool employed by those in dominant positions to oppress and marginalize a group of people.

Kluth et al. (2003), in *Access to Academics for ALL Students: Critical Approaches to Inclusive Curriculum, Instruction, and Policy*, stress that inclusive pedagogy grounded in social justice education is about access to the academy: everyone having an opportunity to learn in the classroom. This includes *all* students, even those who have been labeled incapable of "hard work" and of understanding intellectually challenging ideas. The goal is to go beyond presumption of what one can do as a so-called intellectually challenged student, which is often related to one's ethnic heritage. The proliferation of culturally unaware teachers, IEPs, and poor school settings makes such dynamic learning impossible, as does the labeling and subsequent stigmatization of students who do not effectively learn in the traditional modes of the U.S. school system.

CONCLUSION: ENDING THE NEW EUGENICS AND THE RISE OF HIP HOP PEDAGOGY[3]

if social movements can aid in the critique of the disability rights movement's analysis of domination and oppression, so can the educators in those movements.

---

3 Some of this section is adapted from Anthony J. Nocella (2008), "Emergence of Disability Pedagogy," *The Journal for Critical Education Policy Studies*, 6(2).

Change will only occur through education. As Malcolm X once stated, "Education is the passport to the future, for tomorrow belongs to those who prepare for it today." Nicole Armbrust, author of *Youth with Disabilities in the Juvenile Justice System* (2006), writes, "Education is essential to the rehabilitation of youth offenders. According to the Office of Juvenile Justice and Delinquency Prevention … educating juvenile offenders should be the foundation of juvenile programs. Providing education is one of the most effective ways to rehabilitate youth offenders and reduce recidivism" (p. 9). However, traditional educational methods will not do.

To end what we refer to as the new eugenics movement, teachers, schools, and society must begin to understand the experiences, interests, and culture of youth of color. Social justice activist-educators have been rightfully arguing that we must transform K–12 education by adopting more culturally relevant pedagogy often located in Hip Hop education and culture. Hip Hop pedagogy has the ability to allow teachers and students to critically examine and become aware of the socio-political and economic situations in which many urban youth live (Parmar, 2009). Hip Hop education may engender a more engaging and interesting learning experience for youth traditionally labeled as deviant or unintelligent (Hill, 2009). Finally, Hip Hop pedagogy can critically inform youth of their culture, one that is often left out of textbooks and curriculum decisions, and provide a counter-narrative to the traditional stigmatization of Hip Hop as violent and deviant (Hill, 2009).

In recent years, urban education has become reformist, catering to the typical college student demographic majoring in education—white women—rather than investigating the needs of youth of color. Hip Hop pedagogy can be the place to begin this investigation: "However, to suggest there are critical learning opportunities in hip-hop means that we must first value it as a significant form of social knowledge, produced and constructed by urban youth in various cultural contexts" (Prier, 2012, p. xxx). To illustrate, in "They Schools," Dead Prez raps about the deficits of urban education in that it does relate to youth of color in economically disadvantaged communities:

> Until we have some shit where we control the fuckin' school system
> Where we reflect how we gon solve our own problems
> Them niggas ain't gon' relate to school, shit that just how it is
> Know what I'm sayin'? And I love education, know what I'm sayin'? (2000)

This quote summarizes Hip Hop's common critique of the school system. While acknowledging they love education, Dead Prez is against the current school system, which does not relate to the struggle that economically disadvantaged people of color face on a daily basis. As stated at the start of this chapter, school and education are not synonymous.

Further, the current field of urban education seems to have become more about justifying the cultural incompetence of white teachers than about investigating the realities of those who attend urban schools. As Prier asserts, "Many of these youth have been disengaged, alienated, and displaced from the urban school system a long time ago. They do not see themselves in the official school curriculum" (2012, p. xxxi). For this reason, they are not invested and do not see going to school as a pathway to freedom and success.

As we hope to have demonstrated, urban youth and students with learning differences are getting shortchanged by the thousands, as sanctioned by the government and the majority of school administrators and instructors. Although many Americans view eugenics and school segregation as blights on our country's history, they are still dominant ideologies and practices enacted through the educational system today. While many believe we live in a post-racial society, racism is still very present, but is consistently changing (and rendered invisible) to adapt to the current socio-political environment.

What are our alternatives? Inclusive education, Hip Hop pedagogy, and disability pedagogy, all rooted in social justice, are fine starts. However, the first step is to acknowledge and promote the sad reality that America's public school system is a broken, racist, ableist institution that cannot be reformed and restructured to meet the needs of its survivors. It must be dismantled and completely disengaged from the juvenile justice system and that system's inherent connection to privatization and capital gain (Illich, 1972). Schooling and education are different; the former is an institution and the latter is a series of endless possibilities and discourses that allow for freedom and creativity. The longer we school America's youth, rather than educate them, the longer the citizens of our country will remain cogs in the machinery that promotes normalcy and standardization, not difference, critical thinking, and creativity.

REFERENCES

African-American male teachers a vanishing phenomenon, experts say. (2012, April 27). *WSDU News*. Retrieved from http://www.wdsu.com/African-American-Male-Teacher-A-Vanishing-Phenomenon-Experts-Say/-/9854144/13388350/-/item/0/-/eap29cz/-/index.html

Applebaum, B. (2001). Raising awareness of dominance: Does recognising dominance mean one has to dismiss the values of the dominant group? *Journal of Moral Education, 30*, 1.

Armbrust, N. (2006). *Youth with disabilities in the juvenile justice system*. Minneapolis: Minnesota Justice Foundation.

Armstrong, A. C., Armstrong, D., & Spandagou, I. (2010). *Inclusive education: International policy and practice*. London: Sage.

Armstrong, F., Armstrong, D., & Barton, L. (2000). *Inclusive education: Policy, contexts and comparative perspectives*. London: David Fulton.

Ayers, B., Ladson-Billings, G., Michie, G., & Noguera, P. (2008). *City kids, city schools: More reports from the front row*. New York: New Press.

Barton, L. (2004). The politics of special education: A necessary or irrelevant approach. In L. Ware (Ed.), *Ideology and the politics of (in)exclusion*. New York: Peter Lang.

Bigg, M. (2009, January 14). U.S. school segregation on the rise: Report. Reuters. Retrieved from http://www.reuters.com/article/2009/01/14/us-usa-segregation-idUSTRE50D7CY20090114

Cartaina, J. (2009). *The culture of incompetence: The mindset that destroys inner-city schools* [Electronic version]. Bloomington, IN: iUniverse.

Council for Exceptional Children. (n.d.). Juvenile justice. Retrieved from http://www.cec.sped.org/AM/Template.cfm?Section=Home&TEMPLATE=/CM/HTMLDisplay.cfm&CONTENTID=7869

Dead Prez. (2000). They schools. On *Let's get free* [CD]. New York: Loud Records.

Delpit, L. (2006). *Other people's children: Cultural conflict in the classroom* [Electronic version]. New York: New Press.

Dyson, A. (1999). Inclusion and inclusions: Theories and discourses in inclusive education. In H. Daniels & P. Garner (Eds.), *Inclusive education*. New York: Routledge.

Epstein, K. K. (2005). The whitening of the American teaching force: A problem of recruitment or a problem of racism? *Social Justice*. Vol. 32, No 3, 89–102.

Ferri, B. A., & Connor, D. J. (2006). *Reading resistance: Discourses of exclusion in desegregation & inclusion debates*. New York: Peter Lang.

Giroux, H. A. (2009). *Youth in a suspect society: Democracy or disposability?* New York: Palgrave Macmillan.

Goffman, E. (1963). *Stigma: Notes on the management of spoiled identity*. New York: Simon & Schuster.

Harry, B., & Klingner, J. K. (2006). *Why are so many minority students in special education? Understanding race and disability in schools*. New York: Teachers College Press.

Hawkins, R., Robinson, M., & Sinha, S. (2009). "US schools are more segregated today than in the 1950s." In P. Phillips, M. Huff, and Project Censored (Eds.) *Censored 2010: The top 25 censored stories in 2008–09*, (pp. 16–18). New York, NY: Seven Stories Press.

Hill, M. L. (2009). *Beats, rhymes, and classroom life: Hip-hop pedagogy and the politics of identity*. New York: Teachers College Press.

Howard, T. C. (2010). *Why race and culture matter in schools: Closing the achievement gap in America's classrooms*. New York: Teachers College Press.

Illich, I. (1972). *Deschooling society*. New York: Marion Boyars.

Jorissen, K. T. (2003). Successful career transitions: Lessons from urban alternative route teachers who stayed. *The High School Journal, 86*(3).

Kelves, D. J. (1995). *In the name of eugenics: Genetics and the uses of human heredity*. Cambridge, MA: Harvard University Press.

Kluth, P., Straut, D. M., & Biklen, D. P. (2003). *Access to academics for ALL students: Critical approaches to inclusive curriculum, instruction, and policy*. Mahwah, NJ: Lawrence Erlbuam.

Kohn, A. (1992). *No contest: The case against competition*. Boston: Houghton Mifflin.

Landsman, J., & Lewis, C. W. (2011). *White teachers / diverse classrooms: Creating inclusive schools, building on students' diversity, and providing true educational equity* [Electronic version]. Sterling, VA: Stylus.

Linden, A., & Klandermans, B. (2006). Stigmatization and repression of extreme-right activism in the Netherlands. *Mobilization: An International Quarterly, 11*(2), 213–228.

Nas & Dara, O. (2004). Bridging the gap. On *Street's disciple* [CD] New York: Columbia Records.

Nocella, A. J. (2008). Emergence of disability pedagogy. *The Journal for Critical Education Policy Studies, 6*(2), 77–94.

Orfield, G. (2009). Reviving the goal of an integrated society: A 21st century challenge. *Project Censored.* Retrieved from http://www.projectcensored.org/top-stories/articles/2-us-schools-are-more-segregated-today-than-in-the-1950s-source/

Osgood, P. L. (2005). *The history of inclusion in the United States.* Washington, DC: Gallaudet University Press.

Packard, F. A. (1866). *The daily public school in the United States.* New York: Arno Press.

Parmar, P. (2009). *Knowledge reigns supreme: The critical pedagogy of hip-hop artist KRS-One.* Rotterdam, The Netherlands: Sense.

Phillips, P., Huff, M., & Project Censored (2009). *Censored 2010: The top 25 censored stories in 2008–09.* New York, NY: Seven Stories Press.

Prier, D. D. (2012). *Culturally relevant teaching: Hip hop pedagogy in urban schools.* New York: Peter Lang.

Sleeter, C. E. (2001). Preparing teachers for culturally diverse schools: Research and the overwhelming presence of whiteness. *Journal of Teacher Education.* 52(94), 94–106.

Special Education Policy Issues Project. (2006). Juvenile justice and special education students in Washington State. *Special Education Law Quarterly*, Bulletin 9.

Stenhjem, P. (2005). Youth with disabilities in the juvenile justice system: Prevention and intervention strategies. *Issue Brief, 4*(1).

Strauss, V. (2012, July 9). Texas GOP rejects "critical thinking skills." Really. *The Washington Post.* Retrieved from http://www.washingtonpost.com/blogs/answer-sheet/post/texas-gop-rejects-critical-thinking-skills-really/2012/07/08/gJQAHNpFXW_blog.html

Toppo, G. (2009, July 9). Teach For America: Elite corps or costing older teachers jobs? *USA Today.* Retrieved from http://www.usatoday.com/news/education/2009–07–29-teach-for-america_N.htm

Villegas, A. M., & Lucas, T. (2002). *Educating culturally responsive teachers.* Albany, NY: SUNY Press.

PART FIVE

Behind THE Walls

Poor people, people of color especially, are much more likely to be found in prison than in institutions of higher education.

—ANGELA DAVIS

You can jail a revolutionary, but you can't jail a revolution.

—FRED HAMPTON

CHAPTER FOURTEEN

Prisons of Ignorance

MUMIA ABU-JAMAL

With very few exceptions, few in the world of academia really know anything about the world of prison.

They may know surface, they may know statistics, but below exists another world, where America's *Untermenschen* dwell in a hell that is, more often than not, beyond their experience, and thus beyond their ken.

Beyond the brick and steel and narrow-mindedness that masquerade as the so-called correctional system (where no one is, alas, corrected), there is the world outside, which I shall refer to as the feeder system, that ensures the continuing human seepage that populates prisons.

Let me try to illustrate something, albeit with what some may term anecdotal evidence.

The following are two conversations that the writer had recently with other prisoners, but which feature dizzying similarities:

Conversation I:

1: Dude. You ain't gonna believe what a young buck said to me yesterday.

2: What he say, man?

1: He came up to me, and asked, "Can I ask you a question, oldhead?" I said, "Yeah." And the young boy said, "Was Martin Luther King a rapper?"

2: You lyin', man! Get outta here!

1: I ain't lyin'! I swear 'fore God!

2: "Was Martin Luther King a rapper?" Seriously?

1: Seriously.
2: Well, what did you tella young dude?
1: First, I just stared at him. My mouth was open. I couldn't believe it.
2: Then, whachu do?
1: I told him he better get his stoopid black ass over to that library and do some studyin'!

Conversation II:

1: I'm gonna send you a book, man. Lemme know what you think of it.
2: Whoa! A book?
1: Yeah, man. What's up?
2: I don't do books.
1: What?
2: I ain't into books, oldhead.
1: You ain't into books?
2: Naw, oldhead. I don't spell too good.
1: Dude—you—you gotta be kiddin' me.
2: Naw, oldhead; It's just that, y'know, I have, like, trouble, reading and stuff.
1: Listen man, if you gonna hang wit me, you gotta read; you gotta study. I hope you beat your case, and all that, and get outta here. Seriously. But, you gotta lotta years you gotta do, man. You gonna read this joint; and if you find a word you don't know, or can't breakdown, write it down, and we'll talk about it, dig me?
The Qu'ran say you a student from the cradle to the grave, man, hear me?
2: Alright, alright, oldhead; I'll try.

I expect any academic reader who has never had the distinct experience of incarceration to treat these two conversations with complete and unrestricted disbelief. Indeed, I would be surprised if this were not so.

Yet, for any veteran of these American gulags, anyone who has dwelled in places such as this for any significant period of time, s/he knows that conversations such as these are more common than seaweed on the seashore.

They know that it has the ring of truth.

They know that because either they have personally heard or witnessed such conversations, or they were those who exhibited such profound ignorance at some young, distant age.

Nor should any of us be surprised when we dare to seriously consider the abysmal state of American education.

For decades now, due in large part to the bankruptcy of the political class, and the avariciousness of corporate forces, the U.S. public school system, especially in the nation's Black and Latin@ communities, is barely on life support.

The American political system has been engaged in an overt state of battle since the 1954 U.S. Supreme Court ruled in *Brown v. Board of Education* that racial segregation was unconstitutional. Conservative forces swore they would war against such a ruling, and so they have, using the venality of politicians, and the greed of the corporate powers.

The conservative animus brought to life by *Brown* reached a fever pitch that is somewhat difficult for many today to truly discern, for such overt hatred and antipathy rarely breaks through in modern media culture.

For the sake of clarity we here excerpt just one such comment that gives us some flavor of the passions roiling in the wake of the *Brown* decision.

Tom Brady, a Mississippi circuit court judge, made the following remarks shortly after *Brown* was decided:

> [W]hen a law transgresses the moral and ethical sanctions and standards of the mores, invariably strife, bloodshed and revolution follow in the wake of its attempted enforcement. The loveliest and purest of God's creatures, the nearest thing to an angelic being that tread this terrestrial ball is a well-bred, cultured Southern White woman or her blue-eyed, golden-haired little girl. (as quoted in Bennett, 2002, p. 348)

This is far more than empty political rhetoric. It was the red-hot voice of an entrenched and powerful segment of the white South, determined to resist the U.S. Supreme Court. So much so, that Brady, who, as a judicial officer was sworn to abide by the U.S. Constitution, sent the following message to the nation's highest court in his book, *Black Monday*: "We say to the Supreme Court and to the northern world, 'You shall not make us drink from this cup.' … We have, through our forefathers, died before for our sacred principles. We can, if necessary, die again."

In March of 1956, more than 100 U.S. congressmen issued the Southern Manifesto, declaring "massive resistance" to the Court's edict, and mass white protests rocked cities throughout the South (and, by the way, quite a few in the North, as well).

Did all of that energy dissipate? Or, did it (as all energy does) simply take other forms?

It entered politics. It entered law.

It reentered the nation's bloodstream like an inoculation.

And today one of the country's most intense scholar-activists, Jonathan Kozol, reports that U.S. schools are, several long generations after *Brown*, still largely segregated. Indeed, under this post-*Brown* dispensation, the quality of American education has greatly diminished. Kozol has described the present era as "apartheid schooling" (Kozol, 2002, pp. 18–19). Kozol, in the work *The Shame of the Nation*, interviewed former journalist and law professor Roger Wilkins, who made the following observations on the state of education in many communities of color:

> Any serious effort to reopen the debate about desegregation, is going to be enormously more difficult than the dismantling of apartheid in the South. Apartheid of that era was so gross and open in its manifestations that it was unsustainable within the age that followed World War II. But just as legal segregation in the South was a huge national horror hidden in plain view, so too the massive desolation of the intellect and spirit and human futures of these millions of young people in their neighborhoods of poverty is yet another national horror hidden in plain view; and it is so enormous and it has its own ganglia implanted so profoundly in the culture as we know it that we're going to have to build another movement if we hope to make it visible. (as quoted in Kozol, 2002, pp. 237–238)

How can a Black American child come to age in the 20th or 21st century, in an era of mass communications, and not have the faintest idea who Rev. Dr. Martin Luther King was?

Was Martin Luther King a rapper?

Well, yes—of a sort. He was a master rapper. But he didn't have a bling game. He rapped against war, materialism, and capitalism.

He rapped against racism.

"That's nothing you have to worry 'bout, kid! Get ready for that test we're gonna give ya tomorrow!"

Barely functioning schools are certainly an important element in this process.

Baltimore, Maryland, has a 75% drop-out rate in some neighborhoods. In many U.S. cities the high school drop-out rate averages at 50%.

Yet, as Wilkins has suggested, we do not have a politics that is able to meaningfully address and correct this great social disaster.

As we do not have a politics, we have no public policy designed to deal with this problem.

The former U.S. congressman Jesse Jackson, Jr., was also interviewed by Kozol, with the latter approving his ideas about a U.S. constitutional amendment guaranteeing an education to all Americans. As Kozol notes,

> Congressman Jesse Jackson, Jr., who represents a district in Chicago, has proposed a constitutional amendment that would guarantee the right to public education "of an equally high quality" to every American child and has introduced a resolution in the U.S. House of Representatives to this effect. Jackson's amendment, introduced in March 2003, would establish education as "a fundamental human right" under the U.S. Constitution and, as he described its purpose to me, would essentially strike down *Rodriguez* [*San Antonio Independent School District vs.*][1] and defend the education rights of children that are not defended by the high court's present readings of the equal protection clause of the Fourteenth Amendment.

---

1 The *Rodriguez* case, seen as the Hispanic anti-*Brown*, decided in 1973, denied relief to San Antonio parents seeking equal rights in education as in wealthier districts. The Court ruled 5–4 that such a right was not explicitly found in the Constitution, and thus they had no standing to sue.

> "Today," he said, "we have a 'states' rights educational system' —50 states, 3,067 counties, 95,000 public schools in 15,000 locally controlled districts in which 50 million children go to separate and unequal public schools. We need the assistance of the Constitution to correct this. Until we have it, 'savage inequalities,' to use your words, will not be an aberration in the system—it will be 'the system' as it stands." (Kozol, 2002, p. 251)

Unfortunately, Rep. Jackson has left his seat under a cloud, and his bill never found its way into law, perhaps because business interests did not want it to prevail.

In any event, it is not in the Constitution, and on that basis alone Americans are accepting not just an unequal but a nonfunctional system that simply doesn't work.

However, let us quibble a bit.

Who is to say that it doesn't work? It may not work on its stated terms, but what if its true *sub rosa* function was not to educate the vast majority of children (especially those of Black and brown America)? What if it was designed to provide an informal (yet devilishly effective!) "feeder system" to the vast U.S. prison system?

Or what if its function was to systematically *exclude* huge numbers of young people from the economic and political systems?

If this were its real socio-economic-political role, one would have to say it's working like gangbusters!

Tim Wise is a student of American racism, and a writer of several works on the subject. In his 2010 work, *Colorblind*, Wise writes of the nation's educational challenges:

> Although the premise of "No Child Left Behind" (the Bush administration's signature education bill) is that racial achievement gaps should be closed completely within ten years, the legislation never came with the kind of resource supports needed to make that goal achievable. Although No Child Left Behind requires certain outcomes, it does not mandate that schools must equalize the resources available to all students in order to make those more equitable outcomes likely. Nor did the law—which has so far been continued under the Obama administration, with very little functional change in its specific policy formulations—seek to put an end to the pernicious tracking practices in our schools that all but *guarantee* the leaving behind of children. In fact, many states have adopted norm-referenced tests as determinants of their "annual yearly progress" (mandated by the law), failing to appreciate that norm-referenced tests by *definition* produce a distribution where half of all test-takers will fall below the 50-percentile mark and thus be considered below average. In other words, tests that mandate failure and inequity in achievement are being used under a law intended to promote success and reduce inequity! To advocate equity but maintain structures that, by definition, create inequity is the ultimate contradiction. (Wise, 2010, pp. 108–109)

No Child Left Behind (NCLB), Wise argues, has placed schools under intense pressure, resulting in instructors teaching to the tests rather than other, richer areas of learning, such as those that are practiced in suburban and wealthy private schools. How could NCLB be seen as anything but a device that actually furthers the apartheid school system that covers too much of the nation? Wise (2010) adds:

> High-stakes testing has also created incentives for schools to push lower-achieving students out, rather than keep them in the schools, attempt to educate them and suffer the possible penalty if they fail, in terms of meeting testing requirements. In Chicago, for instance, schools have been expelling low-achieving students even by the age of 16, under the pretense that their academic achievement or attendance records make it unlikely that they would graduate by the age of 21. Rather than resolve to educate such students—almost all of whom are students of color—the schools give up, remove the students and thus boost their test-score profile as a result, with blacks banished from the schools at three times the rate of whites or Latinos. (p. 109)

What happens to a young, uninformed person who is thrown out of school at 16?

What life is there for him, *except* street life? And, surrounded by that which glitters but isn't gold, the false allure of fool's gold that blinds the eye and dulls the sense—that looks easy—what is a youth to do?

And where does s/he go?

We know where they go. They go where the feeder system has designed for them to go.

And once inside, what real options are available?

The answer is, not much, thanks to the passage and signing into law of Bill Clinton's Crime Bill that, among other things, outlawed the usage of Pell Grants for prisoner-students. Clinton amended the Higher Education Act of 1965 with a prohibition of all such grants to those in state and federal prisons.

This, despite the fact that the only demonstrable solution to criminal recidivism is education, which gives people options other than the street life.

Is that the very essence of a feeder system? It certainly looks like it.

In 1995, when the crime bill became law, I wrote that the bill was essentially a $30+ billion boondoggle designed by the neo-liberals to work as a public employment system for predominantly white rural workers.

Today, more than $60 billion is spent on the prison industrial complex (Cole, 2009, p. 42).

And schools are little more than training camps for graduation into oftentimes lifelong confinement to feed the rapacious beast.

We are on the wrong road, and schools, having failed so badly, have played a pivotal role in shaping this dystopian future. Yet it must be said that the realm of popular culture has also played a role of appearing to prize ignorance, despite the illustrious history of intellectual excellence in Black history, á la Du Bois, Robeson, and King—uhhh—wait; was Martin Luther King a rapper?

Unless we seriously elect to reestablish that tradition, or establish our own truly independent primary and secondary schools, the future of Black America will be bleak indeed.

REFERENCES

Bennett, L. (2002). *Before the Mayflower: A history of Black America.* Chicago: Johnson.

Cole, D. (2009, November 19). Can our shameful prisons be reformed? *New York Review of Books,* 41–43.

Kozol, J. (2005). *The shame of the nation: The restoration of apartheid schooling in America.* New York: Three Rivers Press.

Wise, T. (2010). *Colorblind: The rise of post-racial politics and the retreat from racial equity.* San Francisco: City Lights Books.

CHAPTER FIFTEEN

At THE End OF THE Pipeline

Can the Liberal Arts Liberate the Incarcerated?

DEBORAH APPLEMAN, ZEKE CALIGIURI, AND JON VANG

INTRODUCTION

In the United States, incarceration is an epidemic. Incarceration has replaced education as the life course for millions of adolescents and young adults. According to the Higher Education Policy report "Unlocking Potential: Results of a National Survey of Postsecondary Education in State Prisons," an estimated 2.3 million people are incarcerated in the United States (Gorgol & Spensler, 2011). On any given day, more than 1 in 100 adults are in jail or prison (Warren, 2008). As Alexander (2010) so powerfully argues, incarceration has become the new caste system in the United States, and there are powerful systemic mechanisms that ensure a permanent incarcerated underclass, largely composed of men of color. We must join forces to abolish both the mechanisms of social control as well as the prisons that perpetuate such systematic injustice.

We need not look further than our local schools to find one of the primary and precipitating sources of this systematic mechanism of injustice, one that relentlessly serves up adolescent boys to the jaws of incarceration. A school-prison nexus (Winn, 2011) comprises several factors that combine to doom many youth, especially urban youth of color, to a life path where incarceration is almost a near certainty. Meiners (2007), explains it this way: "Trapped in failing schools that are physically deteriorating, disciplined and moved into juvenile justice systems through violations of punitive zero tolerance policies, failing to pass high stakes standardized tests and channeled into special education programs, youth of color are materially and conceptually moved from schools to jails" (p. 16). Waquant cites the decaying urban schools as institutions of confinement, a condition of the "hyperghetto." Noguera (2003) describes the relentless sorting that occurs with children as young as 8 years old. This early onset has prompted organizations such as the Children's Defense Fund to rename the school to prison pipeline the "cradle to prison pipeline" (Children's Defense Fund, 2007).

Thus, we share with the other volume contributors the sense of urgency to dismantle the school to prison pipeline and eventually to dismantle the prison system itself. Yet this chapter has a somewhat different focus. What can be done to sustain the incarcerated while they are in prison? The fact remains that there are tens of thousands of human beings currently incarcerated whose lives and sentences will expire long before the changes called for by education reformers, social justice advocates, and prison abolitionists can be implemented. Therefore, a central component of prison reform efforts must be to ensure that those who are currently incarcerated are provided with access to high-quality educational experiences. We further assert that those educational experiences not be limited to strict technical or vocational training or only to those who will eventually be released. We recognize the need to tend to and to nourish the lives and minds and hearts of those who are serving time, regardless of the length of sentence. We believe that a liberal arts education—one that allows the incarcerated to challenge ideology, write freely, express one's ideals openly, and read widely—is an essential way to help heal and transform the incarcerated and to provide them with the sense of potential and respect that so many of them richly deserve. This chapter, then, explores the critical role that a liberal arts education can play as a transformational alternative for those who are incarcerated.

LOCATING OUR AUTHORIAL STANCES

We offer this exploration from the perspectives of a prison teacher (Appleman), a formerly incarcerated student (Vang), and a currently incarcerated student (Caligiuri). We combine our voices and perspectives from the outside and from the inside, in part to demonstrate the potential and value of intellectual collaboration between the bars of incarceration. We also seize upon this rare opportunity to have the incarcerated speak for themselves rather than have their thoughts be ventriloquized, even from well-meaning allies. We stress that even more than the words we write, our act of writing together defies the constraints that have been placed on the three of us. We come together, reaching beyond the bars that still incarcerate one of us to exercise our right to participate in critical discourse. This co-authorship defies the limitations of incarceration and, we maintain, is a result of the very impulse for liberal arts education that we advocate in the pages that follow.

Jon has recently been released from a high security prison in the Upper Midwest. He says that he always liked school well enough and that he actually had begun a college career before his crime interrupted that trajectory. The stark reality and the grimness of prison stood in sharp contrast to the steady and safe middle-class life to which he was aspiring. When college classes in prison came his way, he jumped at the chance to enroll. He believes that the opportunity to continue his education in prison is a key factor in his ability to rebuild his life on the outside. He also believes that the classes he took in prison fundamentally changed him.

For Zeke, who remains incarcerated in the same correctional facility that Jon once inhabited, the most salient part of his high school experience happened outside of school. Lack of attendance and motivation convinced Zeke that he was uninterested in what schools had to offer. One of the most remarkable students Deborah has ever taught, Zeke scoffs at his high school GPA of 79. His interest in writing and in language blossomed once he was incarcerated. He is now an award-winning poet, essayist, memoirist, and fiction writer.

After a decade as a high school teacher, Deborah was led by circumstance to the classrooms of an elite liberal arts college, where she has taught for twenty-six years. An opportunity later arose for her to teach at a high security prison for men, and the need for doing so was made abundantly clear as she learned about the dramatic de-funding of many prison education programs. A view of liberal arts education through the lens of incarceration has clarified its value for her. She says that Jon and Zeke and her other incarcerated students rival her students at the University of California at Berkeley and at Carleton College in terms of their intelligence, dedication, commitment, and talent. Most important, she has witnessed the fundamentally transformative powers of liberal arts education for the incarcerated. Unfortunately, this perspective is still not widely held among policy makers and the general public, despite the ample evidence we have about the positive effects of education among the incarcerated.

EDUCATION AND RECIDIVISM

The most recognized reason for prison education programs is their effect on recidivism. Study after study vaunts the finding that offenders who participate in educational programs in prison are less likely to reoffend. While this statistic may be a bit of a commonplace, the reasons behind its truth are not often discussed. In addition to job readiness and the attainment of important basic literacy skills, education—especially liberal arts education—can significantly help the incarcerated by increasing their self-efficacy, their confidence, and their sense of themselves as being "more than a felon." According to Vacca (2004),

> Prisoners who attend education programs while they are incarcerated are less likely to return to prison following their release. Since 1990, literature examining the return rates of prisoners, or recidivism, has shown that educated prisoners are less likely to find themselves back in prison a second time if they complete an educational program and are taught skills to successfully read and write. The "right kind" of education works to both lower recidivism and reduce the level of violence. Moreover, appropriate education leads to a more humane and more tolerable prison environment in which to live and work, not only for the inmates but also for the officers, staff and everyone else (Newman et al., 1993).

Arguing for a renewed emphasis on and expansion of prison education programs, Nixon writes:

> Numerous studies have shown that completing postsecondary educational programs while in prison has sweeping effects on the lives of formerly incarcerated individuals. In addition to increased social capital, earning potential and better health outcomes for families and communities, the public safety implications of increased access to higher education cannot be overstated. (Nixon, 2012)

The Bard Prison Initiative web site also recognizes this positive outcome of liberal arts education in prison:

> Graduates of the BPI program have consistently succeeded after release from prison. Some have chosen to work in human service organizations, serving people with AIDS, or becoming professional counselors for residents in city-based alternatives to incarceration. Several alumni have worked their way up to management positions in an innovative, for-profit electronics recycling company. Other graduates have continued their educations, earning scholarships and working toward additional academic and professional degrees. (n.d.)

Although it is true that education deters recidivism, Zeke offers an important reality check:

> For all the emphasis that is put on education as the great recidivism reducer, educational opportunity has a pretty substantial ceiling that people who start from behind end up bumping their heads against. It all looks good, but the programs are oversimplified and don't get people jobs when they get out or keep a person from having to lock into a cage every night for several decades without any relief.

THE STATE OF PRISON EDUCATION PROGRAMS

Despite the incontrovertible evidence of the powerful effects of education on recidivism, education for the incarcerated remains a hard sell. Although there was a flurry of initiatives in the mid-1970s, education programs in prison have diminished or disappeared as a result of restrictions on funding such as Pell Grants and the chilling effects of tough-on-crime legislation. Across the country, funding has dried up for prison programs, especially those located in high or maximum security prisons. As Martin (2009) explains:

> The tough-on-crime era of the 1970s and after ushered in a host of measures that supported the framework of a harsher, more punitive approach to prisoners. ... Mandatory minimum sentencing, three-strikes-and-you're-out sentencing laws, juveniles being tried as adults—all of these were part of the trend. Amid all this, the defunding of education programs for prisoners was a less noticed but related change.

Duffy (2007) further traces the demise of most prison programs:

> Educational programs in prisons actually used to be commonplace. Starting in the 70s, prisoners organized themselves and pushed for educational opportunities within correctional facilities. They were successful. There were 350 college-in-prison programs around the country by 1995, according to BPI's website. Then, as politicians began to present themselves as "tough on crime," the axe fell on most of the programs. Critics wondered why inmates were receiving educational opportunities when so many non-incarcerated Americans already lacked adequate access to college. Congress eliminated Pell Grant eligibility for inmates through the 1994 Violent Crime Control and Law Enforcement Act. Within a few years of the act's passage, only three college-in-prison programs remained.

Offerings in prison have dwindled to just a handful of largely technical courses. Libraries have become sparse and outdated; technology is used only sparingly and is compromised by constant surveillance and worries of security breaches. Many potential students are ineligible for the classes they are so eager to take because of their status as violent offenders. In other words, those who are most likely to benefit from the positive outcomes of post-secondary education are prevented from taking part. The Higher Education Policy report "Unlocking Potential: Results of a National Survey of Postsecondary Education in State Prisons" puts it this way:

> Although research has shown a link between educating prisoners and reduced rates of recidivism, many inmates have struggled to pay for college since President Bill Clinton barred inmates from receiving Pell Grants in 1994. Some private colleges have joined with nearby prisons to offer free, for-credit courses to inmates, but those individual partnerships—while often successful in reducing recidivism on a small scale—don't represent the educational opportunities available to most inmates. (Gorgol & Spensler, 2011)

Zeke also offers a frank assessment of the state of prison programs:

> There was once a thriving narrative of reemergence that existed for those in and coming out of prison. Men and women turned into authors and cultivated successful art careers, or became highly regarded professors or representatives in social movements. The gradual tightening of policy and lawmaking has made much of this almost impossible, even for those with genuinely transformative ideas. It feels like they would love for us to be robots that spout out prearranged statements from a script. They have never taken into consideration just what the loss of time really takes from human beings, or that assume they have any sort of alternate point of view.

> While an education is something that is supposed to last and evolve through an entire lifetime, the value of education in prison can go mostly to waste. It hasn't shown a direct influence in the shortening of sentences or increased opportunities. In many ways education offers lonely accomplishments that sound very good. We have had some magnificent people come in and share their life-changing energies that are lasting and real. But it also needs to be mentioned that while there have been strong efforts to add new programs to and reinforce lasting programs in education departments in the system, there exists a definite ceiling. The focal point of correctional education is still the GED programs which, in themselves, are good and necessary. And while there are classes that lead toward an A.A. degree, they are still sparsely offered—perhaps two classes at a time with large gaps between offerings. Because slots are so scarce, often guys are able to take only a single class at a time, so it is difficult and time consuming to get past that single hurdle. At one point when I was working toward a degree, the entire higher education program was cut. When you get to the parts where the greatest statistical support for success exists, there is really nothing. There aren't Bachelor's and Master's programs available for those who have completed the available programming. Pell Grants, which were at one point one of the primary means for prisoners to continue their educations, were taken from prisoners in the 1990s, thus cutting off a substantial extension to the rehabilitation for incarcerated men and women. Those who are able to continue work are left with very few degree programs to choose from because of the lack of access to online capabilities used primarily by most schools' distance learning programs. Our computer access is very limited as well, and personal writing projects aren't allowed on the scale they could be.

To be sure, there are a few notable exceptions to this dire portrait of prison education programs. Both Bard College and Grinnell College are offering prison programs to present "liberal arts behind bars." Bard College has an extensive program that works with five New York prisons:

> The Bard Prison Initiative (BPI) creates the opportunity for incarcerated men and women to earn a Bard College degree while serving their sentences. The academic standards and workload are rigorous, based on an unusual mix of attention to developmental skills and ambitious college study. The rate of post-release employment among the program's participants is high and recidivism is stunningly low. By challenging incarcerated men and women with a liberal education, BPI works to redefine the relationship between educational opportunity and criminal justice. (Bard College, n.d.)

Duffy explains Bard's motivation this way:

> Bard realized that as a liberal arts college, it could offer inmates at nearby prisons an education that would greatly reduce their chances of re-entering the justice system at a cost far lower than that of continued incarceration. (Duffy, 2012)

Bard has also created the Consortium for the Liberal Arts in Prison, to which Grinnell College belongs. Grinnell offers the first year of college at no cost to incarcerated men and women and has involved both faculty and students. Grinnell describes the mission of its Liberal Arts in Prison program this way:

The program has stayed true to its original vision of reciprocal learning and open intellectual exchange: exchange that enriches lives both inside and outside the fences and affirms the transformative power of a liberal arts education. (Grinnell College, n.d.)

Although these two programs have clearly animated the potential of offering liberal arts to the incarcerated, they exist as isolated beacons of light in an otherwise dark landscape of missed opportunities. So what can liberal arts education do for the incarcerated? Why should this particular kind of education, often associated with elite colleges and students of privilege, be offered to those in prison? Perhaps we should first clarify what we mean by a liberal arts education.

WHAT IS A LIBERAL ARTS EDUCATION?

Harris (2010) describes a liberal arts education as one that teaches individuals how to think, how to learn, how to make sense of the world around them, how to understand the relationship between old knowledge and new knowledge, how to generate creativity. He writes:

> The diverse body of knowledge you will gain from a liberal arts education, together with the tools of examination and analysis that you will learn to use, will enable you to develop your own opinions, attitudes, values, and beliefs, based not upon the authority of parents, peers, or professors, and not upon ignorance, whim, or prejudice, but upon your own worthy apprehension, examination, and evaluation of argument and evidence. … A thorough knowledge of a wide range of events, philosophies, procedures, and possibilities makes the phenomena of life appear coherent and understandable. No longer will unexpected or strange things be merely dazzling or confusing. (Harris, 2010)

Brown University (n.d.) also delineates some important effects or results of a liberal arts education, including enhancing communication skills such as writing and speaking, understanding differences among cultures, evaluating human behavior, embracing diversity, learning what it means to study the past, collaborating fully, experiencing scientific inquiry, developing a facility with symbolic languages, expanding reading skills, enhancing aesthetic sensibility, and applying what one has learned. These are broad intellectual goals, to be sure, but goals that are relevant for the incarcerated as well. As Nixon writes,

> Education should also be considered on its own merit. Put simply: Education is not just a means to myriad positive ends, but an end unto itself. Education—on its own—is worth pursuing, worth having and worth supporting. (Nixon, 2012)

THE VALUE OF A LIBERAL ARTS EDUCATION FOR THE INCARCERATED

Although it may seem counterintuitive, a liberal arts education is particularly well suited to the incarcerated, especially those who are serving life or very long sentences. The lack of specific vocational focus, sometimes viewed as a shortcoming for those on the outside, is actually advantageous for those who are focusing on experiences whose value is not tied to vocational training. For many of the incarcerated, these programs provide a second chance to avail themselves of the value of education, a value that they might not previously have experienced:

> Many prisoners are likely to have poor self-confidence and negative attitudes about education because they viewed their early experiences as being negative. (Paul, 1991)

Both Jon and Zeke confirm that education became much more meaningful to them after their incarceration. Jon writes: High school became boring, and I became more interested in the popularity of the gang lifestyle. During that time in my life, I had so many unanswered questions about being a man and socially interacting with other males and females. Many told me that school was important, but I didn't connect it with why it was important in the job world.

Zeke recollects his high school experience with some irony:

> I never believed anything that was being taught was too difficult to learn. What I think it demanded too much of was time, and it offered too little time for me to process what it was I was supposed to be learning. We sat through six different class periods over the course of seven hours. I personally had an attention span of about forty-five minutes. I also think I was like a lot of fringe students who wanted to be challenged personally on things but didn't want such a life-or-death consequence: success or failure with every course. I wanted to be taught with the expectation that I already understood certain things and that the only way to hold my attention was through continued challenge. I wanted to feel intelligent, but what I was being taught made me feel dumb for trying to make it seem important. Most of this, it should be said, wouldn't have mattered if I myself had a clearer perspective on what I wanted. I think what I needed most was an actual understanding that I wasn't fully capable of understanding what I was really going to want out of life when I got older. I needed to know from someone that there was a harsh, violent world out there that would consume me unless I found ways to make myself more capable. The streets taught me a lot about who I was, just not enough to fight the vastness of the things pushing back against me. Honesty would have been helpful when I was messing up, instead of a sugarcoated, afterschool-special version of the future.

While most of the incarcerated, like Jon and Zeke, had ambivalent feelings about education on the outside, it becomes a cherished experience for most on the inside. At a panel featuring Grinnell's Liberal Arts in Prison Program (February 3, 2013), a recently released former student waxed enthusiastically about what the liberal arts had done for him: "Liberal arts changed me to the core. The liberal arts teaches you how to think. Vocational education may teach you how to perform a job, but liberal arts education teaches you about yourself." Another member of the panel said, "The outside world falls away when you are institutionalized. The world outside of prison becomes an abstract idea. Liberal arts education makes that world come back to you. As you grapple with ideas, you are grappling with the world."

Jon underscores this notion of education reconnecting the isolation of the incarcerated back to "the world":

> Being cut off from much of the world and having a lot of idle time, education is priceless. It is a breath of fresh air and it gives me purpose. Learning and doing something productive makes me feel like my time is not wasted. I wish we had more options and avenues for education. Education is like the parts of a machine. The prison programs are the tools. When you use them together, you can assemble the best chance at succeeding once released from prison. It has been essential to my rehabilitation. Without it, I would most likely still have the same mindset and habits as I did before going into prison.

Zeke offers this assessment of the value of a liberal arts education for the incarcerated:

> It showed me there are levels of accomplishment that I may have missed at points in my life that I can still attain. It also helped repair some of the injuries incurred between my family and me during my years in the Minneapolis Public School system. It gave me an extension of language to communicate who I am and what it is I have experienced. They are not new experiences; people have been in dungeons as long as other humans were able to construct them. The most difficult part has always been communicating to those outside of them why they are wrong, communicating that they are part of all of the things human beings will do to each other. Without knowing it, my education helped to teach me the sociological angles to these things, as well as the psychological and political and economic aspects of why places and experiences like this exist. And even without a single definitive answer, it has helped me to understand my personal place and opinions involved in it.

Ian Buruma, a college teacher who participated in the Bard Prison Initiative, remarks on how education is edifying to the students:

> It was obvious to me, as a teacher, how precious education was to the students, not only because they could practically recite every sentence of the books and articles I gave them to read but also because of the way they behaved to one another. Prisons breed cynicism. Trust is frequently betrayed and friendships severed when a prisoner is transferred without warning to another facility. The classroom was an exception. (Buruma, 2005)

READING AND WRITING IN PRISON

Jon discusses the general value of reading and contrasts reading on the outside and reading while incarcerated: "I have learned that reading is fun when you read about things you are interested in. Reading things in school seemed so boring, especially when they mandated what I had to read. When I read a novel or about a topic that interested me, time flew and I got lost in my thoughts. A great book for me can leave me in tears or feeling free and inspired."

For Zeke, reading while incarcerated has also become a crucial element of his education:

> Jail and prison are different from the streets in that there are substantial chunks of time spent empty or waiting on what is supposed to happen next. When I was first locked up I read whatever I could to keep my mind from stewing over what might happen to my life: mystery or romance novels, magazines, even the orientation packets, just hoping it would eat enough time to get me closer to my next nap. A point came where I realized I wasn't holding onto much of what I took in and was getting very little enjoyment, just more work. So, I started to read literature again, mostly recognizable authors and titles: Hemingway and Steinbeck and Joyce. This coincided with a period where I was anticipating a long stint in segregation over some things that were happening in the makeup of the institution. I started subscribing to a bunch of magazines, a couple of weeklies, and a bunch of monthlies. The segregation trip never came but I got accustomed to an influx of current information, which helped me to understand in more depth how the written word was in a sense a living organism where sometimes ideas and meanings were worthwhile and alive for a while, then they die or turn into something else. It took what I read and applied current and evolving value to what I had already read, which made me a much more active learner. One of the most common things I've recognized in a lot of the people I've done time with, is the tendency to hold on to and argue vigorously for the ideas they get from the few things they actually read. Many guys may only read two or three books a year, so you have guys making life or death declarations over what they read in the only book they read in the previous two or three years. By taking in a larger swath of information, it kept me from becoming one of those people. It made me feel like I was still learning and that the entire world wasn't decided yet. It made me see that there were greater narratives that existed that spanned greater stretches of the human experience that I never completely understood without the commitment to reading and wanting to know more. And that those stories were just as much intertwined with my story and the stories of guys lined up in cells all down the tiers as well. We have no control over where we are born and the circumstances we come up in, but the struggles are universal and that taught me not to overrate the things I might have been going through, but also not to diminish them either.

The study of literature as well as recreational reading has value for the incarcerated. In a literature class, for example, incarcerated students become literary theorists and interpreters of texts. While this is a population that is often accused of lacking empathy, the very act of reading and interpreting a piece of literature and empathizing with the characters seems to expand the empathetic ability of the students. Reading both literary and historical texts from multiple perspectives (Appleman, 2010) helps students read and resist the ideologies that undergird those texts, which in turn enables them to critique their own ideologies as well. And there is no more fiercely ideological place in the world than a prison.

Liberal arts education also helps provide opportunities for the incarcerated to become writers. At the heart of liberal arts education is the emphasis on learning to articulate one's beliefs and ideas through writing. For many inmates, writing becomes a central element, sometimes even the core, of a recrafted identity. For example, Jon writes:

> Since incarceration, writing has become an avenue to navigate through my thoughts and feelings in life. It has become a staple to my communication with loved ones. Writing is a tool of artistic expression and a way to share stories. To me, writing is empowering because words are powerful. I have a greater understanding of words when I am able to break them down like an etymologist and look at the roots and origins of a word.

For Zeke, an unusually gifted writer who has won several national writing awards, writing has become a core part of his identity. He says:

> Prior to my incarceration there was nothing to write for. I always felt like I would write a book one day, but I lived in a mental state where I could barely concentrate long enough to study for a driver's test, let alone imagine and edit any kind of long-form material. I still had no idea what sort of book I might write; it was probably mostly just an avenue that came from a starving ego. Getting locked up meant looking at my life as a sort of pause from the speed I had been accustomed to moving. It made me feel like I still wanted a sort of relevancy to my life, even if it was going to be short or difficult, and I resolved that one of the only ways that could ever be possible was if I left some sort of artistic expression in the universe. I think from the beginning I just wanted people to understand what an unjust system we were living in and that it hurt exceptionally on a personal level to have everything I understood of my life be suppressed to such tiny extremes. I came to understand that most would never even have a channel that would catch the rants and scrambled disappointments of just one of the two-and-a-half-million incarcerated Americans. While others expressed themselves through other forms of visual art, the written word was the only expression I had to say something that might move tangibly into the hands of someone else who wasn't tortured by the same things that tormented me. I was fortunate enough to have educators who came in, told me what I was doing was relevant, and encouraged me to keep going. In time, it started to become a re-humanization process by which I started to re-conceive my own humanity and self-respect. It is easy for those in power, those associated with the law, to tell you that you are wrong and then expect the only way for you to get back right again is to spout off a reinforcement of the ideas that got you locked up rather than constructing ideas of your own.
>
> Writing has become an essential part of who I see myself to be. Being a writer means I can speak for myself. I am also able to speak for those in similar situations and express themes in the world that are perplexing or unjust or that support notions of those whose voices don't get listened to or acknowledged. It has also meant my inclusion within a body of human existence that has been around forever, that framed the world in terms people could see as something other than what existed in their time. I have joined people that have written and rewritten over and over because they cared about what it was they created. Writing connects me spiritually with people in gulags and concentration camps and

> personal exiles who wrote without knowing if they'd be killed or wither away somewhere unheard, who found ways to get their words out of that oppression and into the world. It means that being one of those people means working even if you're not sure someone will ever get to listen to it. It also means something grew up in me. I started somewhere and was able to work my way into someone with a sharper grasp of what he could do. Coming from someone that never completed anything and without any kind of vision of who that person could be, I became someone capable of writing my own universe. Writers are active voices, sometimes even beyond their own lifetimes, and very realistically, it gave me an identity beyond the titles I was given when the judge dropped his gavel and an offender identification number was ironed over my name. Instead of waiting on someone else to come around and tell the story in a way, it is my narrative and the characters are very real, breathing examples of life and experience.

CHANGING PERSONAL NARRATIVES

In prison, these forays into reading and writing, this kind of education, exists in its purest form. There is no external payoff, no job, no material change in circumstances, and often no degree. For the most part, it seems that those who undertake education in prison do so for the purest of reasons—they want to learn for learning's sake and to experience the personal transformation that accompanies education. Inevitably, this desire to transform, to become a better and sometimes a different person, alters the personal narratives of those in prison. This change in personal narrative, in self-definition, is one of the most important aspects of the role of liberal arts education in prison. For those who will re-enter society after being incarcerated, their success and well-being largely depend on their ability to imagine themselves as more than a felon, as more than a criminal.

This ability to craft an alternate identity is equally crucial for those who will remain incarcerated. Liberal arts education offers alternative narratives to those who have defined themselves only by their current circumstances and by what they have done wrong. As one student said, "I am more than what I did twenty years ago. I am a man."

Zeke underscores this point:

> Education made me a writer, a student, a man, an individual outside statistics hidden somewhere. It made me a better son, able to replant seeds over the things I tore down a long time ago. It made me a voice that could articulate what I felt about myself and about this whole experience instead of just a projection of these emotions and feelings. It also made me understand what I could about the future, no matter how difficult it may still seem.

Jon emphasizes the role that education plays in developing more flexible habits of mind. He relates an exercise in our sociolinguistics class when students were asked to move to a different part of the room to inhabit a perspective they didn't believe in. He says that this enabled him to inhabit the perspective of others and to understand points of view that were wildly different from his own. This is really what it means to be educated, he asserts: to understand, from the inside out, a view that stands in opposition to one's own. He continues:

> I believe that one of the most important things anyone can gain from higher learning is the ability to think critically about things in life and embrace your own results from your own thoughts. I say this because I know many who see things in life as either us or them, black or white, Bloods or Crips, Democrats or Republicans, etc. Through that thought process, too many decisions that affect the whole are made by too few, as lines are drawn and followers follow. The ability to take in "What an idea means," "So what does this idea mean to me?" and "Now what do I about this idea?" is one of the most valuable processes that I have gotten from higher learning. The critical part is that I have learned to view the idea from the perspective of another who disagrees with my view and understand their counterarguments. This is the critical thinking that I believe will help end recidivism.

Perhaps even more important than the specific intellectual skills or habits of mind that are transmitted is the changing sense of self-efficacy. Lagemann (2010) quotes a graduate of the Bard program:

> Participating in the Bard program, he said, had not directly helped him get a job, but it had "put the puzzle together" for him and enabled him "to get ready to be different when he got home." As I pressed him to explain, he talked of growing up in Harlem, where his friends in the street always wanted to know "who was putting us down." Bard taught him, he said, to think critically about statements like that. His classes in history and anthropology had enabled him to understand his situation in a social context. "Now," he said, smiling, "I know life is more than 'us versus them.'"

CONCLUSION

The prison industrial system as it currently exists, the shame of our "civilized" nation, is able to continue only because most people are oblivious to the waste of human capital, the astounding level of intelligence and creativity, that exists behind bars. Its daily operations depend on systematized practices of dehumanization to which both Zeke and Jon have alluded. In order to cage human beings, we need to dehumanize them. There are a myriad of ways in which this is systematically done. Inmates are referred to and are directly addressed by an Offender Identification number rather than by name. Movement is closely restricted, even to the point of regulating shower lengths and stints on the toilet. In many places health care is atrocious. Only when men are dehumanized can they be so controlled by other men. This dehumanization exists in direct and vehement opposition to the goals of liberal arts education, which seeks to humanize. This tension, then, between the aims of liberal arts education and the aims of incarceration are ubiquitous in prison education programs to the students and to their teachers.

Despite these inherent contradictions, however, it seems evident that educational opportunities in prison can be, as one of my incarcerated students put it, "a lifesaver."

Zeke writes:

> I had no idea what prison would do to me or what opportunities would or wouldn't be available when I came through the door. I was fortunate enough that there was programming and higher education available to me (although much less now) when I came in. I met instructors and professors that encouraged me to write and learn more. I also met other convicts that were trying to learn more and become something beyond what they were slated to be by the numbers on their ID cards. Education helped me see myself as someone who might have avoided prison had the infinite variables worked themselves out differently.

Zeke writes:

> It also showed me some humanity. It maintained for me the idea that there are still aspects of our society that believed in the rehabilitative spirit in those of us that had in essence been cast away or discarded. The environment offers such sharp contrasts between a population of us face-to-face with our own failures and a community that reinforces those failures by determining what we should be able to have access to and what we should be able to learn and become. We get a clear picture that we are less than human enough to live in cages. So when human beings come in, mostly unpaid, to offer us access to information available in the schools outside these bars, it showed me there was still a little humanity left somewhere.

We often find ourselves at odds with those in the prison abolitionist movement, including several whose voices are contained in this volume. Some say that providing educational opportunities for the incarcerated simply turns activists into unwilling handmaidens of the prison industrial system. "Don't make it easy for them to look good," they say. "You are enabling their ability to maintain such a cruel and immoral system of incarceration, humiliation, and dehumanization." While we agree that the systems of discipline, surveillance, marginalization, and racism that enable the school to prison pipeline and the current prison system must be interrupted, the fact remains that there are hundreds of thousands of men and women whose agile minds languish in the absence of any intellectual challenge or educational opportunity.

As Lagemann asks:

> Have we lost the faith in education that once made the United States a place of opportunity for so many people? I hope not. But demonstrating this faith, and with it continuing optimism about the nation's future, requires extending the national agenda to include college in prison. (2010)

Many of us have indeed lost faith, both in an educational system that seems to track young men into jail and in a criminal justice system that unequally metes out sentences and ignores the importance of education as the only effective deterrent to recidivism.

Through systems of discipline, unequal resources, and systematic racism, tens of thousands of young men, caught in the school to prison pipeline, have been stripped of their civil rights and left to languish in prison. Among the rights they lost on the occasion of their incarceration were the civil right of literacy and the right to an education. Let us work together to dismantle the school to prison pipeline and the relentless cruelty of institutions of incarceration. Until those institutions are transformed, let us work together to create, provide, and sustain educational opportunities for the incarcerated. As one incarcerated college student of the Prison University Project, Chrisfino Kenyatta Leal (2011), exclaimed: "The more opportunities we in prison have to learn to value education and see possibilities for ourselves, the greater the chance we will break the cycle of incarceration not just for ourselves but for future generations to come."

REFERENCES

Alexander, M. (2010). *The new Jim Crow: Mass incarceration in the age of colorblindness*. New York: New Press.

Appleman, D. (2009). *Critical encounters in high school English: Teaching literary theory to adolescents* (2nd ed.). New York: Teachers College Press.

Bard College. (n.d.). Bard Prison Initiative. Annandale-on-Hudson. Retrieved from http://www.bpi.bard.edu

Brown University. (n.d.). *Liberal learning goals*. Retrieved from http://brown.edu/Administration/Dean_of_the_College/curriculum/downloads/Lib_Learning_Goals.pdf

Buruma, I. (2005, February 20). Uncaptive minds. *New York Times Magazine*. Retrieved from http://www.nytimes.com/2005/02/20/magazine/20PRISON.html?pagewanted=print&position=&_r=0

Children's Defense Fund. (2007). *America's cradle to prison pipeline report*. Washington, DC: Author.

Duffy, Z. (2010, October 7). Give prisoners the gift of a Whitman education. *The Pioneer*. Retrieved from http://whitmanpioneer.com/opinion/columnists/2010/10/07/give-prisoners-the-gift-of-a-whitman-education/

Gorgol, L., & Spensler, B. (2011). Unlocking potential: Results of a national survey of postsecondary education in state prisons. *Institute for Higher Education Policy*. Retrieved from http://www.ihep.org/publications/publications-detail.cfm?id=143

Grinnell College. (n.d.). *Liberal arts in prison*. Grinnell, IA. Retrieved from https://www.grinnell.edu/node/10447

Grinnell's Liberal Arts in Prison Program. (February 3, 2013). Panel discussion at the Minnesota History Center, St. Paul, MN.

Harris, R. (2010, October 15). On the purpose of a liberal arts education. *Virtual Salt*. Retrieved from http://www.virtualsalt.com/libarted.htm (Original work published March 14, 1991)

Lagemann, E. (2010, November 28). Doing time, with a degree to show for it. *The Chronicle of Higher Education*. Retrieved from http://chronicle.com/article/Doing-Time-With-a-Degree-to/125482/

Leal, C.K. (2011). The Last Mile: Commencement Address, Prison University Project. Retrieved from http://thelastmile.org/2011/07/commencement-address/

Martin, M. (2009, June 2). What happened to prison education programs? *The Socialist Worker.* Retrieved from http://socialistworker.org/print/2009/06/02/what-happened-to-prison-education

Meiners, E. R. (2007). *Right to be hostile: Schools, prisons and the making of public enemies.* London: Routledge.

Newman, A.P., Lewis, W., and Beverstock, C. (1993). *Prison Literacy.* Philadelphia: National Center of Adult Literacy.

Nixon, V. (2012, December 18). During and after incarceration, education changes lives. *The New York Times.* Retrieved from http://www.nytimes.com/roomfordebate/2012/12/18/prison-could-be-productive/during-and-after-incarceration-education-changes-lives

Noguera, P. (2003, Autumn). Schools, prisons, and social implications of punishment: Rethinking disciplinary practice. *Theory into Practice.*

Paul, M. (1991). *When words are bars: A guide to literacy programming in correctional institutions.* Kitchener, Ontario, Canada: Core Literacy.

Prison Studies Project. (n.d.). *Why prison education?* Cambridge, MA: Author. Retrieved from http://prisonstudiesproject.org/why-prison-education-programs/

Ripley, P. (1993). *Prison education's role in challenging offending behaviour.* Bristol, England: Staff College.

Sieben, L. (2011, May 4). Report describes limits of inmates' access to college education. *The Chronicle of Higher Education.* Retrieved from http://chronicle.com/article/Inmates-Access-to-College/127375/

Vacca, J. S. (2004). Educated prisoners are less likely to return to prison. *Journal of Correctional Education, 55*(4), 297–304.

Wacquant, L. (2000). Deadly symbiosis: When ghetto and prison meet and mesh. *Punishment and Society, 3*(1), 95–134.

Warren, J. (2008, February 28). *One in 100: Behind bars in America 2008.* Washington, DC: Pew Center on the States. Retrieved from http://www.pewtrusts.org/our_work_report_detail.aspx?id=35900

Winn, M. (2011). *Girl time: Literacy, justice and the school to prison pipeline.* New York: Teachers College Press.

CHAPTER SIXTEEN

Transforming Justice AND Hip Hop Activism IN Action

ANTHONY J. NOCELLA II

CULTURE OF VIOLENCE

Conflict and injustice are common in all schools because schools are microcosms of society. Therefore, it is surprising and disappointing that teachers, administrators, counselors, and staff are not required to take courses on how to manage, resolve, and/or transform conflict in schools—from kindergarten to the twelfth grade and beyond. This lack of conflict transformation knowledge is painfully evident. For example, in response to Adam Lanza's shootings at Sandy Hook Elementary School in Newtown, Connecticut, in 2012, where he killed twenty-six people including twenty children, the National Rifle Association (NRA) recommended placing armed guards in every school around the country. So, in the eyes of the NRA, gun violence should be countered with *more guns*. In many economically marginalized, isolated, and disinvested urban communities of color in the United States, this answer is already a reality, including cameras in every corner of the building and metal detectors at every entrance. So far, this solution doesn't seem to be working.

Famed public intellectual Cornel West recognizes this reality and wonders why there is so much outrage and sorrow when white children are shot, but so little outrage and sorrow when youth of color are shot, which, unfortunately, occurs much more regularly. In the wake of the Newtown shooting, West states, "Not a mumbling word when the black folk getting shot. But now Newtown, CT, vanilla side, low and behold. … We have a major conversation. That's wonderful. Each life is precious, but it just upsets me when we're so differential" (Your Black World, 2012). West, far from being insensitive to the Sandy Hook tragedy, is raising the specters of identity and privilege. In general, people in dominant power positions (presidents, the media, celebrities, etc.) tend to cater to dominant identities: white, Christian, able-bodied, male, heterosexual, formally educated, and wealthy. Conversely, people of color, people who identify as LGBTQ, women, the economically marginalized, those not formally educated, and folks with dis-abilities are commonly silenced, marginalized, and/or ignored. These individuals do not receive the same kind of attention and care, even when they are victims of direct violence. This is an injustice, to say the least, and very telling about our society.

In response to rampant violence, some might believe that more prisons are the answer, believing the old assumption that with more criminals off the streets and behind bars, we can have a more peaceful and just society. *But who is a criminal?* Quite often, the answer depends upon who is committing the crime. For example, someone caught with cocaine, considered a high-end drug used by the wealthy, does less prison time than someone caught with crack-cocaine, a low-end drug associated with poverty.

I am very familiar with these debates since much of my own community organizing, activism, and scholarship focuses on problems within the current criminal justice system. My work is grounded in the field of critical criminology, which emerged in the 1960s–1970s out of critical theory and Marxism. In general, critical criminology opposes punitive retribution and exploitive "justice" systems, which are at the cornerstone of the U.S. prison system. For example, in the early 1980s, there were approximately 500,000 adults housed in the U.S. prison system. But by the end of the decade, there were more than a million people incarcerated (Justice Policy Institute, 2000, para. 1). In the 1990s, education was taken out of prisons to save money, and it was replaced with factory jobs that profited corporations (Burton-Rose, Pens, & Wright, 1998; Davis, 2003). These jobs include making circuit boards for computers, office furniture, and clothing. This substitution of jobs for education is a form of incarcerated slavery that funds the prison industrial complex.

Moving forward, the criminal justice system eventually became so overcrowded and unmanageable that there were not enough lawyers, judges, and courtrooms to properly handle all the cases. In the early 2000s, under President George W. Bush, the U.S. prison population grew to more than two million, which actually overextended the prison bed limit (Davis, 2003). With no more room in prisons, the government now commonly imprisons people in their own homes with ankle bracelets and other surveillance devices. This whole operation has developed along a logic of privatization: More and more prisons and prison-services are becoming privately owned. Privatization is said to save taxpayers money and to provide better services than the government can in the area of corrections. With more prisoners in private prisons, profits for these companies increase. In the *2010 Annual Report on Form 10-K* filed with the Securities and Exchange Commission, Corrections Corporation of America (CCA) states: "The demand for our facilities and services could be adversely affected by … leniency in conviction or parole standards and sentencing practices" (2010, p. 19). This means corporations now have a monetary incentive to incarcerate people. We will soon have two classes of people: those who are imprisoned and those who profit from the imprisoned.

Thinking About Alternatives

Prisons, guns, and armed guards are not the answer. Instead, we must start developing skills and alternative systems. Skills can include the ability to communicate, actively listen, build groups and teams of mutual support and understanding, forgive ourselves and others, and develop methods for positively transforming those who have hurt others. These skills must then become core practices in our communities, homes, schools, relationships, and places of work. To do this we need workshops, training, and education on the topics of peacemaking and social justice. Everyone must become involved—politicians, teachers, administrators, students, parents, and workers of all levels.

We must also develop new systems to replace the oppressive systems currently in place. Some alternative systems include peer-mediation programs in the workplace and school, community dialogues around difficult and controversial topics, and more community-based conflict transformation centers that are free and open to the public. If we could accomplish all of this, then perhaps one day we can forgo the need to call police and armed guards, to walk around with assault weapons, or to build more prisons to house more people. In "Poetry Behind the Walls," Parmar, Nocella, and Shykeem (2011) cite the U.S. Constitution's Thirteenth Amendment (1865) to demonstrate that slavery is not a mere historical footnote; rather, it continues in the prison system: "Neither slavery nor involuntary servitude, except as a punishment for crime whereof the party shall have been duly convicted, shall exist within the United States, or any place subject to their jurisdiction" (U.S. Const. Am. 13). Modern slavery manifests as prisoners are "paid from pennies to minimum wage—minus fines and victim compensation—for everything from grunt work to firefighting to specialized labor," making and packaging products for corporations such as Starbucks, Microsoft, and Victoria's Secret (Winter, 2008, para. 1). Recently, Alexander (2012) has reported that "more African Americans are under correctional control today—in prison, in jail, on probation or parole—than were enslaved in 1850, a decade before the Civil War began" (p. 175). The reality of present-day slavery is irrefutable, and it begins with the school to prison pipeline. The school to prison pipeline is simply defined as pushing youth out of school and into the streets to commonly hustle, which often ends in their incarceration. Social critics, educators, and advocates who care about youth of color must address the continuing issue of slavery as well as the historical events that caused and maintain oppression, such as youth incarceration. Hip Hop artists have the potential to participate as a major force in exposing these truths.

WHAT IS HIP HOP?[1]

Hip Hop is one of the fastest growing cultural phenomena in the world, as shown by its recent corporatization by the entertainment industry (Fernandes, 2011). Ogbar (2007), author of *Hip-Hop Revolution: The Culture and Politics of Rap*, writes,

> The international manifestations of hip-hop are considerable. In the last decade, hip-hop expanded its appeal considerably; there have emerged local communities of "head" in the far reaches of the world. Ghanaian hip-life, Panamanian- and Puerto Rican-inspired reggaeton, South African Kwaito, and other hip-hop/local hybrids have made indelible marks on glocal (global/local) youth culture and political expressions. (p. 180)

For mainstream audiences, Hip Hop is synonymous with rap, a musical genre that the police, corporate media, and suburban white middle class often connect with violence, gang activity, and other deviant, nihilistic behaviors. Such assumptions are similar to the stigmatization of other aspects of Black culture throughout U.S. history (Rose, 2008; Watkins, 2005). Hip Hop is unfairly generalized because of the media's tendency to promote rappers whose lyrics are insensitive to women and the lesbian, gay, bisexual, transgender/sexual, queer, intersexual, and asexual (LGBTQIA) community while exalting the "gangsta" lifestyle (Parmar et al., 2011, p. 288).

In contrast to these misconceptions, Hip Hop culture is rooted in African musical customs and emerges from the musical traditions popularized during the U.S. Civil Rights movement (Boyd, 2003; Chang, 2005). Once Africans were brought to the United States as slaves, Marshall (2000) explains that "African-American expressive cultures, especially musical ones, have provided opportunities for resistance, critique, and education since their first syncretic soundings sometime in the sixteenth century" (para. 1). Non-corporate Hip Hop continues to exemplify "resistance, critique, and education" (Marshall, 2000, para. 1). Forman (2007) notes that rap and Hip Hop emerged in the late 1970s and early 1980s within the Black community in the boroughs of New York City not as a call for

1 This section is adapted from Nocella and Socha's "Old School, New School, No School: Hip Hop's Dismantling of School and Prison-Industrial Complexes," to be published in the *International Journal of Critical Pedagogy*.

violence from gang-infested streets, but as a musical genre that hoped to "challenge or disrupt the cultural dominant" through a "combination of defensiveness and willful optimism" (p. 9). Despite this inspiring definition, Hip Hop still gets regularly stigmatized as violent and misogynistic, sometimes with good cause, as many rap lyrics refer to woman as "hos" and "bitches," thus perpetuating misogyny and patriarchy. But these negative messages of some rap lyrics are far fewer than those wider-reaching messages of the dominant white, capitalist, colonized, U.S. imperialist culture that promotes patriarchy, sexism, and homophobia via all forms of media, only *one* of which is corporate Hip Hop (Perry, 2004; Rose, 1994; Williams, 2010). The civilization arising from white European origins argues for competition, control, and normalcy, not for collaboration, interdependence, respect for difference, and equity. However, the latter, positive attributes are celebrated by many communities of color, such as non-corporate Hip Hop.

Indeed, non-corporatized Hip Hop is the only culture that speaks to educating youth of color on a deeper level than merely imparting their pre-slavery and colonialist histories to them (Ball, 2011). Williams (2010) emphasizes the potential power of this "counterhegemonic spirit of hip-hop such as narration of institutionalized racism, internal colonialism, underclass entrapment, and urban poverty, to help explain the external sources of prevalent psychosocial problems among African American youth" (p. 230). Much of non-corporate Hip Hop speaks to the current conditions of poor urban communities, writing and rapping on topics from police brutality to the war on drugs, by such artists as Public Enemy, Nas, KRS-One, Mortal Technique, Dead Prez, The Game, and Mos Def. Hip Hop—through graffiti, dance, rap, fashion, education, deejaying, beat boxing, and locally owned private businesses—tells the story of a people who must now rebuild their communities after periods of slavery, colonization, Jim Crow, the Civil Rights era, and continued institutionalized racism. Part of this rebuilding is to offer what Marshall (2000) calls "an alternative education—a challenge to dominant notions of knowledge and truth" that youth find in traditional Western-Colonial schooling (para. 4), noting that early Hip Hop artists and producers, such as KRS-One, actually referred to their art as "Edutainment" (para. 4). Hip Hop is composed of artists using their medium to identify and criticize social ills while offering alternatives for the oppressed. In his song "Hip Hop Lives," KRS-One (2007) defines the genre as "more than music"; rather, it is "knowledge," and an "intelligent," "relevant movement." Hip Hop, as KRS-One defines it, is about positive and intellectual momentum and is, from its earliest inceptions, a social justice movement with which its listeners became engaged advocates rather than passive listeners (Parmar, 2009).

While many think of protesting, rallies, boycotts, and vigils and forms of activism, resistance, and direct action, there are many other forms of expression as well, as showcased in Hip Hop. Hip Hop culture has four traditional agreed-upon elements: graffiti, emceeing, deejaying, and break dancing. When these elements are transferred into Hip Hop activism they are (1) reclaiming space such as street corners, abandoned warehouses, and parks for break dancing; (2) creating art on walls via wheat pasting on doors, spray painting on billboards, and other forms of graffiti; (3) deejaying by making noise and beats through pencil drumming on a desk in class, bucket drumming on the sidewalk, or beat boxing in the subway; (4) and finally emceeing by getting in the face of a teacher or police officer and telling him/her off, yelling in the school hall, or spitting poetry on a train.

Hip Hop activism is dedicated to four systems of domination: (1) socio-political oppression, (2) criminal justice, (3) monolithic education, and (4) cultural imperialism. Hip Hop culture recognizes that these issues are interwoven and dependent on one another to perpetuate domination. More specifically, Hip Hop activism specifically addresses mass incarceration, police brutality, racism, poverty, and the protection of youth expression. With this need to address the oppression of the criminal justice system, capitalism, and consequent systems of domination, a number of radical youth advocacy grassroots groups are promoting transformative justice, such as the Youth Justice Coalition, Philly Stands Up, Generation FIVE, American Friends Service Committee, and Save the Kids. These organizations organize rallies, candlelight vigils, public forums, teach-ins, and workshops; they also provide services to youth involved with the juvenile justice system. Transformative justice is a prime way that such organizations create alternatives to public school and incarceration systems.

TRANSFORMATIVE JUSTICE

Transformative justice was founded by the late Ruth Morris, a Canadian Quaker and author of *Stories of Transformative Justice* (2000) and *Penal Abolition: The Practical Choice; A Practical Manual on Penal Abolition* (1998). Transformative justice is by far the most progressive method for approaching conflict and social injustice. Transformative justice places issues of inequality, oppression, and domination at the forefront. It takes a systems approach to conflict, recognizing that we are all interconnected: the offender and the victim, one's choices and one's situation, the community and its social structures, power differentials among all involved in a crime. Transformative justice argues that we are all involved in complex relationships of oppressors and oppressed, dominators and dominated (Nocella, 2012). I may be the oppressed in one situation, but I may be the oppressor in another situation. I may be the victim from one perspective, but I may be the offender from another perspective. Transformative justice is not about destroying and building anew, and it's not about creating win-lose solutions common to social revolutions in which the oppressed become the new oppressors (Skocpol, 1995). Instead, transformative justice asks that *everyone* and *everything* change—we as individuals, as well as our systems, structures, and relationships.

Transformative justice addresses not only the specific conflict between victim and offenders, but also the plethora of social issues that come to bear on that conflict. For instance, a 14-year-old boy, who is from a poor neighborhood and identifies as queer, robs a store at 2:00 a.m. Transformative justice not only looks at the crime of burglary, but also looks at why the boy committed the act. Was the boy kicked out of his home by a father who was homophobic? Did the boy need money for food, clothes, or a place to stay? Was he trying to get money to help his younger sister who is also homeless? These questions are addressed in order to understand the whole context, which, unfortunately, involves a great deal of injustice. Our society oppresses and marginalizes those who are poor and queer. Consequently, there are two victims within this scenario—the store owner who was robbed *and* the 14-year-old boy. This is a clear example of how the systems approach of transformative justice breaks down common barriers between victim and offender, creates a much wider understanding of abuse and violence, and tries to bring everyone together in a transformative relationship (Nocella, 2012).

Social justice activists often identify the oppressor as the enemy. While this is understandable, transformative justice actually challenges this perspective: No one is an enemy; instead, everyone needs to be involved in a voluntary, safe, constructive, and critical dialogue about accountability, responsibility, and the initiative to heal. This means that both activists and oppressors, as well as law enforcement, lawyers, judges, prisoners, community members, teachers, students, politicians, spiritual leaders, and others, must come together. It is for this reason that we should be willing to work with a diversity of people in our fight for a better world. Transformative justice looks for the good in others while also acknowledging the complex systems that we all live within.

Below are ten general principles of transformative justice that I have created. My hope is that they crystallize the sentiment of the chapter thus far.

1. Transformative Justice stresses the notion that the current criminal justice system in the United States separates the victim and the offender, which re-victimizes the victim and changes the offender into a victim of the state.
2. Transformative Justice is based on prison abolition.
3. Transformative Justice brings issues of identity back into the realm of justice by addressing socio-political injustices toward women, people of color, gays, lesbians, trans and queer, poor, immigrants, people with disabilities, and other oppressed and marginalized groups.
4. Transformative Justice believes that "crime" is framed by the state and not by the community.

5. Transformative Justice believes in de-institutionalization (empowering people, rather than institutions, to make decisions).
6. Transformative Justice is against violence and punishment.
7. Transformative Justice believes in the value of mediation, negotiation, and community to transform conflicts.
8. Transformative Justice values conflict as an opportunity for growth, progress, and social justice.
9. Transformative Justice identifies crime as conflict. Consequently, social structures and the government are identified as potential offenders.
10. Transformative Justice is for total liberation and the end of all systems of domination.

These ten principles are only a beginning. They must be challenged, extended, critiqued, and redeveloped by fellow peace workers, penal abolitionists, social justice activists, and those from oppressed communities, especially those incarcerated. As a burgeoning concept, transformative justice is open to revision and is adaptable to social changes.

Transformative justice, unlike restorative justice or conflict management and resolution, seeks to challenge all aspects of authoritarianism, domination, oppression, and control within society. For this reason, transformative justice is more than an alternative approach to conflict or to the criminal justice system. Instead, it is a non-dogmatic and process-oriented social justice philosophy for peace that allows for creative approaches in transforming conflict and addressing issues of brutality, assault, abuse, victimization, accountability, responsibility, loss, and healing (Nocella, 2012).

GRASSROOTS ACTIVISM

With chapters in Twin Cities, central New York, Buffalo, Niagara, Chicago, Connecticut, Los Angeles, and Vermont, Save the Kids (STK), a fully volunteer national grassroots organization rooted in Hip Hop and transformative justice, advocates for alternatives to, and the end of, the incarceration of all youth. To end youth incarceration, STK works to dismantle the school to prison pipeline by challenging standardized monolithic compulsory schooling and punitive justice systems. STK is also against able-bodied, heteronormative, patriarchal, white cultural imperialism, such as schools', towns', companies', and cities' recent wave of rules and laws banning the sagging of one's pants. These laws, STK argues, promote racial profiling of youth of color involved in the Hip Hop culture.

By design, STK is *not* a nonprofit organization with paid employees. STK argues that nonprofits do not aid in solving socio-political problems, but rather acerbate them into an accepted occurrence in society, consequently developing the nonprofit industrial complex (INCITE! Women of Color Against Violence, 2009). Instead, it is a volunteer-based organization. We believe that if we are doing something good for people, then the people of the community will find ways to make that something last and grow. However, for a program to flourish, it must be run by those who are directly affected by the program's actions. In this case, we are talking about the families and friends of incarcerated youth and the various community members that are affected by the criminal justice system. Save the Kids is thus run by professors, teachers, activists, community organizers, probation officers, social workers, school counselors, and former prisoners. The purpose is to help people come together and create positive change in their communities, both in the present moment and for future generations.

STK started in 2009 based on a conversation held among four incarcerated youth about how community centers are ineffective in helping the youth of the juvenile justice system. Those four youths at Hillbrook Youth Detention Facility in Syracuse, New York, created Save the Kids. In fact, one particular youth came up with the name, which is the reason it is still used today even though it can be wrongly viewed as paternalistic and patronizing. At the time, I was a graduate student at Syracuse University and a Life Skills Teacher, providing volunteer opportunities for college students to work with incarcerated youth. I helped those four youth start STK, which has ten principles:

1. We believe that all youth need support, love, and skills in order to achieve their goals.
2. We believe that all youth are amazing and wonderful no matter what actions they have committed.
3. We make a clear distinction between actions and kids; actions can be bad, but not kids.
4. We are committed to helping youth because they are our future, and if we do not help them, we will not have one.
5. We believe in respecting all no matter what their gender, ability, race, economic status, sexuality, religion, ethnicity, health, age, or nationality.
6. As a Hip Hop activist organization, we work toward both social justice and the end of all forms of oppression and domination, specifically the school to prison pipeline.
7. As an organization based on transformative justice principles, we strive to promote alternatives to incarceration, such as community-based programs rather than institutionalization.
8. We believe in peace and nonviolence in resolving and transforming all conflicts.

9. We believe in people, not labels; thus, we are inclusive in all of our activities.
10. We promote inclusivity on the basis that everyone in the community should work together in making a peaceful world; STK will work with everyone and anyone in order to achieve that goal. (Save the Kids, 2009)

With so many organizations working to end the incarceration of youth and dismantling the school to prison pipeline on local and national levels, STK is unique because it does not focus on policy or mentoring. Instead, STK operates as a fully volunteer organization with three different programs: (1) publishing research essays on transformative justice, Hip Hop studies, poems, and stories from incarcerated adults and youth; (2) activism such as rallies, protests, and vigils; and (3) educational programs such as youth workshops in detention facilities and public forums on the school to prison pipeline.

One of the projects in the education program is *Poetry Behind the Walls*, a free online publication dedicated to writings by youth incarcerated throughout the United States. The selected writings reproduced here share the common experiences of young people caught in the juvenile justice system. For legal and safety reasons, I do not provide the authors' locations and last names. First, experiences with arrests are explained by Shona (a youth who was incarcerated in Hennepin County Juvenile Detention Center) in "From School to Lock Up" and Kamarei (a youth who was incarcerated in Hennepin County Jail) in "Detained." Another very common experience is articulated by James (a youth who was incarcerated in Hennepin Juvenile Detention Center) in "Locked Up." The juvenile justice system is known for its high recidivism rates; Adrianna (a youth who was incarcerated in Hennepin County Juvenile Detention Center) addresses this commonality in "In and Out." Finally, Donquarius (a youth who was incarcerated in Hennepin County Jail) provides an overarching view of punitive justice in "The Legal System?"

From School to Lock Up
By Shona

I ran away from home 4 or 3
Days and I was due to court
On Wed the 10th 2013 and did
Not show up now Im facing
lock up intill im 19 or 21
But I did not attend
School and was on house
arrest once Befor F or S days
And ranaway once Befor to
go home to my dads house

cause i was in foster hom
and Befor that i was loced
up in the CHS for aggravated robbery.

Detained
By Kamarei

I missed my courtdate and
Now im in Jail.
The only freedom I have is
Within these 12 cells.
I get so angry because I have to ask to go pee
Everywhere I turn I got cameras
watching me.
Everyday im missin my son
I pray to god he doesnt grow
Up playing with guns.
I Really dont know how I should
feel
Because when the Judge
Says detained I figure
the man yall call god is just
not real.

Locked Up
By James

All my thoughts are locked up
All of my friends are locked up
Sometimes I feel like my Soul is locked up
But I know that just my mind is going crazy
My body is locked up but not my mind
I feel like the walls are closing in on me
Some days I don't know what to do
Is there anything I can do
What can anybody else do
Why can't anyone else help me
Why can't I help myself
What did I do to get here
How did I get here
Sometimes I ask myself why I am here
What can I do to not come here
Why do they bring people here
I feel like this place is hell
I feel like this pace is for no man or woman
I feel like the world do not exist

In and Out
By Adriana

It sucks being here when everyone in this facility know me. In a bad way I know how everything works, even know the Address by heart. So Icant even lie about my name. Ive been in DRT, physical olds and escorts, lots of times and I see most people come back and they say I know you, and it sucks being locked up. Even the police, sheriffs, know me when I go to court. Everytime I come back they say, "omg your back" and I'm like I don't wanna hear it.

The Legal System?
By Donquarius

Why the system is so corrupt? Idk.
Why is the Jail the way it is.
locked away like an animal.
Why the innocent get's found guilty for a crime they didn't commit.
Why Jail Staff want's to strip you from your pride and self-esteem.
Want you to feel guilty and stress through your case process playing with your life want to look you away for decades.

The above pieces are not only forms of youth expression, but also words of personal experience and a socio-political statement by youth speaking out against the incarceration of youth, recidivism rates, and the role of schools in those rates. Any argument for or against the current state of juvenile justice without youth participation is destructive and silencing those for whom I and others advocate. Scholars and politicians must begin to cite and quote youth rather than adults when speaking about the experiences and effectiveness of policies that pertain to youth, especially when those policies relate to controlling and oppressing them. Too often, schools and juvenile justice systems argue what is best for youth and society without consulting them. In closing, these systems need to be authentic about valuing the perspectives of youth rather than condescending to them when conducting research.

REFERENCES

Alexander, M. (2012). *The new Jim Crow: Mass incarceration in the age of colorblindness.* New York: New Press.

Ball, J. A. (2011). *I mix what I like! A mixtape manifesto.* Oakland, CA: AK Press.

Boyd, T. (2003). *The new H.N.I.C.: The death of civil rights and the reign of hip hop.* New York: NYU Press.

Burton-Rose, D., Pens, D., & Wright, P. (1998). *The celling of America: An inside look at the U.S. prison industry.* Monroe, ME: Common Courage Press.

Chang, J. (2005). *Can't stop, won't stop: A history of the hip-hop generation.* New York: St. Martin's Press.

Corrections Corporation of America. (2010). *2010 Annual report form 10-K.* Washington, DC: United States Securities and Exchange Commission.

Davis, A. Y. (2003). *Are prisons obsolete?* New York: Seven Stories Press.

Fernandes, S. (2011). *Close to the edge: The search of the global hip hop generation.* New York: Verso.

Forman, M. (2007). Hip-hop ya don't stop: Hip-hop history and historiography. In M. Forman & M. A. Neal (Eds.), *That's the joint! The hip-hop studies reader* (pp. 9–12). New York: Routledge.

INCITE! Women of Color Against Violence (2009). *The revolution will not be funded: Beyond the non-profit industrial complex.* Cambridge, MA: South End Press.

Justice Policy Institute. (2000, May). *The punishing decade: Prison and jail estimates at the millennium.* Washington, DC: Author. Retrieved from www.justicepolicy.org/images/upload/00–05_rep_punishingdecade_ac.pdf

KRS-One (2007). Hip-hop lives. On *Hip hop lives* with Marley Marl (CD). New York: Koch Records.

Marshall, W. (2000). *The (mis)education of a nation: Hip hop's critiques of and alternatives to the education system.* Retrieved from http://www.swaraj.org/shikshantar/papers_miseducation.html

Morris, R. (1998). *Penal abolition: The practice choice; A practical manual on penal abolition.* Toronto: Canadian Scholars Press.

Morris, R. (2000). *Stories of transformative justice.* Toronto: Canadian Scholars Press.

Nocella, A. J., II. (2012). An overview of the history and theory of transformative justice. *Peace & Conflict Review, 6*(1), 1–10.

Ogbar, J. O. G. (2007). *Hip-hop revolution: The culture and politics of rap.* Lawrence: University Press of Kansas.

Parmar, P. (2009). *Knowledge reigns supreme: The critical pedagogy of hip-hop artist KRS-One.* Rotterdam, The Netherlands: Sense.

Parmar, P., Nocella, A., & Shykeem. (2011). Poetry behind the walls. *Peace Review: A Journal of Social Justice, 23*(3), 287–295.

Perry, I. (2004). *Prophets of the hood: Politics and poetics in hip hop.* Durham, NC: Duke University Press.

Rose, T. (1994). *Black noise: Rap music and black culture in contemporary America.* Middletown, CT: Wesleyan University Press.

Rose, T. (2008). *The hip hop wars: What we talk about when we talk about hip hop—and why it matters.* New York: Basic Books.

Save the Kids (2009). *Save the kids ten point principles.* Retrieved from on November 20, 2013. http://savethekidsgroup.org/?page_id=557

Skocpol, T. (1995). *Social revolution in the modern world.* Cambridge: Cambridge University Press.

Watkins, S. C. (2006). *Hip hop matters: Politics, culture, and the struggle for the soul of a movement.* Boston: Beacon Press.

William, L. (2010). Hip-hop as a site of public pedagogy. In J. A. Sandlin, B. D. Schultz, & J. Burdick (Eds.), *Handbook of public pedagogy: Education and learning beyond schooling.* New York: Routledge.

Winter, C. (2008, July–August). What do prisoners make for Victoria's Secret? *Mother Jones.* Retrieved from http://motherjones.com/politics/2008/07/what-do-prisoners-make-victorias-secret

Your Black World. (2012, December). Dr. Cornel West says President Obama, politicians are "cowards" for lack of response to gun violence in the black community. Retrieved from www.yourblackworld.net/2012/12/black-news/dr-cornel-west-says-president-obama-politicians-are-cowards-for-lack-of-response-to-gun-violence-in-the-black-community

PART SIX

Transformative Alternatives

No one is born fully-formed: it is through self-experience in the world that we become what we are.

—Paulo Freire

The learning process is something you can incite, literally incite, like a riot.

—Audre Lorde

CHAPTER SEVENTEEN

Back ON THE Block

Community Reentry and Reintegration of Formerly Incarcerated Youth

DON C. SAWYER III AND DANIEL WHITE HODGE

INTRODUCTION

A few years ago while serving as a facilitator of an alternative summer school program I, Don, became increasingly interested in researching the experiences of Black boys in urban schools. I wanted to understand how these students navigated hostile educational spaces and underserved neighborhoods and how they made sense of their lives. During the summer I was able to work with Black boys who were sent to summer school. Through a partnership with a university professor and a male mentoring and manhood training program, we were approved to run an alternative summer school program that focused on writing and mathematics.

In this chapter we engage in a critical analysis of the systemic problems that increasingly push Black males toward the criminal justice system. There has been an exponential increase in the number of Black men and boys entering the prison industrial complex. Faulty policies and practices have pushed Black males out of school and have created an environment in which they are overrepresented in school suspensions, special education, and prison (Howard, 2008). Through the analysis of three case studies, we deconstruct the practices of systems that oppress and repress populations of color in educational settings that in the end lead to students being imprisoned and having to struggle with reentry into society. We track these experiences through the broader discourse of society related to males of color, schools' educational and disciplinary practices, otherwise referred to as the "school to prison pipeline" crisis, and programs targeted to reintegrate formerly incarcerated youth. Last, we make suggestions for alternative strategies in addressing the problems of incarceration and reentry.

IMAGES OF BLACK-MALENESS IN THE AMERICAN PSYCHE

Concerns about the lived experiences and perceived pathology of Black males have remained important topics for educators, researchers, policy analysts, and the general public. These often unqualified perceptions of Black male pathology tend to be divorced from an analysis of the social and structural obstacles facing many Black males. For instance, in his 2008 edited volume on poor young Black males in society, Elijah Anderson argues, "Living in areas of concentrated ghetto poverty, still shadowed by slavery and second-class citizenship, many Black males are trapped in a cycle that includes active discrimination, unemployment, crime, poverty, prison, and early death" (p. 3). When a few act out violently to these forms of oppression, with media assistance, the implications for other Black men is expansive. As a result, Black males are assumed violent and untrustworthy, simply based on their skin color. The image of the Black male is seen with fear and suspicion.

Duncan (2002) argues that Black males suffer a condition characteristic of a population that is *beyond love*. This is

> a condition of those who are excluded from society's economy and networks of care and thus expelled from useful participation in social life. ... Black males are constructed as a strange population. ... As a group with values and attitudes that are fundamentally different from other students, their marginalization and oppression are understood as natural and primarily of their own doing. (p. 140)

He argues further that Black males are relatively powerless to define their circumstances and as a result are often relegated to a state of being defined by others. Delgado (1996) as referenced in Duncan (2002) states that

> the incessant characterization of Blacks in demeaning terms means that the average member of society virtually equates any one of us with trouble. We come to be seen as absent fathers, welfare mothers, lazy office worker "quota queens," and so on. Once this sets in, we have little chance of appealing to the better natures of persons who hold this unconscious image of us. The image renders us "other." It means people simply don't think of us as individuals to whom love, respect, generosity, and friendliness are due. We are "beyond love." (p. 51)

This description is not abnormal but a common occurrence for Black males in society. Many young males are targeted in decrepit school environments that have become militarized police zones for many urban centers. The schooling environment, which some consider to be a place where gaps can be equalized, is not always conducive to success for Black students (especially males).

National and state academic assessments consistently report that Black adolescent males are performing at lower levels than other groups (Jencks & Phillips, 1998; Ladson-Billings, 2006; Noguera, 2008). In addition, we see that Black adolescent males are disproportionately placed in special education; experience high rates of school suspensions and expulsions; and lead in school dropout rates, unemployment, and juvenile incarceration (Artiles, 2003; Artiles & Trent, 1994; Holzman, 2006). Black males outnumber all other ethnic groups in the prison population and have a rate of incarceration at least five times higher than that of white males. Department of Justice statisticians project that based on current demographics 1 in every 3 African American men can expect to spend some time incarcerated, on probation, or under some type of jurisdiction of the penal system during his lifetime (Howard, 2008). These statistics paint a picture of the failed educational practices and social policies and set the stage for the work needed to counteract the impact of these lived realities faced by young men of color (Sawyer, 2012).

THE PATH TO PRISON: SCHOOL TO PRISON PIPELINE

> The [school to prison] pipeline is so named because it appears actively to collect school-aged youth and funnel them toward a future in prison. The school-to-prison pipeline implicates the educational system in the structuring of a path that leads to incarceration.
>
> —SIMMONS (2009, P. 229)

In an effort to discuss the perils of being involved in the criminal justice system and then facing reentry problems, it is important to take a step back and review the process that youth often follow to prison. The school system is often a funnel for Black and Latino youth and it structures experiences that prime these students for entry into the prison system, also referred to as the "school to prison pipeline" (Meiners & Winn, 2010; Simmons, 2009). Structural racism, the criminalization of Black males, race and class privilege, and zero tolerance policies in school settings contribute to the increasing number of students being directed to prison (Monroe, 2005b). The place where education is thought to take place is also a place where we see other functions of school, such as socializing, social control, and sorting (Noguera, 2003). These latent functions of the school are powerful in helping to determine the educational and life trajectories of the students entrusted to its system on a daily basis and, unfortunately, a life in prison becomes a possibility as a result of these oppressive measures.

The main purpose for public schools in the context of youth of color is to ensure that this population accepts a subordinate role in schools, the economy, and society (Duncan, 2000). Duncan argues the relationship among schooling Black males, the global economy, and the prison industrial complex is significantly related to three main areas: the service industry, popular culture and media, and the curricula in public schools. He argues,

> These domains work through adolescents of color to construct them as a superfluous population for whom society views prison as a reasonable, if not natural option. ... Urban pedagogies are the means by which information, images, symbols, are proliferated in, and disseminated to, urban populations. As is characteristic of all instructional processes, urban pedagogies have intention, direction, and purpose. Pedagogies are designed to forge identities by inculcating in students behaviors, attitudes and values, by mobilizing their fears, joys, and desires, and by shaping their tastes and perceptions. (2000, p. 36)

First, urban pedagogies work through adolescents of color, making them less competitive economically by subjecting them to an education that emphasizes discipline and control rather than gaining meaningful skills. Second, they work upon adolescents of color, impacting their image of themselves and the ways in which society views them, thus making them undesirable as employees. This occurs as various media depict them as violent, lazy, and incompetent. These views allow Black males to be seen as menaces to society for whom prison is more appropriate than a good education (Feirman, Levick, & Mody, 2009; Raible & Irizarry, 2010; Tuzzolo & Hewitt, 2007). Rather than developing strategies to improve the educational standing of urban Black males, there is an alternative "solution" to the issue. As stated previously, zero tolerance policies and the criminalization of Black males allow for these young men to be primed for entry into prison. "The social and economic problems related to nonviable public secondary systems for Black and other racialized youth populations would eventually be solved, in part, by the exponential expansion of the prison industrial complex" (Duncan, 2000, p. 33). Rather than improving education and skill levels to make Black males "more employable," what were once considered jobs that were reserved for poor Blacks can now be outsourced or "in-sourced" to correctional facilities. The prison industrial complex has benefited from increased funding while our most needy urban educational centers have been the victims of repeated budget cuts. For example, from 1984 to 2000 every U.S. state spent six times more funds on prison than on higher education (Meiners, 2011). States have been investing large amounts of their budgets in the maintenance and development of the prison system while students suffer in decrepit educational institutions with most of the disaster being concentrated in urban centers. Approximately $70 billion is spent annually to place adults in prison, hold youth in detention centers, and supervise 7.3 million people on probation and parole (Hawkins, 2010).

In schools, the neediest children are often punished as the system tends to focus on the management of student behaviors and the controlling of their bodies rather than on educating the student (Noguera, 2003). The focus on discipline and punishment is more central to the schools' success, and quality education often takes a back seat to the other priorities of control. Under this regime of control, students are often labeled as behavioral problems, resulting in a stigma that tends to follow them throughout their school experiences. Research shows that the practice of labeling and exclusionary discipline practices have the potential to create a self-fulfilling prophecy that often results in negative student behavior that becomes habitual (Noguera, 2003). As students internalize the label placed upon them by the institution, they are perceptive enough to begin to notice that their educational trajectories will not get them to the same levels as others and begin to view school as a waste of time.

> Once they know that the rewards of education—namely, acquisition of knowledge and skills and ultimately, admission to college, and access to good paying jobs—are not available to them, students have little incentive to comply with school rules. … At a relatively young age students may have so many negative experiences in school that they soon begin to recognize that education is not working. (Noguera, 2003, p. 343)

In addition, the disciplinary practices in schools closely resemble our approach to crime in the larger society. We attempt to remove the "bad apples" before they spoil the rest. These exclusionary practices keep students out of the classroom and are seen as methods that allow the students who "want to learn" the space to do so without being distracted by the students who are assumed to have no interest in learning. Seldom are the institutional barriers to student learning called into question. Schools, for these students, serve as places where oppression and repression are reified. Not only do they face these harsh realities in the world, but also the school reinscribes their second-class citizenship and reproduces systems of inequity. Not only are inequalities reproduced in urban educational spaces, but as previously argued these tactics are also part of the prepping for students to enter the prison industrial complex.

One of the ways in which students are pushed out of school and into prison is through the criminalization of their behaviors and harsh disciplinary practices. Research reveals that Black students receive harsher punishments than their peers, often for committing the same offenses (Monroe, 2005a). The disciplinary inequalities are most evident in relation to Black boys (Ferguson, 2001). When students attempt to resist the draconian policies in school, they are often met with swift punishment. Schools aim to suppress student resistance and use harsh disciplinary practices to maintain a population of docile bodies (Foucault, 1995). Schools make efforts to quell resistance through the increased use of zero tolerance policies. Originally these policies, derived from the 1994 Gun-Free Schools Act, were crafted to deal with more serious violations, but they are often used to control student resistance and minor behavioral issues (Meiners, 2011). As time progressed, federal funding became contingent upon schools adopting these behavioral policies. Schools along with federal mandates have often expanded the policies to include minor infractions (Nolan, 2011). The dependency on zero tolerance discipline policies has not benefited students, as many of the sanctions are tarnished by discriminatory practices that can be traced through race-based biases evident in the system of disciplinary practice. In addition to the rise in suspensions and expulsions for Black youth, with the increase in police occupation of schools, acts of resistance and other behavioral violations have been criminalized. Violations that were once handled by school administrators are now handled by police officers and the courts.

The model used in urban schools with police officers was based on problem-oriented community policing that has extended the criminal justice system into school buildings by creating partnerships with law enforcement agencies (Kupchik & Bracy, 2010). Most of the officers in schools are armed and uniformed; however, some do wear plain clothes. Their presence is supposed to engender a perception of safety and to quell concerns about school violence. The number of police officers is continuing to grow. By 1999, more than half of our nation's public middle and high schools reported having officers. By 2005, the number increased to approximately 68% (Kupchik & Bracy, 2010). An interesting fact is that suburban schools, where many violent incidents have occurred, tend to avoid the heavy reliance on surveillance levied against urban schools (Hirschfield, 2010). According to Hirschfield (2010), the increased presence of police officers and metal detectors in urban schools tends to reinforce racial, gender, and socioeconomic disparities in educational outcomes, school suspensions, and arrests. He further argues that "the resultant disproportionate policing and surveillance of urban minority students functions to prepare such students for their rightful positions in the postindustrial order, whether as prisoners, soldiers, or service sector workers" (2010, p. 40). The school does not only push students into the criminal justice system, but in a way has also come to resemble a pipeline that funnels students to prisons or juvenile correctional facilities.

Black male students are often seen as deficits rather than possibilities and are pushed aside to exist as a superfluous population for which prison seems a real possibility … an inevitable stop on the journey of life. The most important question to address is, "What are we doing to prevent these realities for students?" Unfortunately, the treatment of students in school exposes the reality that some students are on their way to a life of prison and second-class citizenship as if there were nothing that the school could do to change their trajectory. We remain complacent and desensitized to the reality that school practices are clearing a path for certain populations, mainly poor people of color, to march toward entry into the prison industrial complex.

The recent "tough-on-crime" policies have ushered in an increase in youth incarceration, and this increase in people entering the prison system has also increased the number of people reentering society (Mears & Travis, 2004).

According to Mears and Travis (2004) we are facing the reality of reintegrating approximately 200,000 youth and young adults ages 24 and younger who return home each year, and the transition from prison to citizen may be more difficult for young people. Many of these youth are returning to the underserved neighborhoods that were influential in their initially getting "caught up" in the system. In this next section, we concentrate on three case studies of Jason, Mike, and Larry, all of whom were dealing with the process of reentry. The stories of these young men impacted by the system shed light on many hidden difficulties facing people on the path to reentry.

REAL LIVES, REAL ISSUES, AND REENTRY: CASE STUDIES OF JASON, MIKE, AND LARRY

This section examines the effects that prison has on youth and the complications youth have when reintegrating into a society in which work, life, relationships, and community are exponentially made more problematic. As an urban youth worker and advocate for more than twenty years, I, Dan, share three reentry case studies of youth with whom I have had close relationships. The chapter concludes with a brief overview of the issues surrounding reentry for our young people and includes solutions desperately needed to resolve this crisis.

Jason

Jason had recently been released on good behavior from a fifteen-year sentence on a gang enhancement charge in which the district attorney had no physical or material evidence to convict, but received a conviction anyway. Jason was a great student, had a sharp critical mind, and loved sports (basketball and football). He was also a mentor to his younger brother and sister. He worked hard and had dreams of becoming a chef. So what happened? How did this great young man get "caught up" into the tentacles of the prison industrial complex? Was it Jason's decisions? Was it his home life? Was it the geographic location he found himself in? Jason had merely wanted to help a friend who needed a ride across town. This friend, unbeknownst to Jason, had mild gang involvement in the community in which they both lived. During the ride, a rival gang recognized Jason's friend, and a scuffled ensued. A passerby called the police and law enforcement soon arrived. Jason's friend had a concealed weapon and because Jason was "associating with *known* gang members" (direct quote from legal forms) he was arrested. The charge was "force with a deadly weapon" and because he was associated with a "known" gang member, the district attorney added an additional gang "enhancement" charge that ultimately increased the final sentencing time (an enhancement is a charge added into law to add colossal amounts of time to sentences as a deterrent to others to keep them from joining gangs and to keep the "public" safe). Because Jason lived below the poverty line and could not afford an attorney, he was appointed a public attorney (PD). The PD was overworked, as is most often the case, and instead of defending Jason or launching an investigation, or potentially suing the police department, Jason was advised to "plead out." The district attorney proposed that if Jason pleaded guilty and signed a plea form, his sentence would be reduced from the maximum twenty-five years to life to a lighter sentence, fifteen years (seven with good behavior). Faced with the dilemma of going to trial and risking receiving the maximum penalty, Jason ultimately took the plea deal. After serving fifteen years, Jason reentered society as a parolee with a stigma attached to him often associated with ex-felons: thug, lazy, poor decision-maker, uneducated, unreliable, untrustworthy, and unskilled. Along with these stereotypes, Jason faced the challenge of finding employment opportunities that afforded him a fair wage and benefits.

Mike

I first met Mike in the Introduction to Sociology class that I taught at a community college in Southern California. Mike, a 24-year-old African American freshman, wanted to get his life back on track after being in prison for a period of time, and attending college was the first step. Mike caught my attention because he showed great energy, enthusiasm, and active participation and engagement in every class session.

After several private discussions with Mike, I soon found out that he had recently been released from prison. Mike had committed serious crimes that resulted in incarceration. When he was 15 years old, Mike made poor decisions, one resulting in an arrest for D.U.I. Within six months, Mike began hanging around a volatile group of friends, and before long they had conjured up a scheme to home invade a house located in "The Valley"—an upper-middle-class community in Southern California. The targeted home belonged to a first-generation Cambodian family who owned several local businesses. The family, distrustful of banks, was known to keep large amounts of cash at home. After scoping out the property and assuming it was empty, Mike, along with four other friends, entered the home after donning ski masks. Unbeknownst to them, a visiting uncle surprised Mike and his partners upon entry. A scuffle ensued, resulting in the uncle tearing away one boy's ski mask. While the uncle suffered severe injury from the fight, the boys escaped with $150,000 in cash. When the uncle recovered from his injuries, he was able to identify one of the young men, which eventually led to the arrest of all the boys. Mike was convicted of premeditated robbery, a home invasion charge, and attempted murder. He received a strike and was facing fifteen years, but because he was a minor at the time, with a relatively clean record, he was sentenced to eight years but was out in four because of good behavior. The strike, however, remained on his record.

Mike, now age 22, looked back on that time with much regret and shame. He expressed to me on numerous occasions that if he had to do it over again, he would have refused to "make the run" and made better choices. Although Mike was on parole, he found a job and was living with his grandfather. As is routine, parole officers make unannounced home visits to parolees, oftentimes early in the morning. One particular morning at approximately 5:30 a.m., Mike's parole officer made a surprise visit to the house. He had with him a Los Angeles sheriff's officer. Mike, awake but not startled by their presence, felt confident the visit was merely routine as he had nothing to hide. Mike was asked to wait outside his bedroom while both the parole officer and sheriff's officer rummaged through his room. Suddenly, the parole officer yelled, "We got you, you fuck!" Mike ran into the bedroom, only to be accosted by the sheriff's officer and quickly handcuffed. The parole officer said, "Your Black ass thought you could get away with this right? Well, you're going back to jail, asshole!" The parole officer reached into the corner closet and pulled out a very old rifle. Mike responded by telling both officers that the rifle was not his. Mike's grandfather rushed into the room and corroborated his story and explained that Mike was staying in his old room, in which the gun was stored. The officers laughed and told both of them to "shut the fuck up." Mike was then taken back to jail.

Within thirty minutes Mike's grandfather came to the police station with registration papers showing him as the legal owner of the gun. He attempted to explain again that the gun was inadvertently stored in the bedroom closet and took full responsibility for not removing it when Mike moved in. Unfortunately, his explanation fell on deaf ears and they were told the violation would be taken to court. Mike was charged with violating his parole and possession of a deadly weapon. In California, the latter charge counts as a strike and a mandatory twenty-five-year prison sentence. Mike, similar to Jason, was assigned to a PD and was advised to plea out. Despite Mike's pleas that the gun was not his and, more important, there were proof of registration papers to validate his story, the district attorney did not permit this evidence in court—a common practice among district attorneys, especially when individuals have a prior arrest record, which Mike's grandfather had. Instead of taking this to court and facing the maximum sentence, the district attorney offered Mike a plea deal of fourteen years. Mike's PD strongly advised him to take the plea. However, he refused the deal, fired the PD, and with the help of his family, raised enough money to hire a criminal defense attorney.

The case went to trial and lasted ten days. Despite the district attorney's "eyewitness" testimony that Mike was a gang member, his new attorney showed evidence of Mike's clean record since his release from prison. Furthermore, the attorney successfully reentered registration papers as evidence of gun ownership. Ultimately, the jury found Mike not guilty. However, the not guilty verdict came with a price. Mike lost his job as a result of spending a year in county jail waiting for his trial date. He also reported experiencing intimidation from officers on a daily basis. Although Mike maintained a positive attitude and eventually enrolled in community college, he struggled to show up to class on time, had anger issues, and lacked social skills. Another major obstacle was finances. Mike's family spent all of their money hiring an attorney, and while he had won his case, he still needed to get his record expunged of the charges. This would cost additional money that Mike did not have. As for many ex-felons, the absence of a job and a college degree left Mike in a precarious position. After Mike completed my class, I lost track of him and feared the worst given his situation. Approximately one year later, I was happy to receive a call from him one evening. However, the call came from a prison in Northern California. Mike had been arrested for petty theft, and because he was on parole, and never had the charges expunged, he was sentenced to fifteen years in a state penitentiary. Still maintaining a positive attitude, Mike reassured me not to worry, that "life was good," and concluded by saying, "Shit, Dan, my entire adult life all I've ever known is some form of prison. So, this is like home for me." I was speechless and wanted to support him, but I felt helpless. Could Mike have made "better decisions"? Maybe. Oftentimes, the geographical context, social situation, and constructs of oppression targeted at low-income communities, and particularly Black males, affect the "decisions" and behaviors young people make. Limited funding, lack of services to assist in reintegration, and oppressive legal reforms have created challenging obstacles for ex-felons trying to obtain employment, housing, and education. Oftentimes, young people like Mike find themselves caught in a contradictory system that says "do good" yet provides them very little resources, opportunities, and skills to successfully accomplish their goals (Venkatesh, 2006, pp. 8–12).

Larry

Larry's story is a bit different from Mike's and Jason's. Larry is an older African American male who has been in and out of juvenile facilities since the age of 12. Larry's ill fortune finally caught up with him at age 16 when he was caught smuggling cocaine for a drug dealer in South Central Los Angeles. At the time, the now infamous Iran-Contra Scandal was in full swing and many of the large drug dealers in South Central were on the CIA payroll (Webb, 1998). Larry, a pawn in this deadly game, found himself locked up in prison for the next twenty-two years. And from Larry's account, those large drug dealers were given either probation or amnesty, or were set free.

When I met Larry, it was later in life and he had been out of prison for only three months. I met him through another community youth advocate whom Larry was engaged to. The two met through a mutual friend and had been dating (and later became engaged) while Larry was in prison. Larry was thrilled to be out and in a new relationship with someone who, as he put it, "kept me sane."

Still, while Larry was in prison, he was dating another woman, and, consequently, had two young boys from that former relationship (some prisons allow conjugal visits). Larry's motivation to "do good" was high and he was excited to be a part of society again.

Larry's issues, however, were threefold. First, Larry was experiencing what many scholars have referred to as institutionalization (Hattery & Smith, 2007; Kin & Mauer, 2006; Macleod, 1995; Mauer, 2002), in which a person becomes accustomed to the institutionalized lifestyle (e.g., meals, bedtime, and life at programmed times). Larry's adjustment to "life on the outside" was rough. He was used to breakfast at 4:00 a.m., lunch at 10:00 a.m., and dinner by 3:00 p.m. His "new" bed was too comfortable so Larry often slept on the floor. He had a difficult time understanding the eight-hour workday and an even more difficult time adjusting to "daily living." Larry had no one programming his life and did not possess the skills to plan his own day. He was in his late 30s and did not comprehend how to use an alarm clock. Larry's social skills were still that of an imprisoned soul.

Second, Larry was not accustomed to the technology of contemporary society. Larry told me he wept when he walked into a public men's restroom as he did not know how to operate the faucets. When he went into jail faucets still had handles; today, many modern faucets are made with hands-free technology. It was not until another man came in and placed his hands under the faucet that he understood how to use them; and even then it was still confusing. Larry also wondered where all the public telephones had gone. There used to be one on every block and now they were sparse if present at all. And while Larry was aware of cable, the five hundred plus stations often overwhelmed him and he had no concept of high definition technology, smartphones, Wi-Fi, and communication software such as Skype. Larry was at a technological loss.

Third, Larry did not have any employable skills. While Larry was on the last wave of prisoners receiving some college and work training, the training and education he received were subpar at best and did not prepare him in any way for the fast-paced job market in cities such as Los Angeles. While Larry sought work, he did not realize the importance of a résumé or a suit, and he did not realize that many employers simply did not have work for him, even as a dishwasher.

Larry quickly found himself in a bind. While he was excited to have a "new life" with a new woman, he did not know how to deal with the day-to-day routines. Larry also struggled being an example for his two boys, who by then had come to live with him. Larry and I would meet regularly, and his fire and passion were contagious. Yet Larry was socially awkward, had serious anger issues, possessed very little conflict resolutions skills, and was extremely jealous of his fiancé. I would find myself, more often than not, calming Larry down and deescalating situations that would otherwise have been non-issues.

But Larry's biggest concern was income. His fiancé worked for a non-profit with a small budget. His two sons were in high school and all the associated expenses that came with raising teenagers rested on Larry's shoulders (or so he felt). Larry was growing anxious as the wedding loomed. His coping mechanism was to escape for weeks on end without anyone hearing from him, knowing where he was, or having the ability to contact him. Larry also developed an alcohol abuse problem. Things were not looking good. Yet after being admitted to an alcohol abuse program, attending Alcoholics Anonymous (AA), and finding a part-time job which paid him $7.00 per hour, things seemed to be looking up—for the time being.

One afternoon, after being yelled at by his supervisor (who was twelve years younger than he was), after his parole officer called him a "colored man," after finding out his rent was going up by 20%, and after feeling frustrated because his son did not come home for a week, Larry snapped. He drove back into South Central Los Angeles and found himself back in the underground economy. For a while he did quite well: new cars, new housing, new furniture, and even a new marriage. His sons had the clothes and "gear" they so desired and Larry felt as though he were back in action and back to "life."

While Larry did not get "caught" for his underground economic actions, he fell apart socially, emotionally, and spiritually. He became more aggressive with his new wife and began to ignore his sons and their needs. Larry handled conflicts by what Elijah Anderson (1999) refers to as "the code of the street" (e.g., respect by means of aggression and conflict management by way of fists). Eventually, the street life, lack of coping skills, and guilt associated with his street life took a toll on Larry. In one of his "escapes" he left California with his sons for another state to reconnect with his old girlfriend (his sons' mother) and to be, as he would later tell me, in a "better place." His new wife was crushed and I and fellow community activists who were personally involved in his life were saddened by the situation.

What makes Larry's story unique is that while he did not face (and still has not faced, to my knowledge) jail time, the other parts of his life were rough and in need of much repair. Oftentimes, men like Larry find that their social (the ability to interact with others and maintain relationships), cultural (the ability to function in contemporary society and its context), emotional (the skills needed to maintain a basic rhythm of life), and spiritual (the ability to engage with a supernatural realm) skill sets are limited or lacking, thereby placing them at social disadvantages. Moreover, individuals such as Larry often wrestle with psychological issues such as depression, spilt personalities, sleep loss, and suicidal ideations. Larry is becoming a part of a growing number of ex-offenders who are released from prison systems and find great strain reintegrating into society on many social, cultural, economic, and personal levels. Larry is currently living with his former girlfriend and two sons.

REENTRY PROBLEMS

Jason's, Mike's, and Larry's stories are strikingly and regrettably similar to the hundreds of young people whom I have encountered struggling to reintegrate into society and return to "normal" life. The Jasons, Mikes, and Larrys of the world do not find rest in the perceived "rehabilitation" of what prison is supposed to accomplish. Add to this the mainstream public's perception that anyone in prison "deserves" to be there and you have a society that is not very forgiving when the inevitable mistakes are made—or worse, when someone is wrongfully accused of a crime he did not commit and has to contend with having it on his record.

Jamie Fader (2011) argues that one of the main problems facing youth in the process of reentry is that the prison institution has not provided them the services to learn how to "code switch" (p. 30) and learn behavior that will be conducive to entering society at the end of their sentence. Violence and aggressive posturing, for males in particular, is a cultural norm; couple that with prison guard aggression and youth have learned a violent and aggressive mode of social behavior. Once released these youth have not picked up the necessary skills needed to navigate a world, including employment and education, which is not dominated by these codes of the street. Fader (2011) argues that "as long as they lack access to mainstream institutions and support for investing in their own futures, their only option is to remain firmly embedded in street culture" (p. 216).

Every person who has been processed through the criminal justice system has a trail of paperwork that always follows them. These records are available to the public and can be viewed by potential employers, creditors, and landlords. The stigma of a record can have far-reaching effects for these individuals. Merely having a record is often used as a way to keep ex-offenders out of mainstream society without access to quality jobs, housing, and other normal needs. Pager (2008) argues that the State serves as a form of credentialing agency. Similar to a college degree or any other credential, the mark of a criminal record "constitutes a formal and enduring classification of social status, which can be used to regulate access and opportunity across numerous social, economic, and political domains" (p. 73).

What follows is a brief discussion of the major issues facing reentry for young people coming out of the prison industrial complex.

Employment bans: An employment ban is a ban from career-based employment if a felony is present on a person's record. Most job applications ask the applicant to reveal if s/he has ever been convicted of a felony, and more recently, applicants are being asked if they have ever been detained, pulled over, and/or stopped by an officer of the law. These types of bans, while discriminatory (Fader, 2013; Kin & Mauer, 2006), consistently occur and are difficult to prove as discrimination as any employer can give a vague response about why they decided not to hire a particular applicant. Moreover, when race is involved and a conviction of any sort is present on the applicant's record, that person is almost 98% less likely to be hired for a position (Cole, 2009). It is rare to have employment training centers such as Homeboy Industries and Homegirl Café & Catering in Los Angeles, which employ, train, and empower young people reentering society from prison. Consequently, when reviewing an application for employment, employers very rarely hire a convicted felon, and worse yet, it is increasingly becoming the trend not to hire someone with a pending case or an arrest of any sort.

Driver's license ban: As a result of the 1980s and 1990s "war on drugs," the federal government is allowed to deny highway funds to any state that refuses to impose a minimum six-month (maximum three-year) revocation of the driver's license of individuals convicted of a felony drug offense. In states such as California and Illinois, even a gross misdemeanor could warrant such a ban. This adds to the problems facing young people reentering social normalcy (stereotypes of felons, racial stereotypes, family rejection, anger issues, and depression).

Corrupt systems of parolee employment: Oftentimes, a parole officer may assign a parolee to a particular employer for employment. The employment is required in order that the parolee not be sent back to prison. Far too often, these employers use corrupt tactics. They may require the parolee to work long hours for low wages. They may require that a large percentage of the parolee's pay go back to the employer. The parolee may be asked to perform illegal work for the employer, which oftentimes results in the parolee getting caught and receiving another conviction. If the parolee attempts to report any of these activities, he/she is labeled as violating parole and sent back to prison (Mauer, 2002; Pager, 2009; Reiman, 2009; Webb, 1998).

Recidivism: Research has shown that among those released from prison, nearly two-thirds will be charged with new crimes and 40% will return to prison within three years (Pager, 2009, p. 246). Moreover, a parolee is paroled back to the neighborhood of residence, which often means the person goes back to his/her former context and faces the same types of challenges and conditions that aided in getting him/her into prison in the first place. Far too many times, the parolee is simply ill equipped to handle living on the outside and resorts to what is familiar and comfortable: navigating the underground economy.

The poor receive prison while "white collar crimes" are viewed as less arduous: Jeffrey Reiman (2009) concludes:

> The simple fact is that the criminal justice system reserves its harshest penalties for its lower-class clients and puts on kid gloves when confronted with a better class of crooks. … The tendency to treat higher-class criminals more leniently than lower-class criminals has been with us for a long time. (p. 239)

As seen in Jason's story, many low-income families cannot afford the thousands of dollars it costs to hire high-profile criminal attorneys. As a result of the *Gideon v. Wainwright* case in 1963 that established the right of anyone accused of a crime to have legal counsel present even if they could not afford a lawyer, the accused, particularly those who cannot afford to hire counsel, are assigned a PD. As we have seen through Jason's story, many PDs are overworked and are pressured by the district attorney to have their client "plea out" or "settle" to avoid going to trial.

Disenfranchisement: Angela Hattery and Early Smith, in their work on African American families (2007), explain the problem surrounding the seriousness of social disenfranchisement, particularly affecting women:

> Should she live in the majority of states, she will either be permanently disenfranchised or have to engage in a lengthy and complex process to reinstate her right to vote. What are the odds, then, that this mother will be able to successfully reintegrate with her family and not recidivate and wind up back in prison? (2007, p. 271)

Reentry without resources or services to assist ex-offenders gain civil liberties, employment, education, or housing will lead to failure, especially for formerly incarcerated mothers. Further, a 1993 study found that when children were placed with caregivers during their mother's incarceration, 40% of the male teenagers had some involvement with the juvenile justice system, 60% of female teenagers were or had been pregnant, and 33% of all children experienced severe school-related problems (Connor, 2002).

Psychological disorders: As was the case with Larry, those released from long prison terms (five years or more) are faced with emotional issues that they do not know how to deal with or comprehend. Socially constructed identities based on "gender" assignment can cause great challenges for those subscribing to such constructs. For men like Larry, the pressure to be a "real man" by not revealing emotions or vulnerability, or dealing with problems alone rather than asking for help, can be detrimental to the psyche. Depression, withdrawal, the inability to cope, bipolar disorder, schizophrenia, and suicidal ideations plague many young people upon reentry into society (Connor, 2002; Fader, 2013). They have very few places to turn to garner adequate help for these problems, or they simply do not have the economic resources to receive proper help (e.g., adequate health care or psychological evaluations and treatments).

MOVING FORWARD

Far too frequently, young ex-offenders resort to simply going back to prison because society is not equipped to aid in their transition to reintegrate. Jason's story illustrates this point well. The district attorney would not talk with my organization and even though I (Daniel) am an ordained minister and can enter a prison, I was given limitations in my visiting rights with Jason. Moreover, Jason began to lose hope and vision that his life would ever get better. Even when he was released he struggled to find meaningful work, a space that would welcome him, and time to be happy. Fortunately, Jason had a small ray of hope. He had strong familial and community support. Our organization and youth advocates were able to get Jason work through Homeboy Industries and eventually enroll him into college, which led to more opportunities that required him to stay busy and move forward. In addition, we found Jason counseling, which was underwritten by donors. Jason's life seemed to come back and while we are still currently fighting his initial charge, Jason is doing well and working. This was the result in part of the support structure that Jason had, something that many young people do not:

- A family that never gave up
- Proximity to an organization that employs young people reentering society from jail/prison
- Access to therapy and resources
- A variety of mentors and voices in the life of a young person
- Creative arts such as spoken word and graffiti art
- A community who loves without labels
- Access to education
- The belief from other people that the person *can* and *will* make it

While this list is not a five-step process to "better the problem," it is a pathway to creating change in a nefarious system that debilitates and punishes young people for mistakes, often made when they are very young.

To add to these societal structures, laws and public perceptions must change in order to help reentry into society:

- Enhancement laws must be overturned. While only 3% to 4% of prison populations is made up of violent and extremely dangerous individuals, the majority of prison inmates are non-violent drug offenders; enhancement laws are racially, culturally, and class biased (Reiman, 2009)
- Public awareness of the prison phenomena in this country
- Racial awareness and cultural sensitivity training for police officers and district attorneys

- More pro bono criminal attorneys
- Affordable health care
- Laws penalizing employers for overlooking or not hiring someone who has been arrested or detained by the police

Angela Davis (2003) asks an important question, "Are prisons obsolete?" As we continue to hear about the problem of hyper-incarceration and become aware that America is the most imprisoned nation on the planet, we must seriously consider her question and call to action. In her landmark book, *The New Jim Crow: Mass Incarceration in the Age of Colorblindness*, Michelle Alexander challenges not only the prison industrial complex but also the societal structures that aided in placing those labeled as "felons" in prison. Alexander states:

> Rather than rely on race, we use our criminal justice system to label people of color "criminals" and then engage in all the practices we supposedly left behind. Today it is perfectly legal to discriminate against criminals in nearly all the ways that it was once legal to discriminate against African Americans. Once you're labeled a felon, the old forms of discrimination—employment discrimination, housing discrimination, denial of the right to vote, denial of educational opportunity, denial of food stamps and other public benefits, and exclusion from jury service—are suddenly legal. (2010, pp. 2–3)

Alexander reminds us that race and hyper-incarceration have led us to a new form of legal discrimination within the prison walls. She tells us that we have not ended a racial caste in the United States, but merely redesigned it (2010, p. 3).

According to Davis (2003), prison abolitionists are dismissed as impractical, unrealistic people striving for a utopian society. Although people consider abolishing the death penalty, many cannot fathom existing in a society in which imprisonment is not an option to be used as needed. Davis argues that "the prison is considered so 'natural' that it is extremely hard to imagine life without it" (p. 10). If we are honest, we can see that prison has not worked as a place of rehabilitation, or as a deterrent. With most of our prisoners serving time for non-violent drug offenses, the system has to be revamped. Davis (2003) states:

> An abolitionist approach … would require us to imagine a constellation of alternative strategies and institutions, with the ultimate aim of removing the prison from the social and ideological landscapes of our society. … We would not be looking for prisonlike substitutes for prison, such as house arrest safeguarded by electronic surveillance bracelets. Rather, positing decarceration as our overarching strategy, we would try to envision a continuum of alternatives to imprisonment—demilitarization of schools, revitalization of education on all levels, a health system that provides free physical and mental care to all, and a justice system based on reparation and reconciliation rather than retribution and vengeance. (p. 107)

A lot of attention is given to trying to help and educate young people to avoid prison and now increasing attention is given to improving the process of reentry, such as mentoring, after school programs, and youth advocacy groups. More money needs to be given to these types of community programs that help and assist young people before an issue occurs that would warrant prison/jail time. Further, with research and material, such as Alexander and Davis, isn't it about time we begin to heed the problems? Isn't it about time our society reimagines what "rehabilitation" really is? Isn't it about time to give consideration to the idea that prisons should be abolished for some, if not all? Should we not try to imagine alternatives to a society driven by profit, punishment, and prison?

REFERENCES

Alexander, M. (2010). *The new Jim Crow: Mass incarceration in the age of colorblindness*. New York: New Press.

Anderson, E. (1999). *Code of the street: Decency, violence, and the moral life of the inner city*. New York: W.W Norton.

Anderson, E. (Ed.). (2008). *Against the wall: Poor, young, black, and male*. Philadelphia: University of Pennsylvania Press.

Anyon, J. (1997). *Ghetto schooling: A political economy of urban educational reform*. New York: Teachers College Press.

Artiles, A. J. (2003). Special education's changing identity: Paradoxes and dilemmas in views of culture and space. *Harvard Educational Review, 73*(2), 164–202.

Artiles, A. J., & Trent, S. C. (1994). Overrepresentation of minority students in special education: A continuing debate. *The Journal of Special Education, 27*(4), 410–437.

Cole, D. (2009). No equal justice: The color of punishment. In C. A. Gallagher (Ed.), *Rethinking the color line: Readings in race and ethnicity* (pp. 219–225). New York: McGraw-Hill.

Connor, D. F. (2002). *Aggression and antisocial behavior in children and adolescents: Research and treatment*. New York: Guilford Press.

Davis, A. Y. (2003). *Are prisons obsolete?* New York: Seven Stories Press.

Duncan, G. A. (2000). Urban pedagogies and the celling of adolescents of color. *Social Justice, 27*(3), 29–42.

Duncan, G. A. (2002). Beyond love: A critical race ethnography of the schooling of adolescent black males. *Equity & Excellence in Education, 35*(2), 131–143.

Fader, J. J. (2011). Conditions of a successful status graduation ceremony: Formerly incarcerated urban youth and their tenuous grip on success. *Punishment & Society, 13*(1), 29–46.

Fader, J. J. (2013). *Falling back: Incarceration and transitions to adulthood among urban youth*. New Brunswick, NJ: Rutgers University Press.

Feierman, J., Levick, M., & Mody, A. (2009). The school-to-prison pipeline … and back: Obstacles and remedies for the re-enrollment of adjudicated youth. *New York Law School Review, 54*, 1115–1171.

Ferguson, A. A. (2001). *Bad boys: Public schools in the making of black masculinity*. Ann Arbor: University of Michigan Press.

Foucault, M. (1995). *Discipline & punish: The birth of the prison* (2nd ed.). New York: Random House.

Hattery, A. J., & Smith, E. (2007). *African American families*. Thousand Oaks, CA: Sage.

Hawkins, S. (2010). Education vs. incarceration. *Prospect.* Retrieved April 24, 2013, from http://prospect.org/article/education-vs-incarceration

Hirschfield, P. (2010). School surveillance in America: Disparate and unequal. In T. Monahan & R. D. Torres (Eds.), *Schools under surveillance: Cultures of control in public education* (pp. 38–54). New Brunswick, NJ: Rutgers University Press.

Holzman, M. (2006). *Public education and black male students: The 2006 state report card.* Cambridge, MA: Schott Foundation for Public Education.

Howard, T. C. (2008). Who really cares? The disenfranchisement of African American males in PreK–12 schools: A critical race theory perspective. *Teachers College Record, 110*(5), 954.

Jencks, C., & Phillips, M. (Eds.). (1998). *The black-white test score gap.* Washington, DC: Brookings Institution Press.

Kin, R. S., & Mauer, M. (2006). *Sentencing with discretion: Crack cocaine sentencing after* Booker. New York: The Sentencing Project.

Kupchik, A., & Bracy, N. L. (2010). To protect, serve, and mentor? Police officers in public schools. In T. Monahan & R. D. Torres (Eds.), *Schools under surveillance: Cultures of control in public education* (pp. 21–37). New Brunswick, NJ: Rutgers University Press.

Ladson-Billings, G. (2006). From the achievement gap to the education debt: Understanding achievement in U.S. schools. *Educational Researcher, 35*(7), 3–12.

Macleod, J. (1995). *Ain't no makin' it: Aspirations & attainment in a low-income neighborhood.* Boulder, CO: Westview Press.

Mauer, M. (2002). Race, poverty, and felon disenfranchisement. *Poverty and Race Research Council, 11*(4), 1–2.

Mears, D. P., & Travis, J. (2004). Youth development and reentry. *Youth Violence and Juvenile Justice, 2*(1), 3–20.

Meiners, E. R. (2011). Ending the school-to-prison pipeline: Building abolition futures. *The Urban Review, 43*(4), 547–565.

Meiners, E. R., & Winn, M. T. (2010). Resisting the school to prison pipeline: The practice to build abolition democracies. *Race Ethnicity and Education, 13*(3), 271–276.

Monahan, T., & Torres, R. D. (Eds.). (2010). *Schools under surveillance: Cultures of control in public education.* New Brunswick, NJ: Rutgers University Press.

Monroe, C. R. (2005a). Understanding the discipline gap through a cultural lens: Implications for the education of African American students. *Intercultural Education, 16*(4), 317–330.

Monroe, C. R. (2005b). Why are "bad boys" always black? Causes of disproportionality in school discipline and recommendations for change. *The Clearing House, 79*(1), 45–50.

Noguera, P. A. (2003). Schools, prisons, and social implications of punishment: Rethinking disciplinary practices. *Theory into Practice, 42*(4), 341–350.

Noguera, P. A. (2008). *The trouble with black boys: And other reflections on race, equity, and the future of public education.* San Francisco: Jossey-Bass.

Nolan, K. (2011). *Police in the hallways: Discipline in an urban high school.* Minneapolis: University of Minnesota Press.

Pager, D. (2008). Blacklisted: Hiring discrimination in an era of mass incarceration. In E. Anderson (Ed.), *Against the wall: Poor, young, black, and male* (pp. 71–86). Philadelphia: University of Pennsylvania Press.

Pager, D. (2009). The mark of a criminal record. In C. A. Gallagher (Ed.), *Rethinking the color line: Readings in race and ethnicity* (pp. 246–249). New York: McGraw-Hill.

Pettit, B., & Western, B. (2004). Mass imprisonment and the life course: Race and class inequality in U.S. incarceration. *American Sociological Review, 69*(2), 151–169.

Raible, J., & Irizarry, J. G. (2010). Redirecting the teacher's gaze: Teacher education, youth surveillance and the school-to-prison pipeline. *Teaching and Teacher Education, 26*(5), 1196–1203.

Reiman, J. (2009). … and the poor get prison. In C. A. Gallagher (Ed.), *Rethinking the color line: Readings in race and ethnicity* (4th ed., pp. 234–245). New York: McGraw-Hill.

Sawyer, D. C., III. (2012). Stupid fresh: Hip-hop culture, perceived anti-intellectualism, and young black males. In B. J. Porfilio & M. J. Viola (Eds.), *Hip-hop(e): The cultural practice and critical pedagogy of international hip-hop* (pp. 284–301). New York: Peter Lang.

Sawyer, D. C., III. (2013). *"I ain't do nothing!" An analysis of the social and academic experiences of black males in a dismantled middle school.* Unpublished doctoral dissertation, Syracuse University, Syracuse, NY.

Simmons, L. (2009). End of the line: Tracing racial inequality from school to prison. *Race/Ethnicity: Multidisciplinary Global Contexts, 2*(2), 215–241.

Tuzzolo, E., & Hewitt, D. T. (2007). Rebuilding inequity: The re-emergence of the school-to-prison pipeline in New Orleans. *The High School Journal, 90*(2), 59–68.

Venkatesh, S. A. (2006). *Off the books: The underground economy of the urban poor.* New York: Oxford University Press.

Webb, G. (1998). *Dark alliance: The CIA, the Contras, and the crack cocaine explosion.* New York: Seven Stories Press.

CHAPTER EIGHTEEN

Youth in Transition and School Reentry

Process, Problems, and Preparation

ANNE BURNS THOMAS

Discussion of the harsh realities of the school to prison pipeline in America can obscure the reality of youth living and learning every day in these spaces. Educators and activists rail against the tendency to label and track young people as fixed "criminals" or "delinquents" without acknowledging the nature of identities as ever-shifting. Care must be taken, however, because the same can be said of the image and language of the "pipeline," which can serve to homogenize the complex trajectories of young people involved in the juvenile justice system. One aspect that gets little attention is the great number of youth who are being released from detention with the expectation that they will return to school. Whether involved in the system for minor infractions, serious offenses, or miscarriages of justice, each young person who leaves the juvenile justice system is expected to return to a school setting or receive a credential indicating that he or she has completed the requirements for a high school diploma (GED), typically as conditions of release. Other chapters in this volume explore the transition of youth from out-of-home placements to work-readiness programs, which might be combined with academic courses (Laura & Stovall, 2013); this chapter is focused on the expectation that youth will return to a school, either the youth's previous school or an alternative school placement. What characterizes the transition and reentry to school? What are the various supports that are in place for young people through this transition and how effective are they, in reality? What characterizes the teachers and school staff who interact with young people in transition? What kind of preparation have they received to enable young people in these most difficult circumstances to find success in school, however that may be defined?

Out-of-home placements as a result of juvenile justice involvement ranging from alternatives-to-incarceration programs to detention facilities are prescribing involvement in a rigid transition process. These youth are in transition from one form of incarceration to the steps of this process with the very real consequence of returning to detention if they do not succeed, however that success is defined. It is common knowledge that inequities mark the experiences of young people in the juvenile justice system, and several other chapters in this volume describe this systemic failure in great detail. From the overrepresentation of youth of color and students with learning disabilities to the unfair and unequal sentences that young people receive, inequity, racism, and sexism are pervasive enough to call into question the validity of any decision or program associated with the idea of juvenile justice. It is in that context that this chapter looks at the experience of court-involved young people transitioning from an out-of-home placement for the juvenile justice system to schools, either a neighborhood school or an alternative school.

The importance of naming and describing the youth who are the focus of this chapter is critical, particular work. In the Abolitionist Toolkit created by the group Critical Resistance (2013), activists are cautioned that "[words] redefine people and actions in terms of the categories the word represents. In this way, a person becomes a criminal and the act of the state putting someone in a cage becomes justice." Calling the system that youth inhabit the "juvenile justice system" is a far cry from the "prison industrial complex" and all the nuances that each implies. It matters what young people are called and how those names get taken up, and by whom. Many programs that guide the transition from an "out-of-home" placement where the youth has been detained to the school and community where they live refer to the young people as "court-involved." (Clark, 2009; Vasudevan, Stageman, Rodriguez, Fernandez, & Dattatreyan, 2010; Williams, Mukamal, & Tarlow, 2012). "Court-involved," with its implications of partiality (the youth is involved in and with so much more than just the courts) and lack of blame (that can be inspired by terms such as "delinquent" and "offender"), suggests an understanding of the youth in transition that can be tolerated for the purposes of description, but it is clear that this term should be seen as partial and problematic. Even the relatively benign term of "transition" implies a certain linear, progress-oriented stance toward the youth, who, it must be acknowledged, have been in and will be in transition for much of life.

In this chapter, I first describe what school reentry can entail for youth in transition, including the often hostile reception from schools; here I outline the complex range of programs that are meant to guide the transition of young people who are leaving the juvenile justice system, with a focus on the need for a coherent transition planning process. Next, I explore the experiences of youth transitioning to schools and the supports that are necessary, but critically lacking, in the school environment. Finally, I propose that teachers, some of the most potentially powerful figures in the transition process, are woefully underprepared for the challenge of knowing and teaching youth in transition.

In order to look more closely at the experiences of court-involved young people who are returning to school settings while engaging in transition programs designed by state and local governments, some general background is needed to bring the picture into focus. Nationally, approximately 100,000 youth leave out-of-home placements each day (Roy-Stevens, 2004). Who are these young people who are expected to return to school and what might they need to successfully reenter school after being held in confinement for a period of time? Ranging in age from 12 to 19 (depending on local definitions), they have been labeled differently through the years, often with great stigma attached. In the population of court-involved youth engaged in the transition process, youth of color and youth with learning difficulties are grossly overrepresented (Nellis & Wayman, 2009; Williams et al., 2012) and research suggests that this group may be two to three times as likely to suffer adverse mental health conditions as are youth in the population at large (Mendel, 2011). A recent reform effort (Bonnie, Chemers, & Schuck, 2012) indicates that transition programs should enforce "positive legal socialization, reinforce a prosocial identity, and reduce reoffending" (p. vii), which clearly reflects a belief that these youth have negative legal socialization and a negative social identity and are likely to reoffend. Perhaps not surprisingly, nearly 75% of these youth will not reenroll in school (Clark, 2009).

THE NEED FOR SCHOOL REENTRY POLICY

As many authors in this volume indicate, the school can be seen as a source of many of the court-involved youths' issues, including at times the reason for their involvement in the juvenile justice system (Kupchik, 2010). However problematic or unrealistic, the expectation remains that school-age youth in transition should return to school, often the school they attended before the out-of-home placement began. In this context, it may seem helpful to have a range of programs and oversight guiding the process of school reentry, but this hardly proves accurate. In 2008, the Second Chance Act authorized the creation of the National Reentry Resource Center, which collects best practices in transition services. Despite this nationwide effort in data collection and program guidance, huge gaps remain in research and resources dedicated to youth in transition, especially in relation to the return to school. For example, there is no federal policy guiding the transition process; Nellis and Wayman (2009) argue that there is a federal policy that covers the transition of youth who are leaving the foster care system, but no similar policy to regulate the care and requirements of court-involved youth. Calls for a coherent system of policies guiding the transition reflect several issues faced by youth attempting to return to school. Even if a youth is required by the terms of his/her release and probation to be enrolled in school, the transition is far from natural or guaranteed.

Researchers and policy makers have identified several key obstacles to successful transitions for court-involved youth returning to school, including obstacles created by schools (Clark, 2009; Williams et al., 2012). According to the National Reentry Resource Center (Rieland, 2011), "Despite the strong connection of school truancy and dropping out to delinquency, school administrators sometimes challenge reenrollment in school for youth leaving detention because these youth are considered difficult to manage. School district administrators also may feel pressured to discourage reenrollment for youth coming from detention facilities to help their schools meet academic and safety performance goals." The strong climate of accountability and fear-based testing has led many schools to determine that court-involved youth transitioning back to school and community are an excessive burden. Some schools have sought to make it difficult for transitioning youth by questioning the validity of credits earned while in an out-of-home placement (Clark, 2009), further delaying the critical transition period. Sullivan (2004) found, "Young people returning from secure confinement are caught between normative expectations that they attend school and barriers to reentry posed by the structure of educational institutions" (p. 5).

Several states have sought relief from the requirement for local schools to accept transitioning court-involved youth by mandating the creation of alternative schools; in Pennsylvania and Alabama, court-involved youth who are leaving out-of-home placements are required to attend alternative schools. These schools, designed specifically for those deemed not a "good fit" for the traditional school system, are positioned as an attractive option, but have several serious drawbacks that could derail the transition of a court-involved youth. As Upshaw (2008) found, alternative schools may not have quality educational programs and may rely heavily on independent, or virtual, learning, which can be highly problematic for students who are already facing academic difficulties. In addition, some states suspend disability services for students who enroll in alternative schools; for court-involved youth, many of whom have been identified as in need of educational support services, enrollment in an alternative school can be a guarantee of academic failure. Pennsylvania's alternative school requirement was effectively challenged in the courts, but the absence of a federal policy means that this strategy continues to be employed across the country (Nellis & Wayman, 2009; Upshaw, 2008).

The issue of alternative schools for court-involved youth demonstrates the need for a protective policy, perhaps at the federal level, that can be used to leverage resources necessary for school enrollment and success. As Nellis and Wayman (2009) argue, there is a "federal policy on school exclusion (for instance, the

Gun-Free Schools Act requires expulsion for weapons offenses) but there is no federal policy on school re-entry" (p. 18). An even more powerful precedent for a federal policy is the existing federal-level guide for the care and treatment of adolescents leaving the foster care system. In the absence of such a policy for those in the juvenile justice system and the presence of extreme pressures on schools to increase test scores and reduce absenteeism, school administrators will continue to create obstacles to reenrollment for court-involved youth.

Aside from the obstacles created by schools, youth transitioning from out-of-home placement face significant pressures in the return to family and community environments. In this case, the absence of youth voices complicates understanding what exactly the problems with transition to home and community are; from the organization of supportive programs, it seems that an assumption is that youth need mentoring and counseling because the majority of grant-funded best practices stress this step in transition (American Institutes for Research, 2008; Just-Children, 2003; Stephens & Arnette, 2000). Although some recent research calls for "best practices" that include more of the youth's perspective and voice in the structure of the process, these are currently lacking.

TRANSITION FROM WHAT TO WHAT? DEFINING THE PROCESS

Although definitions of the transition process vary, a central focus is on identifying needs of the youth who are in an out-of-home placement and connecting those needs with corresponding community agencies that can address the needs (Matvya, Lever, & Boyle, 2006; Tolbert, 2012). The process is intended to begin while the youth is in the out-of-home placement and should continue through some finite period, at which time the youth will be determined to be "successfully reintegrated" (American Institutes of Research, 2008; Tolbert, 2012). The poorly named but widely disseminated Transition Toolkit 2.0 from the National Evaluation and Technical Assistance Center for the Education of Children and Youth Who Are Neglected, Delinquent or At-Risk describes the needs of youth in this way: "He or she may need an array of support services upon re-entry, ranging from counseling and other mental health services to medical services, as well as additional tutoring or other academic supports to successfully reintegrate" (p. 27).

A search for exemplary programs through the National Reentry Resource Center will inevitably lead to out-of school mentoring programs (such as the Believe in Y.O.U.T.H program in Cobb County, Georgia, and the 180 Degrees Program in St. Paul, Minnesota) and restorative justice efforts (Justice NYC is modeled on a national program). These programs center on identifying mentors in the community to provide additional support to the youth in transition. Some also offer parent and family involvement supports, such as courses and mentoring for families. The majority of policy efforts supporting court-involved youth as they return to school seem to be community based and make efforts to push them into schools, without much programming designed to take place at the schools or in conjunction with schools. The one exception is in the area of records; many transition plans include efforts to transfer the court-involved youth's records between placement and school in a timely fashion in order to minimize obstacles to academic progress (Clark, 2009; Rieland, 2011).

THE TRANSITION PROCESS AT SCHOOL

Since the majority of programs involved in the reentry process are community based, and the role of the school can often be that of gatekeeper rather than as a support, what is the role of the school in the transition process? What should be the role of this process that has the potential to identify young people's needs and match corresponding services and supports to meet those needs? More than one program has drawn inspiration from the process of developing Individualized Education Plans (IEPs) for students with learning disabilities. The National Center on Education, Disability and Juvenile Justice argues, "The Individuals with Disabilities Education Act (IDEA) holds promise for youth with disabilities leaving corrections because it requires their participation in *transition* services" (Just-Children, 2003). Indeed, many corollaries exist between the IEP planning process and the transition for court-involved youth, not the least of which is the absence of data on how exactly these plans guide practice at the school level.

One similarity is the stipulation of many transition programs that a meeting be held between the youth and his/her family, school officials and staff, probation officers, and juvenile justice administrators prior to the young person returning to school. This practice is often cited as an innovative, important step in ensuring a successful transition to the home and school community. The "pre-release school visit" described in the Transition Toolkit 2.0 includes such suggested activities as "an interview with the school principal, discussion of the school rules and any zero-tolerance polices" and an opportunity for youth and his/her parents to sign any codes of conduct that might exist for the school (American Institutes for Research, 2008). The number of assumptions and problematic activities in the description of this one meeting seem designed to challenge the confidence and positive attitude of any young person in transition. First, the voices of youth and any needs that they might present are absent from the conversation; instead, the meeting is dominated by official paperwork and reminder that the youth is under constant surveillance for rule breaking. Next, there is no indication that the school administrators and/or faculty receive any training or education to provide necessary supports to the youth at school. Finally, the requirement that a young person in transition bring a family member to school complicates an already challenging process by placing demands on families that they may not be able to meet for any number of reasons.

As the transition process begins, youth are expected to develop a set of goals for their immediate and long-term future upon release. These goals are a key component of many of the mentoring and support services offered by community programs cited in much of the literature, including many recipients of Second Chance grant funding. Yet how these goals are developed and how much input the youth actually have in their creation is suspect, especially considering the prescribed nature of teaching and learning at schools in the era of high-stakes standardized testing. Fisher, Purcell, and May (2009) researched a drama program for young, court-involved women and found that "creating free spaces and fostering a discourse of 'second chances' in the context of institutions focused on discipline and oftentimes rigidity requires many voices" (p. 340). The school meetings might focus on setting goals for attendance, for credits, or for checking the multiple boxes required of good school behavior as defined by the school and the justice system officials. Yet how will this actually support a young person to participate in school in a meaningful way when faced with the multiple challenges that a court-involved label implies?

Turning to the individuals at the school level who are expected to provide support to court-involved youth, a disturbing trend emerges. The climate of fear that has invaded American schools has caused a marked increase in the nature and number of rules and consequences for students, especially zero tolerance policies. These policies, criticized as unfair, inequitable, and leading directly to more involvement with the juvenile justice system, are so ubiquitous that they are taken for granted at the school level. In fact, a 2004 study found that 93% of teachers and administrators favored zero tolerance policies for their potentially deterrent effects (Kupchik, 2010). Yet zero tolerance policies are far from fairly implemented by the individuals who are being hired or drafted to enforce them at the school level. In his study of zero tolerance policies at four high schools across the country, Kupchik (2010) noted the reliance on male faculty, particularly coaches or other highly masculine figures, to implement discipline. Will these be the individuals that youth in transition turn to when confronted with challenges and difficult choices? How will the youth be received and supported when the goal of faculty and administrators is peace at any price? Where will the "many voices" needed to foster chances for court-involved youth emerge in a process designed with little or no input from the youth whom it intends to serve?

This critique begs the question: What might be beneficial to support youth transition to schools? As Sullivan (2004) argued, "Reentering youth are simultaneously experiencing two sorts of transition, one from confinement back to the community, the other from adolescence to adulthood" (p. 68). Indeed, developmental concerns are critical to understanding supports for youth in transition. In addition, these young people need (as many young people do) space to be autonomous and independent, and the freedom to be critical in schools, since these qualities are severely restricted in any out-of-home placement (Critical Resistance, 2013). Today's schools rarely value these qualities and favor blind obedience (Giroux, 2012), but any program, mentoring, or activity that can provide youth in transition with the space in which they can make important decisions about their own lives and can be critical of the decisions of others can be the foundation of quality support.

WORKING THE TRANSITION: TEACHERS AND COURT-INVOLVED YOUTH

The dilemma of how to "see" and "know" students is faced by almost every teacher at some point in his/her career, which becomes even more challenging when the students are court-involved youth. As a new teacher, I had a student in my class who I came to know as an inventive writer, an inveterate complainer about any assignment, and a wonderful companion who stayed after school with me almost every day to chat, help me straighten up the room, and eat soft pretzels. After seven months of teaching him, I received a folder of information from his previous school that indicated he had been dismissed from school for threatening a teacher with a knife. I was able to forget the information received from this outside source, instead remembering what I had come to know about him from my time as his teacher, and we passed the rest of the year as we had the beginning. Looking back, I wonder how the year would have been different if I had been handed that information on his first day of school. Would I have been able to "know" him as the multifaceted, constantly changing and growing 11-year-old that he was, or would my knowledge of him have been stuck in preconceived notions of what and who court-involved youth were meant to be? Although it happened less than fifteen years ago, it seems like a much simpler time, with less focus on accountability in the forms of meetings with checklists and test-driven success. I'm not at all certain that I would be given the discretion or opportunity to choose how to respond to this "court-involved youth" in the current educational climate. How can teachers be supported to see all youth whom they teach as fully as possible, without relying on labels and convenient scapegoating?

One "best practice" must be the insistence on teacher education programs that include considerable focus on the foundations of education pertaining to diverse populations such as court-involved youth, including sociological perspectives on power, knowledge, and ample training in understanding and critiquing current educational policies (Neumann, 2009). Among other things, courses in the social foundations of education "encourage educators to contemplate their role as transformative intellectuals in the eradication of injustice and advancement of democratic ideals" (Neumann, 2009, p. 85). With the narrowing of the profession of teaching (Giroux, 2012) come fewer opportunities for new teachers who view supporting court-involved youth through the transition process as a paramount responsibility, equal even to administering assessments and completing required lesson plans. An insistence on acknowledging the myriad social and institutional powers at play in the lives of court-involved youth is one concrete step that a teacher can take to provide support for the transition process; as Villegas (2007) argues, "Given the salient role that schools play in shaping students' life chances and the obligation that teachers have to teach all students fairly, teacher education can ill-ignore the conspicuous pattern of disparities in the distribution of school benefits across groups" (p. 371).

Aside from encouraging quality teacher preparation that includes confronting deficit perspectives and advocating for an understanding of the present juvenile justice system as inherently flawed and racially biased, what can be done to train and support teachers to be qualified supporters and advocates for court-involved youth transitioning to school placements? Another concrete step would be to familiarize teachers, both in-service and pre-service, with the expectations associated with transition plans through a focus on the policies in place in each school district. The National Reentry Resource Center provides a "range of practices specific to youth" (Williams et al., 2013) that can be entry points for developing positive goals and relationships, such as the recommendation that youth must be involved in the selection of community mentors. If teachers are aware of this recommendation, they can be advocates supported by federal guidelines as they help youth to identify positive mentors and role models. Further, a critical examination of current policies through a lens informed by social foundations can enable teachers to push back against enrollment obstacles at the school level.

Teachers must be encouraged to take sides in debates of all types, particularly those that impact their students' lives. Giroux (2012) decries efforts to de-intellectualize teaching, noting,

> Unlike many past educational reform movements, the present call for educational change presents both a threat and a challenge to public school teachers that appear unprecedented. The threat comes in the form of a series of educational reforms that display little confidence in the ability of public school teachers to provide intellectual and moral leadership for our youth. For instance, many recommendations that have emerged in the current debate across the world either ignore the role teachers play in preparing learners to be active and critical citizens or they suggest reforms that ignore the intelligence, judgment and experience that teachers might offer in such a debate. (para. 11)

Another promising avenue for inspiration can be found in current arts-based programs for youth. Vasudevan et al. (2010) propose "that for students whose schooling experiences have been fraught with challenges, arts-based programs have the potential to re-cast problematic labels such as 'academic deficiencies' through the lenses of dignity, self-worth and confidence" (p. 55). Although the curriculum in schools continues to be narrowed in ways that remove opportunities for youth to cast and re-cast identities through creative writing, drama, song, and the broader inclusion of the arts, work with court-involved youth in schools should include chances for youth to explore their identities, to dream, and to inspire others. If teachers and administrators working to support court-involved youth upon their transition to schools see their role as involving and encouraging this critical expansion of the possibilities for and with youth, the entire process can become one that welcomes and encourages youth voice in expressing needs, finding support, and achieving success.

PROCESSING THE PROCESS: CONCLUDING THOUGHTS

Efforts to ease the transition of court-involved youth back to school must begin with an acknowledgment of the inequitable conditions of schools and the justice system in this country. Although work to reduce the number of youth being returned to out-of-home placements by creating more programs of support are laudable, they must be seen as part of a larger abolitionist perspective (Critical Resistance, 2013) rather than an end goal. Teachers and other school administrators who will work with youth in transition should be prepared to critically resist images of court-involved youth who might be served by static processes of goal-setting, check-ins, and completed objectives. Although policies that protect youth in transition from obstacles to school reenrollment and that provide support for youth to receive services from community organizations are a good first step, we do not currently know enough about the black-box of school reentry to feel confident in the process. Additional research, especially ethnographic studies and first-person accounts, of the experiences of youth in transition can begin to demonstrate the very real gaps between who youth in transition are and how they are perceived in schools.

REFERENCES

American Institutes for Research. (2008). Transition Toolkit 2.0: Meeting the educational needs of youth exposed to the juvenile justice system. National Evaluation and Technical Assistance Center for the Education of Children and Youth Who Are Neglected, Delinquent, or At Risk.

Bonnie, R. J., Chemers, B. M., & Schuck, J. (Eds.). (2012). *Reforming juvenile justice: A developmental approach*. Washington, DC: National Academies Press.

Clark, K. (2009). *Improving public school re-entry for youth involved with the juvenile justice system.* [powerpoint] Eugene: University of Oregon.

Critical Resistance. (2013). *Words matter: Thoughts on language and abolition*. Abolitionist Toolkit. Retrieved from http://criticalresistance.org/resources/the-abolitionist-toolkit/

Feierman, J., Levick, M., & Mody, A. (2009). The school-to-prison pipeline ... and back: Obstacles and remedies for the re-enrollment of adjudicated youth. *New York Law School Law Review, 54*, 1115–1129.

Fisher, M. T., Purcell, S. S., & May, R. (2009, July). Process, product and playmaking. *English Education, 41*(4), 337–355.

Giroux, H. (2012). The war against teachers as public intellectuals. *Truthout*. Retrieved from http://truth-out.org/opinion/item/13367-the-corporate-war-against-teachers-as-public-intellectuals-in-dark-times

Griffin, P., Steele, R., & Franklin, K. (2007). Aftercare reality and reform. *Pennsylvania progress*. Pittsburgh, PA: National Center for Juvenile Justice.

JustChildren. (2003, November). *A summary of best practices in school reentry for incarcerated youth returning home*. Charlottesville, VA: Legal Aid Justice Center.

Kupchik, A. (2010). *Homeroom security: School discipline in an age of fear*. New York: NYU Press.

Laura, C., & Stovall, D. (2013). Checking the pit stops: Job Corps as intermediary in the school-to-prison pipeline. In A. Nocella, P. Parmar, & D. Stovall (Eds.), *From education to incarceration: Dismantling the school to prison pipeline*. New York: Peter Lang.

Matvya, J., Lever, N. A., & Boyle, R. (2006, August). *School reentry of juvenile offenders*. Baltimore, MD: Center for School Mental Health Analysis and Action, Department of Psychiatry, University of Maryland School of Medicine.

Mendel, R. M. (2011). *No place for kids: The case for reducing juvenile incarceration*. Baltimore, MD: Annie E. Casey Foundation.

Nellis, A., & Wayman, R. H. (2009). *Back on track: Supporting youth re-entry from out-of-home placement to the community*. Washington, DC: Youth Reentry Task Force of the Juvenile Justice and Delinquency Prevention Coalition.

Neumann, R. (2009). Highly qualified teachers and the social foundations of education. *Phi Delta Kappan, 91*(3), 81–88.

Richardson, T., DiPaola, T., & Gable, R. K. (2012, October). *Former juvenile offenders re-enrolling into mainstream public schools*. Paper presented at the 43rd annual meeting of the Northeastern Educational Research Association, Rocky Hill, CT.

Rieland, J. (2011). *Education in the world of work* [Powerpoint presentation]. Washington, DC: The National Reentry Resource Center, Council of State Governments Justice Center.

Roy-Stevens, C. (2004). *Overcoming barriers to school reentry* [Fact sheet]. Washington, DC: Office of Juvenile Justice and Delinquency Prevention. Retrieved from https://www.ncjrs.gov/pdffiles1/ojjdp/fs200403.pdf

Stephens, R. D., & Arnette, J. L. (2000). From the courthouse to the schoolhouse: Making successful transitions. *Juvenile Justice Bulletin*. Office of Juvenile Justice and Delinquency Prevention.

Sullivan, M. L. (2004). Youth perspectives on the experiences of reentry. *Youth Violence and Juvenile Justice, 2*(1), 56–71.

Tolbert, M. (2012). *A reentry education model supporting education and career advancement for low-skill individuals in corrections.* Washington, DC: U.S. Department of Education, Office of Vocational and Adult Education.

Upshaw, H. (2008, January). Alternative schools: Promise or peril for youth leaving the juvenile justice system. *Youth Law News.* National Center for Youth Law.

Vasudevan, L., & Campano, G. (2009). The social production of adolescent risk and the promise of adolescent literacies. *Review of Research in Education, 33*(1), 310–353.

Vasudevan, L., Stageman, D., Rodriguez, K., Fernandez, E., & Dattatreyan, E. G. (2010, Summer). Authoring new narratives with youth at the intersection of the arts and justice. *Perspectives on Urban Education, 7*(1).

Vasudevan, L., & Wissman, K. (2011). Out-of-school literacy contexts. In D. Lapp & D. Fisher (Eds.), *Handbook of research on teaching the English language arts* (3rd ed., pp. 97–103). New York: Routledge.

Villegas, A. (2007). Dispositions in teacher education: A look at social justice. *Journal of Teacher Education, 58*(5), 370–380.

Williams, D., Mukamal, D., & Tarlow, M. (2013). *Employment and education FAQs.* National Reentry Resource Center. Retrieved from http://www.nationalreentryresourcecenter.org/faqs/employment-and-education

CHAPTER NINETEEN

A Reason to Be Angry

A Mother, Her Sons, and the School to Prison Pipeline

LETITIA BASFORD, BRIDGET BORER, AND JOE LEWIS

Don't be so fearful of anger or cynicism from students. I often felt that only one attitude was allowed [in this class]—a happy, cheerful, hopeful attitude. My sense was that you wanted to squelch hostility or cynicism. However, there is a place for these feelings.

This critique appeared in the anonymous course evaluations that I (Letitia) collected on the last day of teaching Education and Cultural Diversity at a small private liberal arts university in a Midwest metropolitan area. My first reaction was to feel defensive. I had been making genuine efforts to expose the class to the nature, causes, and effects of prejudice and to help them understand its profound impact on our K–12 classrooms. I had also tried to infuse the class with some sense of optimism, in the hopes of inspiring my students to foster meaningful change in their future classrooms. This student was directly challenging my approach, and I was forced to ask: Had I been teaching the entire class through Pollyanna glasses? Had I been too afraid of anger and rejection from students who had never been exposed to institutional racism in our schools? Though I had called for critical discourse, had I also inadvertently discouraged "too much" critique of our schools?

My second reaction was to guess who had written the critique, and I was certain it had come from Bridget. Bridget was an older, white, non-traditional student in the class. During class discussions she had routinely drawn attention to the harsh realities of discrimination and zero tolerance policies in our public schools. Bridget was especially concerned about the profound effect of the school to prison pipeline on African American males. As the mother of two bi-racial sons who she felt were the victims of a racist, classist, and punitive schooling system, she spoke about white privilege with the kind of lived experiences that most of the class (overwhelmingly white and in their mid-20s) did not have and could not fully grasp (or so I assumed). Bridget had shown clear concern that the future teachers sitting next to her might leave the class, our program's one required course on cultural diversity, without a full awareness of some of the disturbing truths about our schools.

Recovering from my initial defensiveness, I recognized that Bridget's critique was deserved. Throughout the class, I had tried to tamp down Bridget's passion so that the other "more sheltered" students would not feel too intimidated by her. I had also tried to balance her ardent, sometimes cynical and distrustful, tone with a more "measured," "composed," and "constructive" one. By doing so, I had actually denied our class an invaluable opportunity to hear Bridget's first-hand account of her sons' experiences in school that led ultimately to their incarceration. In other words, I had denied my students a direct, powerful, and very real account of the school to prison pipeline, a frightening development in our public school system that is in dire need of critical examination. I had also steered us away from one of those culturally courageous conversations (Browne, 2012; Singleton & Linton, 2006) that we need to be having in our teacher education programs and in schools in general.

Two weeks later, I received a call for proposals for this book and I immediately thought of Bridget. Here was a chance for her to share some of those lived experiences with an audience that understood the profound impact of the school to prison pipeline and was seeking to achieve meaningful change. Here too was a chance for me to further examine what my own teaching had failed to achieve. Bridget and her two sons agreed to write the chapter with me. Using Bridget's final course paper as a starting point—a paper that focused on the detrimental effects of exclusionary discipline and the importance of culturally responsive teaching—I then sought out Bridget's reflection, as well as her sons' stories, for theorizing the school to prison pipeline. Later, I invited Joe Lewis, a university colleague, to help us craft the chapter further.

This chapter attempts to accomplish two things at once. First, it seeks to scrutinize and theorize the school to prison pipeline through the lived experiences of Bridget and her two sons. The goal here is to fully expose the institutional racism and classism that feed the pipeline and to illustrate its very real impact on real people. Second, the chapter begins to consider what K–12 schools and schools of education must do to resist and ultimately dismantle the school to prison pipeline. We argue that there is a need for us to be more vigilant in preparing future teachers to eschew problematic practices in their own teaching and to face down institutional forms of racism and classism. We also argue for a return to culturally relevant, student-centered teaching, a classroom and schoolwide practice that places meaningful relationships at its core and strives to educate and nurture the *whole* student.

Because the school to prison pipeline is in such dire need of exposure and critique, we write this chapter from a critical theoretical perspective. Building from the seminal work of Paulo Freire (1970/2002), critical pedagogues have argued for a continual need to expose and critique societal inequities. They see such critique as central to the work of public schooling and they envision schools, in their ideal form, as important public spaces to model, learn about, and promote social justice (see Apple, 1995; Friere & Macedo, 1987; Giroux, 2006, 2012; Kincheloe, 2008; McClaren, 2006; Shor, 1992, 1996). Perhaps most important, critical pedagogues view schools as an essential social space from which to take meaningful action in response to societal inequities; here, teachers and students become agents of social change, learning not only to "read the world," but to transform it as well (Freire & Macedo, 1987). Critiques of the school to prison pipeline also call for a lens of critical race theory, since the pipeline is so clearly linked to institutional forms of racism and classism. Here, we have turned to the work of Gloria Ladson-Billings (1992, 1995, 1997), Beverly Daniel Tatum (1997/2003), Lisa Delpit (2008), and bell hooks (2001, 2010) to help us better understand white privilege and the various forms of micro-aggression that people of color may encounter in our schools.

BACKGROUND ON THE WRITERS

Bridget and Her Sons: Bridget is the white mother of two bi-racial sons, Jordan and Philip. Of his bi-racial identity, Jordan shared that in school, "I wasn't considered bi-racial; I was considered black. I could identify with being black, so I hung with blacks." Bridget describes herself as a single mother, and describes the father of Jordan and Philip, who is African American, as "basically an absent father" who was "not too available for either Philip or Jordan." She raised her children in the heart of a large metropolitan area in the Midwest. When her children started going to school, Bridget was, in her own words, a "college dropout," "on welfare," and "not a very confident mother." Of schools, she said, "I was pretty trusting of the school system when my sons first entered. … I thought it would be good for my kids to be in school and be guided by people better educated and more mature than myself." Today, Bridget is pursuing her master's degree and teaching license in English as a Second Language. She is currently teaching English in China.

Because of expulsions and sometimes by choice, Jordan and Philip attended a variety of public, magnet, charter, and alternative schools in this city. Describing these schools as "definitely urban," Bridget recalled one elementary school her children attended where a little girl on the playground was grazed by a bullet when a round of gunfire went off in the street. Jordan was expelled from his first school when he was 8 years old. His first experience in the juvenile detention center was at age 14. Now 25 years old, Jordan is currently serving ten years in a federal prison. He was caught at age 19 with crack cocaine and a loaded gun; mandatory minimum sentencing requires a five-year sentence for each charge. He is scheduled to be released in April 2016. Philip, now 26 years old, first went to the juvenile detention center at the age of 15. He went to prison in 2007 on a gun charge and was released in 2009.

Letitia: Letitia is a white, middle-class woman who works as an assistant professor of education at the small private liberal arts university where Bridget is pursuing her master's degree. She is also the mother of two young girls, both white, who attend public schools in the same metropolitan area where Bridget's sons attended school. Letitia met Bridget in her Education and Cultural Diversity class in the summer of 2011. Since that time, she has corresponded with Bridget and her sons through regular mail and email, where they have shared their stories.

Letitia asked Bridget, Jordan, and Philip to share their thoughts about their schooling experiences and their perspectives on what schools did or did not do to improve the lives of students who might be at risk for the school to prison pipeline. She received two letters from Jordan while in prison, an email from Philip, and a series of emails from Bridget. Since that time, they have responded to follow-up questions and have reviewed the completed chapter to make sure it is an accurate representation of what they have shared.

Joe: Joe is a white, middle-class man and an assistant professor of education at the small liberal arts university noted above. Working with pre-service teachers, he has experienced some of the same challenges that Letitia describes in her teaching. As the father of two young African American girls, he has witnessed many "small" instances of institutional racism in the public schools and has come to see that, collectively, such occurrences can create a major barrier to success for students of color. Like Letitia, he is committed to fostering meaningful change through his teaching, though he often struggles to decide what this should look like. For this chapter, Joe helped provide an overarching theoretical narrative about the experiences and perspectives of Letitia, Bridget, and her sons.

THE SCHOOL TO PRISON PIPELINE

The metaphor of the school to prison pipeline (STPP) underscores the fact that our public school system often acts as a conduit toward incarceration rather than a space for opportunity, growth, and learning. Nancy Heitzeg (2009) describes the pipeline as a "growing pattern of tracking students out of educational institutions … and, directly and/or indirectly, into the juvenile and adult criminal justice systems" (p. 21). STTP researchers draw attention especially to institutional forms of racism and classism that serve as key features of the pipeline, which overwhelmingly affects the lives of low-income youth of color, especially boys and young men. It steadily and relentlessly siphons them out of our school system and into our prison system and often makes them members of our nation's "under-caste," a term intended to signify a permanent lower-class status (Alexander, 2011).

Before examining the causes and damaging effects of the school to prison pipeline, it is important to step back and note two disturbing trends in U.S. incarceration over the past 40 years:

1. As a direct result of the so-called war on drugs, levels of incarceration in the United States have risen at staggering rates. According to Michelle Alexander, "Since 1970, the number of people behind bars has increased by 600 percent" (as cited in Sokolower, 2012). In raw numbers, this means "the U.S. penal population [has] exploded from around 300,000 to more than 2 million. The United States now has the highest rate of incarceration in the world, dwarfing the rates of nearly every developed country" (Alexander, 2011, p. 11).
2. The "get tough war on drugs" and resulting increase in incarceration rates has targeted low-income communities of color almost entirely. Alexander (2011) points out that "the overwhelming majority of the increase in imprisonment has been poor people of color, with the most astonishing rates of incarceration found among black men" (p. 12). Meanwhile, crime rates do not explain the rise in incarceration. "Rates of imprisonment—especially black imprisonment—have soared regardless of whether crime has been rising or falling in any given community," writes Alexander (2011, p. 12). Further, "the drug war has been waged almost exclusively in poor communities of color, despite the fact that studies consistently indicate that people of all races use and sell drugs at remarkably similar rates" (p 13).

Just what is going on here? In her book *The New Jim Crow: Mass Incarceration in the Age of Colorblindness*, Alexander (2012) argues that the moniker of "criminal" (or "budding criminal") has replaced the n-word as an acceptable way to identify those individuals who "need" to be removed from mainstream society, held in captivity, and/or denied their basic civil rights. She explains:

> In the era of colorblindness, it is no longer socially permissible to use race, explicitly, as a justification for discrimination, exclusion, and social contempt. So we don't. Rather than rely on race, we use our criminal justice system to label people of color "criminals" and then engage in all the practices we supposedly left behind. Today it is perfectly legal to discriminate against criminals in nearly all the ways it was once legal to discriminate against African Americans. … We have not ended racial caste in America; we have merely redesigned it. (p. 2)

Because our public schools reflect society, a version of this same kind of discrimination has filtered down into our schools. In the same way that poor men of color are targeted for arrest and incarceration on a societal level, boys and young men of color are in much greater danger of experiencing disproportionate discipline and exclusionary or repressive punishment in our schools. They tend to be targeted and labeled as "problems" in school; they are frequently pushed out of mainstream classrooms; they experience suspension and expulsion at disturbingly higher rates; and they often wind up in the school to prison pipeline.

In what follows, we examine the school to prison pipeline in greater detail by highlighting three important causes: (1) disproportionate and exclusionary discipline practices that particularly target young African American males; (2) the "zero tolerance" policies developed by the federal government and instituted in the public schools as a reaction to drug use and gun violence; and (3) the slow erosion of the teacher-student relationship as the essential feature in effective student-centered education. In each case, we examine the specific cause of the school to prison pipeline in relation to the lived experiences of Bridget's sons, Jordan and Philip.

DISPROPORTIONATE, EXCLUSIONARY, AND REPRESSIVE DISCIPLINE

In "What Discipline Is For: Connecting Students to the Benefits of Learning," Pedro Noguera (2008) takes a close look at disciplinary practices in our public schools and discovers that "a disproportionate number of students who receive the most severe punishments are students who have learning disabilities, are from single parent households, are in foster care, are homeless, or qualify for free or reduced-price lunch. In many schools, these students are disproportionately students of color" (p. 132). In other words, we tend to punish and push away those students who are most in need of social services and steady, reliable adult guidance. Fenning and Rose (2007) have examined exclusionary discipline practices such as suspension and expulsion over the past three decades and document a clear overrepresentation of youth of color, particularly African American males. They also note "a direct link between these exclusionary discipline consequences and entrance to prison … for these most vulnerable students" (p. 536). (See also Solomon, 2004; Rashid, 2009; and Christle, Jolivette, & Nelson, 2005, for further analysis of exclusionary discipline practices and their detrimental consequences.)

Both Jordan and Philip experienced disproportionate and exclusionary discipline in school. Between seventh and eleventh grades, Philip estimated that he was suspended from school close to forty times and expelled from school twice. He recalled being suspended for "doing immature things that kids do." For example, Philip was once suspended for three days for sticking up his middle finger at a school authority figure. Like Philip, Jordan had numerous suspensions and expulsions, starting in third grade when he was suspended, then expelled and required to transfer to another school (this incident is described in detail below).

The most obvious problem that results from the habitual use of suspension and expulsion is that it disconnects students from the classroom and disrupts their learning. This disconnect can be especially detrimental if it occurs frequently or over a long period of time. Students who miss a lot of class time fall behind and have difficulty catching up. In addition, if students are frequently suspended and not in school, this allows for greater periods of unsupervised free time and may actually increase the likelihood of criminal behavior. Equally damaging is the stigma created by multiple experiences of suspension and/or expulsion. Feelings of shame, humiliation, and anger may set off an irreversible downward trajectory. Students may begin to distrust their teachers and school. They may feel rejected and unwanted, resulting in a much higher risk for dropping out permanently.

After the ongoing experience of feeling "singled out" by teachers and staff and "punished for any little thing I did," Philip admitted to cultivating a negative self-image, because it appeared to be expected of him:

> *Once my teachers characterized me as a "troubled kid," I felt I had to continue to be that way, upholding an image I thought was cool, but an image I did not create by myself. I began to go to school to start trouble and I was a part of the troubled kids. Going in and out of suspension for kids is like going in and out of jail for adults. It becomes acceptable in one's life and leads kids to believe they are a part of the trouble, so they should just stay that way.*

Exclusionary discipline can have devastating effects because it pushes students away, rather than seeking to redirect problematic behavior and offer meaningful alternatives. Philip explains:

> *I've been suspended for fighting and cursing but never offered anger management. I've been suspended for smelling like marijuana but never offered chemical dependency rehabilitation. Kids from impoverished neighborhoods have other issues outside of school other than trying to get their education. Isn't it up to the schools to support all students and help them in all aspects of life?*

In many schools, we over-rely on embarrassment and exclusion as quick-fix disciplinary tactics, rather than seeking to build long-term relationships with our students and guide them toward more responsible choices. Often, the disciplinary action of exclusion is wholly unrelated to the actual act of misbehavior. Repetitive experiences with exclusionary discipline can result in students building up resistance to its deterrent effects (which are already limited). Noguera (2008) argues that schools "must accept responsibility for racial disparities in discipline patterns" and seek alternatives, such as positive behavior support systems. We must "stop using discipline as a strategy for weeding out those [we] deem undesirable or difficult to teach and instead use discipline to reconnect students to learning" (p. 138).

This important change might begin with a thoughtful critique of "zero tolerance" policies in our schools.

ZERO TOLERANCE POLICIES

Zero tolerance policies were developed in the 1990s by the federal government as a means to prevent drug use and gun violence in our schools. The initial intent of such policies was to reduce and/or prevent significant and intolerable infractions like selling illicit drugs or carrying dangerous weapons. Today, zero tolerance policies are so overused that students often receive severe punishments for misunderstandings, mistakes, or minor infractions. Myriad research studies have documented the misuse and abuse of zero tolerance policies and exposed them as a root cause of the school to prison pipeline. (See, for example, Brownstein, 2009; Evans & Lester, 2012; Heitzeg, 2009; Solomon, 2004; Youth United for Change/Advancement Project, 2012.) These same studies demonstrate a clear pattern of schools doling out the most severe disciplinary measures to boys and young men of color. Below, we reference some of the more disturbing scenarios described in these studies and relate the specific experiences of Jordan and Philip with zero tolerance policies.

In one case, a 10-year-old boy diagnosed as having Emotional and Behavioral Disturbance (EBD) got angry at his classmates who were repeatedly teasing and harassing him, even choking him in one instance. The boy yelled, "I could kill you!" to his tormenters. As a consequence, he was detained by the school and arrested by police for making terroristic threats (Brownstein, 2009). Before the advent of zero tolerance policies, such an infraction might have led to a meeting with the student's parent(s) or guardian(s) and a search for meaningful strategies to help him cope with such emotionally charged situations. A complete and thoughtful response might have also attempted to address the initial mistreatment of the student himself by his classmates. Instead, a zero tolerance policy led to a disturbing oversimplification of the situation, a clear lack of meaningful, compassionate response, and immediate involvement by the police.

Youth United for Change (2012) have studied the deleterious effects of zero tolerance policies in Philadelphia. They argue that such policies "have not been limited to serious offenses that pose an ongoing threat to school safety. Instead, they are routinely used for relatively minor, or even trivial, behavior" (p. 2). Below, the group describes some of the most egregious incidents of overzealous enforcement in the Philadelphia schools:

> Robert, an 11-year-old … in his rush to get to school on time, put on a dirty pair of pants from the laundry basket and did not notice that his Boy Scout pocket knife was in one of the pockets until he got to school. … Robert was arrested, suspended, and transferred to a disciplinary school. (p. 8)

> Kevin, a 10th grader, was "caught" with a small pair of scissors in his backpack while going through the school's metal detector. He had forgotten to remove it after wrapping Christmas presents at his girlfriend's house the night before. Kevin was arrested, suspended, and transferred to a disciplinary school. (p. 8)

> Gerald, 15, was arrested, suspended, and sent to an alternative education program for having a butter knife in his backpack. He only learned it was there when he was entering school and placed his bag on the scanner as he walked through the metal detector. … He was handcuffed to a chair until the Philadelphia Police came and arrested him. (p. 8)

These examples are extreme, but they effectively illustrate two important points about zero tolerance policies: (1) They leave little or no space for intelligent, caring, well-meaning adults to assess specific incidents contextually and arrive at a reasoned response that considers the best interest of everyone involved. (2) As our society has become increasingly paranoid about safety and security, our schools have begun to feel and look more like prisons.

Bridget recalled an incident when her then 8-year-old son Jordan was suspended and later expelled from his school for what she believed was an overreaction to the school's zero tolerance policy:

> *One day in Mrs. Johnson's*[1] *classroom, they were celebrating birthdays and some of the kids joked about giving birthday spankings. Apparently, this kind of talk concerned Mrs. Johnson, so she gave an earnest lecture about how there would be no hitting or spanking in the classroom. She reminded them that the school had zero tolerance for hitting and if you hit someone you would be sent to the principal's office and could be suspended or expelled. Now to Jordan, I guess her words seemed hypocritical. He had told me many times before that Mrs. Johnson showed favoritism toward the girls in his class. The girls in the classroom had repeatedly hit, pinched, and poked him without consequences. So in response to her lecture, he proceeded to get out of his seat, walk up to Mrs. Johnson, slug her in the arm, and said, "Can I go to the office now?" Since she had just given the class a lecture on zero tolerance for hitting, she had to follow through.*

The school responded to this incident by giving Jordan the longest possible suspension of ten days. Even more surprising was what followed. In an official meeting, the principal, an African American woman, informed Bridget that her son would be transferred to a new school effective immediately because he had acted in a "threatening" and "violent" manner. Bridget was never consulted on the transfer (though she later learned that the district policy mandated that parents or guardians be consulted in such cases). She recalled feeling "powerless" as her son's future was irrevocably altered, and she remembered feeling a clear class and racial bias against her son and the black father of her children, even though the principal herself and the teacher involved were also African American:

---

1 Pseudonyms have been given to all teachers and schools.

> *I felt a lot of contempt from [the principal] at that meeting. There was no respect from her whatsoever. I really felt that they did not respect me because I was a single mom, unmarried and my kid's father was black and very South Side Chicago. I wondered if it might have been a mistake to bring Jordan's father along because she seemed to have even more contempt for him. After the meeting, Jordan's father stated the same [concern] to me. He also felt her contempt and disrespect and thought that Jordan was being treated harshly because he was a black boy. It was very familiar to him.*
>
> *I was certain that Jordan got railroaded. He was being viewed as a "violent black male" at the age of eight. He was never given the opportunity to state his perspective of what had happened with Mrs. Brown. He was never asked how he felt about his class or his teacher. There was no discussion of natural consequences related to the actual incident. There was no discussion with Jordan about how to change his behavior. He was given no opportunity to learn about making amends, reconciliation, or forgiveness. For [the principal], this was just an open and shut case and a simple matter of zero tolerance. Thus began the nightmare.*

As Bridget has prompted us to do above, we must ask difficult questions about race, gender, and class in this scenario: Would a white 8-year-old student have received the same punishment? Had Jordan been white, would his behavior have been described as "violent" or might it have been interpreted and therefore handled differently? What if Jordan had been a girl? Though the purpose of a "zero tolerance" policy is to promote consistent enforcement of the rules, this incident illustrates that there are almost always contextual factors that call for interpretation and nuanced response. Study after study has demonstrated that zero tolerance policies are used largely to push "problematic" students out of the school (and often into the prison pipeline). But what makes these students problematic? With a teaching force that is 83% white and overwhelmingly female (Fenning & Rose, 2007), we need to consider the role that race and gender play in determining for whom we have "zero tolerance." Is the real problem a general societal fear of, and paranoia about, black and brown males? We note again that the teacher and principal involved were African American themselves. Has a form of "black on black" racism occurred here? What role did socio-economic class play in the situation?

The male student of color stuck in a "zero tolerance" paradigm may eventually begin to give up hope. Overzealous disciplinary response can lead to further incidents of "acting out" and increases the likelihood of academic failure. Unless a caring adult can make a meaningful connection, despair may set in. Eventually, dropping out becomes the only viable option, greatly increasing the likelihood of criminal behavior and, ultimately, prison time. Both Jordan and Philip experienced this exact trajectory—the school to prison pipeline.

Zero tolerance policies have increased the use of policing tactics on school campuses, as well as the actual physical presence of police and armed security guards. In her book *Lockdown High: When the Schoolhouse Becomes a Jailhouse*, Annette Fuentes (2011) points out that "children and adolescents spend the majority of their waking hours in schools that have increasingly come to resemble places of detention more than places of learning. From metal detectors to drug tests, from increased policing to all-seeing surveillance, the public schools of the twenty-first century reflect a society that has become fixated on crime, security, and violence" (Introduction, p. ix). Fuentes notes that our societal paranoia about school safety has steadily increased during a period when the actual number of violent incidents has declined. And "in a strange paradox that is so American, children are considered both potential victims, vulnerable to dangers from every corner, and perpetrators of great violence and mayhem, demanding strict, preventive discipline" (Introduction, p. ix). In *Disposable Youth*, Henry Giroux (2012) argues that "punishment and fear have replaced compassion and social responsibility as the most important modalities mediating the relationship of youth to the larger social order. … Youth, particularly young people marginalized by class and color, appear to live in a state of perpetual and unending emergency" (p. xv), exacerbated by constant surveillance at school.

A visible police presence on a school campus can amplify emotional tension for boys and young men of color, even those who do not have criminal records. They may feel that they are always under suspicion of criminal behavior, an atmosphere that makes productive learning more difficult and may actually encourage oppositional attitudes. The daily attitudes and practices of a campus police and security force can strongly influence this atmosphere. Jordan spoke about this in relation to one of his high school experiences:

> *The police presence was very strong at Harriet High School. The police had their own office at that school and officers would take you in there and put on their black gloves and threaten you. They would even arrange drug busts. I was taken to the office one time for an altercation with the school principal and the police threatened me down there.*

Students who feel marginalized by the dominant culture of the school and threatened by constant surveillance and monitoring may also choose to adopt a counterculture. Here, a sense of identity and belonging develops through collective resistance to a perceived oppressive power structure (see Basford, 2010; Lee, 2001; Ogbu, 1987; Tatum, 1997/2003). Countercultures are often viewed as rebellious, subversive, and threatening to teachers, administrators, and the police, who then react in extreme ways to punish the "perpetrators" (see Heitzeg, 2009; Raible & Irizarry, 2010; Solomon, 2004). Again, a downward spiral occurs that may force many young men of color out of school and into the prison pipeline.

For Jordan and Bridget, a series of troubling incidents and disturbing trends gradually eroded their trust in teachers and the school system:

In first grade, Jordan observed his teacher attempt to molest a fellow student. When Jordan told the principal what he had seen, he was accused of lying and suspended from school. A few years later, Jordan and his mother read a newspaper article about this same teacher, who had been officially accused of molestation at school.

In eighth grade, Jordan and his friend got into a physical fight with a white student who had called them "niggers." Bridget recalled that the school seemed determined to prove that Jordan and his friend were lying and that the fight that followed was unprovoked. "From this incident," she shared, "I was told that my son was a 'high risk' student. ... I was confused, angry, and losing trust fast."

As Jordan grew older, he became aware of some of the systematic discriminatory patterns in school. He saw how his African American peers were typically placed in the lower-level tracks and noticed that higher-income students always seemed to "get a pass." He saw a predominantly white teaching staff struggle to connect with a mostly nonwhite student population, which often led to cultural misunderstandings and escalating tensions in the classroom. At times, a teacher or administrator might interpret the actions of a student of color as being disruptive or menacing when the student himself did not realize that the behavior was problematic. Such misunderstandings could lead to reactionary discipline and set off a chain of escalating responses.

Jordan would eventually be permanently removed from the city school district and transferred to Zander, a charter school for kids in trouble with the law. The incident that led to his removal began with a shouting match between Jordan and the school's vice principal. Bridget recalled:

> *This VP [vice principal] was really old school. He had a reputation for knocking kids around in his office, even girls. He brought Jordan into his office because Jordan was being too loud in the hallway. Jordan got mouthy and so a cop was called. Before the cop got there, the VP hit Jordan and Jordan hit him back. The cop pulled Jordan off the VP, but only saw Jordan hit the VP.*

Bridget reported the incident to the administration and demanded an investigation. Eventually, the investigator concluded that the vice principal's behavior had been inappropriate. By this time, Jordan had already been transferred to Zander.

Reflecting on Jordan's experience with "zero tolerance," we see a school culture that puts young black males on the defensive for simply being young black males. We see a school administrator acting unprofessionally at best (illegally and immorally at worst). We see a discipline system that pushes the student away, rather than seeking to rehabilitate or reestablish a meaningful connection. We see parents who feel judged and powerless in the face of non-negotiable school policy. In short, we see a school use "zero tolerance" as an excuse to give up entirely on a student and a family. In Jordan's case, the effect was permanent. Eventually, after going through several school programs including a fifteen-month detention in a local county home school, Jordan, before the age of 20, was arrested for possessing crack cocaine and carrying a loaded gun. He received a mandatory ten-year prison sentence (five years for each charge). Today, he remains in jail. Our point here is not to suggest that Jordan was guiltless—clearly he was a challenging student to reach and he made a series of bad choices. Our point is simply to ask (for Jordan and for every other student who may wind up in the school to prison pipeline): How might this have been otherwise, and what do we need to do in schools to make a change for the better?

FOSTERING MEANINGFUL RELATIONSHIPS IN SCHOOLS

Of course we want our schools to be physically safe spaces. But a functioning community of learning also requires emotional safety and trust. Meaningful education can occur only when students are free to take risks, make mistakes, try out new ideas, experiment with different forms of expression, and learn to thoughtfully critique the status quo. Students *do* need structure, but they also need to feel that they belong. This requires a welcoming space that is not only tolerant of difference, but also actively supports and nourishes it. And it begins with genuine opportunities for students to develop meaningful relationships—with one another, of course, but also with adult mentors, be they teachers, administrators, advisers, coaches, counselors, maintenance and cook staff, or even security guards. In a true community of learning, every adult in the building should seek to foster meaningful relationships with kids. Every student should feel accepted and connected, not pushed away, mistreated, or "left behind."

Easy enough to say. But how do we achieve this in our schools? One important response is to ensure that all students have access to highly qualified, effective teachers. Another is to be certain that our teachers are adequately supported. In her extensive research on public schools in the United States, Linda Darling-Hammond (2010) has found that effective teachers are *the* primary factor influencing student success. She also points out that "teachers are the most inequitably distributed school resource" in our nation (p. 40). "By every measure of qualification," writes Darling-Hammond, "less-qualified teachers are found in schools serving greater numbers of low-income and minority students" (p. 43). This is not to deny that there are many dedicated, talented teachers working in our urban public schools. But it *is* to underscore a general trend: When talented teachers encounter daunting class sizes, inadequate resources, less-than-effective school leadership, and prison-like working conditions, they are, of course, more likely to leave such settings for better resourced, more supportive, and uplifting environments. Those who remain are more likely to become burned out, apathetic, and cynical. We believe that Darling-Hammond's call for highly qualified teachers in all schools is essential but *not* sufficient. Highly qualified teachers can only fully succeed in culturally responsive communities of learning that support and empower them, rather than blaming them for low standardized test scores. Transforming our schools will also require highly qualified school leaders and a broader community effort that recognizes the need to fully resource and support its schools, teachers, students, and families.

Jordan reflected on how much his teachers mattered to his overall success in school and noted a general lack of dedication and inspiration:

> *A lot of teachers that I had did not seem to be as dedicated as they should have been. It seemed an arduous task to teach us. My fourth grade teacher used to leave the class all the time and be gone for a while. He'd leave the class in the care of a [paraprofessional] aide. I remember Mr. Kary, my seventh grade teacher, who used to just put movies in the VCR and let us watch them day after day, often leaving us for almost the whole class period. Sometimes he would stay and go to sleep after drinking his coffee. He never interacted with the class.*

Bridget felt that school was often too easy for Jordan, and that many of his teachers seemed "frustrated" and "worn out." Jordan described himself as "smart" and said that he was often "extremely bored" in school:

> *The schoolwork was too easy. I needed more to do; however, my requests for more work were unsuccessful. Some teachers were vexed by my request for more work and I would always be told just to wait. This was not good for me as a child because I would get very anxious and have to find something to do.*

Jordan admitted that class sizes were large at the schools he attended and that it was often difficult for teachers to address the needs of "far too many kids in one classroom." Still, he maintained that it was critical for teachers to do more to engage students in the curriculum.

> *Ms. Drew would send me to the office and leave me there for what seemed like hours. I used to sit there in the office and watch staff make copies at the printer next to me. The only time I did not get kicked out of that class was when Ms. Drew read the book* Where the Red Fern Grows *by Wilson Rawls. It was something I liked. But most of the time, no one ever asked me what I liked or what kept me interested.*

This is worth restating: "Most of the time, no one ever asked me what I liked or what kept me interested." How is this possible in schools that supposedly strive to leave no child behind?

Not all of Jordan's experiences in school were bad. In sixth grade, Jordan had one of his best teachers. Bridget described this teacher as a "savvy, young black man who developed a good rapport with Jordan all year." It is important to note that during that year, Jordan was never suspended, nor could he recall going to the principal's office. Jordan explained:

> *Mr. Dirk was dedicated to his job. He tended to the needs of each student so that we all could learn and stay interested. His class was eclectic and all of the students benefited. In addition to keeping me from getting into trouble, he would ask me to come talk to him when he saw a problem arising,*

> *which kept me from getting into rebellious behavior. He took the time to help every individual student in class with whatever they needed help with.*

Jordan emphasized that teachers who developed caring and responsive relationships with students were better able to work with them on academic skills. He valued teachers who were skilled at honoring the students' perspectives and experiences and helping them to "choose" academic excellence for themselves.

TOWARD CULTURALLY RESPONSIVE COMMUNITIES OF LEARNING

How is it that Mr. Dirk and other teachers like him are able to reach students consistently and create productive communities of learning in their classrooms? In "Lessons from Teachers," Lisa Delpit (2008) describes what she has learned "from watching and talking with extraordinary teachers who regularly perform magic" (p. 115) in some of the most challenging urban settings. Among the many specific suggestions that Delpit delineates, she revisits three central themes. First is the importance of having high expectations for all students. "See their brilliance," she emphasizes. "Do not teach less content to poor urban children; … teach more!" (p. 115). Regardless of the particular curriculum or methodology, Delpit calls on all teachers to "demand critical thinking" (p. 118). Second is the importance of really knowing your students. "Recognize and build on [their] strengths," (p. 123) writes Delpit. "Use metaphors, analogies and experiences from [their] world" (p. 124). "Honor and respect [their] home culture" (p 130). Finally, and perhaps most important, is the need to build a true sense of supportive community—in the classroom, in the school, and beyond: "Create a sense of family and caring in the service of academic achievement" (p. 125). "Foster a sense of [their] connection to community—to something larger than themselves" (p. 132). Delpit's advice is strikingly similar to Jordan's description of effective teaching above.

In the same collection of essays, Gloria Ladson-Billings (2008) argues that culturally relevant teaching is not "primarily about what to do," but is, instead, a way of thinking and being in relation to students (p. 163). Her book *The Dreamkeepers* (1997) examines the practices of successful teachers of African American students. Here, she argues that practicing culturally relevant teaching is a "way of 'being' that [should] inform our ways of 'doing'" (p. 176). Both Delpit and Ladson-Billings envision a form of rigorous academic achievement that "has nothing to do with the oppressive atmosphere of standardized tests, … scripted curricula, … and the intimidation of students, teachers, and parents," but is primarily about building a community of learning that "cultivate[s] the students' minds and support[s] their intellectual lives" (Ladson-Billings, 2008, p. 168).

Ladson-Billing also calls teacher preparation programs to task, pointing out that "[m]ost pre-service teachers enter a program that ghettoizes issues of diversity. Somewhere in a separate course, students are given 'multicultural information,'" much like the course that Letitia teaches (described in the introduction to this chapter). "It is here that students often become confused, angry, and frustrated because they don't know what to do with the information" (Ladson-Billings, 2008, p. 172). Though such courses may succeed in generating some of the cognitive dissonance that beginning teachers need to experience (about race, class, gender, and other differences), they often do not succeed in helping teacher-candidates to work through that dissonance productively and apply it meaningfully to their practice. Clearly, we need to do a better job in teacher preparation of nourishing culturally relevant dispositions and pedagogies over the course of an entire program and, ultimately, an entire teaching career. In particular, we need to prepare our teacher candidates to be agents of change in schools: to recognize and seek to dismantle institutional forms of racism and classism; to advocate for students of color, English language learners, GLBT students, and others who may feel marginalized or threatened by a dominant school culture; to use a wide variety of instructional strategies that respond to the particular needs and interests of students; to be willing and able to reflect critically on their teaching practice, recognize shortcomings, and make meaningful changes.

We conclude this chapter by returning to the words of Philip:

> *Kids from impoverished neighborhoods have other issues outside of school other than trying to get their education. Isn't it up to the schools to support all students and help them in all aspects of life?*

The answer, of course, is yes. We need teachers and school leaders who are prepared and adequately supported to respond not only to every child, but also to the whole child. Schools can (and should) be spaces where youth develop not only academic skills, but collaborative and cross-cultural communication skills as well. School curricula and a variety of extra-curricular opportunities can (and should) emphasize peer mediation, conflict studies, restorative and social justice initiatives, and service learning opportunities. For students like Philip and Jordan, schools must be spaces for healing, rehabilitation, and empowerment, not preparation for prison. For students who come to school with greater financial resources and cultural capital, schools must challenge their understandings of privilege and social justice and nudge them toward becoming agents of social change.

As teacher educators, we must call attention to—not evade or minimize—such dangerous trends as the school to prison pipeline. We must prepare our teacher-candidates to be actively antiracist and culturally responsive in their teaching. And when a student like Bridget enters our classroom, we must let her speak … even when, perhaps especially when, she is angry. For we have learned from her, and from Jordan and Philip, that she has every right to be angry.

REFERENCES

Alexander, M. (2011). The new Jim Crow. *Ohio State Journal of Criminal Law, 9*(1), 7–26.

Alexander, M. (2012). *The new Jim Crow: Mass incarceration in the age of colorblindness.* New York: New Press.

Apple, M. (1995). *Education and power* (2nd ed.). New York: Routledge.

Ayers, W. (2004). *Teaching toward freedom: Moral commitment and ethical action in the classroom.* Boston: Beacon Press.

Basford, L. (2010). From mainstream to East African charter: Cultural and religious experiences of Somali youth in U.S. schools. *The Journal for School Choice: Research, Theory, and Reform, 4*(4), 485–509.

Browne, J. R., II (2012). *Walking the equity talk: A guide for culturally courageous leadership.* Thousand Oaks, CA: Corwin Press.

Brownstein, R. (2009). Pushed out. *Teaching Tolerance, 36*, (Fall 2009). Retrieved from http://search.proquest.com/docview/61814374?accountid=28109

Children's Defense Fund. (2011). *Portrait of inequality 2011.* Retrieved from http://www.childrensdefense.org/programs-campaigns/black-community-crusade-for-children II/bccc-assets/portrait-of-inequality.pdf

Christle, C., Jolivette, K., & Nelson, C. (2005). Breaking the school to prison pipeline: Identifying school risk and protective factors for youth delinquency. *Exceptionality, 13*(2), 69–88.

Darling-Hammond, L. (2006). Securing the right to learn: Policy and practice for powerful teaching and learning. *Educational Researcher, 35*(7).

Darling-Hammond, L. (2010). *The flat world in education: How America's commitment to equity will determine our future.* New York: Teachers College Press.

Delgado, R., & Stefancic, J. (2001). *Critical race theory: An introduction.* New York: NYU Press.

Delpit, L. (2008). Lessons from teachers. In W. Ayers, G. Ladson-Billings, G. Michie, & P. Noguera (Eds.), *City kids, city schools: More reports from the front row.* New York: New Press.

Evans, K. R., & Lester, J. N. (2012). Zero tolerance: Moving the conversation forward. *Intervention in School and Clinic, 48*, 108.

Fenning, P., & Rose, J. (2007). Overrepresentation of African American students in exclusionary discipline: The role of school policy. *Urban Education, 42*(6), 536–559.

Freire, P. (1970/2002). *Pedagogy of the oppressed* (Myra Bergman Ramos, Trans). New York: Continuum.

Freire, P., & Macedo, D. (1987). *Literacy: Reading the word and the world.* London: Routledge.

Fuentes, A. (2011). *Lockdown high: When the schoolhouse becomes a jailhouse.* London: Verso.

Giroux, H. (2006). *The Giroux reader: Cultural politics and the promise of democracy* (Christopher G. Robbins, Ed.). Boulder, CO: Paradigm.

Giroux, H. (2012). *Disposable youth: Racialized memories and the culture of cruelty.* New York: Routledge.

Grant, C., & Ladson-Billings, G. (Eds.). (1997). *Dictionary of multicultural education.* Phoenix, AZ: Oryx Press.

Heitzeg, N. (2009). Education or incarceration: Zero tolerance policies and the school to prison pipeline. *Forum on Public Policy Online*, 2009 (2). Retrieved from http://search.proquest.com/docview/61806559?accountid=28109

hooks, b. (1994). *Teaching to transgress: Education as the practice of freedom.* New York: Routledge.

hooks, b. (2001). *Salvation: Black people and love.* New York: HarperCollins.

hooks, b. (2010). *Teaching critical thinking: Practical wisdom.* New York: Routledge.

Kincheloe, J. (2008). *Knowledge and critical pedagogy: An introduction.* London: Springer.

Ladson-Billings, G. (1992). Reading between the lines and beyond the pages: A culturally relevant approach to literacy teaching. *Theory into Practice, 31*, 312–320.

Ladson-Billings, G. (1995). But that's just good teaching! The case for culturally relevant pedagogy. *Theory into Practice, 34*(3), 159–165.

Ladson-Billings, G. (1997). *The dreamkeepers: Successful teachers of African-American children*. San Francisco: Jossey-Bass.

Ladson-Billings, G. (2008). "Yes, but how do we do it?": Practicing culturally relevant pedagogy. In W. Ayers, G. Ladson-Billings, G. Michie, & P. Noguera (Eds.), *City kids, city schools: More reports from the front row*. New York: New Press.

Lee, S. (2001). More than "model minorities" or "delinquents": A look at Hmong American high school students. *Harvard Educational Review, 71*(3), 505–528.

McLaren, P. (2006). *Life in schools: An introduction to critical pedagogy in the foundations of education*. Boston: Allyn & Bacon.

Noguera, P. (2008). What discipline is for: Connecting students to the benefits of learning. In M. Pollock (Ed.), *Everyday antiracism*. New York: New Press.

Ogbu, J. (1987). Variability in minority school performance: A problem in search of an explanation. *Anthropology and Education Quarterly, 18*, 312–334.

Olsen, L. (1997). *Made in America*. New York: New Press.

Raible, J., & Irizarry, J. G. (2010). Redirecting the teacher's gaze: Teacher education, youth surveillance and the school-to-prison pipeline. *Teaching and Teacher Education, 26*(5), 1196–1203.

Rashid, H. (2009). From brilliant baby to child placed at risk: The perilous path of African American boys in early childhood education. *Journal of Negro Education, 78*(3), 347–358.

Shor, I. (1987). *Freire for the classroom: A sourcebook for liberatory teaching*. New York: Heinemann.

Shor, I. (1992). *Empowering education: Critical teaching for social change*. Chicago: University of Chicago Press.

Shor, I. (1996). *When students have power: Negotiating authority in a critical pedagogy*. Chicago: University of Chicago Press.

Singleton, G., & Linton, C. (2006). *Courageous conversations about race: A field guide for achieving equity in schools*. Thousand Oaks, CA: Corwin Press.

Sokolower, J. (2011–2012, Winter). Schools and the new Jim Crow: An interview with Michelle Alexander. *Rethinking Schools*, 26(2). Retrieved from www.rethinkingschools.org.

Solomon, R. (2004). Schooling in Babylon, Babylon in school: When racial profiling and zero tolerance converge. *Canadian Journal of Educational Administration and Policy, 33*. Retrieved from http://search.proquest.com/docview/61859546?accountid=28109

Stop the school-to-prison pipeline. (2011–2012, Winter). *Rethinking Schools, 26*(2). Retrieved from http://www.rethinkingschools.org/archive/26_02/edit262.shtml

Sturgis, C. (2003). *Dismantling the school-to-prison pipeline*. Paper presented at the Shaping the Future of American Youth: Youth Policy in the 21st Century conference. Retrieved from http://search.proquest.com/docview/62160728?accountid=28109

Tatum, B. (1997/2003). *"Why are all the Black kids sitting together in the cafeteria?" and other conversations about race*. New York: Basic Books.

Youth United for Change/Advancement Project. (January 2011). Zero tolerance in Philadelphia: Denying educational opportunities and creating a pathway to prison. Retrieved from http://b.3cdn.net/advancement/68a6ec942d603a5d27_rim6ynnir.pdf

PART SEVEN

Building Alternatives to Punitive Justice

In other words. It is a privilege to ignore the consequences of race in America.

—Tim Wise

Transformative justice sees crime as an opportunity to build a more caring, more inclusive, more just community. Safety doesn't lie in bigger fences, harsher prisons, more police, or locking ourselves in till we ourselves are prisoners.

—Ruth Morris

CHAPTER TWENTY

Ending THE School TO Prison Pipeline/Building Abolition Futures

ERICA R. MEINERS

DEPARTURES

Years ago, while at Stateville Correctional Center in Illinois as a monitor with a local advocacy organization, a man I was talking with about the quality of his food and his access to educational programs asked me what I did for a living. Overseen by a corrections officer a few feet away, I said that I worked at a university, and he asked me what I studied. I said something vague—education, prisons, and our nation's ill-conceived commitment to incarceration—and his response still sticks in my brain. "So, you make a living being an expert about my situation."

For over 10 years I have been working in anti-prison movements and in teacher education programs. I have spoken, taught, written, and organized around a constellation of related issues: rights for those released from prisons and jails, educational access inside and outside of prisons, the school to prison nexus (the policies, ideologies, and local practices that move a select group of young people from schools to prisons), the need for paradigm changes and bigger visions—prison abolition—and more. I have taught in many kinds of free community programs, but I have also been paid to give talks. I even wrote a book, *Right to be Hostile: Schools Prisons and the Making of Public Enemies* (Meiners, 2007). For this scholarly work, in part, I received tenure at my unionized university and now make a good salary with health and dental benefits. While at times I still deny any association with this label, I can be an "expert" on our nation's commitment to incarceration and on the school to prison pipeline.

After 10 years of this work I am in two conflicting places. I am angry at the waste in postsecondary institutions, or the seemingly careless ways in which we dispense our many resources—time, labor, legitimacy, skills—and at the glacial pace of change, except when the state apparatus morphs to appropriate our labors and to move the goalposts. But, always, I am astonished at the ability of people, in particular those most vulnerable, to work, to learn, to have love for themselves and each other, and to build change.

At the risk of appearing arrogant, as 10 years of labor is a hiccup in time when other people work their lives for justice that they do not see, after a decade I need a reality check. Where is the movement to interrupt the school to prison nexus? As the university pays my rent, this is an important question for me to ask because my aim is not simply to be a better expert in this area. I suspect this is true for all of us who work on issues related to punishment, incarceration, and education. I have yet to meet the person who is for the school to prison pipeline, or is advocating for an increase in school suspensions, or is conducting research to document why education should not be offered in prisons, or is collecting data to demonstrate that black female youth really are inherently more violent or dangerous than white female youth, or is writing about why we should provide school security guards tasers. Given that some form of collective liberation is our goal, where are we on this path? If I return to Stateville in a few years, to the same tier and the same man, what can I say I am doing or my field has achieved?

Following this partially confessional preamble, this article has several aims: First, I make a case for analysis, advocacy, and engagement that places prison abolition on the horizon for those invested in educational justice who are committed to interrupting the flow of young people toward prisons and jails. Second, I offer a somewhat unorthodox and very brief state of the field of research and advocacy surrounding school to prison work. Finally, I identify four ongoing tensions within this field of work that is, by definition, theoretically focused on social justice. I close with a push for us to continually evaluate our professional investments, and invite us to consider how they constrain our ability, as Angela Davis often says, "to ask questions that see beyond the given" (2005, p. 23). And, for those of us with "safe" gigs (tenure-track labor) who have the privilege of time and resources, what is our responsibility to participate in building transformative schools and communities?

THE CARCERAL NATION AND WHY ABOLITION

As many other chapters in this special issue have outlined, the United States has the dubious distinction of locking up more people than any other nation. With 5% of the world's population and 25% of the total prison population, the number of people incapacitated in the United States has increased since the 1970s, not because of an increase in violence or crime, but because of policies including three strikes and you are out legislation, mandatory minimum sentencing, and the war on drugs (Alexander, 2010; Davis, 2003; Gilmore, 2007; Mauer, 1999; Pew Center on the States, 2008). Who is harmed by this expansion of our prison nation is not arbitrary: the over two million people locked up and warehoused in prisons and jails across the United States are poor, mentally ill, under- or uneducated, non-gender conforming, non-citizens, and/or non-white.

Activists, organizers, academics, and those directly impacted have popularized the term "prison industrial complex" (PIC) which refers to the creation of prisons and detention centers as a perceived growth economy in an era of deindustrialization, and as "a set of symbiotic relationships among correctional communities, transnational corporations, media conglomerates, guards' unions and legislative and court agendas" (Davis, 2003. p. 107). These economic and social changes shape prison expansion, and subsequently naturalize prisons as inevitable. I also use the term "carceral state" to highlight the multiple and intersecting state agencies and institutions that have punishing functions and effectively regulate poor communities: child and family services, welfare/workfare agencies, public education, immigration, health and human services, and more (Roberts, 1997; Wacquant, 2009).

While the term "PIC" typically refers to connections between jails, the economy and the political sphere, research demonstrates that education must be included in this definition. With the increased use of surveillance and incarceration tools—for example, metal detectors, surveillance cameras, school uniforms, armed security guards, and on-site school police detachments—urban schools look and feel a lot like detention centers. In addition, the growth of an incarceration nation clearly impacts education, funneling the limited pool of tax dollars from social service programs to the carceral state. Between 1984 and 2000, across all states and the District of Columbia, state spending on prisons was six times the increase of spending on higher education (Justice Policy Institute, 2002). As budgets for corrections expand and funding for higher education contracts, the State's visions about the future of select youth are clear.

The term "school to prison pipeline" aims to highlight a complex network of relations that naturalize the movement of youth of color from our schools and communities into under- or unemployment and permanent detention. This is not a novel phenomenon. Public education in the United States has historically aggressively framed particular populations as superfluous to our democracy yet imperative for low-wage work, or jobs available after full white employment. With First Nations residential schools, apartheid segregation, and chronically inequitable access to state resources, public education has and continues to funnel targeted non-white and poor youth toward nonliving wage work, participation in the street, or the permanent war economy and prison. While these educational outcomes are not new, the expansion of our prison nation in the United States over the last three decades has strengthened policy, practice, and ideological linkages between schools and prisons. White supremacy has always been central to our nation's public education system and to our carceral state.

As is the case with many pressing justice issues—healthcare, housing, food—resisting the carceral state requires that organizers and scholars practice the following "both/and": social service and social change. Services are desperately needed for young people who are locked up, and yet equally important are structural and paradigmatic shifts that alter the contexts that produce such high levels of incarceration in the United States. I frame this tension between the need to provide services and the need to make structural reforms as a reform/abolition tension. Or, short-term reforms are needed to address the real conditions and real needs of actual people caught up in the system, but this is not enough. Many, as Angela Davis writes, are raising the question of abolition (2003).

Critical Resistance, a national antiprison organization, defines prison abolition as "the creation of genuinely safe, healthy communities that respond to harm without relying on prisons and punishment" (Critical Resistance, n.d.). Prison abolition does not mean that there will be no violence. Rather, it acknowledges that prisons are not a just, efficient, or moral solution to the problems that shape violence in our communities. As we have reduced or eliminated social assistance programs, and criminalized the options that poor people possess to cope with untenable situations, the majority of those in prisons and jails are poor people. In Illinois in 2002, 90% of women caught up in the system were locked up for nonviolent crimes, largely related to poverty and addiction (Kane-Willis, et. al. 2006, p. 4). As California (CA) State Senator Gloria Romero stated (CA is the state with the world's two largest prisons for women), "California can't build [more prisons as] its way out of this problem" (Romero, as cited by Braz, 2006, p. 87).

While abolition is not a utopian dream but a necessity, simultaneously reform work is required because there are real bodies in need of immediate resources. For example, in schools students are under- or overdiagnosed with a "behavior disorder," there are grotesque disproportionalities in who gets suspended and expelled, and police presence in select urban schools has been naturalized. As longtime feminist anti-prison activist and scholar Karlene Faith writes, this requires those invested in change to negotiate reform and structural change work. Every reform raises the question of whether, in Gramsci's terms, it is a revolutionary reform, one that has liberatory potential to challenge the status quo, or a reform which may ease the problem temporarily or superficially, but reinforces the status quo by validating the system through the process of improving it (Faith, 2002, p. 165). Faith reminds us of the necessity of doing the "both/and" where everyday local work may involve engaging reforms, but where it is also useful to place, understand, and connect these reforms to a larger movement. Or, if we are keeping our eyes on the prize, what is the prize? Liberation and justice for all, including the young people in juvenile detention centers, or cleaner prisons that have better due process? Better school suspension and expulsion policies that just remove the "right" bad kids from schools, or communities and school systems that do not prioritize identifying and punishing "bad" kids?

Building for abolition is neither clean nor easy. It is by definition transformative and multifaceted work as scholar and antiviolence worker Beth Richie identifies:

> The work for prison abolition is at once a policy issue, a community accountability issue, a family issue, and an issue that must be understood to be deeply personal. It is about health, neighborhood, the environment, U.S. position in global markets, youth empowerment, spirituality, the upcoming election, interpersonal relationships, identity politics, and many more things. (Richie, 2008, p. 24)

As Richie outlines, and as this chapter documents, to build stronger communities we must transform our conceptions of what makes us secure, and what makes our lives and communities just. This has specific implications for educators.

A STATE OF THE FIELD

Over the last decade, there has been a growth in analysis and scholarship surrounding the school to prison pipeline (Browne, 2003; Duncan, 2000; Meiners, 2007; Simmons, 2009; Winn, 2010). Yet, as previously noted—and this merits reemphasizing—the targeted under- or uneducation of particular populations is nothing new, and the United States has always tracked poor, non-white, nonable-bodied, noncitizens and/or queers[1] toward under- or uneducation, nonliving wage work, participation in a permanent war economy, and/or permanent detention. The *School to Prison Pipeline: Structuring Legal Reform* (Hewitt, Kim, & Losen, 2010) identifies some of the key components: special education, school discipline, criminalization of students, monstrous resource disparities, and unequal access to educational opportunities in alternative schools. And these are interlocking: students with select "soft" disability categories are targeted for suspension and expulsions, and these same students are often pushed into alternative schools (because they have been suspended or expelled), or have been caught up in schools that are hyperpoliced.

Research has consistently documented how school suspension, expulsion, and classification of a student as "special education" are moderate to strong predictors of undereducation and future incarceration (Advancement Project, 2010; Duncan, 2000; Losen & Orfield, 2002; Skiba, Michael, Nardo, & Peterson, 2002). School

1 Queer encompasses not just gay, lesbian, bisexual, and transgendered, but all nonheteronormative and nongender-conforming identifications.

suspension rates for African-American male students are consistently significantly higher than for their white and female counterparts, and scholarship documents the overrepresentation of youth of color in our nation's juvenile justice systems and in school-based disciplinary actions, as early as preschool (Ayers, Dorhn, & Ayers, 2001; Gilliam, 2005; Gregory, Skiba, & Noguera, 2010; Polakow, 2000; Skiba & Knesting, 2002; U.S. Department of Education). These gendered and racialized practice of removing students from an educational setting is the most dramatic educational sanction available, and starts in preschools, as a 2005 survey of 40 states' prekindergarten programs indicates (Gilliam, 2005, p. 3).

In addition to radical disproportionality in school suspension and expulsions, school to prison pipeline work highlights how students of color are overrepresented in "soft" disability categories (Harry & Klingner, 2005; Losen & Orfield, 2002; McNally, 2003; Smith & Erevelles, 2004), warranting two formal investigations (1982 and 2002) by the National Academy of Sciences. In *Why Are There So Many Minority Students in Special Education?* (2005), Harry and Klingner document how "soft" categories—that is, categories reliant on assessment practices that are much more subjective—are differentially interpreted across states, and researchers have found that these categories are clearly not applied uniformly within schools and districts. The use of each of these categories also shifts across time, a further indication of "a sign of the instability and ambiguity of the categories themselves" (Harry & Klingner, 2005, p. 4). Not unlike the subjectivity of school-based disciplinary actions, where disrespect or acting out move children into the category of a disciplinary problem, a number of subjective factors are responsible for placing largely male youth of color in these soft disability categories. Classification as special education masks segregation, and pathologizing "students of color as disabled allows their continued segregation under a seemingly natural and justifiable label" (Reid & Knight, 2006, p. 19). An entire special issue of Educational Researcher (2006) examined racial (and gendered) disproportionality in special education and aimed to invite readers to think about how these flexible practices of classification educationally disqualify certain communities.

Building from critical work on how disability places students on tracks toward undereducation, related work examines schools as punishing sites within larger economic and political structures (Anyon, 1980; Robbins, 2008; Saltman & Gabbard, 2003). Scholarship also analyzes the linkages between capitalism, and more currently, neoliberal policies and education, creating punishing educational futures (Anyon, 2005; Apple, 2010; Kumashiro, 2008; Lipman, 2004). Numerous smaller ethnographic studies document the gendered and racialized production of disposable youth (Ferguson, 2000; López, 2003; Winn, 2010) and this research is inextricably linked to work that outlines the foundational inequities of public education in the United States by many including James Anderson (1988), Jeannie Oakes (1985), and William Watkins (2001). Of course, my summary is woefully ahistoric. Significant scholarship—from Carter G. Woodson to bell hooks—continues to identify the complex roles of white supremacy in education, highlighting the old story of tracking and unequal access to educational opportunity for African-American, First Nations, and Latino students.

Investigation in overlapping fields also identifies that incarceration and education are directly linked. Decreases in education correlate with higher rates of incarceration, most dramatically for African-American males (Petit & Western, 2004). Research suggests that just one more year of high school would significantly reduce incarceration (and crime) rates, and raising the male high school graduation rate by 1% would result in the nation saving, by one economist's analysis, $1.4 billion (Lochner & Moretti, 2004). Numerous studies demonstrate that education, in particular higher education while locked up, reduces recidivism (Fine et al., 2001; Steurer, Tracy, & Smith, 2001; Taylor, 1992; U.S. Department of Education, 1995), yet Pell Grants were removed in 1994 for people incarcerated. The Illinois Consortium on Drug Policies has calculated that, in 2002, if postsecondary programs were offered to incarcerated men and women, then Illinois could have saved "between $11.8 and $47.3 million" from the reduced recidivism rates (Kane-Willis et al., 2006, p. 4).

Networks and organization have emerged to focus research and resources around the school to prison pipeline, to convene high-profile meetings, and to translate research into more accessible materials for mainstream audiences: Advancement Project (http://www.advancementproject.org http://www.stopschoolstojails.org/); American Civil Liberties Union (http://www.aclu.org/racial-justice/school-prison-pipeline); Charles Hamilton Houston Institute for Race and Justice (http:// www.charleshamiltonhouston.org/Projects/Project.aspx?id=100005); Civil Rights Project/Proyecto Derechos Civiles (http://www.civilrightsproject.ucla.edu/); Dignity in Schools (http://www.dignityinschools.org/); and Southern Poverty Law Center (http://www.splcenter.org/what-we-do/children-at-risk). Advocacy organizations that work on juvenile and educational justice issues in many states have developed initiatives, for example, the Juvenile Justice Project of Louisiana's Schools First! Project (http://jjpl.org/new/?page_id=19) centering the school to prison pipeline as an organizational focus.

Grassroots and youth-centered community groups across the United States have placed interrupting the schoolhouse-to-jailhouse track on their advocacy agenda. Youth-led projects including Chicago's Blocks Together, teacher-facilitated journals such as Rethinking Schools and smaller conferences such as Educational for Liberation have all provided leadership, analysis, and movement building around challenging discriminatory educational policies at the local and state level that track youth to prisons. Notably, the "schools not jails" movement was initially a staunchly youth-led movement, with a fierce critique of the "status quo of schooling"—including nonrelevant curriculum and a sharp analysis of the unequal forms of schooling available to urban youth—yet some of this analysis gets lost in more mainstream scholarship on the relationships between education and incarceration that simply posits schooling as the antidote to carceral expansion, without linking the two structures (Acey, 2000).

TENSIONS FOR SCHOLARSHIP WITHIN THE FIELD

With this quick summary of the field, I turn to highlight four specific challenges involved in interrupting the school to prison nexus and building abolition futures. I write this for audiences with at least one or two limbs in educational spaces: students and teachers. These are both movement strategy and research questions, primarily based from my local and national work, reading and engagement. These tensions are ones I struggle with myself, and they are offered here in the service of building stronger collective movements and paradigms for justice work. More importantly, I offer these as central concepts to track for those committed to ending our nation's overinvestment in a carceral state, and ending the school to prison pipeline.

These tensions are intersecting theoretical and movement building questions. (1) How do we negotiate work that often centers youth or juveniles as "exceptional" within the larger mess of the criminal justice system? (2) How do we negotiate shifting state structures capable of appropriating our justice work? (3) Why is it important to also focus labor on how to change and build practices and paradigms of public safety that are not reliant on punishment, isolation, and stigma? And finally, (4) How do we center an intersectional lens in our organizing and research? For each, I offer a short theorized summary, with brief examples where possible, of what these questions resemble in practice.

EXCEPTIONALITY, OR THE DIFFERENCE DIFFERENCE MAKES

Research and organizing within the framework of the school to prison pipeline struggles with the tensions involved in working with and challenging a portion of a system and a structure that is flawed; this becomes particularly troubling as this labor and focus is reliant on prioritizing a category, "youth," that is also constructed and flexible. Scholarship and advocacy in this field often starts with a shared understanding that youth are different than adults. This a priori case for a kind of exceptionalism creates problems for both wider justice movements, and for work with youth as well.

These categories—childhood, youth, juvenile, adult—are anything but natural or static. Debates about where to draw the chronological (and culpable) line repeatedly surface in mainstream media; less visible yet equally important is the evidence used to rationalize any boundary by the media, "child savers," psychological experts, and other parties across the political spectrum. For example, "emerging adulthood," the new development category that elongates adolescence, surfaced in 2010 in mainstream media at the same time the Supreme Court debated the constitutionality of sentencing juveniles to life without parole (LWOP) for nonmurder crimes (the death penalty for juveniles was abolished in the United States in 2005). Science and experience were used to scaffold both constructions. "Emerging adulthood," psychologists identify, is demarcated by delay of "common" adult experiences—employment, leaving the parental home, marriage, child birth—and other seemingly naturalized life-stage markers. In writing the Court's 6–3 decision to render LWOP unconstitutional for those who commit crimes under age 18, the New York Times cites Justice Stephens's decision:

> "Knowledge accumulates," he wrote. "We learn, sometimes, from our mistakes." (as cited in Liptak, 2010)

Neurological research was also circulated in material that supported efforts to render the death penalty unconstitutional for juveniles by the American Bar Association (2004). Psychology, experience, and neurology legitimate "delay," and are organized as evidence that juveniles need protection and should not receive the death penalty, or that 26-year-olds ("emerging adults") should be able to continue to access their parents' health insurance and remain dependent on state or parental management and intervention.

In particular, for youth, experience becomes a double bind. Remaining innocent (the defining category of childhood) requires the negation of experience (sexual, life, and other), and therefore knowledge becomes tricky for children. As McDermott, Goldman, and Varenne (2006) aptly point out in their research on the construction and circulation of "learning disability" within educational spaces, the child can be the unit of concern, but not the unit of analysis (2006, p. 12). When the child becomes the unit of analysis the contextual factors that shape and produce this artifact, the child, and her condition as "disabled," are erased.

Exceptionality and youth are also circulated in other arenas. Innocence and safety (for select children only) are repeatedly deployed to expand policing and surveillance. How many times at a meeting having to do with education or criminal justice is the good of the children, or children's futures, raised? While "protection" of "innocence" (of course only available to the few) is used to expand the carceral state, anxieties surrounding the laboring futures for "our children" are also often a key plank of prison expansion.[2] Yet, these political and economic futures

2 For a more extensive discussion on the local economics of prison expansion, see Gilmore (2007). Gilmore documents how a small California town, Corcoran, lobbied for a prison,

are always predicated on a particular racialized, heteronormative, gendered logic. Clearly, those interested in prison construction are imagining futures where their sons are on the "right" side of the prison bars, and not futures where their daughters work in an all-male prison. Childhood is at the heart of prison expansion as false promises of safety and employment, particularly for our most "innocent" (children) are repeatedly used to expand a prison nation.

Interestingly, where I have observed and felt this tension around youth, criminality, and exceptionalism most directly in the last year has been in relation to work in immigration justice organizing—specifically surrounding the Development, Relief, and Education for Alien Minors Act (DREAM Act). Living in a community and working at a university with a large number of undocumented people, and as a legal resident alien myself, has educated me about the U.S. border, and I have participated in legalization movements since I arrived in the United States on a tourist visa. First introduced in 2001, the DREAM Act was created to offer undocumented youth potential pathways for legalization in the absence of any comprehensive immigration reform proposal. As this book goes to press, the 2010 DREAM Act (there have been many iterations over the last 10 years) permits undocumented youth who finish two years of community service or two years in the military and are of "good moral character" access to potential pathways for legalization. While I support the advocates for the DREAM Act, I also persistently raise questions. The DREAM Act trades on tropes of "innocence" and "merit," directly linked to student identity. These strategies reinforce the idea that there are "real" criminals and undeserving or guilty immigrants who should legitimately be denied access to pathways for legalization. The DREAM Act (the 2010 version is also a de facto racial and economic draft) also separates a population that typically accrues the most sympathy—students—and provides this limited group access to pathways for legalization, thus possibly making it difficult to pass a wider legalization initiative for other undocumented groups that are less "attractive" including day laborers, domestic workers, and those over 30.

Justice movements struggle with exceptionality, or what is the difference that makes a difference? Motherhood continues to be circulated in efforts to push for changes in sentencing and conditions for women who are locked up. Narratives and images of transwomen in men's prisons who are denied access to hormones or the right to serve their sentence in women's institutions are circulated to instigate change. These are critical and vital issues. Exceptionality, as noted, is particularly prevalent in work related to the school to prison pipeline. We love children, want to center children and youth as different from adults, and our entire body

---

and providing local economic futures for young people was offered as the rationale for a prison (pp. 171–172).

of developmental literature reinforces developmental differences. Yet, there are costs to the deploying and framing of populations as different, special. This use of difference can also limit other ways of knowing/knowledge and organizing. If juveniles are protected because of immature brain development, does this make the rest of us culpable and can only access punishment?

The challenge for those of us with extra time who are paid to think is to ask what the circulation of these identities makes visible and what is obscured. Yet, as I write this I am daily reminded of the unequal ways in which state and interpersonal violence is deployed in our own lives and communities. "Disproportionality" does not capture the reality of who is actively targeted for state and interpersonal violence: women, queers, and those gender nonconforming, poor people, brown–red–black people, people with disabilities, and/or others on the margins.

Nancy Fraser addresses this challenge directly in her work, writing about when our tactics result in recognition but not redistribution (of resources, state systems, and more) (Fraser, 1997). For Fraser, justice strategies all too often agitate for recognition (a liberal multicultural model), thus inviting additive responses that are not capable of transforming systems of power, oppression, and privilege.[3] In addition, recognition can often only be on a single axis (race, gender, or sexuality). Asking juveniles or children to be viewed differently than adults does not transform the larger contexts that punish particular communities. This is also the reform/abolition question—in a different outfit. Abolition visions can get translated into reformist strategies because organizing can be about compromise, and the tactics deployed attempt to trigger public feelings (outrage, sympathy, pity) that can limit and constrain work. Public and private affect (and corresponding campaigns) are often produced through the "specialness" of particular populations.[4] Organizing and research on the school to prison nexus, with a center on youth, is particularly challenged by the very framings that make this work and these interventions possible.

THE SHIFTING STATE

As prison reform organizations lobby—particularly for populations afforded "exceptionality" status, including pregnant women and juveniles—for "alternatives" to incarceration, it is important to trace how these alternatives are created,

3 For example, simply asking select "good" gays to be recognized as equals by the state does not redistribute access to all the important resources attached, for example, to marriage.

4 And I believe that this is how, in antiprison movements, those "too bruised by history" (Berlant, as cited in Rhodes 2005, p. 402) such as those convicted of sexual assault or child pornography, get dropped out of the movement.

developed, and implemented and to track the relationships of these alternatives to the carceral state. The construction of alternatives to incarceration also offers us the opportunity to engage with the changing conceptions of the state and the corresponding ways identities are sutured, often through affect, to these new state practices/formations. As political scientist James Ferguson argues, the state is not a static entity: "The state, in this conception, is not the name of an actor, it is the name of a way of tying together, multiplying, and coordinating power relations, a kind of knotting or congealing of power" (1994, p. 273).

By alternatives to incarceration and punishment, I refer to a range of programs like the "culture of calm" in Chicago Public Schools (Huston, 2010), and more widely, the limited moves in some school systems to include forms of restorative justice, and the extension in many states to include boot camps and military programs into their menu of public educational options. I also include the growing number of programs that are often mandated for "at risk" youth: anger management (men) and self-esteem (women). Academics and those invested in prison reform (or educational reform) are often called to support these alternatives, and we often evaluate, grant write, and endorse these options because these are "alternatives" to prison or detention for young people (Carr, 2010; Haney, 2010).

Yet these alternatives, provided by community-based, nonprofit entities that wield considerable power, participate in forming a neoliberal state capable of "government from a distance" (Rose, 1999). It is not immediately clear whether these programs extend or soften the carceral state, or if they are alternatives. The relationships between these programs and the state are nuanced. These alternatives form networks of power that remind us that the decentralization key to neoliberal policies does not mean that the state withdraws; rather, the state's relationships and abilities to negotiate power, to "govern" from a distance, shift, and potentially expand. A key concern is whether young people are made more vulnerable by supporting and implementing, for example, the proliferation of anger management programs in lieu of in-school detentions.

I use the geographer Jennifer Wolch's term, "shadow state," to describe the foundations, nonprofit organizations, for-profit entities, and other nongovernmental forces that essentially fulfill functions that were once identified as the purview of the state (Wolch, 1990). Instances of the shadow state include when tax exempt private foundations and not-for-profit corporations fund and run schools that are still legally framed as public school (e.g., charter schools where students must be admitted via lottery). Men and women are paroled from prison and receive housing from religious nonprofit associations and are court-mandated to counseling services conducted by "in-training apprentices" from the local for-profit colleges and institutes. These "service agencies," often staffed by women in low-paying nonunion jobs, do not have to be accountable to any public, just to its unelected board members, or the invisible or too visible big-ticket donors. The constellation of these organizations forms a shadow state to deliver central services, and also participates in changing what counts as the state.

In the realm of alternatives to incarceration or punishment, arenas of service continue to emerge, often linked as forms of therapeutic self-governance: anger management programs, self-esteem workshops, etc. In her study of women locked up in community-based alternatives to incarceration, and staff members who work in these programs, Haney (2010) documents the strength and growth of therapeutic governance, or the augmentation of "recovery" programs and cultures within the carceral state, particularly for populations, such as women, pregnant teens and juveniles. These forms of therapeutic governance are predicated on the assumption that the body at stake is not eligible for a rights-based discourse, but instead requires forms of governance to manage an outlaw's desires and feelings. I am particularly interested in how these new nonprofit organizations—or hybrid or satellite states as Haney terms them (2010)—manage affect. In Haney's work, the therapeutics of carceral self-governance are explicitly gendered and racialized and naturalize a correspondingly gendered, heteronormative, and racialized dependency discourse.

Yet, it would be a mistake to ascribe too much power to these programs. And while I am not romanticizing resistance of the oppressed, in my years of work, I've found ventriloquation is a key skill when negotiating governmental structures, such as teachers, social workers, welfare or workfare caseworkers, principals or truancy, and parole officers on a daily basis. But, simultaneously, when recovery culture (anger management, self-esteem, or twelve-step programs) is the only healing paradigm available—these programs (sometimes) work. And by work I mean that youth have a place to stay, some support to get clean, and tools (largely from each other) to negotiate the new punitive state practices.

Crucial questions remain as we move into this terrain: How do these programs facilitate or advance our collective goals of liberation? How able is the state to appropriate "do-gooder" desires to extend the state's reach, in particular those initiatives targeted at juveniles? For example, when "community"" programs such as Alcoholics Anonymous become court mandated and/or state organized, potentially radical, democratic, and healing practices are transformed. When schools start to offer restorative justice practices, and these practices are tied to juvenile justice systems, there must be assessments about what is won and what is lost with these moves. These should not be investigations that limit us but rather challenge and question our work.

BUILDING SAFE COMMUNITIES AND SCHOOLS

Parents want security guards and surveillance cameras in schools because they perceive schools as unsafe spaces. Teachers want detention and a school discipline officer because they don't know what to do with students in their classrooms who harm themselves or their peers. People often want more police on the streets and tougher laws because they want to feel safe. People want, need, and deserve safe schools and communities, but what makes these spaces feel and be safe or unsafe?

The prevailing contemporary carceral logic recycles the false notion that safety can be achieved through essentially more of the same: more guards, fences, surveillance, suspensions, punishment, etc. Inviting abolition futures pushes us to name how this "more of the same"—building more youth detention centers and prisons, funneling more youth into suspensions or expulsions, placing more police and cameras in schools—will not make schools safer, or our communities stronger. We must reclaim definitions of safety. Scholars that are invested in work that interrupts and transforms the school to prison nexus must build other futures and participate in rethinking safety.

Building safer schools requires challenging mass incarceration policies but also grappling directly with questions and feelings of safety, and in particular, how a gendered and often racialized fear (e.g., of sexual assault of white women and children) is publicly deployed to augment the prison system. Our classrooms are not immune from these stereotypes and fears. Our schools receive and can reproduce powerful mythologies: violent teenaged super-predators, crack babies, "bad and lazy" parents, and disordered and dangerous youth.

The work to challenge mass incarceration as a public safety strategy is also made difficult by how "common sense" the ideas of both incarceration and exclusion appear, as well as the real lived experiences of violence and unsafety of many. But shifting from a punishment- and detention-based approach to a definition of safety that incorporates relationships and community inside and outside our schools requires engagement with the lived experience of being and feeling safe. This is complicated and vital work. We need research and organizing that explores what schools and communities are doing to create safe and strong communities without relying on more detention rooms, truancy officers, surveillance cameras, and school security guards.[5]

Unpacking carceral logic from feelings and experiences of being unsafe or fearful can demonstrate how punishment logic masks the real question: how do we build stronger and safer communities? This is local and affective work, and we must do this together. As many, from Audre Lorde (1984) to Feel Tank Chicago point out, politics and political engagement is a "world of orchestrated feeling" (Feel

5 Formal and ad hoc groups are focused on this nationally and I track their work: Story Telling and Organizing Project/Creative Inventions and the Audre Lorde Project/Safe Outside the System. Locally, I am involved with Project Nia, a group providing transformative justice. Accountability is difficult. We don't have great tools but abolitionist organizations are at the forefront of trying to imagine and build new tools.

Tank, 2008, p. 3). Addressing questions of fear and safety in a landscape where sexual and other forms of harm are endemic is difficult, because building responses to these forms of state and interpersonal violence necessitates multifaceted labors. We must consider how our responses mobilize disgust, defensiveness and pity, and to subsequently use this thinking to shape our organizing efforts. In schools, these practices are no different, and we need allies willing to focus research and other labors on the fledgling restorative and transformative justice practices that are happening in schools: peace circles, peer juries, motivational interviewing, and many other forms of building relationships and community. Ending the school to prison pipeline requires building other sustainable frameworks for public safety.

NEGOTIATING INTERSECTIONALITY

An intricacy in my organizing, service providing, and scholarship is the challenge to practice and center intersectional work within a context where our labor and analysis are often reactive, while juggling to make short-term reforms within a landscape that requires longer-term structural and paradigm shifts. Legal theorist Kimberlé Crenshaw developed the term "intersectionality" to refer to the multiple ways that power and privilege intersect (Crenshaw, 1994). Intersectionality recognizes how identities—ethnicity, gender, sexuality, ability, race—are mutually constitutive. For example, white supremacy is not an adequate frame to name the oppression of black women because oppression is simultaneously experienced based on class and gender. Thinking through white supremacy requires an understanding of how heteronormativity and misogyny are central to animating and reconfiguring white supremacy. An intersectional lens, in analysis or organizing, is tough as we may understand ourselves and how we are embodied as intersectional—for example, as a queer black transman or as a disabled woman—but this is not how our civil rights and justice movements and our service organizations are typically organized.

As an example, I point to the scarcity of intersectional work within the school to prison pipeline, specifically work that includes gender and sexuality within an analysis, or within organizing. This is particularly problematic when sexuality and gender are central to the movement of youth, in particular youth of color, into incarceration. Sexual and gender violence toward girls shapes school push-out, and researchers have linked interpersonal sexual violence as a "powerful indicator" of future incarceration for young girls (Simkins, Hirsh, Horvat, & Moss, 2004; Winn, 2010). Sexually righteous young women, including pregnant and parenting teens, are offered no protection for their sexual lives in school and are punished if they exceed the state's impoverished expectations (Fine & McClelland, 2006). Not surprisingly, research identifies that gay, bisexual, and lesbian youth are more likely to be punished by courts and schools, even though they are less likely than straight peers to engage in serious crimes, and "consensual same-sex acts more often trigger punishments than equivalent opposite sex behaviors" (Himmelstein & Bruckner, 2011, p. 50).[6] For example, in 2006, K. K. Logan, a teenaged transwoman in Gary, Indiana, was told she could not wear a dress to her prom, only a "nice ladies pant-suit," and in 2010 Constance McMillen was told she could bring a same-sex date or wear a tuxedo to her Mississippi high school prom (Advocate Editors, 2011; Strom, 2010). While frequently erased from mainstream media or not viewed as substantive issues, Logan and Constance offer us high-profile examples of lesbian, gay, bisexual, transgendered, and queer (LGBTQ) and nongender-conforming youth resisting the gendered and sexualized forms of punishment in their schools. Scholarship and organizing on the school to prison nexus must account for the myriad of ways in which schools actively discriminate, and concurrently push-out, LGBTQ and nongender-conforming youth and how sexual violence targeted at women participates in augmenting the school to prison nexus.

My goal is not to add queer lives and bodies, or to engage in a hierarchy of categories or oppressions, or to advance homonormativity—but to stress how gender and sexuality are always central to how we understand the school to prison nexus. In many areas of educational justice work, gender, and sexuality are still ignored, viewed as superfluous or detractors to the real issue (race or class), or as unnecessary research complications or variables (Meiners & Quinn, 2009; McCready, 2004; Rofes, 2005).

Understanding intersectionality is incredibly important as we think through our strategies to respond to injustices in schools and communities. A failure to encompass an intersectional lens in our analysis of the problems or in our intervention strategies can result in the animation of significant and longer-term structural problems. Or, short-term good intentions can lead to unintended consequences down the line. For example, as antibullying legislation and policies gain recent measures of success, specifically those that recognize the decades-long failures to provide even a measure of "safety" for lesbian, gay, bisexual, transgendered, and queer (LGBTQ) and gender nonconforming youth in schools, all too often these policies heavily sanction perpetrators. The turn to a criminalization of perpetrators of this "antigay" violence in schools results in more school sanctions, more punishment, and potentially more push-out in an educational context where school

6 This research by Himmelstein and Bruckner follows a decade of work by advocacy organizations including the Gay, Lesbian and Straight Educators Network (GLSEN) that clearly outlines how LGBTQ and gender nonconforming youth are also disproportionately targeted for suspension and expulsions and also denied the right to an education (e.g., see Kosciw and Diaz 2009).

disciplinary actions disproportionately harm youth of color. Our "remedies" have collateral damages. In part, this is also the limitation of tinkering around the edges of paradigms, and the setback of small-scale reforms, rather than structural and systemic transformations. Intervention in the movement of youth of color from schools to prisons is intersectional work.

COLLECTIVIZING FOR ABOLITION FUTURES

I have attempted to describe some of the difficult places I see at this moment in antiprison scholarship and organizing, specifically the work linked to the school to prison nexus. As this chapter summarizes, our weakness include tensions around exceptionality, specifically our desires to center children and youth, and concurrently how carceral practices continue to change the face of the state and require us to be vigilant and to track how alternatives to incarceration are organized. We are also challenged to build sustainable and viable decarceration initiatives and to develop ways to make schools and communities safer, without augmenting a carceral state, and to address state and interpersonal violence, while integrating LGBTQ lives and feminist standpoints.

The transformations required appear overwhelming. As articles in this special issue highlight, there is a wide range of organizing and scholarship underway, but the depth and breadth of the transformation needed is tremendous. In their survey of legal reforms surrounding the school to prison pipeline, Hewitt et al. (2010) repeatedly remind readers that neither the "right" analysis nor legal reform will create just communities or schools, but rather movements and organizing might. I find it helpful, when I think I am stuck and there is not much I can do, to think about how social change works, and to consider the kinds of roles possible for university-based workers.

Indigenous rights scholar and activist Andrea Smith invites activist scholars to see ourselves as workers in justice movements before scholarship, and names the importance of collectivizing and being able to recognize ourselves and build cultures within universities:

> The point is that if we are going to challenge the individualist system, we need to engage in collective action through relationships built on mutual responsibility and accountability. The system can handle thousands of "oppositional" academics who do work on their own; it is not until these thousands begin to act collectively that the system can be challenged. (Smith, 2009, p. 41)

I imagine Smith's call for collectivizing could take many forms, because we know that research is not confined to colleges and universities, nor is there a best or only recipe for producing justice-mobilizing scholarship inside institutions (if only it was hermeneutics or statistics that could snap away white supremacy). Instead, Smith asks us to imagine and to practice collective models, and to build and strengthen collective pathways for justice work in our institutions. These initiatives could be framed methodologically, if, for example, instead of producing more research on the experience of youth behind bars, or more reports on why young people are locked up, we shifted our gaze to studying up (Nader, 1972) and organized to document how organizations and institutions work to naturalize carceral outcomes for select youth.

Perhaps more importantly, Smith's charge suggests the myriad of assets we possess—not simply research skills but other labor, research, and pedagogical tools—and asks us who we hold ourselves accountable to at the end of the day—our scholarship or justice movements? Generally, scholars are professionalized to produce academic products to get and to keep our jobs, to build our expertise, and to advance our disciplines or the field. But what if we built networks that moved us to ask—how am I accountable to movements? To a larger collective that is struggling to make a way out of no way? If we are conducting work with human subjects we must go through an Institutional Review Board (IRB) process (generally to protect the institution from any liability). What if we developed processes that asked the question—how is the work linked to other justice-mobilizing scholarship? Or, how will this work redistribute resources or access to life pathways? Changing to whom and how we are accountable can move us away from "research of convenience" to research that responds to express material, political, or historical need(s). Our networks could develop pathways between organizations, people, and institutions to focus work. For example, these networks could channel resources, graduate students who want experience doing research, with people and organizations that need this labor. Collectivizing moves against so much of what the academy emphasizes—individual expertise and success (or failure)—but as resources continue to diminish inside universities for justice work, pooling our labors is a strength. This is how we build justice movements, abolish democracies, and end the school to prison nexus.

ACKNOWLEDGMENTS

Many thanks to Bill Ayers, Laurie Fuller, Jean Hughes, Toussaint Losier, Therese Quinn, the editors of this special issue—Amy Swain and George Noblit—and to the fierce peeps at Critical Resistance.

REFERENCES

Acey, C. (2000). This is an Illogical statement: Dangerous trends in anti-prison activism. *Social Justice Journal, 27*(3), 206–211.

Advancement Project. (2010). *Test, punish, and push out: How "zero tolerance" and high-stakes testing funnel youth into the school-to-prison pipeline*. Washington, DC.

Advocate Editors. (2011). Ind. School district settles with trans student. *The Advocate*. Retrieved from http://www.advocate.com/News/Daily_News/2011/01/28/Ind_School_District_Settles_With_ Trans_Student/

Alexander, M. (2010). *The new Jim Crow: Mass incarceration in the age of colorblindness*. New York. NY: The New Press.

American Bar Association (Juvenile Justice Center). (2004, January). *Cruel and unusual punishment. The juvenile death penalty: Adolescence, brain development and legal culpability*. Washington, DC. Retrieved from http://www.abanet.org/crimjust/juvjus/Adolescence.pdf.

Anderson, J. (1988). *The education of blacks in the South, 1860–1935*. Chapel Hill, NC: University of North Carolina Press.

Anyon, J. (1980). Social class and the hidden curriculum of work. *Journal of Education, 162*, 67–92.

Anyon, J. (2005). *Radical possibilities*. New York, NY: Routledge.

Apple, M. (2010). *Global crises, social justice, and education*. New York, NY: Routledge.

Ayers, W., Dorhn, B., & Ayers, R. (Eds.). (2001). *Zero tolerance: Resisting the drive for punishment in our schools*. New York, NY: The New Press.

Braz, R. (2006). Kinder, gentler, gender responsive cages. *Women, Girls and Criminal Justice*, 87–91.

Browne, J. A. (2003). *Derailed: The school to jailhouse track*. Report. Washington DC: The Advancement Project.

Carr, E. S. (2010). *Scripting addiction: The politics of therapeutic talk and American sobriety*. Princeton, NJ: Princeton University Press.

Crenshaw, K. W. (1994). Mapping the margins: Intersectionality, identity politics, and violence against women of color. In M. A. Fineman & R. Mykituk (Eds.), *The public nature of private violence* (pp. 93–118). New York, NY: Routledge.

Davis, A. (2003). *Are prisons obsolete?* New York, NY: Seven Stories Press.

Davis, A. (2005). *Abolition democracy: Prisons, democracy, and empire*. New York, NY: Seven Stories.

Duncan, G. A. (2000). Urban pedagogies and the celling of adolescents of color. *Social Justice: A Journal of Crime Conflict and World Order, 27*(3), 29–42.

Faith, K. (2002). Reflections on inside/out organizing. *Social Justice, 27*(3), 158–167.

Feel Tank Chicago. (2008). Retrieved from Manifesto. http://www.feeltankchicago.net/.

Ferguson, A. A. (2000). *Bad boys: Public schools in the making of black masculinity*. Ann Arbor, MI: University of Michigan Press.

Ferguson, J. (1994). *The anti-politics machine: "Development," depoliticization and bureaucratic power in Lesotho*. Minneapolis, MN: University of Minnesota Press.

Fine, M., Boudin, K., Bowen, I., Clark, J., Hylton, D., Martinez, M., et al. (2001). *Changing minds: The impact of college in prison*. Retrieved from http:www.changingminds.ws

Fine, M., & McClelland, S. (2006). Sexuality education and desire: Still missing after all these years. *Harvard Educational Review, 76*(3), 297–338.

Fraser, N. (1997). *Justice interruptus: Critical reflections on the "postsocialist" condition*. New York, NY: Routledge.

Gilliam, W. (2005). *Prekindergarteners Left Behind: Expulsion Rates in State Pre Kindergarten Programs*. FCD brief series No. 3. Retrieved August 10, 2010 from http://www.fcd-us.org/PDFs/ ExpulsionFinalProof.pdf.

Gilmore, R. W. (2007). *Golden gulag: Prisons, surplus, crisis, and opposition in globalizing California*. Berkeley, CA: University of California Press.

Gregory, A., Skiba, R., & Noguera, P. (2010). The achievement gap and the discipline gap: Two sides of the same coin? *Educational Researcher, 39*(59).

Haney, L. (2010). *Offending women: Power, punishment, and the regulation of desire.* Berkeley, CA: University of California Press.

Harry, B., & Klingner, J. K. (2005). *Why are there so many minority students in special education?: Understanding race & disability in schools.* New York, NY: Teacher College Press.

Hewitt, D., Kim, C., & Losen, D. (2010). The school to prison pipeline: Structuring legal reform. New York, NY: NYU Press.

Himmelstein, K., & Bruckner, H. (2011). Criminal-justice and school sanctions against non-heterosexual youth: A national longitudinal study. *Pediatrics, 127*(1), 48–57.

Huston, W. (2010). CPS creates 'calm' environment for students. *Chicago Defender.* Retrieved from http://www. chicagodefender.com/article-7032-cps-creates-lscalmrs.html.

Justice Policy Institute. (2002). *Cellblocks or classrooms? The funding of higher education and corrections and its impact on African American Men.* Retrieved from http://www.justicepolicy.org/images/upload/0209_REP_CellblocksClassrooms_BBAC.pdf.

Kane-Willis, K., J. Janichek, & D. Clark (2006). Intersecting voices: Impacts of Illinois drug policy. *Illinois drug policy consortium.* Chicago: Roosevelt University, 1–65.

Kosciw, J. G., & Diaz, E. D. (2009). *Shared differences: The experience of lesbian, gay, bisexual and transgendered students of color in our nation's schools.* New York, NY: GLSEN.

Kumashiro, K. (2008). *The seduction of common sense: How the right has framed the debate on America's schools.* New York, NY: Teachers College Press.

Lipman, P. (2004). *High stakes education: Inequality, globalization, and urban school reform.* New York, NY: Routledge/Falmer.

Liptak, A. (2010). *Justices limit life sentences for juveniles.* New York Times. Retrieved from 2010/05/18/us/politics/18court.html (Accessed June 10, 2010).

Lochner, L., & Moretti, E. (2004). The effect of education on crime: Evidence from prison inmates, arrests, and self-reports. *American Economic Review, 94*(155).

López, N. (2003). *Hopeful girls, troubled boys: Race and gender disparity in urban education.* New York, NY: Routledge.

Lorde, A. (1984). *Sister outsider: Essays and speeches.* New York, NY: The Crossing Press.

Losen, D. J., & Orfield, G. (Eds.). (2002). *Racial inequality in special education.* Cambridge, MA: Harvard Education Press.

Mauer, M. (1999). *A race to incarcerate.* New York, NY: New Press.

McCready, L. (2004). Understanding the marginalization of gay and gender non-conforming black male students. *Theory Into Practice, 42*(3), 136–143.

McDermott, R., Goldman, S., & Varenne, H. (2006). The cultural work of learning disabilities. *Educational Researcher, 35*(6), 12–17.

McNally, J. (2003). Black over-representation in special education not confined to segregation states. *Rethinking Schools Online, 17*(3).

Meiners, E. (2007). *Right to be hostile: Schools, prisons and the making of public enemies.* New York, NY: Routledge.

Meiners, E., & Quinn, T. (2009). Doing and feeling research in public: Queer organizing for public education and justice. *International Journal of Qualitative Studies in Education, 23*(2), 147–164. .

Nader, L. (1972). Up the anthropologist. In D. Hymes (Ed.), *Reinventing anthropology* (pp. 284–311). New York, NY: Vintage Books.

Oakes, J. (1985). *Keeping track: How schools structure inequality.* Birmingham, NY: Vail-Ballou Press.

Petit, B., & Western, B. (2004). Mass imprisonment and the life course: Race and class inequality in U.S. incarceration. *American Sociological Review, 69*(2), 151–169.
Pew Center on the States Public Safety Performance Project. (2008). *One in 100: Behind Bars in America 2008*. Retrieved from http://www.pewcenteronthestates.org/uploadedFiles/One%20 in%20100.pdf.
Polakow, V. (2000). *The public assault on America's children: Poverty, violence, and juvenile injustice*. New York, NY: Teachers College Press.
Reid, D. K., & Knight, M. G. (2006). Disability justifies exclusion of minority students: A critical history grounded in disability studies. *Educational Researcher, 35*(6), 18–23.
Rhodes, L. (2005). Changing the subject: Conversation in supermax. *Cultural Anthropology, 20*, 388–411.
Richie, B. (2008). Dismantle, change, build. *Left Turn, 30*, 24.
Robbins, C. (2008). *Expelling hope: The assault on youth and the militarization of schooling*. New York, NY: State University New York Press.
Roberts, D. (1997). *Killing the black body: Race, reproduction, and the meaning of liberty*. New York, NY: Vintage Books.
Rofes, E. (2005). *Status quo or status queer: A radical rethinking of sexuality and schooling*. New York, NY: Rowman and Littlefield.
Rose, N. (1999). *Powers of freedom: Reframing political thought*. New York, NY: Cambridge University Press.
Saltman, K. J., & Gabbard, D. (Eds.). (2003). *Education as enforcement: The militarization and corporatization of schools*. New York, NY: Routledge/Falmer.
Simkins, S., Hirsh, A., Horvat, E., & Moss, M. (2004). The school to prison pipeline for girls: The role of physical and sexual abuse. *Children's Legal Rights Journal, 24*(4), 56–72.
Simmons, L. (2009). End of the line: Tracing racial inequality from school to prison. *Race/Ethnicity: Multidisciplinary Global Perspectives*, 2(2), 215–241.
Skiba, R. J., & Knesting, K. (2002). Zero tolerance, zero evidence: An analysis of school disciplinary practice. In R. J. Skiba & G. G. Noam (Eds.), *New directions for youth development (no. 92: Zero tolerance: Can suspension and expulsion keep schools safe?)*. San Francisco, CA: Jossey-Bass.
Skiba, R. J., Michael, R. S., Nardo, A. C., & Peterson, R. L. (2002). The color of discipline: Sources of racial and gender disproportionality in school punishment. *The Urban Review, 34*(2), 317–342.
Smith, A. (2009). Native studies and critical pedagogy. In J. Sudbury & M. Okazawa-Rey (Eds.), *Activist scholarship: Antiracism, feminism and social change*. Boulder, CO: Paradigm Publishers.
Smith, R. M., & Erevelles, N. (2004). Toward an enabling education: The difference that disability makes. *Educational Researcher, 23*(8), 31–36.
Steurer, S. J., Tracy, A., & Smith, L. (2001). *Three state recidivism study*. Lanham, MD: Correctional Education Association.
Strom, S. (2010). Mississippi A.C.L.U. Rejects $20,000 for alternate prom. *New York Times*. Retrieved from http://www.nytimes.com/2010/04/01/us/01prom.html.
Taylor, J. (1992). Post-secondary correctional education: An evaluation of effectiveness and efficiency. *Journal of Correctional Education, 43*(3), 132–141.
U.S. Department of Education. (1995). *Pell grants for prisoners: Facts/Commentary*. Washington, DC: Office of Correctional Education.
Wacquant, L. (2009). *Punishing the poor: The neoliberal government of social insecurity*. Durham, NC: Duke University Press.

Watkins, W. (2001). *The white architects of black education: Ideology and power in America, 1865–1954.* New York, NY: Teachers College Press.

Winn, M. (2010). *Girl time: Literacy, justice, and the school-to-prison pipeline.* New York, NY: Teacher's College Press.

Wolch, J. R. (1990). *The shadow state: Government and voluntary sector in transition.* New York, NY: The Foundation Center.

CHAPTER TWENTY-ONE

A New Choice of Weapon

Activism Through Hip Hop and Restorative Justice

ARASH DANESHZADEH

IT AIN'T HARD TO TELL: THE EUGENICS OF TRAFFICKING EUROCENTRIC LIES

There is a relationship between the literary stories that represent "triumph" and historical accounts of oppression. Who tells the story, how they tell it, what details are selectively removed, which others are emphasized or outright falsified determine how one interprets history. In the enduring words of hip hop artist Inspectah Deck, "life as a shorty shouldn't be so rough" (Wu-Tang Clan, 1993). American schools have played a prominent role in manufacturing an image of Black youth as "other" than human—destitute, needy, unruly, savages. There is something troublingly ironic about an education system that perpetuates the myth of a normative achievement gap, while minimizing the role that the counterintelligence program of the FBI (COINTELPRO) had on normalizing Black pain. The criminality of Black youth in the U.S. education system is proportional to the perceived danger of Black resistance, self-definition, and independence. These three variables are forged in the mantle of critical storytelling.

In U.S. schools, power and privilege determine the relationship between teaching and learning. Who is classified to tell the story is just as important as who plays the role of hero in an epic saga. Students internalize perceptions of their learning ability with their existential power. Storytelling, with the hopes of transmitting parables to youth, has been a common vehicle for teaching historical literacy since time immemorial. Historical literacy, of course, is paramount to unpacking the truth about where we come from, particularly, in any society that blurs the atrocities of transatlantic slavery and the ongoing struggle for civil rights. You may recall a recent case in Texas, in which a textbook manufacturer referred to enslaved Africans as "workers" (*The New York Times*, October 2015).

In the United States, there are ample cases where individuals received starkly contrasting punishments for committing nearly the same offenses, conceivably because of the color of their skin, which in turn plays into whether or not they are perceived as a threat. Most recently, our attention was turned to the judicial cases of Brock Turner and Cory Batey. Turner was a young, White, male standout swimmer at Stanford University. Batey was a young, Black, male standout football player at Vanderbilt University. Turner was accused of sexually assaulting an unconscious woman behind a garbage dumpster. Batey was accused of sexually assaulting an unconscious woman in a dormitory room. After their respective trials, both men were found guilty of multiple felony charges, yet Turner's 6-month jail sentence was strikingly different than Batey's 15- to 25-year prison sentence.

An array of scholars of color including Amos Wilson, bell hooks, Asa Hilliard III, Uma Jayakumar, and John Henrik Clarke have provided deep insights into how ubiquitous European norms are in America and how these norms have fostered the permanence of White supremacist ideologies in our society. Wilson (1993) argued that in order for Black people (and we argue, communities of color as a whole) to embark on the journey toward a knowledge of self, they must first have an accurate knowledge of European history. An understanding of the oppressor's history can lead to a greater awareness of how the oppressor has been able to falsify the history of the oppressed. In her 2009 TedTalk, *The Danger of a Single Story*, Chimamanda Ngozi Adichie further explained how people with power all too often get to write the narrative for those who lack power. The cases of Brock Turner and Cory Batey and countless others reinforce Wilson's and Adichie's assertions and demonstrate how communities of color have been impacted by Eurocentric norms and how Black bodies, in particular, have been existentially weaponized through the legal system, seeing them as threats first and humans second. Hence, in this section we contend that the school to prison pipeline exists because of White Supremacist norms and wish to highlight the impact that nonconformity to White racial frames of achievement has had on Black youth.

The anchoring weight of slavery continues to ground schools by design and implementation, 151 years after the 13th Amendment to the Constitution was ratified. Tracing the cartography of this postindustrial and "emancipated" America, we find more legislative attention paid to material production than social liberation, which gave rise to federally sanctioned projects aimed at upholding and securing kyriarchal power structures imbued by White colonial settlers (Butchart, 1980). For example, Freedman Schools in the south, specifically appropriated by

Congress as pedagogical sites for those recently emancipated from slavery, were not engendered with the same level of sociopolitical respect as schools reserved for their predominantly white counterparts. In 1870, Congress created the Freedman Bureau, charged with subsidizing and stocking the rudimentary provisions for teaching and learning such as schoolrooms, transportation, and books for Black teachers and youth in the south. However, despite comprising over half of Georgia's school-going population at the time, and the obligation to pay taxes toward state education coffers, Freedman School families and students were still excluded from enjoying many of the amenities offered by de facto public institutions originally created for White students (Anderson, 1988).

While educational sites and their operations have undergone dramatic reconstruction paved by legislation and collective practice over decades, the iterations of schooling converge on one seminal point: to maintain the dominant paradigm of capitalism as transmitted through the cultural tenets of White Supremacist heteropatriarchy (hooks, 1994). The mission to protect the majoritarian narrative of power is riddled within school textbooks (Ravitch, 2013), funding algorithms (Rose & Weston, 2013), and leadership structures (Museus & Jayakumar, 2012) that herald a racial apartheid through coded and duplicitous language. This language provides the culturally subtractive (Valenzuela, 1999) and White-systemic frameworks (Feagin, 2009) that objectify youth and, over time, balkanize students in lockstep with the dominant economic and racial hierarchy. What is most endemic to the historical organization of schools is the outright erasure, by homogenizing and gutting contributions of people of color through eugenic projects such as the Carlisle Indian Industrial Schools (Adams, 1997), and other boarding schools specifically designed to cleave youth from their communities and culturally sterilize First Nation youth, reifying the European colonial vision of physical and psychological conquest. Scholars have emphasized the relationship between exhuming the intellectual ancestry and cultural literacy of youth and liberatory space-making in schools. King, Swartz, Campbell, Lemons-Smith, and Lopez (2014) highlight the process of "othering" or socially isolating youth from academic contexts, by denying access to what Tara Yosso (2005) coins as cultural wealth, particularly resistance capital. King et al. (2014) argue that White Supremacist infrastructure of schools maintains hegemony by seizing a child's knowledge of community and by hyperindividualizing the experience of learning. They write:

> Denials or restrictions of freedom to some are in sync with the cultural tenets (e.g., duality, a hierarchy of human worth, might makes right, social isolation and fragmentation) that underpin European/White traditions and practices … Due to these cultural tenets, individually oriented cultures were and are inclined to make exclusionary claims about maintaining culture, with the conservation of the dominant culture viewed as achievable only by separation from and subjugation and exploitation of other cultures. Standard social studies materials cloak the claims advanced by European/White colonists and Enlightenment

> philosophers by portraying land theft and enslavement—with all the cultural disruptions they entailed—as inevitabilities of colonial settlement, expansion, and economic development. They were outcomes of the European assertion that only they had the right to maintain culture. A "re-membered" text on freedom and democracy connects alterity and dominant themes, and in so doing, shifts the student of freedom and democracy from sole assertions of supremacist inevitability to examining sets of assertions. (King et al., 2014, pp. 68–69)

The quote above illustrates the duplicitous actions and practices employed by many institutions—including schools—as they relate to freedom and oppression. Today's schools, in relation to their colonial counterparts that predominantly served White aristocratic males, offer a tacit binary that demarcates the line between the subjugated pupil and the unsubjugated dominant group. That is, offering the *illusion* of participation without transmogrifying the colonial requisites that socially quarantine students historically left out of the academic edifice. Antonio Gramsci captures the contradiction of marginalization by participating within systems built by our oppressors. Cited by Hoare and Smith (1971), Gramsci deftly explains that "the normal exercise of hegemony" on the educational terrain is "characterized by the combination of force and consent, which balance each other reciprocally without force predominating excessively over consent" (p. 80). The message behind this quote does not age well, given the volatile imbrications of school disciplinary policy in the mid-nineteenth century.

WHAT GOES AROUND: IMPLICATIONS FOR SCHOOL LEADERSHIP AND ORGANIZATIONAL BEHAVIOR

It is important to remind administrators, teachers, and students that teaching historical accounts and positional power in the classroom are not mutually exclusive, but symbiotically paired like the effect of location upon real estate prices. If you are teaching Black youth from a space of intersecting privilege (e.g., white, heterosexual, upper-middle class, male), it becomes important to center students in the texts so that your unearned privilege does not derail a potentially uplifting moment of historical literacy. Too often, individual icons such as Martin Luther King and Rosa Parks are superimposed onto Black students as passive and inanimate props for white integration stories.

But what about the communities that inspired King and Parks? Their political nuances, critical development, and vast ocean of community influences are filtered through a netting that removes all texture—replaced with carefully curated aesthetic. An aesthetic that appreciates Martin Luther King for his eloquent rhetoric, and Rosa Parks for her searing opposition to a bus driver—rather than the radical story of how the community mobilized, despite painful opposition from the U.S. government in the form of COINTELPRO, prior to the bus boycotts and union walkouts. While teachers often appropriate Dr. Martin Luther King as an interracial sympathizer, the facts surrounding his death are often manufactured by an ideology, which seeks to destroy any implication that American imperialism was responsible for his demise and for the overall declaration of war upon the Black community. The irony behind this academic tampering: In 1999, the King family won a civil trial against the U.S. government for conspiracy to assassinate Dr. King (Potash, 2007). Why is this history lesson not as readily accessible to youth, particularly Black children, whose historical points of reference are still grounded in respectability and obedience?

Any remote association with Black resistance is engulfed, chewed up, and spit out as a breach of decorum and personal responsibility. This example of historical cherry picking presents a sterilized image of classrooms as neutral factories of compliance. Any inquiry, particularly from students well versed in historical literacy or antiracist artistic expression, poses a threat to the fabric of reproducing society in its current image. The truth is, our classrooms are political spaces where battles for representation (beyond the symbolic) are waged. Nonetheless, stories of organized Black revolutionaries are swept up like doll houses during a tornado, splintered, and dissipated like dust across a child's consciousness. Education policy makers must examine whose power is squarely positioned at the center of our historical textbooks, and privileged as the aspirational goal for students. When discussing student learning, power reprises its role as inseparably married to the privileges wrought by being a teacher.

Scholars find that, over time, schools have doubled-down on their draconian and eugenic roots—which materialize as disproportionate suspensions and expulsions of Black youth. As Henry Giroux (cited by Nocella, Parmar, & Stovall, 2014) contends, "if youth were once viewed as the site where society deposited its dreams, that is no longer true. Punishment and fear have replaced compassion and social responsibility as modalities mediating the relationship of youth to the larger social order" (p. 73). This is particularly true for Black youth, whose disproportionate rates of surveillance and hypercriminalization signals a reprogrammed version of human sorted coded in ambivalent language of school security, intrapsychic objectification, and individual responsibility. According to Nancy Heitzeg (cited by Nocella et al., 2014):

> Black students make up only 18% of students, but they account for 35% of those suspended once, 46% of those suspended more than once, and 39% of all expulsions. In addition, Black and Latino students represent more than 70% of the students arrested or referred to law enforcement at school (Eckholm, 2013). This racial over-representation then manifests itself in both higher drop-out rates for students of color (students from historically disadvantaged minority groups have little more than a fifty-fifty chance of finishing high school with a diploma) as well as the racialized dynamic of the legal system (Losen & Gillepsie, 2012). (p. 23)

Following the Brown versus Board decision of 1954 which racially integrated schools, credentialed Black teachers across the nation were fired in droves, leading to a separation of youth from their cultural wealth. Toppo (2004), using National Education Association data, provided a staggering account of the deleterious consequence that the landmark decision had on Black neighborhood schools:

> In 1954, there were 82,000 black teachers; however, during the 11 years after the court ruling, some 38,000 Black teachers and administrators lost their jobs. After desegregation, 90 percent of Black principals lost their jobs, mainly in southern states. Qualified Black teachers were often replaced with less qualified white teachers according to researcher Carol Karpinski; indeed, 85 percent of black teachers had college degrees compared to 75 percent of white teachers. (p. 2)

The Brown legislation also served as a watershed moment creating an opportunity for Europeans and their White descendants to represent the academic constructs of all achievement while simultaneously denying Black teachers and administrators an opportunity to provide relevant possibilities for Black children. The Brown decision helped advance another negative effect: dispossession of the Black community from having political ownership over shared institutions. That is, obstacles like job security and harassment interfered with concerned parents and community members who wanted equitable stakeholdership in school leadership, which would allow them to derive the pillars of student outcomes in America. Drawing upon the canonical and empirical library of organizational scholars, it becomes abundantly clear that children of the Black diaspora, in addition to other historically looted and dehumanized populations, continue to be subjected to racial segregation in schools. Assimilation is advanced through sleight-of-hand logic that physically orients Black youth in White Supremacist school structures, where dominant culture reigns over curriculum, classroom behavior management, and presumed ability of students, while shrouded in superficial conceptions of post-Brown decision inclusion and neoliberal versions of multicultural diversity. Schools are not the sole progenitors for human sorting and commodified existence through the codification of labor—a universalized and interlocked process of subjection referred to as the necropolitical apparatus of oppression (Mbeme, 2003).

A distinct constellation of segregation practices connects the culture of school organization with the ostentation of Black suffrage. Schools become action arms of subjugation. Sadiya Hartman (1997) asserts that the everyday privilege enjoyed by White people in America is inextricably linked to segregation evidenced by everyday practices in schools. Hartman (1997) describes the paradox of segregation after the Brown decision as the badge of slavery, which was protected by a statute that insisted on providing "for the equivalent treatment of the races, as though the symmetry of [Brown decision] itself prevented injurious and degrading effects" (p. 194). According to Hartman and others, the Brown decision was intent on granting the social benefits of White privilege, to those students who could mimic and in essence, participate in upholding its capitalistic agenda; and, in accordance to youth from non-White communities, "culturally suicidal" zeitgeist (Tierney, 1999).

Over the years, a number of scholars have attempted to identify the structures that leverage and promulgate the retributive state of schools—as they pertain to Black youth. One example is African American Male Theory (AAMT), which resurrects a number of canonical subtexts as touchstones, to articulate the relationship between the "pre and post-enslavement experiences" and the "spiritual, psychological, social, and educational development" of Black boys and men (Bush & Bush, 2013, p. 6). AAMT is underpinned by numerous other frameworks including Black Feminist and Womanist Theory (Cannon, 1988; Collins, 2000), which illustrates the intersectional dynamic of ecological systems (e.g., poverty, racism and identity formation being precipitates of interconnected environments)—captured by Urie Bronfenbrenner (1989)—as well as Tribal Critical Race Theory (TribalCrit; Brayboy, 2005), that represents the veritable bridge between desecration of indigenous land, natural resources, and cultural literacy, and the false binaries (e.g., Black as proxy for criminal) common to the daily experiences of many non-White populations. A result of findings that magnify the urgent need to redress school conditions, unfairly and subjectively punishing Black youth, is an emergent movement toward alternative policies and positive behavior approaches to school discipline (Sugai & Horner, 2009). Victor Rios (2011) suggests that this Youth Control Complex rigidly targets Black, First Nation, and Latinx youth in order to reclassify the racial undercaste manufactured by generations of post-colonial persecution. One of Amos Wilson's (1978) most salient arguments is the notion that desegregated schools that fail to modify their colonial, or White Supremacist, norms of academic decorum will be unable to meet the needs of non-White students. In fact, as Wilson contends, anglonormative standards heighten the problem of Black youth isolation, because:

> Discontinuity between Black life and school life breeds resistance, hostility, disinterest, etc., in the Black child. Much of what is taught in school meets his needs. It would be expecting too much however, of the schools, white schools in particular, to bridge the gap between black life and school life and to provide the black child with the achievement drives which are essentially the products of the child's cultural-familial background. (p. 234)

This quote makes an important distinction between physical inclusion and epistemological inclusion. Harper and Hurtado (2007) explain that in order to create academic opportunities for historically marginalized populations like Black youth, educational institutions must create opportunity for students, themselves, to play an instrumental role in fostering *pluralistic* constructs of achievement and definition for model behavior. Without an intentionally multicultural approach to leadership, school norms will continue to uphold a White Supremacist ethos and advance monocultural values. Transculturation (Ortiz, 1995) is a term used in place of assimilation, adaptation, and acculturation and describes a more fluid process of self-identification and belonging which favors organizational pluralism over cultural homogenization. In transculturation, Black youth and institutional values are merged together in a dynamic system that allows the student to navigate between the two. Without the active and ongoing co-ownership of school governance, Black youth will remain suspended in a double-edged context of superficial integration while organizationally isolated by myopic carceral outcomes. Wilson (1978) articulates the pitfalls of schools that fail to alter their historically White pillars of control, and the corollary psychosocial gymnastics that Black youth are tacitly coerced to perform in order to meet these standards:

> Attending school for the Black child is often a schizoid process. He is called upon to alienate himself abruptly from his culture and he must maintain a precarious psychic balance between a Black and white world, belonging to neither. It is little wonder that the Black student rebels against this neurotic process which demands that he become not-self and shed his identity in order to succeed. (p. 234)

While we agree unequivocally that there is no singular or monolithic Black experience, the mere acceptance and affirming of Black youth contexts can play a vital role toward harvesting critical dialogue. Restorative Justice is one model of community-centered discipline, which excavates the cultural mistrust (Terrell & Terrell, 1981) and dispossession (Fine & Ruglis, 2009) that Black youth have experienced within myriad (historically) eugenic institutions, including schools. We use the term "Restorative Justice" (RJ) generally to encapsulate an assortment of terms such as "restorative approaches," "restorative practices," and other related iterations as conveyed by the literature.

REPRESENT: HIP HOP ACTIVISM AS CASE STUDIES

One activist group from Fremont, California is *Hip Hop Chess Federation* (HHCF). HHCF employs a nexus of martial arts, chess, and hip hop pedagogy to enact leadership and self-definition among systems-impacted youth (read: formerly incarcerated). The chessboard serves as a microcosm for community. It also represents the fallacy in quotidian education that your success is inspired by *becoming* King. An allegory lauding the merits of social isolation is a direct contradiction from the revolutionary bedrock of liberatory education, which invokes the collective power of community pieces, against a common enemy. This self-aggrandizing portrait of success is buttressed by the capitalistic notion encouraging students to surmount their cultural literacies, because achievement cannot be shared among peers. In the interest of this chapter, literacy is defined as the historical definitions of *self*, rooted in understanding race, gender, class, and other normative identities as constructed within a cultural ecology of synchronized domination and oppression.

In this society, we are trained to believe that academic "success" can be only hoarded, as our education system intentionally triages for patent winners and losers. One consequence of this reductionist view of collective solidarity is the normalization of community divestment. Sloughing entire layers of historical understanding is actually seen as a strategy toward success. We center Whiteness, patriarchy, and settler colonialism by telling students that they were admitted into a college, "despite growing up in the ghetto," which is pathologized as a proxy for Blackness. Similarly, in chess, students are told to count the most valuable pieces in accordance with a rubric of settler colonialism; rendering pawns as merely disposable players who make the occasional cameo during protracted matches. A Western framework that problematizes pawns, and makes Queens a transactional gambit to sustain the longevity of the King, barters with identity.

Taking a more critical lens, we must peel from the layers of historical rust that stifles a student's social mobility. Miring students in the minutia of political and social competition moves the illusion that they are individuals first, and communities are merely instruments for self-marketing. Black history is hijacked, reconstructed, and expelled as a finite canon of individual transcendence. Black excellence is merely a reflection of individuals who demonstrated personal "grit" or perseverance, despite overwhelming odds. As a result of the grit narrative, individual successes throughout Black history fail to consider the manner in which oppressive ideology overly determines policy that shapes community outcomes. Teaching Black history as more than a positivist and towering beacon of more-to-less stakeholders flies in direct opposition to the perception that power and privilege are independent of one another in the classroom. "Ubuntu" is a Zulu word that means "I am because we are" and captures a liberatory strand of teaching. This model posits that our position as individuals is gained by our appreciation of the stories and critical understandings of our ancestors. Without exercising liberating and critical literacies, students tacitly amputate a political connection to their cultures. A connection that renders them as powerful partners within an intergenerational war for the redistribution of provisional wealth. In his groundbreaking work, *The Developmental Psychology of the Black Child* (1978), Dr. Amos Wilson distinguishes between schools that subsidize a highly educated servant (to capitalism) and those that seek to promote Black mobilization. He writes that the Black child is taught to have a sense of dependency on her historical storytellers (i.e., schools) and, thus, can only exercise enough power to perpetuate the desires of those who center an image of Black domination and youth control.

Eminent social psychologist Dr. Claude Steele (2010) explains that the threats to Black student identity are external, albeit internalized. He adds that if people on the street heard someone whistling classical musician Antonio Vivaldi, that the violence prone, "unrefined" Black youth image would not reflexively come to mind. What's more, even other Black youth are less inclined to assume a Black peer is the whistler. Our values and images of "high white society" will always emerge in the classroom. Black children are 18 times more likely than White children to be incarcerated as adults and comprise 58% of all children sentenced to prison as adults in the United States (Poe-Yamagata & Jones, 2007). Black students are "personally responsible" for their actions at an age when white students still benefit from assumptions of their innocence. A school environment that conditions Black youth for perpetual "fight or flight" mode cannot offer time for reflection. As a result, we must not think of Vivaldi as the metric for what distinguishes an academically "successful" Black child from her peers. Instead, it is incumbent upon educators and radical scholars to wean from the phantom value systems that commercially, and socially, distinguish between Vivaldi and hip hop artists, Rapsody or Kendrick Lamar. Until then, pawns will never live to be Queens.

IF I RULED THE WORLD: RESTORATIVE JUSTICE AND SPACE-MAKING IN HIP HOP

Restorative Justice is a framework of community growth and liberatory practices, and a hallmark of many indigenous communities. The genealogy of restorative practices in a broad swath of the Western world is grounded in the traditions of the Maori people, native to New Zealand (Zehr, 2005). In this participatory ethos, counternarratives and equitable stakeholdership between youth and adults create spaces unsanctioned by common Western systems of financial incentives or carceral punishment. Neoliberal appropriations of restorative justice in schools have flattened the community-centered texture and critical lens in which conflict is framed. If Black and First Nation youth are seen as restoration projects, then restorative justice will ascribe to a deficit-lens that hyperindividualizes activism as an issue of Black "respectability," while simultaneously absolving subtle and pervasive violence, also called the necropolitical apparatus, wrought within historically blighted communities by the legacy of settler colonialism. Restorative Justice is a zeitgeist that migrates activism toward ecological concerns that condition violence espoused and perpetuated by a necropolitical state. Activism undergirded by a restorative lens creates bilateral communication between various stakeholders within a community (including youth), unhinged from the veiled threat of retribution, and reinforced by a Fanonian theory of safety (Leonardo & Porter, 2010), which—in the context of schools—has also been described as a pedagogy of love or critical communication pedagogy (Cummins & Griffin, 2012).

If school is an expression of social inclusion, then youth punishment represents the symbiotic underside of systemic exclusion. Partially subsidized by federal School Improvement Grant (SIG) coffers, a rare model of inclusive and preventative Restorative Justice was resurrected. O'Connell employed an all-hands-on-deck approach to discipline. This Tier One model of school-based interventions harnessed an epistemologically pluralistic and ecologically macrosystemic bevy of stakeholders. Students were no longer susceptible to suspension or expulsion for subjective and minor infractions, unless they were found in violation of more documentable and provable violations that involved drugs, weapons, or physical assault. The goal of this model was to cultivate a Third Space (Gutierrez, 2008) of school leadership, unsanctioned by the veiled threat of retribution, where students and practitioners work in concert to find mutually beneficial solutions to systemic issues, like poverty and truancy, rather than in top-down opposition. By employing a larger consortium of community-school partners, that included student ambassadors of RJ training, parent liaisons, and local community-based agencies from a variety of specializations (i.e., college and career counselors from TRIO and GEAR UP Programs, transcendental meditation experts, Hip Hop/spoken word artists, urban gardeners, chess masters, mural artists, mental health clinicians, case managers for formerly incarcerated youth, et cetera), O'Connell was able to create classrooms that fostered long-term and active participation by students and families. Counselors also played a central role in moving this restorative mission forward. A different counselor was allocated to each grade level and responsible for facilitating an RJ class that was beholden to restorative ideals of equity and community building. Counselors led group discussions on a student-led Community Practicum Project (CPP). The CPP was meant to synthesize curriculum garnered in the students' other foundational classes, while allowing students the space to forge blended learning from their personal and academic experiences. The RJ class required teachers, counselors, and community-based organizations to work in small learning teams with assigned student ambassadors to ensure that curriculum was informed by the consciousness of its students. As a result, O'Connell's emerging Restorative Justice CPP's have made strides in redressing systemic issues around The Mission and San Francisco, including but not limited to: subsidized transportation for youth displaced by gentrification, eye glasses for families and youth who cannot afford federal health care, and free soil lead testing and soil for families whose gardens were found to be high in toxins. This approach to restorative curriculum not only shifted the locus of control from schools to community, but also engaged students as partners, pivoting away from the hyperindividualized focus on youth (mis)behavior and, instead, transforming the conditions of the students' immediate environments.

The successes of John O'Connell should serve as an example of the possibilities of an RJ program. However, many Tier Two and Three RJ programs, if left unchallenged, may potentially paint Black children with wide brushstrokes that converge them into one entry point of identity. Separating race, gender, and class from one another provides a shortsighted portrait of how these intersecting identities "mutually construct" a matrix of domination (Collins, 2000, 218) that is upheld by RJ for-deficit programs. As George Lipsitz highlights (2007), the possession of Whiteness provides an aggregate of landmines that hinder the access of Black youth to equitable learning opportunities. Thus, a critical RJ program that incorporates elements of community as a tool for subversion, "acknowledges the need for multiple counterstories and counteractions that challenge the dominant narrative within and across different spheres of influence" (Jayakumar & Adamian, 2015, p. 36). A mutual engagement of students, families, and community partners toward critical RJ begins with the fundamental understanding that students must negotiate aspects of their identities in order to meet Eurocentric and necropolitical metrics of academic and interpersonal success.

There are radical groups which have attempted to utilize the restorative lens of activism. One such grass roots organization is Communities United for Restorative Youth Justice (CURYJ), of East Oakland, California. This organization seeks to promote ecological and pedagogical healing to populations impacted by systemic injustices that range from land desecration to gang injunctions. There are several pillars to restorative activism, ascribed by CURYJ leaders, according to their 2016 Mission Statement:

1. Training and Technical Assistance: To other grass roots agencies to support the expansion and implementation of indigenous methodologies of addressing violence.
2. Youth Participatory Action Research: Engaging young people in the generation of new knowledge about their own communities is critical to building grassroots movements that are rooted in the experiences of those who are oppressed. Developing data that addresses the needs of the community and speaks the language of government institutions is a powerful tool for the next generation to build.
3. Restorative Justice Circles: Engaging communities to address violence through indigenous healing practices. With the acknowledgement of our internalized oppression individuals begin to restore their perspective and begin to unlearn the harmful behavior that mainstream society perpetuates.
4. Community Applied Research and Action: On the ground documentation of police harassment and gentrification can generate important information in building movements for self-determination in our communities. Documentation of the positive impact of alternatives to incarceration such

as restorative justice can be used as evidence fight for successful solutions to violence. CARA is at the foundation of our policy work, and is essential to building our community's leadership and skills to sustain our movements. This effort has brought propositions, such as Proposition 57 in 2016, to light that seek to eradicate the common practice of direct liberty file by District Attorneys who aim to try youth as adults; instead shifting the responsibility to juvenile court judges to make that demarcation of adult defendant (p. 1).

REFERENCES

Adams, D. W. (1997). *Education for extinction: American Indians and the boarding school experience, 1875–1928*. Lawrence, KS: University of Kansas Press.

Adichie, C. N. (2009, July). *Chimamanda Ngozi Adichie: The danger of a single story* [Video file]. Retrieved from https://www.ted.com/talks/chimamanda_adichie_the_danger_of_a_single_story

Amstutz, L. S., & Mullet, J. H. (2005). *The little book of restorative discipline for schools: Teaching responsibility; creating caring climates*. Intercourse, PA: Good Books.

Anderson, J. D. (1988). *The education of Blacks in the south, 1860–1935*. Chapel Hill, NC: University of North Carolina Press.

Annie E. Casey Foundation. (2011). *No place for kids: The case for reducing juvenile incarceration*. Baltimore, MD: Richard A. Mendel. Retrieved from http://www.aecf.org/m/resourcedoc/aecf-NoPlaceForKidsFUllReport-2011.pdf

Bell, D. A. (1980). Brown v. Board of Education and the interest-convergence dilemma. *Harvard Law Review, 6*(92), 518–533.

Bensimon, E. M. (2005). Closing the achievement gap in higher education: An organizational learning perspective. *New Directions for Higher Education, 131*, 99–111.

Bireda, M. R. (2010). *Cultures in conflict: Eliminating racial profiling* (2nd ed.). Lanham, MD: Rowman & Littlefield Education.

Brayboy, B. M. J. (2005). Toward a Tribal critical race theory in education. *The Urban Review, 37*(5), 425–446.

Bronfenbrenner, U. (1989). Ecological systems theory. In R. Vasta (Ed.), *Annals of child development* (Vol. 6, pp. 187–249). Greenwich: JAI Press.

Bush, L. V., & Bush, E. C. (2013). Introducing African American male theory. *Journal of African American Males in Education, 4*(1), 6–17.

Butchart, R. E. (1980). *Northern schools, southern Blacks, and Reconstruction: Freedman's education, 1862–1875*. Westport, CT: Greenwood Press.

Cabrera, N., Watson, J. E., & Franklin, J. D. (2016). Racial arrested development: A critical analysis of the campus ecology. *Journal of College Student Development, 57*(2), 119–134.

Cannon, K. (1988). *Black womanist ethics*. Atlanta, GA: Scholars Press.

Collins, P. H. (2000). *Black feminist thought: Knowledge, consciousness, and the politics of empowerment* (Vol. 2). Boston, MA: Unwin Hyman.

Collins, P. H. (2006). *From Black power to Hip Hop: Racism, nationalism, and feminism*. Philadelphia, PA: Temple University Press.

Collins, P. H., & Bilge, S. (2016). *Intersectionality*. Malden, MA: Polity Press.

Council of State Governments Justice Center. (2011). *Breaking schools' rules: A statewide study of how school discipline relates to student's success and juvenile justice involvement.* Texas A&M University, Public Policy Research Institute. New York, NY: Council of State Governments Justice Center.

Cummins, M. W., & Griffin, R. A. (2012). Critical race theory and critical communication pedagogy: Articulating pedagogy as an act of love from black male perspectives. *Liminalities: A Journal of Performance Studies, 8*(5), 85–106.

Delgado, R. (1990). On mindset and metaphor. *Harvard Law Review, 103*(8), 1872–1877.

Delpit, L. (2008). *The skin that we speak: Thoughts on language and culture in the classroom.* New York, NY: The New Press.

Duneier, M. (2016). *Ghetto: The invention of a place, the history of an idea.* New York, NY: Farrar, Straus, & Giroux.

Eckholm, E. (April 12, 2013). With police in schools, more children in court. *New York Times*, p. A1.

Feagin, J. R. (2009). *The white racial frame: Centuries of racial framing and counter-framing.* New York, NY: Routledge.

Fine, M., & Ruglis, J. (2009). Circuits and consequences of dispossession: The racialized realignment of the public sphere for U.S. youth. *Transforming Anthropology, 17*(1), 20–33.

Fronius, T., Persson, H., Guckenburg, S., Hurley, N., & Petrosino, A., (2016). *Restorative justice in U.S. schools: A research review.* San Francisco, CA: WestEd Justice & Prevention Research Center. Retrieved from http://jprc.wested.org/wp-content/uploads/2016/02/RJ_Literature-Review_20160217.pdf

Gay, G. (2006). Connections between classroom management and culturally responsive teaching. In C. Evertson & C. S. Weinstein (Eds.), *Handbook for classroom management: Research, practice, and contemporary issues.* Mahwah, NJ: Erlbaum.

Giroux, H. A. (2015). *Education and the crisis of public values: Challenging the assault on teachers, students, and public education.* New York, NY: Peter Lang.

Gonzalez, N., Moll, L., & Amanti, C. (2005). *Funds of knowledge: Theorizing practices in households, communities and classrooms.* New York, NY: Taylor & Francis.

Gregory, A., Skiba, R. J., & Noguera, P. A. (2010). The achievement gap and the discipline gap: Two sides of the same coin? *Educational Researcher, 39*, 59–68.

Gutierrez, K. (2008). Developing a sociocritical literacy in the Third Space. *Reading Research Quarterly, 43*, 148–164.

Harlow, C. W. (2003). *Education and correctional populations.* U.S. Department of Justice, Bureau of Justice Statistics Special Report, NCJ 195670.

Harper, S. R., & Hurtado, S. (2007). Nine themes in campus racial climates and implications for institutional transformation. *New Directions for Student Services, 120*, 7–24.

Harris, C. L. (1993). Whiteness as property. *Harvard Law Review, 106*(8), 1710–1791.

Hartman, S. (1997). *Scenes of subjection: Terror, slavery, and self-making in nineteenth century America.* New York, NY: Oxford University Press.

Hoare, Q., & Smith, G. N. (1971). *Selections from the prison notebooks of Antonio Gramsci.* London: Lawrence & Wishart.

hooks, b. (1994). *Teaching to transgress: Education as the practice of freedom.* New York, NY: Routledge.

Howell, J. C. (2009). *Juvenile delinquency: A comprehensive framework* (2nd ed.). Thousand Oaks, CA: Sage.

Irvine, J. J. (1990). *Black students and school failure: Policies, practices, and prescriptions.* New York, NY: Praeger.

Jayakumar, U. M., & Adamian, A. S. (2015). Toward a critical praxis for educational research: Lessons from affirmative action and social science advocacy. *Journal Committed to Social Change on Race and Ethnicity, 1*(1), 22–58.

Johnstone, G. (2002). *Restorative justice: Ideas, values, debates.* Portland, ME: Willan Publishing.

Kearney, M. S., Harris, B. H., Jacome, E., & Parker, L. (2014). *Ten economic facts about Crime and incarceration in the United States.* Policy Memo, The Hamilton Project.

King, J. E., Swartz, E. E., Campbell, L., Lemons-Smith, S., & Lopez, E. (2014). *"Re-membering" history in student and teacher learning: An Afrocentric culturally informed praxis.* New York, NY: Routledge.

Leonardo, Z., & Porter, R. K. (2010). Pedagogy of fear: Toward a Fanonian theory of "safety" in race dialogue. *Race, Ethnicity and Education, 13,* 139–157.

Lipsitz, G. (2007). The racialization of space and the spatialization of race: Theorizing the hidden architecture of landscape. *Landscape Journal, 26*(1), 10–23.

Lopez, I. H. (2006). *White by law: The legal construction of race.* New York, NY: New York University Press.

Losen, D., Hodson, C., Keith, M. A. II, Morrison, K., & Belway, S. (2015). *Are we closing the school discipline gap?* Los Angeles, CA: The Civil Rights Project. Retrieved from https://civilrightsproject.ucla.edu/resources/projects/center-for-civil-rights-remedies/school-to-prison-folder/federal-reports/are-we-closing-the-school-discipline-gap.

Losen, D. J., & Gillespie, J. (2012). Opportunities suspended: the disparate impact of disciplinary exclusion from school. *Civil Rights Project*: University of California at Los Angeles.

Mbembe, A. (2003). Necropolitics. *Public Culture, 15*(1), 11–40.

Museus, S., & Jayakumar, U. M. (2012). *Creating campus cultures: Fostering success among racially diverse student populations.* New York, NY: Routledge.

Nocella, A. J., Parmar, P., & Stovall, D. (2014). *From education to incarceration: Dismantling the school-to-prison pipeline.* New York, NY: Peter Lang.

Noguera, P. (2008). *The trouble with Black boys: And other reflections on race, equity, and the future of public education.* New York, NY: Wiley.

Noltemeyer, A. L., Ward, R. M., & Mcloughlin, C. (2015). Relationship between school suspension and student outcomes: A meta-analysis. *School Psychology Review, 44,* 224–240.

Ortiz, F. (1995). *Cuban counterpoint: Tobacco and sugar.* Durham, NC: Duke University Press.

Potash, J. (2007). The FBI war on Tupac Shakur and Black leaders: U.S. intelligence's murderous targeting of Tupac, MLK, Malcolm, Panthers, Hendrix, Marley, rappers & linked ethnic leftists. Baltimore, MD: Progressive Left Press.

Poe-Yamagata, E., & Jones, M. A. (2007). And justice for some: Differential treatment of youth of color in the justice system. *Oakland: National council on crime and delinquency.* Retrieved from http://www.nccdglobal.org/sites/default/files/publication_pdf/justice-for- some.pdf

Ravitch, D. (2013). *Reign of error: The hoax of privitization and the danger to America's public schools.* New York, NY: Random House.

Rios, V. M. (2011). *Punished: Policing the lives of Black and Latino boys.* New York, NY: New York University Press.

Rose, H., & Weston, M. (2013) *California school district revenue and student poverty: Moving toward a weighted pupil funding formula.* Sacramento, CA: Public Policy Institute of California.

San Francisco Unified School District. (2012). *San Francisco Public School (Progress Report AY 2011–2012).* San Francisco. Retrieved from http://www.sfusd.edu/en/assets/sfusd-staff/about-SFUSD/files/2011-2012-progress-report.pdf

Skiba, R. J., Horner, R. H., Chung, C.-G., Rausch, M. K., May, S. L., & Tobin, T. (2011). Race is not neutral: A national investigation of African American and Latino disproportionality in school discipline. *School Psychology Review, 40*(1), 85–107.

Steele, C. (2010). Whistling Vivaldi: And other clues to how stereotypes affect us. New York, NY: W. W. Norton.

Sugai, G., & Horner, R. (2009). Defining and describing school-wide positive behavior support. In W. Sailor, G. Dunlap, G. Sugai, & R. Horner (Eds.), *Handbook of positive behavior support* (pp. 307–326). New York, NY: Spring Science and Business Media.

Terrell, F., & Terrell, S. (1981). An inventory to measure cultural mistrust among Blacks. *Western Journal of Black Studies, 5*, 180–185.

Tierney, W. G. (1999). Models of minority college-going and retention: Cultural integrity versus cultural suicide. *The Journal of Negro Education, 68*(1), 80–91.

Toppo, G. (2004). Brown vs. Board of Education: Thousands of Black teachers lost jobs, *USA Today*. Retrieved from http://usatoday30.usatoday.com/news/nation/2004-04-28-brown-side2_x.htm

Triplett, N. P., Allen, A., & Lewis, C. W. (2014). Zero tolerance, school shootings, and the post-Brown quest for equity in discipline policy: An examination of how urban minorities are punished for white suburban violence. *Journal of Negro Education, 83*, 352–370.

Tsui, J. C. (2014). Breaking free from the prison paradigm: Integrating restorative justice techniques into Chicago's schools juvenile justice system. *Journal of Criminal Law and Criminology, 104*(3), 636–665.

U.S. Department of Education Office for Civil Rights. (2014). *Civil Rights Data Collection: Data Snapshot (School Discipline)*. Washington, DC: U.S. Department of Education for Civil Rights. Retrieved from http://ocrdata.ed.gov/Downloads/CRDC-School-Discipline-Snapshot.pdf

U.S. Department of Education Office for Civil Rights. (2016). *Civil rights data collection: A first look (key data highlights on equity and opportunity gaps in our nation's public schools)*. Washington, DC: U.S. Department of Education for Civil Rights. Retrieved from http://www2.ed.gov/about/offices/list/ocr/docs/2013-14-first-look.pdf

Valencia, R. (1986, November). *Minority academic underachievement: Conceptual and theoretical consideration for understanding the achievement problems of Chicano students*. Paper presented to the Chicano Faculty Seminar, Stanford University.

Valenzuela, A. (1999). *Subtractive schooling: U.S.-Mexican youth and the politics of caring*. New York, NY: State University of New York Press.

Van Ness, D. (1993). New wine and old wineskins: Four challenges of restorative justice. *Criminal Law Forum, 4*(2), 251–276.

Voussoughi, S., & Gutierrez, K. (2010). Studying movement, hybridity, and change: Toward a multi-sited sensibility for research on learning across contexts and border. *National Society for the Study of Education, 113*(2), 603–632.

Weier, S. (2014). Consider Afro-Pessimism. *American Studies: A Quarterly, 59*(3), 419–433.

Welch, K., & Payne, A. A. (2010). Racial threat and punitive school discipline. *Social Problems, 57*, 25–48.

Wilson, A. N. (1978). *The developmental psychology of the Black child*. New York, NY: Afrikan World InfoSystems.

Wilson, A. N. (1993). *The falsification of Afrikan consciousness: Eurocentric history, psychiatry, and the politics of white supremacy*. New York, NY: Afrikan World InfoSystems.

Woolfolk, A. (2016). *Educational psychology* (13th ed.). Upper Saddle River, NJ: Pearson.

Wu-Tang Clan (1993). C.R.E.A.M. On Enter the Wu-Tang (36 Chambers) [LP]. New York, NY: Loud Records. November 9, 1993.

Yosso, T. J. (2005). Whose culture has capital? A critical race theory discussion of community cultural wealth. *Race, Ethnicity, and Education*, *8*(1), 69–91.

Zehr, H. (2002). *The little book of restorative justice*. Intercourse: Good Books.

Zehr, H. (2005). *Changing lenses: A new focus for crime and justice*. Scottdale: Herald Press.

CHAPTER TWENTY-TWO

Youth of Color Fight Back

Transforming Our Communities

EMILIO LACQUES-ZAPIEN AND LESLIE MENDOZA

INTRODUCTION TO THE YOUTH JUSTICE COALITION, LOS ANGELES[1]

The **Youth Justice Coalition (YJC)** is working to build a youth, family, and prisoner-led movement to challenge race, gender, and class inequality in Los Angeles County's and California's juvenile *in*justice systems. Our goal is to dismantle policies and institutions that have ensured the massive lockup of people of color; widespread police violence, corruption, and distrust between police and communities; disregard of youths' and communities' constitutional and human rights; the construction of a vicious school to jail track; and the buildup of the world's largest network of juvenile halls, jails, and prisons. The YJC uses direct action organizing, advocacy, political education, transformative justice, and activist arts to mobilize system-involved youth, families, and our allies—both in the community and within lockups to bring about change. In 2003, at a series of three meetings sixty-two people—who were or had been arrested, detained,

1 Emilio Lacques-Zapien is one of the adult organizers of Youth Justice Coalition and Leslie Mendoza is a youth organizer of Youth Justice Coalition. Much of this article was taken directly from the Youth Justice Coalition official website—http://www.youth4justice.org/.

incarcerated, and/or deported, and/or who were leaders of groups working inside juvenile halls, probation camps, jails, or prisons—came together to discuss the impacts of the system on Los Angeles and *prioritized four organizing campaigns:*

1. **Exposing & dismantling the war on gangs as a war on youth of color** including challenging the lack of due process and community input in the implementation by police, sheriffs, and the courts of gang suppression tactics including gang injunctions and gang databases that serve to sweep thousands of youth into the system without notification, appeal, removal, or resources.
2. **Improving conditions of confinement** for youth at L.A. County juvenile halls, county jails, state prisons, and the Division of Juvenile Justice, including organizing for the shutdown of DJJ and its replacement by community-based youth development and rehabilitation centers, and ending the use of extreme sentences for youth (including Juvenile Life Without the Possibility of Parole—JLWOP).
3. **Reducing the county's use of detention and incarceration** by 75% within ten years, including closing dilapidated and inhumane county and state lockups.
4. **Pushing the county to develop community-based owned and operated alternatives** to school suspension/expulsion, arrest, court, detention, and incarceration (Youth Justice Coalition, 2013).

We believe that the youth are already the most powerful people both to turn this system upside down and to create a more just society now, and for generations to come.

EDUCATIONAL DISCRIMINATION AGAINST SYSTEM-INVOLVED YOUTH: CONDITIONS OF THE SCHOOL TO PRISON PIPELINE

In order to understand why we do this work, we have to understand the conditions that our youth face on a daily basis to recognize the community conditions that create the school to prison pipeline. Once suspended, expelled, arrested, and/or incarcerated, many youth face discrimination in reenrolling in school—sometimes barred from entire districts. In addition, youth often come home from lockups without transcripts and IDs, the documents essential for enrollment. System staff offer too little support to help youth and their families find a school placement, while simultaneously threatening that without school, youth face violation and reincarceration. Few resources exist in schools or communities that can serve as alternatives to school suspension and expulsion, court, detention, and incarceration.

Finally, system-involved youth are often treated differently in traditional schools, being checked with handheld metal detectors in class in front of their peers, pulled out of class or stopped in the halls for probation checks, locker and back pack searches, pat downs, and interrogations. Often, youth who have been arrested or locked up are forced into underfunded and inferior probation, continuation, or alternative schools. Zero tolerance and other disciplinary policies are often even harsher in many of these schools and many youth are pushed out and/or violated and sent back to lockups for truancy and other minor problems.

We at the YJC recognize that the system too often fails our youth of color in L.A. County. What our youth need most are schools and community centers that address both their educational needs and the community conditions of South Los Angeles. Therefore, in the fall of 2007, the YJC founded **F.R.E.E. L.A. (Fighting for the Revolution to Educate and Empower Los Angeles) High School** for youth ages 16 to 24. The goals of F.R.E.E. L.A. High School are to:

Build stronger youth leadership through a curriculum that trains young people in developing basic academic and life skills, direct action organizing, campaign research, media and communications, arts activism, public policy development, advocacy, and transformative justice to heal from violence and to prevent future violence.

Eliminate barriers and discrimination for system-involved youth to enroll in high school; to train youth in organizing and public policy development; to produce alternatives to the criminalization, suspension, expulsion, and arrest of students; and to challenge the policing and intense prison-like environments existing in too many schools in poor communities and communities of color.

Support the youth development and educational needs of YJC members and other youth. The school serves as an alternative to detention and incarceration for youth who face confinement, an educational site for youth who have been suspended or expelled from schools or entire districts, a school for youth returning home from lockups, and a more respectful and smaller program for youth who have left traditional schools discouraged.

The curriculum at F.R.E.E. L.A. High is integral to our youth community organizing work. Our F.R.E.E. L.A. High students represent the heart and soul of why we do this work.

Finally, in 2009 we established our first space in South Central Los Angeles. We named it *Chuco's Justice Center* in memory of Jesse "Chuco" Becerra, one of the YJC's youth organizers who was killed in September 2005. Chuco's Justice Center serves as a youth and community space, resource center, and gathering place for organizers, artists, educators, and organizations building a social justice movement in Los Angeles. In addition, many of our students become *LOBOS—Leading Our Brothers and Sisters Out of the System*—YJC youth organizers who receive stipends to coordinate the YJC's organizing campaigns. For most youth, LOBOS positions are their first jobs outside of the underground economy, as well as many young people's first opportunities to travel outside of Los Angeles.

TRANSFORMATIVE JUSTICE: COMMUNITY-BASED MODELS OF JUSTICE

At the Youth Justice Coalition, we practice transformative justice as a way to find solutions to issues that young people deal with on a day-to-day basis. We utilize this model as an alternative method of creating more humane and holistic public safety instead of law enforcement, incarceration, courts, and the criminal *in*justice system. When an incident or problem occurs within our members, we quickly de-escalate the situation, we let the people calm down, and we then take them home if necessary. When the people affected and harmed are ready to talk we bring them back into a "Transformative Justice Circle" where everyone affected has a support person, whether it's a friend, family member, or community member and we talk about the real issues that caused the incident to happen and work to create solutions from our circle, including follow-up. Sometimes multiple circles are needed over an extended period of time depending on the situation. Transformative justice has to be flexible because people are complex and our communities have been suffering from many forms of oppression for centuries. We understand that TJ is a process of *un-learning* oppressive behavior and *de-colonizing* and *transforming* our behaviors, minds, bodies, and spirits.

Here we highlight the differences between criminal and juvenile court's systems of handling conflict versus transformative justice practices at the YJC:

Criminal and Juvenile Court:
What law was broken?
Who broke it?
What punishment is warranted?
Competition between lawyers—assumes two opposing sides.
Assumes guilty and innocent parties—victim and perpetrator
Not responsible for determining or addressing root causes of conflict

Transformative Justice for YJC:
Who was harmed?
What are the needs and responsibilities of those involved?
How do all affected parties together address needs and repair harm?
Is non-adversarial. Seeks an outcome all parties can agree to.
What is the root cause of the conflict?
What community and/or societal change is needed to change relationships, conditions, and power?

Transformative justice also:

- Addresses the harm caused to all parties involved, as well as to the community at large.
- Also addresses root causes; challenges and seeks to end *in*justice and inequities that lead to violence and crime.
- Focuses on improving existing relationships and building new relationships in order to prevent future conflict/harm.
- *Replaces prosecution, punishment, and incarceration.* Serves as a true diversion from the system—does not use the return of police, court, or custody as a threat for participation.
- Transfers problem-solving skills to individuals—and communities can be trained to use peace-building skills.
- Similarly, recognizes that all of us can do harm to others, and allows for all people to be held accountable regardless of their status position, authority, age, race, or wealth.
- Does not assume there are wholly "innocent" and "responsible" parties and rejects language such as "victim" and "offender" that assumes simplified ideas of "guilt" and "innocence."
- Similarly, does not use labels for anyone involved, and seeks to recognize the humanity in all people—does not use the disempowering terms such as ward, juvenile, minor, inmate, offender, victim, convict, gang/gang member, pregnant teen, addict, or derogatory terms for law enforcement.
- Gives people an opportunity to explain if they were wrongfully accused. Does not require that people plead guilty or accept responsibility in order to participate.
- Uses a strengths-based approach rather that a deficit-based one, focusing on youth/people as assets rather than on identifying a person's pathologies and "fixing" them. (Mcgill, 2012)

Community interventionists, also known as peace-builders, also serve as mediators to help support youth and communities to change cycles of violence and oppression in their daily lives and neighborhoods. Police officers often create fear and mistrust due to racism, brutality, and officer-involved shootings of community members, and are usually not current members of the communities they patrol. Peace-builders are usually members of the communities that they serve and also understand the race, class, gender, neighborhood, and familial dynamics of that particular region. Peace-builders are utilized by the YJC as an alternative model of public safety instead of police and law enforcement in our communities and schools.

YOUTH EMPOWERMENT

When I think about youth empowerment, I think about youth being strong and confident in who they are. At such a young age, we face so much hate from law enforcement or school personnel. Personally, organizing for me in Los Angeles is a very difficult task. I'm a young person of color as well. Not only am I targeted by police harassment and incarceration, but my family also runs the risk of being deported back to Mexico because of their immigration status. The city, state, and nation don't realize that young people are the future of the world. School security, metal detectors, and random searches: This is what the school to prison pipeline looks like. The state implements policies that make youth experiences in the California school system the worst in the United States, which leads many of us to either drop out or be pushed out of school.

At the Youth Justice Coalition, we do our very best to bring the power back to young people. We have a "Street University" class that is taught by the organization, teaching young people how to become youth organizers. We learn what rights we have when we get stopped by the police, as well as how to conduct a civil disobedience to push our campaigns further. The youth create campaigns that are youth led and run. Our youth conduct research and find out who our ancestors really are and learn where they came from and the culture that ties it all together. Youth create a list of bills that we would like to see turn into laws. Thanks to the young people in our center and at the juvenile halls, county jails, and prisons, there are currently seven bills that are up in the state legislature, all relating to young people in the criminal *in*justice system and in our schools. F.R.E.E. L.A. also has a class called Troublemakers, which tells the stories and history of movements and about the people who moved them, not only the leaders. The goal of all these organizing classes is to make youth feel empowered and to educate them on who they really are.

We always close our meetings, actions, and events with a famous chant by Black, "We Must Love Each Other and Protect Each Other, We Have Nothing to Lose but Our Chains!" The youth can feel all the positive energy from the day and the days coming, but most of all the power comes from all the work of past movements and our ancestors who led them. Hope is not lost when you enter the doors of Chuco's Justice Center (L. Mendoza, personal communication, July 3, 2013).

YOU CAN'T BUILD PEACE WITH A PIECE

Our work has become even more powerful as we have extended our youth organizing solidarity onto a national scale. Initially, the "You Can't Build Peace with a Piece" campaign was going to be primarily focused on creating a basic response against the proposed federal legislation by California Senator Barbara Boxer called "Save Our Schools (SOS)" (Boxer, 2013) that would allow federal military and armed National Guard soldiers to help with policing and patrolling of schools in the United States. This and other harmful legislation was being proposed by reactionary political movements in response to the tragic school shootings at Sandy Hook Elementary School in Newtown, Connecticut, in December 2012. But what came out of our coalition was a document even more extensive and powerful than we had envisioned.

The "You Can't Build Peace with a Piece" statement expanded and grew into a National Youth of Color collective document outlining how current policies centered on how "public safety" contributes to the school to prison pipeline, gun violence, incarceration, school push-out, and institutionalized racism. Just as critically, our youth also provide concrete alternatives and solutions centered on community interventionists, holistic education, transformative justice, youth centers, discipline policies, and even transportation, providing our vision of true public safety for youth and students of color across the United States. Championed by the Dignity in Schools National Campaign, the Advancement Project, the Youth Justice Coalition, Alliance for Educational Justice, NAACP, Legal Defense Fund, the ACLU, and several other social justice organizations, the National Statement became a thirty-eight-page document with hundreds of public signatures from youth, allies, organizers, community members, and organizations from all across the country. Here we outline its introduction and key youth solutions. The statement was written, composed, researched, and edited primarily by youth of color organizers and community members from all across the United States. The full document with signatures can be found on the Youth Justice Coalition web site (Youth of Color Across the United States, 2013).

NATIONAL STATEMENT BY YOUTH OF COLOR: ON SCHOOL SAFETY AND GUN VIOLENCE IN AMERICA

We *can* imagine the pain and suffering that the youth and families in Newtown, Connecticut, are experiencing. As youth growing up on some of America's deadliest streets, we are all too familiar with gun violence and its impacts. Too many of us have been shot and shot at. We have buried our friends and our family members. Nearly all of us have been to more funerals than graduations. No one wants the violence to stop more than we do.

But, we have also seen how attempts to build public safety with security systems, armed police, and prisons have failed. *We want college prep, not prison prep.*

President Nixon declared the War on Drugs and enacted the first use of zero tolerance laws in communities. President Reagan expanded the War on Drugs and his Secretary of Education, William Bennett, enacted zero tolerance in schools. School shootings were used as an excuse to expand these policies at the local, state, and federal level, most famously by President Clinton following Columbine. For forty years, federal, state, and local dollars have gone toward the massive buildup of police departments, juvenile halls, jails, prisons, immigration enforcement and detention, and border security, while simultaneously our school and higher education budgets have been severely cut. And, locally, zero tolerance policies have resulted in the takeover of school security by police departments and school resource officers.

As a result, in communities of color throughout the nation, students now experience a vicious school-to-jail track. Despite the fact that school shootings have overwhelmingly happened in white schools, youth of color have paid the price. We have been handcuffed and humiliated in front of other students and staff for "offenses" as small as being late to school; detained in police interrogation rooms at our school; expelled from school for carrying nail clippers, markers, or baseball caps; and arrested—even in elementary schools—for fights that used to be solved in the principal's office. With our backpacks searched and our lockers and cars tossed, at the end of a billy club or the butt of a gun, knees down–hands up, or face down on cold concrete or burning asphalt—we have experienced the true face of "public safety." These policies haven't protected us, helped us to graduate, or taught us anything about preventing violence. They have taught us to fear a badge, to hate school, and to give up on our education. We understand too well that guns *in anyone's hands* are not the solution. *You can't build peace with a piece.*

The movement to end the school-to-jail track, mass incarceration, and deportation of youth of color *is our generation's civil and human rights struggle.* Throughout the nation, our efforts are pressuring school districts and state legislatures to dismantle unfair discipline practices that force youth out of school, and to move instead toward positive student supports that not only dramatically increase school safety but also improve graduation rates. The tragic shooting at Sandy Hook Elementary School must not interrupt this progress or return us to policies and practices that are racist, inhumane, and unjust.

The "National Statement of Youth of Color" calls on **all federal, state, and local officials to:**

1. **End zero tolerance** and other policies that take away school-based decision-making and force schools to suspend, expel, and arrest students in order to be in compliance with the law or to receive federal or state funding.
2. **Eliminate willful defiance, disorderly conduct, and other minor infractions** as punishable by suspension, expulsion, ticketing, or arrest.
3. **Reject efforts to expand police and military in our schools** as well as razor/barbed wire, security gates, metal detectors, surveillance, and increased use of handcuffs and police detention inside and around our campuses. Replace school police and school resource officers with intervention/peace-builders and the other alternatives listed below.
4. **Reject efforts to increase criminal penalties, mandatory minimums, gun enhancements, and the transfer of more youth into adult courts** that will unfairly target youth of color for extreme sentencing and decades of incarceration.
5. **Fund Positive Behavioral Interventions and Supports (PBIS)**—specific strategies that educators can use to reward positive student behavior, hold students accountable for our actions in ways that keep us in school, cause self-reflection and growth, and improve our relationships with school staff.
6. **Fund Community Intervention/Peace-Builders in schools**—trusted community leaders who are trained to provide safe passage to and from schools; create a safety perimeter in and around schools especially during breaks and lunch; reach out to students who are regularly late or missing from school; work with youth who are acting out in class or on campus; prevent inter-group or inter-neighborhood conflict—often contributing to or stemming from neighborhood conflicts that, if unresolved, can lead to serious violence in the community; rumor control to prevent future violence and retaliation; run violence prevention, conflict mediation, and restorative/transformative justice meetings; and make home visits to students who are struggling in school.
7. **Fund Restorative/Transformative Justice (RJ/TJ) in schools**, which develops the skills of students, staff, and other community members in conflict mediation and problem solving, de-escalation of violence, and

techniques to defuse bullying, harassment, and disrespect. RJ/TJ involves students and others in solving problems such as truancy, fights, bullying, theft, intoxication, vandalism, and failure to follow school directives without resorting to suspension, expulsion, ticketing, and/or arrest. In addition, youth and staff learn skills that we can use to improve relationships and solve conflicts outside of school.

8. **Support the development of schools as Community Centers** open year-round, after school and on weekends to extend the school day, build public safety, and increase student attendance and achievement through homework help, tutoring, college preparation, counseling and health/mental health care (many community schools have on-site health/mental health clinics), job training and placement, arts and recreation, even night school for parents and older family members. Schools that operate as community centers also increase family involvement in schools, leading to improved student relationships with parents/guardians and increased graduation rates.
9. **Provide every student pre-school through college with a metro/bus/public transportation pass** to ensure we have transportation to and from school, while also providing unlimited transportation to essential resources throughout our communities including employment, housing, food, health care, etc.
10. **Ensure that every young person on probation or parole and all youth coming home from lockup are immediately enrolled in a quality education program**, and end the illegal blocking of system-involved youth from schools and entire districts. In order to ensure immediate enrollment, ensure that everyone who spends three or more weeks detained or incarcerated leaves lockup with a state ID, birth certificate, social security card, immunization records, medication (if needed) and connection to health/mental health referrals, updated transcript and test scores, and a voter registration card (optional). For undocumented youth, we must leave lockups knowing the risks of deportation especially for convicted people and with referrals for immigration assistance.
11. **End the discrimination against undocumented youth**, the cooperation of school districts and local law enforcement with Immigration and Customs Enforcement (including the Secure Communities Program), and eliminate barriers to all immigrant youths' access to education and student supports from pre-school through college. (Youth of Color Across the United States, 2013)

Finally, the "You Can't Build Peace with a Piece" national network decided as a collective to launch a National Week of Action during the first week of April entitled "April Fools' Week of Action—Youth of Color Say Stop Foolish Policies, No

More Police in Schools!" (Dignity in Schools, 2013). During this week, we took a stand against these oppressive policies with rallies, call-in days, youth concerts, press conferences, forums, and petitions in Los Angeles, California, New York, New York, Chicago, Illinois, Washington, D.C., Greenville, Mississippi, Raleigh, North Caroline, Miami, Florida and others cities. Ultimately, the bill was not enacted and the power of youth of color organizing prevailed! This victory was just one piece of the larger goal to end the school to prison pipeline, and our communities can't stop and won't stop fighting back.

CONCLUSION: STEPS IN COMMUNITY ORGANIZING

"From Isolation to Action"

For me, community organizing has been both extremely difficult and extremely beautiful at the same time. It has been draining, frustrating, consuming, challenging, and simultaneously empowering, life-changing, incredible, and spiritual. My organizing experiences at the YJC have been revolutionary, strategic, practical, and transformative all within one campaign. Too often in our society we experience *ageism*—given the fact that adults dominate almost all sectors of government, decision-making, allocation of resources, and enjoy the privilege of having respected voices in most groups, organizations, and government entities. We believe that youth experiences, struggles, and stories will speak for themselves. Therefore, we work to empower young people to find their own voice so that both the real truths about our society's ills and the real solutions can shine through the voices of youth. This is one of the many ways we strive toward *loving the youth* (E. Lacques-Zapien, personal communication, July 3, 2013).

Finding Our Voice

Most people—including young people—struggle in silence. We deal with everything we experience in our lives and everything we see in the world mostly in isolation. *Change* begins when people begin to find their voice. Finding a voice can mean many things, from talking to friends and family, testifying publicly at hearings or conferences, rhyming or singing about conditions, writing poetry or stories about experiences and feelings, or any other avenues that can help people humanize their experiences.

Unfortunately in the United States, where consumer culture collides with the rights of individualism, almost all of our ideology is focused on blaming or exposing the individual person, and on *fixing you*—instead of on exposing unjust conditions and the inhumane treatment of people and *fixing the system*. In capitalist America, the industry of psychology, psychiatry, and talk shows dominates *voice* in America. Having a voice in this context doesn't often lead to a conversation about oppressive conditions or one about racism, sexism, homophobia, ableism, classism, and many other forms of oppression. In other words, having a voice doesn't guarantee that a person will fight for personal or community liberation. But, several things can enable or inspire people to progress from finding their voice to taking *action*.

Action looks and develops differently for different people. However, there are some patterns that persist that we have laid out here:

1. *Triage:* People see suffering or *in*justice and try to ease it. Hopefully, over time they work to build the capacity in people and communities to address things on their own. For example, this is how the YJC would see our service work, such as the legal education, street outreach, peer support, housing, and court support that people are currently engaged in, as well as the alternatives to arrest, court, and incarceration that people are developing for the future. For organizers, the goals for this work are contrary to traditional social service or missionary models that often build dependence on programs and institutions rather than independence and a more collectivist, anti-capitalist way of addressing our problems. Organizers usually try to teach service while doing it, and raise the expectation that what you gain, you then have a responsibility to pass on to other people. Service work continues, because there are always new people to reach out to, and you have to meet people's immediate—and sometimes crisis—needs before they can fight to change the conditions that cause suffering in the first place.

   We try to instill challenging and critical thinking skills in our work and service so that youth and community members can eventually get a sense that the root causes of societal problems must be addressed. Power needs to be challenged, upset, and redistributed. Therefore, people need to start questioning and talking about *power*.
2. *Power:* At the Youth Justice Coalition, we work on building an organized discussion about power dynamics through several different tactics and avenues:

   a. Street, Juvenile Hall, and Prison Outreach and Education
   b. Political Education Workshops, Including (1) Systems of Oppression, (2) Law Enforcement History, (3) What Is the Prison Industrial Complex? (4) Juvenile and Prisoner *In*Justice Practices, (5) History of Prisoner Movements and Resistance
   c. Youth Organizer Leadership Roles
   d. Leadership Training About Organizing Skills, Strategies, Tactics, and Goals Settings

e. Films, Readings, and Literature About Resisting Incarceration
f. Documentation of Issues, Experiences, Data, and Events
g. Analyzing Mainstream Media and Its Messages
h. Creating People's Grassroots Forms of Media

These are all strategies for people to go from analyzing power to reclaiming it and feeling empowered to take action themselves. Organizing seeks either to push the system, with the goal of *reforming* institutions, services, and/or policies, or to *rock* the system with a goal of *dismantling or revolutionizing* institutions, services, policies, and/or entire systems or communities.

We also rely heavily on three specific strategies in our organizing:

1. *Base-Building:* Mobilizing and educating people on the issue and supporting them to develop and implement an action plan in response. Almost all event organizers participate in workshops or conferences, street or door-to-door outreach, an action or a march, even a cookout or communal barbeque. All these tactics are intended in part to build and educate constituency.
2. *Advocacy:* Through constituency- and coalition-building efforts, organizers are also able to push policy makers to back the demands of a particular campaign. Sometimes policy makers become allies. Sometimes they are the main or secondary target of a campaign. Other times they will actively oppose your campaign. We must also keep in mind that oftentimes decision-makers can also be deterrents to your work because of the oppressive systems they serve under, and at times can be confined only to offering solutions under current laws or within the criminal *in*justice system. Their role is usually determined through research and power analysis conducted during the action planning process.
3. *Movement Building with Allies:* This is often done with other youth and adult activist groups to build a stronger voice to push for your campaign's specific goals and to ignite the overall vision and goals of the coalition(s). When doing coalition work, organizers often rely on some members to do the insider work (less confrontational, consensus-building work). Other members in the coalition keep pressuring the targets through direct action. But all members usually mobilize their people to make some noise with a unified message and goals. Examples of tactics are press conferences, rallies, letter writing, petitions, legislative visits, civil disobedience, shutting down meetings, flash mobs, taking over public space, and many more.

We hope that some of these organizing tools and ideologies will provide some insight and help you take the power back to your own communities. Increasingly across the world, activists are working to dismantle institutions, change policy, kick incompetent or oppressive officials out of office, and in some cases topple governments. But then what? Perhaps an even more difficult challenge is envisioning—*and then building and running*—something new. Because at the end of the day we do believe that another world is possible.

A world where racism, sexism, patriarchy, ableism, classism, colonization, homophobia, ageism, slavery, fascism, and all forms of oppression slowly become de-constructed and dismantled head-on as a daily practice for all members of society. A world where borders are obsolete and prison bars are just a dark piece of our history. A world where people of color are not enslaved by incarceration, but are celebrated for the beauty, power, and ancestry that we proudly carry on our backs and in our hearts. A world where we don't turn to violence and enforcement to solve our communities' problems—we solve them ourselves, with transformative justice, patience, honesty, and de-colonization. A world where we love ourselves, love our youth, and love our communities. We do this work with justice in our minds and love in our hearts. Thank you for taking this journey with us (E. Lacques-Zapien, personal communication, July 3, 2013).

REFERENCES

Boxer, B. (2013, January 24). Official Web site of Senator Barbara Boxer [Press releases]. Retrieved from http://www.boxer.senate.gov/en/press/releases/012413.cfm

Dignity in Schools. (2013, April 4). You can't build peace with a piece April Fools' week of action! [Weblog]. Dignity in School Campaign. Retrieved from http://www.dignityinschools.org/blog/you-cant-build-peace-piece-april-fools-week-action

Mcgill, K. (2012, July 23). YJC know justice, know peace. Part 3. Youth Justice Coalition Retrieved from http://www.slideshare.net/KimZilla/know-justice-know-peace-part-3?from_search=19

Youth of Color Across the United States. (2013, March 4). Youth of Color response to school shootings. *Youth 4 Justice.* Retrieved from http://www.youth4justice.org/ammo-tools-tactics/yjc-reports

PART EIGHT

Tactics for Abolition

I Can't Breathe

—Eric Garner

For the master's tools will never dismantle the master's house. They may allow us to temporarily beat him at his own game, but they will never enable us to bring about genuine change.

—Audre Lorde

CHAPTER TWENTY-THREE

Tactics and Strategies to Organize for Abolishing the School to Prison Pipeline

ANTHONY J. NOCELLA II

Too often when examining the school to prison pipeline (STPP) activists and organizers look for policy change, but that approach tends to be a slow process considering the oppressive and complex nature of the educational system. What is being advocated here is an entire abolition of the STPP. Specifically, both the school and prison systems need to be abolished for their historical systemic repression and oppressive methodologies that promote violence and are themselves violent. This chapter is dedicated to providing the reader activist tactics in creating grassroots change. I will begin with discussing the STPP and then move into explaining the steps of social change by Martin L. King Jr. and Gandhi. I will introduce tactics on how to organize with the oppressed public education forums including ground-rules, and finally conclude by including strategies for participatory activism toward social change fighting political repression, and protecting yourself with security culture.

Before moving forward to discuss activist tactics, it is critical to stress that those activists must be educated about the STPP. The STPP is a systematic socio-political process that pushes select youth out of school and on to the streets, often to be targeted by law enforcement, where many end up in juvenile detention. The following are the top organizations studying and researching the many problems of the STPP: Families and Friends of Louisiana Incarcerated Children, Campaign for the Fair Sentencing of Youth, Child Defense Fund, American Civil Liberties

Union (ACLU), Center for Community Alternatives, Dignity in Schools, Campaign for Youth Justice, The Annie E. Casey Foundation, Youth Justice Coalition, Black Youth Project, Power U, Racial Justice Now, National Association for the Advancement of Colored People (NAACP), and Advancement Project. Another organization in which I am the National Co-Coordinator is Save the Kids, founded in 2009 by four African-American boys residing in a New York juvenile detention facility. It is the only national fully volunteer grassroots group to create alternatives to—and end—the criminalization and incarceration of youth and the STPP.

PROBLEMS OF THE STPP

According to Save the Kids, there are five common elements of the STPP: (1) Criminalization, (2) Policing, (3) Punitive Discipline, (4) Oppressive/Rigid Education, and (5) Cultural Incompetent Personnel.

1. The first element, criminalization, refers to the stigmatization of targeted youth through laws and norms that are based on their behavior, dress, ability, socializing, identity, and community in which they live. A prime example includes the current public shaming of young Men of Color who wear large pants without belts. In the aftermath of the murder of Trayvon Martin, there was dialogue about the presumed threat of young Black men wearing hooded sweatshirts.
2. The second element is the policing of youth. This refers to the surveillance and social control of youth by law enforcement and those in disciplinary roles. Notable examples of this type of surveillance include New York City's infamous "Stop and Frisk" past law and other aggressive policing policies that result in a heavy police presence in poor neighborhoods and Communities of Color.
3. The third element, punitive discipline, refers to the punishment of youth which includes detention, sitting in the hall or corner, involuntary labor, in and out of school suspension, incarceration, home arrest, and probation. The punitive actions have become the result of the ever-expanding adoption of zero tolerance policies by school systems.
4. An oppressive Monolithic Education system is the fourth element in the formation of the STPP. This element refers to the curriculum, pedagogy, and practices that promote and are grounded in the dominant ideology and culture. This type of education distances itself from the history and experiences of its marginalized students. When this element is combined with the final factor, the cultural incompetence of those who serve our youth, they become intractable obstacles to learning and a catalyst for the rise in push-out rates.

5. Cultural incompetence refers to non-diverse, mis-educated or non-representative personnel in both the juvenile justice and school systems that do not relate, understand, or identify with marginalized identities. (Save the Kids, 2015)

SOLUTIONS TO THE STPP

The five general solutions to parallel the problems noted above include:

1. Inclusionary policies and practices that challenge stigmatization;
2. Providing freedom, trust, and independence from authority and law enforcement rather than surveillance;
3. Supporting and adopting restorative and transformative justice, mediation, conflict management/resolution/transformation to replace punitive practices;
4. Allowing the communities culture and marginalized groups history to reflect the curriculum which should be developed by each school rather than a national standardization movement and corporate textbooks; and
5. All personnel within the criminal justice and school systems must reflect and come from the community they are serving.

The overall goal of the STPP is absolute control and punishment when needed, while reeducating the future population (i.e., youth) that reinforces the dominant and dominated binary within society. As such, the STPP is a tool of a repressive government; it is about social control through the criminal justice system and propagation through the school system. A historic example is the early Christian boarding schools for Native youth in the United States. Those that did not cut their hair, learn English, and become Christian found themselves as identified by the U.S. government as "bad Indians" and law enforcement would soon find a way to lock them up through racist laws. Such laws permeate schools today in the form of regulating dress codes, such as making it illegal to sag one's pants in cities such as New Orleans, Chicago, Atlanta, Detroit, Miami, and Jacksonville (Ferris, 2014).

My goal in this chapter is to offer tactics and strategies that will inspire the reader to be an effective activist and social change agent. When selecting tactics the question is not, *What are the best tactics*? but instead, what *tactics do you feel comfortable and want to perform?* When answering that question, adopt the tactic(s) and build a strategy (Del Gandio & Nocella II, 2014). We are inspired by the process in which Martin L. King Jr. and Mohandas (more commonly known as "Mahatma") Gandhi built their strategy for nonviolent social change:

MARTIN L. KING JR. SIX STEPS FOR SOCIAL CHANGE

Martin L. King Jr's six-step plan for social change (King, n.d., 2003, 2010a, 2010b) includes the following:

1. *Information gathering* entails conducting research and finding everything you can on your opposition and issue.
2. *Education* entails educating the community and people in your group or organization about the information you and others found through your research.
3. *Personal commitment* refers to the idea that all of whom are involved in the cause and effort should affirm the amount of time, energy, resources, and legal resources/ramifications they are willing to risk/give.
4. *Discussion/Negotiation* means that once you have a critical mass of committed folk, a meeting is arranged with the opposition to discuss your demands and alternatives. At this point you are hoping they change without escalation tactics.
5. *Direct Action* results when the opposition does not change, and escalating activist tactics are employed to pressure the opposition to meet your demands.
6. Finally, *reconciliation* is a result after escalated pressure on the opposition wherein the opposition is compelled to comply with the demands.

GANDHI'S FOUR STEPS FOR SOCIAL CHANGE

While Martin L. King Jr. had six micro-steps for social change, Mahatma Gandhi noted in general four macro-steps to social change in his book *Freedom's Battle* (2010):

1. Ignore You: The stage which the group or individual is not looked at as having power, a legitimate argument, or the ability to create change; as a result, those in power do not give space or place to the group wanting change.
2. Stigmatize You: Those in power identify those that are different to discredit them so they are not given space and place to create change.
3. Repress You: After a particular time period and growth of the group that wants change are recognized as a threat in creating change, they are specifically targeted and repressed by those in power in the form of arrest, incarceration, assassination, framing, fabricated criminal charges, and infiltration and division of social movements.

4. Accept You: If the group or movement is not destroyed by repression, and the fight for change by the group or movement continues to grow and garner mass public creditability, those in power regress and accept the change.

ELEMENTS OF CONFLICT

No matter the issue, all social change centers on a specific conflict. It is important to know how to analyze a conflict because it will allow those working for social change to understand all the elements involved. According to Nocella, Chiprin, Antar, and Page (2014), conflict has three elements which includes:

1. Relationship: The specific individuals, groups, and communities involved.
2. Subject: The topic that brings the individuals, groups and communities together.
3. Process: The history, present and future interactions of the individuals, groups, and communities involved.

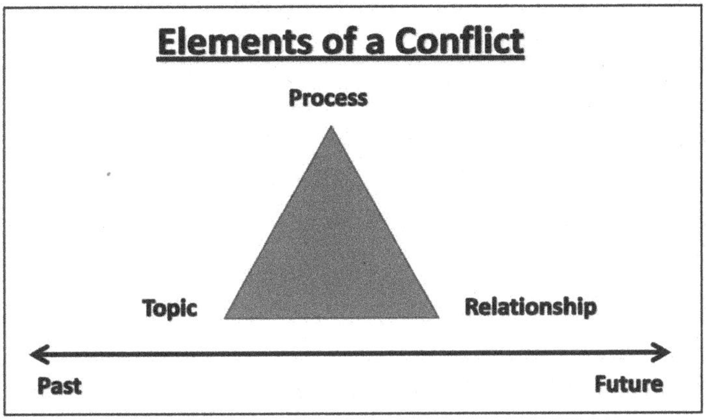

Figure 23.1. Elements of a Conflict.

Each of these three elements can be broken down through developing a flow chart which links all the direct and indirect relationships between corporations, lobby groups, government representatives and agencies, and political parties. Or we can develop multiple lists of why all the groups, individuals, and communities are interested in the topic, or make a timeline of when all the relationships interacted and why. It is important to discuss how to create social change because too often theorists, teachers, authors, politicians, spiritual leaders, and professors inform you about a sociopolitical problem, but fail to provide action plans on how to solve the problem.

WORKING TO BE IN SOLIDARITY WITH OPPRESSED PEOPLE

No matter who you are, you can always be in solidarity with another struggling and oppressed group/movement. The following are fifteen points to consider when building relationships among people, groups, and movements, especially if you have more privileges than those you are working with when fighting to dismantle the STPP:

1. Be invited to the struggle.
2. Listen.
3. Articulate one's commitment.
4. Explain one's skills.
5. Explain motivation and personal goals.
6. Be willing to follow and never lead.
7. Be willing to not get credit, but give credit to non-dominant voices.
8. Be willing to take accountability and own one's supremacy and domination.
9. Be willing to be challenged and called out.
10. Be willing to learn new processes and cultural practices.
11. Be willing to take more risks.
12. Be willing to do more.
13. Be willing to not take money or other benefits.
14. Challenge acts by white individuals and agencies that tokenize, patronize, and co-opt.
15. Be willing to leave and not blame others.

TWENTY-STEP PROCESS FOR ORGANIZING A PUBLIC EDUCATION FORUM

The following is a list of how to organize a successful event, which will help spread information and educate the public about the issue that the group is concerned about:

1. Pick an event theme with a title and a description.
2. Establish an event committee of 2 to 3 people and sponsors.
3. Establish a length of time such as, 1 hour, 3 hours, day long, weekend long, week long, and format of the event such as, workshop, roundtable, teach-in, Skype, film screening, lecture, debate, open mic, or conference.

4. Invite and confirm speakers on the topic from the community, universities, schools, and other institutions/organizations.
5. Receive biographies, professional titles, and full name of the speakers.
6. Lock in a location and time that is accessible and in a location that the public can easily find. Think about the bus schedule and parking situation.
7. Develop a flyer and send it out to the event committee, speakers, and sponsors for approval.
8. Promote and advertise through e-mail, media (such as radio and newspapers), Facebook, Twitter, blogs, phone calls, speaking in classrooms and organizations, and texting.
9. On the day and week of the event, repromote.
10. On the day and week of the event, reconfirm speakers.
11. An hour before the event, make sure all the event committee members are at the event location on time.
12. An hour before the event, organize chairs, food, video camera, banners, and a welcoming/information table.
13. An hour before the event, the cofacilitators should practice explaining the purpose, goal, schedule, and presenters' bios.
14. An hour before the event, the cofacilitators should decide how the discussion will be facilitated after the presenters are finished. If possible, call on people with marginalized identities, try not to call on the same person more than once, and do not allow anyone to speak for an excessively long period of time.
15. Make sure the event starts and end on time.
16. Make sure to thank everyone for presenting, organizing, attending, etc.
17. Make sure to tell everyone about the next event or to tell them where to find out about future events.
18. Make sure to tell people how to get involved with this issue.
19. Make sure to send out, via social media and e-mails, thank yous to those who attended.
20. Make sure to quickly post pictures and videos of the event on social media.

GROUND RULES

Here are a set of common and useful ground rules to use in meetings of the group.

1. Volunteer yourself only
2. No put downs of yourself or others, even in a joking way
3. One mic (one person speaks at a time)
4. Vegas (whatever said in a space, does not go beyond those that heard it)

5. Participate
6. Step up, step down (those that have more privilege speak less in a space)
7. 3 then me (do not speak until at least three people spoke)
8. K.I.S.S. (Keep It Short and Sweet)
9. Keep an open mind
10. Assume the best
11. Don't yuck on my yum (do not put down what someone else likes)
12. Don't take anything personal
13. Attack the idea not the person

FIGHTING REPRESSION[1]

Through Nocella's experience in activism and in conducting an extensive literature review, he has developed five general responses to repression by activists and socio-political groups. They are: *canceling*, *concluding*, *coping*, *confronting*, and *combating*. He labels them the *5Cs of Responding to Repression* (Nocella, 2013). The following describes each of the 5Cs of responding by activists or groups to repression.

1. *Canceling* is the abrupt elimination of all dissent activity.
2. *Concluding* is the gradual closure of all dissent activity, though not cancellation because people are still in jail, processing court cases, paying fees, or conducting counter-suits.
3. *Coping* is to keep constant, but not retreat or lose sight of, one's overall goals; hence, it is a form of managing repression.
5. *Confronting* is to publicize the fact that an individual(s) or group(s) is being repressed, but not take aggressive legal or illegal steps to eliminate the repression, usually due to a lack of resources or public support. In some cases, publicity eliminates the repression and may even advance the cause. Dissidents in this form of response are concerned with the overall goals of the group or movement.
5. *Combating* is to advance the goals of the group/movement, to take legal or illegal measures to eliminate repression, and to achieve justice for already implemented repression against them. For instance, this may involve a countersuit against the city police or the FBI. Not only are activists aggressively advancing their cause, they are seeking to achieve legitimacy through their legal and/or illegal actions.

---

1 This section "Fighting Repression" was taken from Anthony J. Nocella's chapter "The Rise of the Terrorization of Dissent" in the book *The End of Prisons: Reflections from the Decarceration Movement* (2013).

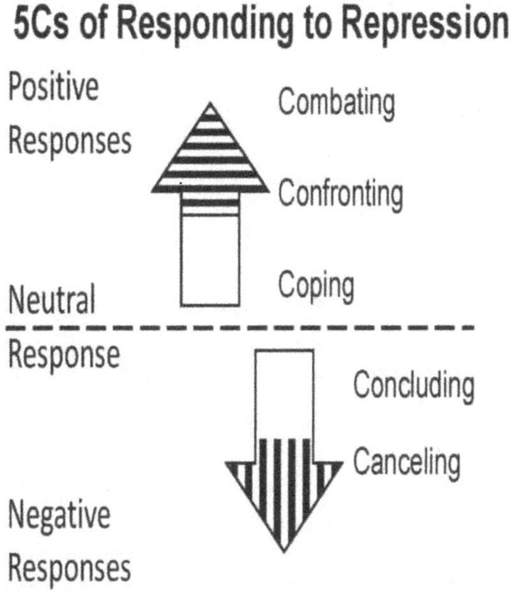

Figure 23.2. 5Cs of Responding to Repression. (Nocella II, 2013).

Of course, responding to repression is never clean-cut or divided solely into five identified responses. Responses often will fall in between and can shift from one response to another in a moment's notice. However, the 5Cs of responding to repression provide an important conceptual foundation. It must be stressed that, at this point, activists have not drawn any significant distinction regarding such responses.

Each of the responses is potentially in the repertoire of the activist or group and can be used to address a particular event, campaign, group, or complete social movement. Further, these responses could be used to explain a diversity of actions. For instance, while an event could be cancelled at a university, and the student group could be coping with academic repression (Best, McLaren, & Nocella, 2010), the overall movement could be more organized and confrontational to State power. Activists' use depends on many factors, particularly the goal and strategy of repression by the government toward them. Activists or groups, except in the case of imprisonment and assassination, always have agency in deciding how to respond to repression. In the case of an informant in an activist group/movement, it is very important to stress how activists have agency and that the state does not entirely determine or eliminate choice from the individual. This is not to say that the U.S. government and its law enforcement officers conduct their acts legally; they do not. Officials admit that, willingly or not. A case-in-point is COINTELPRO, which aided in the assassination, torture, framing, and division of activists and groups between mid-1950s to the early 1970s (Churchill & Wall, 2002a, 2002b).

It is true that it is sometimes impossible to win one's freedom or political campaign in the face of intense repression where the government is not "playing fair." But one must never deny that s/he has agency, which is defined here as the power to determine one's own choice. This does not mean one always has the power to determine the outcome, but people have the choice to decide how to believe and act. Activists and groups throughout time have stressed their agency in many forms, including the use of quotations.

In the case of Shaka Sankofa, a Black, poor, male prisoner who was executed by the state of Texas, he defended his innocence, speaking brilliantly about the horrors of racism and classism in the United States. Before being executed, Sankofa gave his last statement witnessed by Reverend Jesse Jackson, Al Sharpton, Bianca Jagger, and others, with thousands of supporters from around the world gathered outside the walls. He stated, "You can kill a revolutionary, but you cannot stop the revolution" (Mathúna, 2000). Even knowing he would soon be strapped to a cold metal table with his arm pulled tight with a lethal injection, Sankofa eloquently and strongly proclaimed that he, and every revolutionary, has agency.

Each response by an activist group or activist depends on the political climate, available resources, perceived possible consequences (e.g., collapse of organization, imprisonment, or fines), and, most importantly, the tactic used by authorities. Practice Theorists, such as French sociologist Pierre Bourdieu, argue that actions are not independent from systematic and individual motivations and practices. Further, the concept of cultural capital refers to the ability of an individual to move in and out of societies, groups, and communities that s/he affects and is influenced by not because of financial value, but because of his/her/their value s/he/they offer others, such as, his/her/their knowledge experience, or social relationships on a particular topic.

The 5Cs of repression are not the final determinate of one's response, but a beginning point for developing a general framework of identifying how one responds. Furthermore, each response, while dependent on the strategy and tactic of repression employed by the state or private agency, is determined by the activist or group. Therefore, someone's agency cannot be entirely taken away or manipulated by external forces, even while one's physical body can be imprisoned or killed. This framework for response will help show how the members of a movement respond to repression.

Information on repression from one organization or group is shared to another and then another, until that information on that event is spread throughout the world to every social justice activist. This information gives activists possible solutions on how to respond to similar situations. How does a movement respond to a grand jury? Do we speak to cops? Do we call the media when our house is raided? Do we have a press release for when we are framed? To understand these questions we must understand the type of repression, how the victim responded to the repression, and the result of this response. From these factors we can determine what actions are best to take in the future. It is only through activists sharing their experiences that this information can be analyzed and written about, and then applied to social justice movements as a whole.

TACTICS OF FIGHTING REPRESSION

There are many tactics in creating change, but not all tactics are applicable or relevant, but some essential ones to gain attention and control the narrative include:

1. Using social media including Facebook, Twitter, Instagram, LinkedIn, Tumblr, Snapchat, Academia.edu, Myspace, Flickr, Pinterest, Google+, Vine, YouTube, Yik Yak, and Reddit to name a few to spread information about an event or injustice;
2. Having a large network to tell about an event or injustice through listservs, phone-banks, and mass mail and e-mail;
3. Having resources such as printer, chalk, posters, banner, paint, markers, bullhorn, sound system, flyers, stickers, websites, business cards, buttons, shirts, postcards, e-mail, phone-numbers, and office equipment to assist in organizing events; and
4. Developing an organization with bylaws, mission, purpose, goals, strategies, tactics, subcommittees, and regular meetings to create events and to gather information.

The four most effective tactics to resist repression beyond just controlling the narrative include:

1. Occupying places short term such as chalking sidewalks and buildings, protest in classrooms, halls, dorms, sidewalks, streets, and quads and long term such as creating blockades in the front of entrances of buildings, roadways, walkways, and takeover buildings, rooms, and offices.
2. Promoting a boycott by doing mass walkouts or strikes as well as transfer to another school.
3. Mapping out administration and school leadership's vulnerabilities and protest locations where they and their friends and families frequent such as their churches, homes, country clubs, work, restaurants, cafes, doctors, movie theatres, and grocery stores.

4. Developing a smear campaign by creating flyers, posters, memes, stickers, buttons, shirts, and graffiti to bring light to the specific injustices and private unethical acts that the people that are responsible for the academic repression.

BASIC SECURITY CULTURE

Security culture is the actions an organizer and activist should adopt to be safe against infiltration, sabotage, division, and other forms of repression by the government, school, and corporations.

1. Keep your computer, home, office, locker, phone, tablet, vehicles, etc., always locked, organized, and clean so if someone was to enter your home you would likely know.
2. Don't brag about your or other's activism, especially illegal activity, if to family, friends, partners, or other people that have done time.
3. Only do civil disobedience and other illegal activism with people you know very well including where they grew up, work, went to school, and currently live and who their friends and family are.
4. Don't joke or speak about illegal activities. This will aid in spot lighting more attention onto you from law enforcement.
5. Use encrypted software and shorthand communication beyond just writing to protect what you or others are planning.
6. Develop methods in nominations of people into a collective, group, or project to establish one's level of safety and security.
7. Strive to build trust based on honesty and building an open relationship.
8. Don't ask others about their involvement with illegal action.
9. Don't date people or do actions with people you are dating. This will possibly increase the complexity of risk that is taking place.
10. Strive to never have a paper trail of your activism that is "illegal" such as not typing on a computer, e-mail, or piece of paper.
11. Have your meetings in a secure and nonsurveilled location.
12. Do not promote or support rumors about anything about anyone. Strive to end them or address them quickly and efficiently.
13. Minimize on internalized social movement politics, which aids in information gathering of law enforcement, which could be used against activists.
14. Avoid working with people you don't like rather than publicizing your dislike of them.

15. Know your legal/illegal limits based on job, friends, children, family, organization(s), and movement.
16. Respect and learn each individual's security expectations and abide by them.
17. Leave no trace, meaning leave nothing in your home, car, on your phone, computer, or drop anything at events or locations that might aid in incarceration or information gathering of you or others.
18. All messages with the organization including listservs, board-members, volunteers, and coordinators, directors, and social media messages should have the following note at the bottom of all messages discussing events, programs, projects, and general information about the group. All messages about the group should be private and should not be forwarded or discussed with others:

    CONFIDENTIALITY NOTICE: This communication (including any attachments) is intended only for the use of the intended recipient and may contain information that is privileged and confidential. This communication along with all verbal, social media, and digital communication about all _______________ (the name of the organization here) business and _______________ (the name of the organization here) volunteers is private and not to be shared or discussed visually, forwarded, verbally or digitally with others such as friends, family, or members of _______________ (the name of the organization here). If you are not the intended recipient, you are notified that any use, dissemination, forwarding, distribution, or copying of the communication is strictly prohibited. Please notify the sender immediately by e-mail if you have received this communication in error and delete this e-mail and all copies of this e-mail from your system. Thank you.

REFERENCES

Best, N., McLaren, P., Nocella A. J. II. (2010). *Academic repression: Reflections from the academic industrial complex*. Oakland, CA: AK Press.

Churchill, W., & Wall, J. V. (2002a). *The COINTELPRO papers: Documents from the FBI's secret war against dissent in the United States*. Cambridge, MA: South End Press.

Churchill, W., & Wall, J. V. (2002b). *Agents of repression: The FBI's Secret wars against the Black Panther Party and the American Indian Movement*. Cambridge, MA: South End Press.

Cummins, M. W., & Griffin, R. A. (2012). Critical race theory and critical communication pedagogy: Articulating pedagogy as an act of love from black male perspectives. *Liminalities: A Journal of Performance Studies, 8*(5), 85–106.

Del Gandio, J., & Nocella II, A. J. (2014). *Educating for action: Strategies to ignite social justice*. British Columbia, CA: New Society Publishers.

Fernandez, M., & Hauser, C. (2015, October 6). Texas mother teaches textbook company a lesson on accuracy. *The New York Times*, A10.

Ferris, S. (2014). Florida town cracks down on sagging pants problem. *The Washington Post*. Retrieved from https://www.washingtonpost.com/blogs/govbeat/wp/2014/07/20/florida-town-cracks-down-on-sagging-pants-problem/?utm_term=.ee4ac6650bf4

Gandhi, M. (2010). *Freedom's battle: Collected writings and speeches*. New York, NY: WP Press.

King, M. L. Jr. (2003). *A testament of hope: The essential writings and speeches of Martin Luther King Jr.* San Francisco, CA: HarperOne.

King, M. L. Jr. (2010a). *Where do we go from here: Chaos or community?* Boston, MA: Beacon Press.

King, M. L. Jr. (2010b). *Strength to love*. Minneapolis, MN: Fortress Press.

King, M. L. Jr. (n.a.). *Six steps of social change*. Retrieved from http://www.thekingcenter.org/king-philosophy#sub3

Leonardo, Z., & Porter, R. K. (2010). Pedagogy of fear: Toward a Fanonian theory of "safety" in race dialogue. *Race, Ethnicity and Education, 13*, 139–157.

Mathúna, S. M. (2000). Shaka Sankofa murdered by the state of Texas. Flame. Vol. 5. Summer. Retrieved from http://www.fantompowa.net/Flame/shaka_sankofa.htm

Nocella II, A. J. (2013). The rise of the terrorization of dissent. In M. E. Nagel & A. J. Nocella II (Eds.), *The end of prisons: Reflections from the decarceration movement*. New York, NY: Rodopi.

Nocella, A. J. II, Chiprin, M., Antar, A., & Page, A. (2014). Transformative justice and conflict transformation. In J. D. Gandio & A. J. Nocella II (Eds.), *Educating for action: Strategies to ignite social justice*. British Columbia, CA: New Society Publishers.

Poe-Yamagata, E., & Jones, M. A. (2007). *And justice for some: Differential treatment of youth of color in the justice system*. Oakland, CA: National Council on Crime and Delinquency. Retrieved from http://www.nccdglobal.org/sites/default/files/publication_pdf/justice-for-some.pdf

Potash, J. (2007). *The FBI war on Tupac Shakur and Black leaders: U.S. intelligence's murderous targeting of Tupac, MLK, Malcolm, Panthers, Hendrix, Marley, rappers & linked ethnic leftists*. Baltimore, MD: Progressive Left Press.

Save the Kids. (2015). *About STK*. Retrieved from http://savethekidsgroup.org/about-stk/

Steele, C. (2010). *Whistling Vivaldi: And other clues to how stereotypes affect us*. New York, NY: W. W. Norton & Company.

Wilson, A. N. (1978). *The developmental psychology of the black child*. Brooklyn, NY: Afrikan World InfoSystems.

Wu-Tang Clan. (1993, November 9). C.R.E.A.M. On *Enter the Wu-Tang (36 Chambers)* [LP]. New York: Loud Records.

Zehr, H. (2005). *Changing lenses: A new focus for crime and justice*. Scottdale, PA: Herald Press.

CHAPTER TWENTY-FOUR

Abolition Strategies for Teachers Fighting Academic Repression in the Corporate-Academic Industrial Complex

PRIYA PARMAR

As educators we are politicians; we engage in politics when we educate. And if we dream about democracy, let us fight, day and night, for a school in which we talk to and with the learners so that, hearing them, we can be heard as well.

—Paulo Freire (1998, p. 68)

Washing one's hands of the conflict between the powerful and the powerless means to side with the powerful, not to be neutral.

—Paulo Freire (1985, p. 122)

What is the purpose of education? Is it to "educate" or "school?" Is it to inspire academically and intellectually prepared, politically and socially aware and active citizenry—[educate]? Or, is it to produce complacent, cynical citizenry who know their place in society—[school]? Do our school curricula in all subjects overrepresent certain cultures and underrepresent others? Are we teaching from prepackaged, scripted lessons/units or textbooks that sell so-called truths and serve as the final authority on what is right and wrong? Are we privileging certain populations of students and marginalizing others? Are we indoctrinating students to act in prescribed manners that revere dominant cultural values over others? What is our role as educators in this quest to "educate" or "school" our students? What are our expectations of the diverse populations we teach? Do we believe in all of our students? Do we accept, celebrate, and include their knowledge, expertise, language/dialect, and culture into our lesson planning?

I start with quotes from Brazilian educator, philosopher, scholar, activist, and cultural worker, Paulo Freire (1921–1997) whose commitment and passion was to create a truly democratic society, one that reflects an education system that is inclusive and equitable, where students are not schooled, but educated. In the spirit of Freire (and others similar to him), themes suggested in this volume push for resistance against hegemonic and dominant forces within educational institutions and beyond. As Freire's life work demonstrates, educators must demand and work toward a liberatory or revolutionary education, one grounded in a *critical pedagogy* in all content areas with a focus on addressing social injustices. This does not mean content matter is water—downed, or glossed over. Instead, it is the opposite. A critical pedagogy requires educators to be experts in their subject area, to teach with (critical) rigor and high expectations, to contextualize their teaching as much as possible, and to be inter- and intradisciplinary incorporating marginalized and underfunded or -utilized content such as the arts into their teaching. This brief and oversimplified description is only the tip of the iceberg of a critical pedagogy.

A critical pedagogue prepares lessons that challenge hegemony, explores injustices, and names the people or parties responsible. Let's not sugarcoat by using coded, deficit-implying terms such as "at-risk" or "disenfranchised"; instead, let us name the oppressor and the oppressed. Let's name the privileges some have over others ... and why they exist. Let's include the study of whiteness in all subjects, but especially when it's time to incorporate multicultural education. Let's name policies, practices, beliefs, and values laden in white supremacist ideologies. It should be noted the study of whiteness and white privilege does not seek to marginalize or alienate white people. It is intended to examine how power—political, economic, religious, or gender—is constructed and how it benefits some and oppresses others. Let's identify the biases found in our curriculum and textbooks and include marginalized or excluded identities and knowledge. Let's name—and resist—the publishing companies and state or federal agencies responsible for mandating such curricula and textbooks. Let's teach students to question, to challenge the "norm," to reject complacency and cynicism, and inspire social and political activism, or agency. Let's create awareness of cultural, economic, and political (re)production, and specifically, how power within each operates by asking "who benefits?" It is the goal of a critical pedagogy for educators to take risks, to create *critical consciousness*, or as Freire termed it, *conscientização*, to resist against the normalizing and privileging of dominant ideologies and structures, and to actively fight, protest, and replace systems of oppression in favor of ones that are truly democratic, empowering, and equitable for all (Freire, 1970, 2000).

In the face of misguided educational reform efforts focusing on standards- or outcomes-based education (e.g., "Education 2000" initiated by President George

H. Bush, "Goals 2000" by President Bill Clinton, "No Child Left Behind Act" (NCLB) of 2001 by President George H. W. Bush, or President Barack Obama's 2015 "Every Student Succeeds Act" (ESSA)) I recognize the extreme pressures placed on teachers and administrators to measure academic performance primarily by enforcing high-stakes standardized testing. The educational–political landscape may soon worsen if we do not take collective action. As I am writing, the P-16 educational community is rigorously protesting and calling their elected state senators to cast a "NO" vote to current President Donald Trump's Secretary of Education cabinet nominee, Betsy DeVos. DeVos, a billionaire businesswoman hailing from Michigan, has a long history in that State supporting, creating, and funding educational initiatives and laws that favor corporatized charter schools and the privatizing of public schools that require the use of public funds to pay for private school tuition in the form of vouchers. What's more appalling is DeVos has zero teaching experience.

As policymakers, many of whom have very little to no experience in education, work on instituting data-driven, quick-fix, systematic reform efforts focusing on student and teacher accountability, or privatizing public education in favor of corporate charter schools, very little attention is devoted to analyzing and developing curriculum that is culturally and linguistically relevant and focused on social justice issues. By social justice, I am referring to, but not limiting it to, the critical analysis of environmental-, criminal-, economic-, racial-, gender/sexuality-, linguistic-, educational justice. As educators are clearly aware, there are no quick-fixes in this profession. Critical pedagogues understand the complex and nuanced nature of the educational system, work to create a responsible learning environment that targets the needs of a vast range of students, and account for the multidimensional factors and interconnected components that contribute, encourage, and support successful student performance (Parmar & Krinsky, 2013).

I understand and empathize with the frustration, concern, fear, and anger teachers may feel in the current educational climate, especially if one's teaching style or philosophy is opposite of school administrators or current political education regimes. As I wrote earlier, we must take strategic, collective risks in our teaching, resist and act against policies that harm our students, and work to change—or abolish—the system. Toward the end of this chapter, I will include learning activities for any content area teacher to consider implementing into their teaching. But first, it must be emphasized, critical pedagogy transcends outside the walls of the classroom and school building.

We must reach out—call, write, e-mail, visit in person—our legislators and demand our voices be heard. Boycott, protest, or picket legislation or outside interest (private) groups that work to enforce policies that work against our (teachers, students, parents) interests. Participate in community-based and national organizations that are already fighting against antiteacher/antistudent practices and educationally—restrictive and—harmful policies that lead students through the prison pipeline. Educators must be proactive in our teachers unions, taking on leadership roles within the union and school setting. This cannot be emphasized enough considering the current political climate in which the goal is to abolish all unions! I understand that some unions have been accused of cronyism or become so bureaucratic that members become cynical and estranged from union activity. We cannot succumb to cynicism and passivity. We must unite with like-minded colleagues and parents to form collectives. We must be elected into leadership roles within the union. We must work strategically and intelligently to penetrate the "powers" within; if union leadership is not serving your interests, rally, demand change, or VOTE them out! I write this knowing you are inundated with "busy work"—grading, teaching-to-the-test, adhering to student and teacher assessment measures, writing student evaluations, managing student and parent relationships, and, equally important, dealing with our own emotional turmoil created by all of the above and forces beyond. It is not expected that you alone change the system, nor would it be encouraged. If it hasn't been made clear already, the contributors in this volume urge you to form collectives or join existing ones, unite with fellow educators including those positioned in other grades or subjects, connect with professors in colleges/schools of education, invite community organizations and organizers into your schools, welcome parents into your classroom and work with—not against—them in enhancing academic performance.

As a teacher educator, much of my work involves collaborating with my P-12 colleagues in designing and implementing curriculum grounded in critical pedagogy in their respective content area. We serve as coauthors for articles or books that highlight initiatives to bridge the theory-practice gap that is so often argued as missing or forgotten in (P-12) education. I encourage teachers to create their own authentic assessment measures (which most do anyway) that they can collect, record, and report to their colleagues and administrators, or to present at national educational conferences. Keep files of lesson plans and units, document your pedagogy, and use qualitative methods to log student performance and attendance to show administrators and higher officials evidence of academic improvement (ibid).

Inspired by Paulo Freire and grounded in the theoretical framework of critical pedagogy, the ideas suggested below supplement the philosophy explained throughout the chapter. Modifications are obviously necessary depending on grade, subject, and students' needs. Readers are urged to explore the liberatory and revolutionary potential of implementing a critical pedagogy by reading the overwhelming number of published books and articles written by critical scholars-activists.

PHILOSOPHICAL CONSIDERATIONS

- First and foremost, accept and respect who your students are and where they come from. This includes their racial, cultural, socioeconomic, linguistic, and dialectical background. If they choose to reveal their gender identity, accept, respect, and address them by their chosen preference.
- Students are subjects, not objects, therefore, students are *knowledge producers*. All students are passionate about something. Find out what it is, and encourage them to share it with you and/or their peers. Ask them to teach you, the teacher.
- Set high expectations for all students, regardless of their placement in ability groups or tracks. Do not succumb to deficit thinking teaching. All students are capable of learning if we know what their needs are.
- Differentiate your instruction to meet the needs of diverse learners, including those with special needs and English Language Learners. Incorporate student-centered, project- or inquiry-based learning. Resist using worksheets, or rote, memorization-style activities in your teaching.
- Invite opportunities to incorporate their interests into your lesson planning, or ask them to bring in "texts" found in different youth culture mediums—popular culture, media, digital or social media, newspapers, magazines, television, films, video games, music, and so forth—that meet the criteria and themes of the content being studied.
- Freire advocated for using a "problem-posing" approach which directs attention toward power relations at the micro-level (schools to local communities) and the macro-level (larger society, national, and global).
- The teacher's role is that of facilitator. Instruction is dialogic and intersectional. This means students' voices are heard and valued. Power is shared between students and teacher(s). Don't be confused. The teacher is the authority in the classroom but does not act in an authoritarian manner. Content is the primary focus but teaching is contextualized, and the classroom is structured.

PEDAGOGICAL CONSIDERATIONS

- Engage students in inquiry-based or problem-posing projects that require the research, analysis, and critique of policies and practices of power institutions. Examples of such institutions include: governmental agencies, local or federal, impacting human and nonhuman life; education from preschool to higher education; criminal justice and policing policies;

farming and agricultural industries, including harvesting of crops, greenhouse effects, forestry, factory farming and animal welfare, hunting, and fishing; mainstream, corporate media and alternative media; financial/banking/Wall Street; family; political; religious; and economic institutions. These projects must include opportunities for students to socially reconstruct perceived injustices and engage in participatory action against them.

- o This could include letter writing campaigns, organizing and distributing petitions, boycotting and protesting, registering complaints to local and federal agencies, organizing food drives, recycling efforts, or the like. The possibilities are endless!
- o In your own school, do students have power to make decisions affecting school or classroom rules (and consequences)? What role, if any, do they play in curriculum development or lesson planning with the teacher? Are there opportunities for involvement? Can we create opportunities?
- o Are we examining our textbooks and other educational texts for bias and omissions? Whose experiences or cultures are represented in our history classes? Which authors are we reading in the English classroom? Do they represent diverse backgrounds, or are they representing the canon? Which scientists and mathematicians are included in our textbooks? Can we research those inventors, philosophers, or heroes that are left out of our textbooks? And why are they left out? Let's study and critique marginalized or excluded knowledge, voices, and experiences. Are texts promoting stereotypes of any group of people? Is linguistic bias present when describing Native Americans, women, or disabled populations?
- o Are students involved in decision making of the cafeteria food menu? After-school programming? If not, how can they get involved?
- o Is there student government in the school? How much decision making do they have with teachers and administrators in creating and instituting school policies?
- o Can students engage in student-led news reporting through the Public Address (PA) system at designated times throughout the school day?
- o Are students given opportunities to create Public Service Announcements (PSA) and play them for all students and educators in the school?
- o Can students create mural(s) on school walls? Or, can they design websites or social media networking limited to members of the school community?

- Critical literacy and critical media literacy. Students should be aware of the ideologies, biases, and power structures embedded within texts. Texts can be traditional content area textbooks, literature from the canon and beyond, popular cultural texts or media texts (music, film, television, internet, newspapers, magazines, videogames, manga, comics, spoken word, and so on) or formal institutional texts such as policies or legal documents from power institutions named above. Popular culture or media texts are powerful mediums to incorporate into your lessons because often times they address and respond to social unfairness and biases. The younger generation has used social media as a powerful vehicle to document, organize, and rally against social injustices and we as educators must capitalize on the tech-savvy strengths and expertise our students possess by incorporating more technology into our teaching. When deconstructing texts, the focus is on representation, misrepresentation, and underrepresentation (adapted from Parmar & Krinsky, 2013). Ask students to consider the following:
  - o Are multiple perspectives represented?
  - o Whose voices are represented?
  - o Whose voices are missing?
  - o What does this representation mean to me?
  - o Which "groups" are represented in the text? How are they represented?
  - o Does this representation reflect my "group" (peer group, class, race, ethnicity, gender, sexuality, ability level, etc.) fairly or accurately?
  - o How are these depictions or representations (of the group) formed? Where does it come from? The author? Policymakers? Corporations? Media? The public?
  - o Through whose perspective (or eyes) is the text telling the story from?
- Reconstructing texts (adapted from Parmar & Krinsky, 2013). Help students name the inherent biases found within the text and allow them to analyze content through multiple perspectives. Reconstruct the text by replacing certain factors such as race, class, culture, gender, age, ability, sexuality, setting, or theme.
  - o Change the *sex* of the main characters (or any characters) to determine if the meaning changes in any way. Consider changing heterosexual characters to LGBTTSQQIA characters and vice versa.
  - o Change the *race, class, ethnicity, ability or age* of the characters to determine if the meaning changes. Ask students to think about how characters would be described and depicted if any of these elements were to change. How would the overall story change?

- o Change the *setting of the text* to a different time, place, or social class. How would the story differ in meaning if the setting took place in an urban, suburban, or rural environment? How would the story change if it took place in medieval, modern, or contemporary times?
- o Change the major or obvious *theme(s)* of the story and replace with opposite theme(s). Allow students to change themes in the story so they are able to connect personally with the characters and content. Discuss how this changes the outcome of the story and author's intent.

– Community organizing efforts that explore environmental or food justice issues.
- o Document conditions within your community or neighborhood. Note the presence of garbage cans. Are they overflowing or tidy? Are recycling receptacles available?
- o Are billboards in good condition? What products are advertised on the billboards?
- o Are buildings, storefronts, roads, and sidewalks in good condition? Is there graffiti? Are there potholes?
- o Are homes in good condition? Are homes eligible for solar options?
- o Are there hazardous waste plants nearby? If so, how close are they located to residential areas?
- o What types of grocery stores are available to me? Whole, fresh foods and vegetables? Organic foods? National chain grocery stores? Corner stores?
- o What restaurants occupy my neighborhood? Family-owned, authentic cuisine or fast-food chains? Which ones? How many?
- o What kinds of public transportation are available? If there are buses or subways, are they in good condition?

– Students should be encouraged to take pictures, interview community members, and if possible, collaborate with community organizations to plan campaigns or drives that create awareness and transforms or remedies the issue for the betterment of the community. Students could plan a presentation or news report to create awareness of such conditions to their peers in school. They could create a documentary and post it on YouTube or other social media sites. Or they could invite their local politicians or newspaper reporters to their school for a viewing and question/answer session.

– Criminal justice system. Students can analyze, calculate, and graph statistical data pertaining to local or national crime rates. Data can be deconstructed by focusing on specific populations or demographics and critical questions as already mentioned above can be adjusted and applied.

- o Policing policies such as "stop and frisk" can be examined for the possibility of profiling toward targeted populations based on age, race, gender, and economic status.
- o Frequency of arrests and number of those arrested based on racial or economic status could be analyzed and questioned.
- o Access to quality representation once in the criminal or juvenile justice system should be explored. Examination of prison sentences based on severity of crime committed and who commits them should be analyzed.
- o Media (mis)representation of high profiled cases should be examined for unfair and bias reporting. Examine language used to describe perpetrators and victims of crime. Is there evidence of linguistic bias? Are words such as "thugs," "animals," "looters," or other negative and stereotypical language used to characterize certain demographics?
- o Creating a documentary or other form of presentation (performance theatre, role-playing scenarios, digital websites or blogs) that reports and analyzes harmful trends in policing and arrests could be presented to local law enforcement officials and politicians who are invited to the school for a viewing. Actions such as this could help build or strengthen the police-community relationship.

REFERENCES

Freire, P. (1970, 2000). *Pedagogy of the Oppressed.* New York, NY: Continuum.

Freire, P. (1985). *The Politics of Education: Culture, Power, & Liberation.* Granby, MA: Bergin & Garvey Publishers.

Freire, P. (1998). *Teachers as Cultural Workers: Letters to Those Who Dare Teach.* Boulder, CO: Westview Press.

Parmar, P., & Krinsky, H. (2013). *Critical Literacy in English Literature: Primer.* New York, NY: Peter Lang Publishing.

CHAPTER TWENTY-FIVE

Seven Considerations FOR "School" Abolition

DAVID STOVALL

The following document puts forward some practical considerations when thinking about "school" abolition. For the purposes of this account, "school" is understood to be the set of dehumanizing processes that reward young people for order and compliance instead of supporting critical analysis while providing necessary skills to change our conditions. Rooted in the U.S. colonial project of empire, genocide, and slavery, these "schools" were never intended to educate people of color or the general populace. Instead, much of the instruction that takes place in these buildings occurs with the purpose of anesthetizing the masses. Systemically, we are clear that the good teachers we had during our K–12 experience were not effective *because* of the current system, but were good teachers *in spite* of it. In this abolition of "school," our project is to lift up education in all the arenas in which it occurs. For us, the operative question is as follows: *Can school be a place where education happens?*

In learning from our comrades who are engaged in the project of prison abolition, it should be understood that in the practical sense we are not solely talking about the destruction of buildings currently used as schools. What we are asking for, however, is a systemic account of "schooling" in historically disinvested and isolated communities. Because these spaces are primarily populated by low-income/working class people of color, we must also contend with the idea that this population has been declared disposable by the state. In recognition of this dynamic, a "school" abolition, similar to prison abolition, would seek to end the conditions that sustain and support white supremacy through an endemic system of training rooted in dehumanization and white supremacy. Instead, we need to approach the dynamic of "school" abolition as one that challenges the idea that what happens in these "schools" is intended to continually denigrate, marginalize, and isolate those who have historically had the least.

Because "school" abolition at this point is mostly aspirational and incomplete, below is a set of considerations to engage in the attempt to build spaces where education is supported over "school."

1. Challenge and resist the proliferation of corporate charter school networks in historically disenfranchised communities.
2. Build resistance in communities and among educators against vouchers.
3. Build resistance in communities and among educators against teacher merit-based pay.
4. Support efforts to challenge the proliferation of high-stakes standardized testing in historically, disinvested, marginalized, and isolated schools.
5. Support the movement for quality education in neighborhood schools.
6. Support efforts to preserve and grow the work of critical educators inside and outside of traditional school spaces.
7. Build spaces where teachers and community members can support each other in the fight for quality education.

The following organizations have information on these seven considerations:

- Journey for Justice Alliance (www.j4jalliance.com)
- Teachers for Social Justice Bay Area (www.t4sj.org)
- Teachers for Social Justice Chicago (www.teachersforjustice.org)
- New York Collective of Radical Educators (www.nycore.org)
- Students at the Center (New Orleans)
- Peoples Education Movement (Bay Area)
- Peoples Education Movement (Los Angeles)
- Fair Test (www.fairtest.org)
- Grassroots Education Movement (New York)
- Grassroots Education Movement (Chicago)
- Educator's Network for Social Justice (Milwaukee)
- Teacher Activist Groups (www.teacheractivistgroups.org)
- Free Minds Free People (www.fmfp.org)

Afterword

BERNARDINE DOHRN

The cruelest, most pernicious development in domestic social and legal policy in the past two decades has been the widened, faster, broader School to Prison Pipeline—a policy that targets young students of color in their schools and criminalizes normal childhood and adolescent behavior. It is the task of every student, parent, teacher, and community member to educate one another and themselves about this brave new reality, and to dismantle that pipeline immediately. This volume tells you what, why, and how. And perhaps it is useful, at the end, to remember the clear ethical reasons for tearing it down.

When thinking clearly about the future, as young people require us to do, one would think that there would be 100% agreement with the following statement: **We should never punish children by depriving them of an education.** Yet zero tolerance policies, which transformed schools across the nation in the mid-1990s, did precisely that. School misbehavior—talking, taunting, pushing, shouting, fighting, and graffiti—were transformed into crimes. Schools became sites of searches and surveillance, police patrols and arrests, locker inspections and drug testing. Police presence in schools does not improve public safety, nor do search machines, cameras, or student identification tags. Police presence does increase student arrests, criminal and delinquency prosecutions, and exclusion (suspension and expulsion) from schools.

The promoters of zero tolerance, an odd coalition of prosecutors and police, politicians and teachers' unions, frightened parents and high crime communities, unsuspecting advocates of neighborhood safety in the whirlwind panic about super-predators and violent youth, lawyers on school boards fearful of risk—all participated in varying degree with a promised solution. The answer was to barricade previously open public schools. Funding streams were available for search machines, electronic surveillance, police presence in schools, locked doors, and closed campuses. The dreaded word "accountability" became a watchword; children must be *accountable* for their (mis)behavior. Accountable by being arrested, handcuffed, brought to police stations and booked, charged, and convicted, and suspended and expelled. Schools would have codes of conduct. Laws criminalizing every sort of behavior for adults would be enforced against children in school.

And a series of laws unique to children, called status offenses—which criminalize certain behaviors that are not classified as being criminal for adults, such as "willful defiance" or "incorrigibility"—became grist for school disciplinary measures such as suspension and expulsion.

But schools across the country were the safest places for children. Never mind that there was no evidence of the underlying problem, nor any evidence to support the solution. Police and judges knew that most youth arrests took place in the hours immediately after school and before evening. Child protection advocates knew that the most dangerous place for children in America was in the family home. Not all schools were equally safe, but despite the high profile but extremely rare school shootings of the late 1990s, schools were the safest place for children.

How then did zero tolerance in schools come about? Oddly enough, as if the prison industrial complex were not devouring young people of color at a sufficient rate, in 1995 a federal effort to discourage the possession of high caliber guns in children's hands led to the insertion of a single sentence in the federal Elementary and Secondary School Act, conditioning the flow of federal funds to local public schools on compliance. Children with handguns in school must be expelled. The next year, the word "handguns" was amended to "weapon" and there was no looking back. Anything could become a weapon in the hands of a schoolchild; punitive disciplinary codes became the size of telephone books, and the race to arrest, suspend, and expel was on.

This chain of events was part of a larger agenda by powerful forces to destroy public education and public school teachers (and their unions). The proliferation of publicly financed charter schools, Teach For America (TFA) as an alternative to career teaching, high-stakes testing of elementary school and adolescent children, and the urgent need to hold teachers (the lazy, incompetent teachers) accountable, the Common Core, and costly teacher evaluations resulted. This assault on public education and the children and families who attend urban schools (not suburban public schools), led by billionaires turned "educators," amounts to a siege launched from multiple fronts. No Child Behind Left Behind and the re-branded Race to the Top were grounded on a narrow reading of what learning and knowledge are, and were hyped despite obvious fraudulent and faked test scores. Any simple comparison of the schools for the rich and powerful—take the University of Chicago Laboratory Schools and Sidwell Friends' School, for example—and the bitter medicine and rigid punishments for urban public schools reveals the ugly, slick, and racist sales job involved in what was called "school reform."

As this book reveals, the other great agenda at work has its origins in the slave trade and the systems and structure of North American racism. The fierce and uninterrupted struggle to obtain equal education for black children, for Native American children, for immigrant children, for youth with disabilities, and for excluded children continues in new clothing today. Now, one of the major contemporary weapons of separate and unequal education is school discipline. Under the guise of zero tolerance and safety, African American students and students of color are suspended and expelled from schools and from access to an equal public education. The data from these eighteen years of zero tolerance policies in schools are unequivocal. Children of color are disproportionately suspended and expelled and arrested in schools—almost entirely for minor misbehavior.

In effect, we carry on with two systems of education, much as we have two systems of justice for youth. One system is crushing, caging, and punishing. The other is forgiving, remedial and restorative, and ensuring of a productive future.

No one wanted to defend the public school *status quo*—much about public education needed rethinking; equalizing; revamping; upgrading; parity in buildings, equipment, and financing; and economic and hiring stability. A new generation of highly educated and passionately dedicated long-term teachers must be recruited, mentored, supported, and retained.

But take my hometown, Chicago, which can claim the highest number of documented school-based arrests of any school district in the country. Almost twenty years of zero tolerance has not produced safety, but it has created the flow of urban children into police stations and criminal/juvenile courts, and out of schools. Returning to your home school after arrest and suspension is not automatic; it is rare.

In the 2011–2012 school year, police arrested 4,928 students in the Chicago Public Schools. This was an average of 29 student arrests in schools each day. In New York City Public Schools, the average arrest was 5 per day, although there are twice as many students in NYC public schools. Worse, 82% of those Chicago school-based arrests were for misdemeanors, the most minor of offenses or crimes. Whether the charges are dismissed or lead to convictions, the students are excluded from school during this period.

And the impact of zero tolerance is, and has always been, discriminatory. In Chicago, although African American students are 45% to 46% of the student body, 75% of school arrests are of African American children. That amounts to the continuing annual arrest of 19 Black students every day. Further, almost half,

47%, are students 15 years old and younger. And significant numbers who are arrested are youth with disabilities, English-as-a-second-language students, and traumatized students.

The continuing policy of zero tolerance has resulted in high push-out and drop-out rates, and low academic achievement (how can a student continue with algebra or biology if he or she is out of school for 30 days?). We have an unhealthy, prison-like school climate with students not getting the help they need, but instead being punished, harshly disciplined, deprived of an education, and driven out of school.

Most parents, communities, teachers, and principals reject this unfair, castigating, crushing set of policies and practices. Zero tolerance is not inevitable. As this powerfully evocative book shows us, schools, principals, teachers, and communities can opt out, can employ restorative and transformative justice principles for infractions and rule-breaking, and can create school environments that are imaginative, creative, inclusive, challenging, and engaging for all students.

Change requires us to take another path, to dismantle the school to prison pipeline and its lockstep role in the domestic national security state. As we forge more school environments of cooperation and understanding, of listening and participation, equality and innovation, art and humor, the discipline issues will take their (minor) place. Dismantle and create!

Appendix

Organizations and Resources

CALIFORNIA

ACLU of Northern California, San Francisco: www.aclunc.org
ACLU of Southern California, Los Angeles: www.aclu-sc.org
Black Organizing Project, Oakland: blackorganizingproject.wordpress.com
Black Skeptics Los Angeles, Los Angeles: www.blackskeptics.org
CADRE, Los Angeles: www.cadre-la.org
California Conference on Equality and Justice, Long Beach: www.cacej.org
Canvass for a Cause, San Diego: www.canvassforacause.org
Children's Defense Fund, California: www.cdfca.org
Coleman Advocates, San Francisco: www.colemanadvocates.org
Equality Federation Institute, CA: www.equalityfederation.org
Justice for Families
Labor/Community Strategy Center, Los Angeles: www.thestrategycenter.org
Public Counsel Law Center, Los Angeles: www.publiccounsel.org
Restorative Schools Vision Project, Sacramento: www.restorativeschoolsproject.org
San Francisco Youth Commission, San Francisco: www.sfbos.org/index.aspx?page=5585
Youth Committee of Building Healthy Communities, Long Beach: www.bhclongbeach.org/youth-committee
Youth Justice Coalition, Los Angeles: www.youth4justice.org

COLORADO

Padres & Jóvenes Unidos, Denver: www.padresunidos.org

CONNECTICUT

Hearing Youth Voices, New London, CT: www.hearingyouthvoices.com

DELAWARE

ACLU of Delaware: www.aclu-de.org

DISTRICT OF COLUMBIA

American Civil Liberties Union of the Nation's Capital: aclu-nca.org
Advocates for Justice and Education, Inc.: www.aje-dc.org
Center for Law and Education: www.cleweb.org
Critical Exposure: www.criticalexposure.org
Lawyers' Committee for Civil Rights Under Law: www.lawyerscommittee.org
NAACP Legal Defense and Educational Fund, Inc.: www.naacpldf.org

FLORIDA

Power U Center for Social Change, Miami: www.poweru.org
SOUL Sisters Leadership Collective, North Miami: www.soulsistersleadership.org

GEORGIA

Atlanta Community Engagement Team, Atlanta: www.atlcet.org
Gwinnett STOPP, Gwinnett County: www.gwinnettstopp.org

ILLINOIS

Advance Youth Leadership In Power, Chicago: www.accessliving.org
Blocks Together, Chicago: www.btchicago.org

Chicago Coalition for the Homeless, Chicago: www.chicagohomeless.org
POWER-PAC/COFI, Chicago: www.cofionline.org
Project NIA, Chicago: www.project-nia.org
The Woman of God's Design Ministry, Chicago: www.wogd.org

LOUISIANA

Community Education Project of New Orleans: www.cepneworleans.org
Families and Friends of Louisiana's Incarcerated Children, New Orleans: www.fflic.org
Center for Ethical Living and Social Justice Renewal, New Orleans: www.celsjr.org

MASSACHUSETTS

Boston-area Youth Organizing Project, Boston: www.byop.org
The EdLaw Project, Boston: www.edlawproject.org
Youth on Board/Boston Student Advisory Council, Boston: www.youthonboard.org

MICHIGAN

Harriet Tubman Center/Youth Voice, Detroit: www.tubmanorganizing.org
Student Advocacy Center of Michigan, Detroit, Jackson, Ypsilanti: www.studentadvocacycenter.org

MINNESOTA

Minnesota Minority Education Partnership (MMEP): www.mneep.org
Save the Kids, Minneapolis: www.savethekidsgroup.org

MISSISSIPPI

Action Communication and Education Reform, Inc., Duck Hill: www.acerms.org
Activists with a Purpose Plus, Grenada
Citizens for a Better Greenville, Greenville

Citizens for Educational Awareness, Kilmichael
Countywide Family Development Center, Laurel, MS
Fannie Lou Hamer Center, Eupora
Legacy Education and Community Empowerment Foundation, Forest
McComb Youth Council NAACP, McComb
Nollie Jenkins Family Center, Lexington: www.nolliejenkinsfamilycenter.org
Sunflower County Parents and Students, Indianola
Tougaloo M.A.N.U.P. Project, Jackson
Tunica Teens In Action, Tunica County: www.tunicateensinaction.org
Youth Innovation Movement Solutions, Tupelo

MISSOURI

Missouri GSA Network, St. Louis: www.mogsanet.dreamhosters.com

NEW JERSEY

Paterson Education Fund, Paterson, Paterson: www.paterson-education.org
Parent Education Organizing Council, Paterson: www.peocnj.org
Statewide Education Organizing Committee, Trenton/Jersey City: www.seocnj.org

NEVADA

H.E.R.O.S.

NEW YORK

Center for Community Alternatives, Brooklyn/New York City/Rochester/Syracuse: www.communityalternatives.org
Citizen Action of New York, Albany: www.citizenactionny.org
Dignity in Schools—www.dignityinschools.org
Desis Rising Up and Moving, Queens: www.drumnyc.org
Erie County Restorative Justice Coalition, Buffalo, NY
Girls for Gender Equity: www.ggenyc.org
Justice for Families

Make the Road New York, Brooklyn/Queens: www.maketheroad.org
NAACP Legal Defense and Educational Fund, New York: www.naacpldf.org
National Economic and Social Rights Initiative, New York City: www.nesri.org
New Settlement Parent Action Committee, Bronx
Palisade Preparatory PTSA, Yonkers, NY
Sistas and Brothas United, Bronx: www.sistasandbrothasunited.org
Teachers Unite, New York City: www.teachersunite.net

NORTH CAROLINA

Blue Ribbon Youth Leadership Institute, Chapel Hill: yli.chccs.k12.nc.us/home
Education Justice Alliance, Wake County: www.eja-nc.com
Southeast Asian Coalition, Charlotte www.facebook.com/SoutheastAsianCoalition
Youth Organizing Institute, Durham: wakeyouth.wordpress.com

OHIO

Ohio Poverty Law Center, Columbus: www.ohiopovertylaw.org
Racial Justice NOW!, Dayton: www.rjnohio.org
Toledoans United for Social Action, Toledo: www.toledoansunited.org
West Dayton Youth Task Force, Dayton: www.facebook.com/wdytf/

OREGON

Portland Parent Union, Portland: www.wix.com/simplysheilas/portland-parent-union
Resolutions Northwest, Portland: www.resolutionsnorthwest.org

PENNSYLVANIA

ACLU of Pennsylvania, Philadelphia: www.aclupa.org
Action United, Pittsburg: www.actionunited.org
Education Rights Network, Pittsburgh
Philadelphia Student Union, Philadelphia: www.philadelphiastudentunion.org
School Discipline Advocacy Services, Philadelphia: www.sdasphiladelphia.com
Youth United for Change, Philadelphia: www.youthunitedforchange.org

RHODE ISLAND

Young Voices, Providence- www.youngvoicesri.org

SOUTH CAROLINA

South Carolina Appleseed, Columbia: www.scjustice.org

TEXAS

Texas Appleseed: www.texasappleseed.net

VIRGINIA

Advocates for Equity in Schools- Henrico Coalition, Sandston
I Vote for Me, Henrico
Prom Bring It, Glen Ellen: www.facebook.com/PROM.BRING.IT
Mothers and Others, Richmond: www.mothersandothersva.org

WASHINGTON

League of Education Voters, Seattle: www.educationvoters.org
Seattle Young People's Project, Seattle: www.sypp.org

WISCONSIN

ExpresARTE, Madison
Freedom Inc., Madison: www.aboutfreedominc.com
YWCA of Madison: www.ywcamadison.org

CHILD DEFENSE—*CRADLE TO PRISON PIPELINE FACT SHEET*

http://www.childrensdefense.org/library/data/cradle-to-prison-pipeline-overview-fact-sheet-2009.pdf

CAMPAIGN FOR YOUTH JUSTICE—*YOUTH JUSTICE AWARENESS MONTH: GUIDE TO PASSING A RESOLUTION*

http://www.campaignforyouthjustice.org/images/Guide_to_Passing_a_YJAM_Resolution.pdf

ACLU—*LOCATING THE SCHOOL TO PRISON PIPELINE*

https://www.aclu.org/sites/default/files/field_document/asset_upload_file966_35553.pdf

DIGNITY IN SCHOOLS: *INVESTMENT IN EDUCATION VS. INCARCERATION*

http://www.dignityinschools.org/sites/default/files/EducationvsIncarceration_1.pdf

DIGNITY IN SCHOOLS—*WHAT IS SCHOOL PUSHOUT?*

http://www.dignityinschools.org/sites/default/files/Dignity%20in%20Schools%20Fact%20Sheet2014Compressed-Sample.pdf

Contributors

Mumia Abu-Jamal is an African-American writer and journalist, author of six books and hundreds of columns and articles, who has spent the past thirty years on Pennsylvania's death row and now in the general population, wrongfully convicted and sentenced for the murder of Philadelphia Police Officer Daniel Faulkner. His demand for a new trial and freedom is supported by heads of state, Nobel laureates, distinguished human rights organizations, scholars, religious leaders, artists, and scientists.

Dean L. Adams is currently a Visiting Assistant Professor in the Women and Gender studies department at University of Toledo. Dean has a Ph.D. in Special Education with a certificate in Disability Studies, and Gender Studies from Syracuse University, and has co-authored chapters on identifying and stopping the bullying of kids with disabilities in schools, critiquing the use of aversives to modify behavior in humans and animals, as well as the intersection of disability, gender, race and the school to prison pipeline. Current projects explore the intersections between transgender studies and disability studies.

Deborah Appleman is the Hollis L. Caswell Professor and chair of educational studies at Carleton College. Professor Appleman's recent research has focused on teaching college-level writing and literature courses at a high-security correctional facility for men. She is the author of *Reading Better, Reading Smarter: Adolescent Literacy* and the *Teaching of Reading; Reading for Themselves: How to Transform Adolescents into Lifelong Readers Through Out-of-Class Book Clubs*;

Teaching Literature to Adolescents; *Critical Encounters in High School English: Teaching Literary Theory to Adolescents* (winner of the Richard A. Meade Award); and *Braided Lives: An Anthology of Multicultural American Writing*.

Four Arrows, aka Don Trent Jacobs, Ph.D., Ed.D., is author of *Teaching Truly: A Curriculum to Indigenize Mainstream Education* (2013); editor *of Unlearning the Language of Conquest* (2006), and coauthor with Greg Cajete and John Lee of *Critical Neurophilosophy and Indigenous Wisdom* (2009) among other acclaimed books. He is currently a faculty member in the College of Educational Leadership and Change at Fielding Graduate University. He was named by AERO one of twenty-seven visionary educators for their book, *Turning Points*, and is recipient of the Martin Springer Institute for Holocaust Studies 2004 Moral Courage Award.

William Ayers, formerly Distinguished Professor of Education and Senior University Scholar at the University of Illinois at Chicago (UIC), has written extensively about social justice and democracy, education and the cultural contexts of schooling, and teaching as an essentially intellectual, ethical, and political enterprise. His books include *A Kind and Just Parent; Teaching Toward Freedom; Fugitive Days: A Memoir; On the Side of the Child; Teaching the Personal and the Political; To Teach: The Journey, in Comics; Teaching Toward Democracy; and Race Course: Against White Supremacy.*

Letitia Basford, Ph.D., is an assistant professor in the School of Education at Hamline University. Her teaching and research interests focus on students' equitable access to education, with a focus on culturally responsive and reform-based pedagogy. Her work has been published in the Review of Research in Education, Journal of School Choice, Journal of Southeast Asian American Education and Asian Advancement, and elsewhere. Prior to joining the faculty at Hamline University, Letitia was a coordinator of a teen parent center and a middle school English as a Second Language teacher in California.

Bridget Borer, who is from the Midwest region of the United States, is a single mother of two mixed race (European and African American) adult sons, one of whom is currently incarcerated in a federal prison. She is also a graduate student studying for her master's in ESL at Hamline University in St. Paul, Minnesota, as well as her ABE licensure for the state of Minnesota. She is currently working as an English language instructor at a university in Guangdong, China.

Zeke Caligiuri is an accomplished writer of nonfiction, fiction, and poetry. He has won first prize in the PEN writing awards for memoir and has also won writing awards for his poetry. He has spent much of his time trying to rebuild injured family structure through education and self-reflection. He is currently working on his Bachelor of Arts Degree in sociology and has taken part in several writing collectives during his incarceration. He has recently written a full-length memoir about growing up in South Minneapolis. He writes from outside stereotypes to communicate themes of loss, regret, and the effects of isolation in prisoners and their families. He hopes to help change social perceptions about the redemptive value of the individual.

Arash Daneshzadeh, Ph.D. recently held the role of Associate Director of Urban Strategies Council in Oakland, California. He has served as an equity-oriented scholar practitioner for the past 17 years. He has held roles as a teacher in Alameda high schools and community colleges as both faculty and dean. The crux of his praxis converges on the intersections between carceral studies, restorative justice, hip hop pedagogy, identity formation, and organizational theory. He contributes as a lecturer at the University of San Francisco—School of Education (Department of Leadership Studies), as well as faculty for the Prison University Project at San Quentin State Penitentiary.

Bernardine Dohrn, academic, activist, and children's rights advocate, is retired Clinical Associate Professor and was founding director of the Children and Family Justice Center of Northwestern University School of Law, Bluhm Legal Clinic. She is author and coeditor of three books: *Race Course: Against White Supremacy* (coauthored with William Ayers) (2009), *A Century of Juvenile Justice* (2001), and *Resisting Zero Tolerance: A Handbook for Parents, Teachers and Students* (2000). Dohrn serves on the boards of the Burns Institute, the Campaign for the Fair Sentencing of Youth, the Advisory Board of the Children's Rights Division of Human Rights Watch, the Midwest Human Rights Coalition, and the Kovler Center for the Victims of Torture.

Amanda Fields is an Assistant Professor of English and Writing Center Director at Fort Hays State University. She co-edited *Toward, Around, and Away from Tahrir: Tracking Emerging Expressions of Egyptian Identity* (Cambridge Scholars Publishing, 2014) and has published articles in *Community Literacy Journal, Journal of Adolescent Research,* and *Sexuality Research and Social Policy* as well as book chapters. "Performing Urgency: Slamming and Spitting as Critical and Creative Response to State Crisis" won the 2016 *Kairos* Best Webtext Award. She is also a Pushcart-nominated creative writer whose work has been published in *Indiana Review, Brevity, Superstition Review,* and others.

Stephanie S. Franklin, Esq., is the Founder, President, and CEO of Mecca's Place, Inc., an organization that provides legal representation to approximately 3,300 children in child welfare proceedings in Maryland. Franklin sits on the Maryland Legislative Subcommittee on Child Abuse and Neglect and other statewide and local child welfare committees. She has received awards and recognition for her work and has published on issues pertaining to the intersection of child welfare and criminal justice. Franklin will be published in the *Freedom Center Journal* in the spring of 2014 on her work with black girls.

Annette Fuentes is the author of *Lockdown High: When the Schoolhouse Becomes a Jailhouse* (Verso, 2011), an investigation into the myths and realities of school violence and the harsh disciplinary codes and policing that are undermining public schools' mission to educate. Fuentes has been a reporter, editor, and opinion writer for newspapers, magazines, and online outlets, writing about education, health care, and social welfare issues. From 1998 to 2006, she taught news reporting at Columbia University's Graduate School of Journalism. Her chapter is adapted from her book.

David Gabbard, Ph.D., joined Boise State University in 2013, and is currently in Curriculum, Instruction, and Foundational Studies, and was previously the Chair of the Department of Bilingual Education. Before coming to Boise State, he was on the faculty of the College of Education at East Carolina University. Most noted for his work as a critical educational theorist and policy analyst, Dr. Gabbard's research has reflected his quest to understand the phenomenon of compulsory schooling as an instrument of statecraft created, in part, to enforce the conditions of a market society. Hopeful that public schools might one day come to serve more genuinely democratic values, Dr. Gabbard's scholarship, teaching, and service focuses on nurturing critically reflective and democratic dispositions in teachers. His research interests are in cultural studies, curriculum and instruction, new literacies, and anarchist pedagogy.

Henry A. Giroux holds the Global TV Network Chair Professor at McMaster University and is a Distinguished Visiting Professor at Ryerson University. His most recent books include *Twilight of the Social: Resurgent Publics in the Age of Disposability* (Paradigm, 2012), *Disposable Youth: Racialized Memories and the Culture of Cruelty* (Routledge, 2012), *Youth in Revolt: Reclaiming a Democratic Future* (Paradigm, 2013), and *The Educational Deficit and the War on Youth* (Monthly Review Press, 2013); *America's Disimagination Machine* (City Lights) and *Higher Education After Neoliberalism* (Haymarket) will be published in 2014. His web site is www.henryagiroux.com.

Nancy A. Heitzeg, Ph.D., is a Professor of Sociology and Codirector of the Critical Studies of Race/Ethnicity Program at St. Catherine University, St. Paul, Minnesota. Professor Heitzeg has written and presented widely on issues of race, class, gender, and social control, with attention to the school to prison pipeline and the prison industrial complex. Professor Heitzeg is coeditor of an online series, *Criminal InJustice*, devoted to encouraging public education, dialogue, and action on issues of mass criminalization and incarceration.

Frank Hernandez is an Associate Professor and Dean of the College of Education at the University of Texas of the Permian Basin. His research interests include the intersection of identity and school leadership, equity and social justice, the principalship, and Latinos and school leadership. His research has been published in journals such as Educational Administrative Quarterly, Journal of School Leadership, and Education and the Urban Society. During his fifteen years in public education, Dr. Hernandez has served as a classroom teacher, an assistant principal, a principal, and a district coordinator of multicultural programming throughout several Midwestern urban school districts.

Daniel White Hodge, Ph.D., is the Director of the Center for Youth Ministry Studies and Assistant Professor of Youth Ministry at North Park University in Chicago. His research and community engagement explore the intersections of faith, critical race theory, justice, Hip Hop culture, and youth culture. His two books are *Heaven Has a Ghetto: The Missiological Gospel & Theology of Tupac Amaru Shakur* (VDM 2009) and *The Soul of Hip Hop: Rimbs, Timbs, & a Cultural Theology* (IVP 2010). His latest book is *The Hostile Gospel* (Haymarket, 2018).

Jennifer M. Hoenig, Ph.D., is a Senior Researcher in the Office of Research and Evaluation in the Bureau of Mental Health at the New York City Department of Health and Mental Hygiene. Jennifer leads the analysis of complex survey data examining the mental health of New Yorkers. Jennifer's current research focuses on social and environmental factors that influence mental health as well as mental health disparities.

Emilio Lacques-Zapien is a Youth Organizer with the Youth Justice Coalition. He works primarily on movement building, ending police violence and terrorism against communities of color, and redirecting suppression funding in L. A. County back to youth development. Emilio has a hunger and passion for immigrant rights and freedom fueled by the experiences of his undocumented family members from Michoacan, Mexico. He hopes to one day open a youth center in Mid-City Los Angeles modeled after the YJC that also focuses on recreation and sports, art and theatre, social justice, and anticapitalist collectivist living practices.

Nekima Levy-Pounds is a professor of law at the University of St. Thomas School of Law in Minneapolis and the Director of the Community Justice Project, a civil rights legal clinic. Levy-Pounds trains law students to use the law as a adult health, with a focus on sexual orientation and gender identity. He is chair of the Board of Directors of the Sexuality Information and Education Council of the United States (SIECUS), a fellow and former Board member of the National Council on Family Relations, an elected member of the International Academy of Sexuality Research, and was President of the Society for Research on Adolescence.

Don C. Sawyer III is currently a faculty member in the department of sociology at Quinnipiac University in Hamden, Connecticut, where he is teaching the university's first sociology course dedicated to Hip Hop culture. His scholarly focus is on race, urban education, Hip Hop culture, and youth critical media literacy. His research adds to the work of scholars interested in finding solutions to the plight of students of color in failing school districts and aims to center the often silenced voices of urban youth as experts with the ability to understand and articulate their lived experiences.

Shannon D. Snapp is an Assistant Professor in Psychology at California State University, Monterey Bay (CSUMB). She received her Ph.D. in Developmental Psychology at Boston College and completed her postdoctoral training at the University of Arizona. She uses interdisciplinary and mixed-methods research to examine practices and policies that support and hinder underrepresented young people's well-being, with a focus on the experiences of LGBTQ youth, youth of color, and youth whose identities and experiences intersect. She directs the "Support Young People Project" at CSUMB and teaches classes on social justice and love and intimacy.

Kim Socha, Ph.D., is author of *Women, Destruction, and the Avant-Garde: A Paradigm for Animal Liberation* (Rodopi, 2011) and is a contributing editor to *Confronting Animal Exploitation: Grassroots Essays on Liberation and Veganism* (McFarland, 2013). She has also published on topics such as Latino/a literature, surrealism, critical animal studies, and composition pedagogy, and she is currently working on a book about secularism and animal liberation. Kim is an English professor and activist for animal liberation and social justice causes. She volunteers with Save the Kids and is on the board of the Animal Rights Coalition and the Institute for Critical Animal Studies.

Damien M. Sojoyner is an Assistant Professor in the Department of Anthropology at the University of California, Irvine. He researches the relationship among the public education system, prisons and the construction of Black masculinity in Southern California. In addition to his work appearing in many popular media forms, he has written articles in scholarly journals such as Transforming Anthropology, Race, Education, and Ethnicity, and the Berkeley Review of

Education. His book, entitled *First Strike: Prison and Educational Enclosures in Black Los Angeles*, was released in 2016 by the University of Minnesota Press.

David Stovall, Ph.D., is Professor of African-American Studies and Criminology, Law and Justice at the University of Illinois of Chicago. Currently his research and community engagement investigates the intersections of Critical Race Theory, school/community relationships, the relationship between education systems and housing markets, youth culture, community organizing, and education. In addition to his university appointment, he is also a volunteer Social Studies teacher at the Greater Lawndale High School for Social Justice (SOJO).

Anne Burns Thomas is an assistant professor in the Foundations and Social Advocacy Department in the School of Education at SUNY College at Cortland. In addition, she is the coordinator of Cortland's Urban Recruitment of Educators (C.U.R.E) program, a comprehensive program designed to prepare qualified teachers for work in high need urban schools. A former middle school teacher in Philadelphia, her research interests include the nature of support for new teachers in urban schools, urban teacher education, and teacher research. Recent publications include "Finding Freedom in Dialectic Inquiry: New Teachers' Responses to Silencing," Teachers College Record, April 2009.

Jon Vang is the oldest child of Hmong immigrants from Laos. Being the first generation, he struggled with the clash of cultures, which led him to join gangs and try to live the criminal lifestyle. His choices resulted in eight years spent in the prison system. He used the prison programs for reflection and growth. Now he uses his skills to create positive change in the community and to change lives. He leads a support group for people who have previously been incarcerated. One of his projects is a social entrepreneurial venture to employ ex-felons.

Maisha T. Winn is the Susan J. Cellmer Chair in English Education in the Department of Curriculum and Instruction at the University of Wisconsin at Madison. She is the author of *Girl Time: Literacy, Justice, and the School-to-Prison Pipeline*; *Writing Instruction in the Culturally Relevant Classroom* (with Latrise Johnson); *Black Literate Lives: Historical and Contemporary Perspectives*; and *Writing in Rhythm: Spoken Word Poetry in Urban Classrooms*; and has also co-edited *Humanizing Research: Decolonizing Qualitative Inquiry with Youth and Communities* (with Django Paris) and *Education and Incarceration* (with Erica R. Meiners).

COUNTERPOINTS

Studies in Criticality

General Editor
Shirley R. Steinberg

Counterpoints publishes the most compelling and imaginative books being written in education today. Grounded on the theoretical advances in criticalism, feminism, and postmodernism in the last two decades of the twentieth century, Counterpoints engages the meaning of these innovations in various forms of educational expression. Committed to the proposition that theoretical literature should be accessible to a variety of audiences, the series insists that its authors avoid esoteric and jargonistic languages that transform educational scholarship into an elite discourse for the initiated. Scholarly work matters only to the degree it affects consciousness and practice at multiple sites. Counterpoints' editorial policy is based on these principles and the ability of scholars to break new ground, to open new conversations, to go where educators have never gone before.

For additional information about this series or for the submission of manuscripts, please contact:

Shirley R. Steinberg
c/o Peter Lang Publishing, Inc.
29 Broadway, 18th floor
New York, New York 10006

To order other books in this series, please contact our Customer Service Department:

(800) 770-LANG (within the U.S.)
(212) 647-7706 (outside the U.S.)
(212) 647-7707 FAX

Or browse online by series:

www.peterlang.com